John Paul Stevens

John Paul Stevens

Defender of Rights in Criminal Justice

Christopher E. Smith

LEXINGTON BOOKS
Lanham • Boulder • New York • London

Published by Lexington Books
An imprint of The Rowman & Littlefield Publishing Group, Inc.
4501 Forbes Boulevard, Suite 200, Lanham, Maryland 20706
www.rowman.com

Unit A, Whitacre Mews, 26-34 Stannary Street, London SE11 4AB

British Library Cataloguing in Publication Information Available

Library of Congress Cataloging-in-Publication Data

TO COME. (Below is a placeholder.)
Aesthetics and modernity : essays / by Agnes Heller ; edited by John Rundell. Test test test test test test test test test test test test test.
p. cm.
Includes bibliographical references and index.
ISBN 978-0-7391-4131-1 (cloth : alk. paper) -- ISBN 978-0-7391-4132-8 (pbk. : alk. paper) -- ISBN 978-0-7391-4133-5 (electronic)
1. Aesthetics. 2. Postmodernism. I. Rundell, John F. II. Title.
BH39.H445 2011
111'.85--dc22
2010037457

∞™ The paper used in this publication meets the minimum requirements of American National Standard for Information Sciences Permanence of Paper for Printed Library Materials, ANSI/NISO Z39.48-1992.

Printed in the United States of America

For Charlotte

Contents

Preface

During the first decade of the twenty-first century, I observed the publication of books about several Supreme Court justices, including Harry Blackmun, David Souter, Sandra Day O'Connor, Anthony Kennedy, Antonin Scalia, and Clarence Thomas. In light of their importance and influence as decision makers on the nation's highest court, they are all worthy subjects for scholars' attention and analysis. As I read these books, however, I was struck by the fact that none of these justices had served on the Court as long as John Paul Stevens. All but Souter were destined to serve more than twenty years on the Court, yet they received book-length analytical attention prior to approaching Stevens's thirty-plus years of service. At the time that these books appeared in print, Stevens had been the subject of only a few scholarly works: one book on his judicial philosophy written after his first decade on the Supreme Court;[1] a book about his role as an attorney for an Illinois investigatory commission;[2] a few book chapters; and various narrowly focused law review articles. There was a notable lack of comprehensive attention to Stevens and his role and impact on the Court. And I knew why. Or, at least I knew why I had neglected Stevens in my own work. The neglect of Stevens was not based on his lack of importance. Too often, like many of my colleagues in law, political science, and criminal justice, I am attracted to topics that are relatively easy because they are controversial, small-scale and manageable, and readily accessible. Tackling larger topics of exceptional importance can involve grappling with complexity or spending years digging through never-ending reams of material. Historians are accustomed to such work. I am not. The publish-or-perish environment of academia can create incentives and rewards for addressing small, discrete subjects that grab attention as part of current controversies or provide the basis for near-term publications. Long-term projects and complex subjects create extra burdens and risks as well as delayed gratification and rewards.

Why did justices other than Stevens receive earlier or more in-depth attention? Unlike the self-proclaimed originalists, Scalia and Thomas, Stevens was a complex figure whose approach to constitutional interpretation was not easily pigeonholed into a one-dimensional characterization for ease of criticism or praise. Unlike the so-called "centrist" justices, O'Connor and Kennedy, he did not have a reputation as a pivotal figure on the Court who cast outcome-determining votes on key issues. Unlike Souter, the author of 358 opinions during his nineteen years on the Court, Stevens was the most prolific opinion author in Supreme Court history. He ultimately wrote more than 1,400 opinions; a body of work that loomed as a daunting challenge for any scholar to analyze.[3] In addition, as a still-serving justice, Stevens had not invited detailed analysis of his life and career as had his retired colleagues Blackmun, through the unusually early availability of his papers in the Library of Congress, and William Brennan, through detailed interviews with a handpicked biographer. Indeed, as an exceedingly modest man, Stevens was in his thirty-second year on the Court before ABC News could trumpet the fact that they would broadcast his first-ever network television interview in January 2007.[4] Reflecting his modesty, even that groundbreaking interview saw Stevens talking more about the president who appointed him, the then recently deceased Gerald Ford, than about himself.

The relative neglect of Justice Stevens by scholars at the same moment that other justices were the subjects of in-depth analysis triggered my decision to give him the attention that he deserved. The foregoing observations are not meant to provide a basis for me to pat myself on the back. Indeed, they serve to highlight the fact that I failed to achieve my original objective. As I waded through his huge body of judicial opinions and spent time digging through his colleagues' papers at the Library of Congress, I found myself overwhelmed, not merely by the amount of available material, but also by the complexity and importance of his work and impact on so many issues. I came to the conclusion that I, too, would neglect Justice Stevens through the very act of attempting to analyze him in a single book. As a result, I retreated to a specific focus within my own topical area of expertise: constitutional rights in the context of criminal justice. Thus, this book is merely a contribution to the understanding of Justice Stevens's impact and importance. The comprehensive analysis of such a long-serving, historically important figure will require the work of many authors examining a wide array of legal issues. Fortunately, as I embarked on the project, others also turned their attention to Justice Stevens through a biography[5] and several symposia issues of law reviews.[6] I am relieved that other authors are filling the gaps in coverage left by my failure to write the originally intended, complete, and definitive book on Justice Stevens.

When I decided to write a book on Justice Stevens, I immediately wrote to him to ask if he was willing to be interviewed. I did so despite already possessing a substantial collection—suitable for framed display or sale on eBay—of signed letters from other justices declining my requests for interviews over the course of two decades. To my surprise, he immediately wrote back and invited me to the Supreme Court to meet with him. I am eternally grateful for his generosity in permitting me to interview him on two occasions. As a longtime teacher of college classes on the Supreme Court and constitutional law, I will always treasure my memories of these rare opportunities to walk down the back corridors of the Court and spend time with a justice inside his chambers. More importantly, these opportunities to interview Justice Stevens provided insights and information that never would have been obtainable by merely reading opinions, articles, and documents. In addition, I gained a personal sense of his knowledge, intelligence, and thought processes as well as his generosity, warmth, and modesty. Throughout this project, Justice Stevens was genuinely interested in ensuring that I produce my own independent analysis of his work, role, and impact. I admire his desire to avoid influencing my conclusions. Thus I owe my deepest debt of gratitude to Justice Stevens for his interest, openness, and patience throughout this project. I am also grateful to members of the Stevens family who provided background information.

I am indebted to many people who contributed in various ways to this long-term project. Within the scholarly community, I am eternally grateful to my mentor, the late George F. Cole of the University of Connecticut, whose guidance and influence built my career in academic writing. Many colleagues with whom I have coauthored books and articles over the years have made significant contributions to my understanding of Justice Stevens and his impact on constitutional law: Joyce Baugh of Central Michigan University; Thomas Hensley of Kent State University; Charles Jacobs of St. Norbert College; Scott Johnson of Frostburg State University; Madhavi McCall of San Diego State University; Michael McCall of San Diego State University; and David Schultz of Hamline University. I sought and gained valuable advice from senior colleagues, especially Harry Hirsch of Oberlin College and Lawrence Baum of Ohio State University, as well as from scholars who were formerly Justice Stevens's law clerks, especially Diane Marie Amann of the University of Georgia and Joseph Thai of the University of Oklahoma. These scholars made invaluable contributions but they bear no responsibility for my analysis, conclusions, or errors.

I am grateful to my colleagues in the Michigan State University School of Criminal Justice for their contributions to an environment conducive to scholarly productivity, including immediate past director of the school, Ed McGarrell, for facilitating a brief sabbatical as I was conducting research. Several students helped to organize topical lists and descriptions of Justice

Stevens's opinions, although much of their work was not ultimately used when the book's focus narrowed to criminal justice cases. In particular, I would like to acknowledge James Looby, Leah Longuski, and Melanie Morley for their assistance.

My knowledge of legal issues and constitutional law as well as my analysis of Justice Stevens were informed by observations and insights that I gained from conversations over the years with friends and mentors in the legal community: Abraham V. Hutt; Christopher S. Auguste; Lisa Peebles; Pamela S. Horowitz; Thao Tiedt; the late Hon. Richard Enslen, U.S. District Judge (W.D. Mich.); the late Hon. Doyle Rowland, U.S. Magistrate Judge (W.D. Mich.); the Hon. Virginia Morgan, U.S. Magistrate Judge (retired) (E.D. Mich.); and the Hon. James Carr, U.S. District Judge (retired) (N.D. Ohio). I learned a great deal from Linda Greenhouse of the *New York Times* and Yale Law School through reading her insightful work on the Supreme Court and observing her live interview with Justice Stevens at a Public Citizen dinner during the summer of 2013. I also admire and appreciate her willingness to respond to the occasional email message from a very distant acquaintance. In addition, I am grateful for the hospitality and encouragement of my dear friends Gabrielle Virgo and Ernest Carter during my research trips to Washington, D.C.

Portions of chapter 5 were originally published in "Justice John Paul Stevens: Staunch Defender of *Miranda* Rights," *DePaul Law Review* 60 (2010): 99–140. Portions of chapter 8 were originally published in "Justice John Paul Stevens and Capital Punishment," *Berkeley Journal of Criminal Law* 15 (2010): 205–60. I am grateful to these law reviews for permission to use this material in the book.

My children were still in high school when this project began. They are now college graduates nearing completion of their graduate degrees and soon to enter their professional careers. I am grateful for the love and support of future social science scholar, Alicia Smith-Tran, and future lawyer and legal scholar, Eric Smith. I am similarly grateful for the inspiration and encouragement of my parents, Robert L. and Carol Payne Smith. Most of all, I am grateful to Charlotte, my wife of thirty-one years, to whom I dedicate this book, for her patience and support—and willingness to listen to three books' worth of thoughts about Justice Stevens over the better part of a decade.

NOTES

1. Robert Judd Sickels, *John Paul Stevens and the Constitution* (University Park, Pa.: Pennsylvania State University Press, 1988).
2. Kenneth Manaster, *Illinois Justice: The Scandal of 1969 and the Rise of John Paul Stevens* (Chicago: University of Chicago Press, 2001).

3. Lee Epstein, Jeffrey A. Segal, Harold J. Spaeth, and Thomas G. Walker, *The Supreme Court Compendium: Data, Decisions, and Developments*, 5th ed. (Washington, D.C.: Congressional Quarterly Press), 654.

4. Jan Crawford Greenburg, "Exclusive: Supreme Court Justice Stevens Remembers President Ford," ABC News online, January 2, 2007, accessed July 6, 2015, http://abcnews.go.com/Nightline/story?id=2765753.

5. Bill Barnhart and Gene Schlickman, *John Paul Stevens: An Independent Life* (DeKalb, Ill.: Northern Illinois University Press, 2010).

6. *Fordham Law Review* 74 (2006): 1557–2369; *UC Davis Law Review* 43 (2010): 713–1070; *Georgetown Law Journal* 99 (2011): 1263–1324.

Chapter One

Introduction

Two weeks before Justice John Paul Stevens reached his milestone ninetieth birthday in April 2010, he sent a letter to President Barack Obama announcing his resignation effective at the close of the U.S. Supreme Court term in June. In a career that spanned nearly thirty-five years on the nation's highest court, Stevens was a prolific author of judicial opinions. In addition to 396 majority and plurality opinions, he wrote more dissenting opinions (720) and concurring opinions (389) than any other justice in the Court's history.[1] As the third longest-serving justice, Stevens helped to shape the Court's decisions affecting the most contentious issues of his era, including capital punishment and rights for terrorism suspects. He was not merely an equal participant among the nine decision makers on the Court. Instead, commentators acknowledged his special importance and influence in their characterizations of his role and performance: "master strategist";[2] "leader of the [C]ourt's liberal wing";[3] "independent-minded jurist";[4] and "strongest, most articulate voice on the [C]ourt defending the rights of criminal defendants and racial, religious, and other minorities."[5] Stevens's intellect and judicial opinions also made him the object of special respect, admiration, and, presumably, influence among justices with whom he shared judicial values as well as those who frequently disagreed with him. For example, his frequent ally, Justice David Souter, reportedly told friends that Stevens was the "smartest" justice on the Supreme Court.[6] Justice Antonin Scalia, who often dueled with Stevens in their respective opinions on various issues, identified Stevens as his "favorite sparring partner" because of their mutual respect in responding to, rather than dismissing, their points of disagreement.[7]

This book seeks to illuminate and analyze the role and influence of Stevens by focusing on his involvement in cases affecting criminal justice. Criminal justice cases help to demonstrate the role of Stevens within the changing Supreme Court as the appointment of new justices in the 1970s and thereafter shifted debates and decisions. Criminal justice issues, such as capital punishment, prisoners' rights, and *Miranda* warnings, split the Court and the country along political and cultural fault lines that were parallel to the divisions produced by noncriminal justice issues such as abortion, affirmative action, and separation of church and state. Criminal justice cases also illuminate Stevens's approach to decision making, especially his case-by-case approach to decision making and his emphasis on the concept of liberty. While several other justices focused on creating broad rules that they would apply notwithstanding detrimental human consequences from those rules, Stevens treated individual cases as problems to be solved in light of both the commands of law and the effects on people's lives.

A LEADING LIBERAL ON THE SUPREME COURT

The role and influence of any justice are shaped by the historical era and political context in which the justice serves on the Supreme Court. In particular, a justice's legacy is determined not only by his or her own votes and opinions in cases, but also by the specific legal issues presented to the Court and the philosophical orientations and personalities of the other justices with whom an individual justice interacted and made decisions. Justice Stevens joined the Court in 1975 as the fifth of ten consecutive new appointees placed on the high court by Republican presidents. He arrived at an early point in the significant compositional shift from the rights-expanding Warren Court era (1953–1969) to the conservatizing periods of the Burger Court (1969–1986) and the early years of the Rehnquist Court (1986–2005). Although the subsequent mix of Republican and Democratic appointees to the Rehnquist Court and Roberts Court (beginning in 2005), who arrived in 1993 and thereafter, had a less uniformly conservatizing impact, they perpetuated the Court's tilt away from the expansion and protection of rights in criminal justice cases. Thus, the entire context of Stevens's long career was defined by the Court's diminution of individuals' rights in the justice process, driven largely by political events that placed Republicans in the White House at most moments when vacancies arose on the high court.

In this chapter and the throughout the book, the terms "liberal" and "conservative" are used to characterize specific Supreme Court decisions and voting patterns of individual Supreme Court justices. These are problematic labels, yet they are commonly used by judicial scholars who study the Supreme Court. For purposes of categorizing votes in such cases, judicial scholars and the Supreme Court Judicial Database use imprecise characterizations that define "liberal" votes as those supporting individuals against government and those endorsing the protection of rights for women and political minorities, whether racial, ethnic, or religious. Conversely, "conservative" votes are those that support the government against individuals and favor business interests over those of labor unions and consumers.[8] These definitions are problematic for issues associated with political conservatives' support for specific individual prerogatives that clash with assertions of governmental authority. In particular, political conservatives' support for property rights, gun ownership rights, and the "free speech" right of corporations and other organizations to spend money on political campaigns leads to counterintuitive classifications of case outcomes. These specific issues create an anomalous aspect of judicial scholars' formal scorekeeping for Supreme Court justices' votes. The universal labeling of support for individuals as "liberal" in individual-versus-government disputes is inconsistent with general understandings about the positions of self-identified political conservatives and political liberals in contemporary society. Justice Stevens is credited with "conservative" votes for these three contentious issues due to his endorsement of the legality of government regulation of land use, firearms, and financial aspects of election campaigns. These votes reduced his percentage of "liberal" votes in scholars' categorizations. Yet in the eyes of the news media, political commentators, and the public, he actually enhanced his reputation as the Court's leading liberal by writing the major opinions on these issues that directly confronted and opposed the policy objectives of ideological Republican politicians and activist conservative jurists.

For example, Justice Stevens's extensive dissenting opinions provided detailed refutations of the majority opinions by Justices Antonin Scalia and Samuel Alito in the decisions that established an individual right to gun ownership under the Second Amendment. A narrow majority of justices made the Second Amendment right applicable against both federal and local regulations in, respectively, *District of Columbia v. Heller* (2008) and *McDonald v. City of Chicago* (2010). In *Heller*, by providing a detailed historical justification for interpreting the Second Amendment as protecting only states' prerogative to arm their organized militias, Stevens directly challenged Scalia's originalist claims about a personal gun-ownership right.

Notwithstanding the complexity and limitations of applying the labels "liberal" and "conservative" to Supreme Court justices and their decisions, these are widely used terms with generally understood meanings for nearly all rights issues in criminal justice. Thus they are useful for describing and analyzing Stevens's decisions and opinions as a Supreme Court justice.

Among the twelve new justices appointed by Republican presidents from the end of the Warren Court era in 1969 through the early Roberts Court era in 2006, Stevens stood out for his support of constitutional rights claims. The Supreme Court Judicial Database indicates that Stevens's votes in cases classified under the categories of Criminal Procedure, Civil Liberties, Civil Rights, First Amendment, and Due Process favored individuals more frequently than did the votes of Republican appointees from the Burger-era and thereafter with whom he served. In voting on outcomes for cases in these categories, Stevens's support for individuals stood at 65.4 percent. By contrast, the two appointees from this era whom commentators frequently described as defining the middle of the Court, Justices Sandra Day O'Connor and Anthony Kennedy, had rates of 36 percent and 37.1 percent, respectively. Not surprisingly, Stevens had even greater contrasts with consistently conservative justices such as Clarence Thomas and Antonin Scalia, whose respective rates in support of individuals' rights claims were 23.2 percent and 28.3 percent. Among justices who served in the Burger Court era or thereafter, only liberal Warren Court holdovers Justices Hugo Black (73.7 percent), William Brennan (79.6 percent), William O. Douglas (88.3 percent), and Thurgood Marshall (81.6 percent) had career voting records that exceeded Stevens's record for frequency of support for individuals' rights.[9] Justice Black retired several years before Stevens joined the Court and Stevens was appointed to replace Douglas. Thus among the justices with whom he actually served, Stevens trailed only Brennan and Marshall in the liberalness of his voting record on rights issues. Because Brennan and Marshall retired in 1990 and 1991 respectively, for the final two decades of his career Stevens shared the title of "most liberal justice" with Democratic appointee Ruth Bader Ginsburg (65.9 percent).[10] Thus Jeffrey Rosen observed in 2007, "In criminal-law and death-penalty cases, Stevens has voted against the government and in favor of the individual more than any other sitting justice."[11]

Two Republican appointees from Stevens's era also had voting records reflecting support for rights claims in more than half of the cases in these categories, Justices Harry Blackmun (52.5 percent) and David Souter (62.8 percent). Like Stevens, Blackmun and Souter were often harshly criticized by Republicans politicians and commentators for not consistently reflecting within their judicial opinions the values and policy priorities of the political party with which they had been affiliated and that engineered their appointments to the Supreme Court. Despite the fact that the voting records of all three justices sharply distinguished them from the other Republican appointees with whom they served, Stevens differed significantly from Blackmun and Souter in his path to a liberal voting record and his role on the Court.

As scholars have demonstrated, Blackmun and Souter became markedly more liberal over time in their decision making concerning criminal justice and other issues. As one careful empirical analysis noted, "Indeed, Souter is the new Blackmun—that is, a Justice who . . . has grown strikingly more liberal with nearly each passing term."[12] Justice Blackmun observed that "I suspect that when one goes on the Supreme Court of the United States his constitutional philosophy is not fully developed."[13] Indeed, this observation seems true for both Blackmun and Souter. In the case of Blackmun, his authorship, identification with, and defense of the right of choice for abortion in *Roe v. Wade* (1973) profoundly affected his thinking and apparently contributed to a shift in his voting record on rights issues.[14] For Souter, the range of issues presented to the Supreme Court was broader than those he saw as a state attorney general and state supreme court justice in New Hampshire. In addition, Souter's respect for precedent, including Warren Court precedents concerning rights in criminal justice, may have pushed his voting record in a liberal direction as he addressed many cases in which his more conservative colleagues sought to shrink the scope of rights by aggressively jettisoning prior precedents.[15]

By contrast, although Stevens changed his views concerning certain issues, such as capital punishment and affirmative action, as the chapters of this book will argue, he arrived at the Supreme Court with well-formed judicial values as a result of his life experiences and work as a practicing attorney and federal appellate judge. He also articulated unique viewpoints about specific issues and these viewpoints placed into circulation ideas that have the potential to shape the law in future cases. Moreover, upon the retirement of Blackmun in 1994, Stevens frequently became the senior justice supporting individuals' rights for the final sixteen years of his career. As a result, Stevens played a key role in marshaling support for specific positions, crafting opinions, and, when in the majority, assigning authorship of the Court's opinions to preserve or strengthen constitutional protections for criminal suspects, defendants, and convicted offenders. Because of the Court's composition and decision-making trends during the decades in which he served, Stevens had limited opportunities to contribute to the expansion of rights in criminal justice. However, he played a crucial role in resisting other justices' efforts to diminish rights and, in so doing, left a rich legacy of opinions from which current and future judicial officers may draw in crafting their own decisions that protect individuals' rights.

APPOINTMENT TO THE SUPREME COURT

In 1975, the *New York Times* described John Paul Stevens as developing "a solid and scholarly, if unspectacular, approach to law" through "two decades of private law practice in Chicago, primarily in antitrust and corporate fields."[16] Standard snapshot characterizations of his legal career consistently described him as "a lawyer . . . specializing in antitrust cases."[17] These characterizations reflected Stevens's image at the moment that President Gerald Ford nominated him for a seat on the Supreme Court. Based on perceptions of his five-year record as a judge on the U.S. Court of Appeals, the former business lawyer Stevens was widely viewed as a moderately conservative judge who was likely to lean in a conservative direction in his decisions on the Supreme Court. Although a few commentators acknowledged that "Stevens' legal outlook may . . . prove unexpected,"[18] most characterizations were consistent with the image conveyed by the description in the *New York Times*. For example, an article in the *Chicago Tribune* pegged him as "destined to join the right-center of the [C]ourt lineup—somewhere between . . . the conservative end of the bench and the outnumbered liberals, Justices William Brennan and Thurgood Marshall."[19]

In the politics of that post-Watergate moment, President Ford sought to restore the public's confidence in government by selecting an experienced lower court judge who embodied the qualities of integrity, professionalism, and competence.[20] Ford resisted suggestions from conservative Republicans that his choice of an appointee be guided by political ideology. Indeed, such a selection would have created risks of rejection by the Democrats in the U.S. Senate, much like the rejections of President Richard Nixon's two appointees, Clement F. Haynsworth, Jr. and G. Harrold Carswell, just a few years earlier.[21] A scholar who interviewed the Ford-era White House officials involved in the selection of Stevens found that "[f]rom the outset, Ford was determined to name a respected moderately conservative jurist."[22]

The Ford administration sought to portray Stevens as a conservative in order to please Republican politicians and constituents who perceived the recently concluded Warren Court era (1953–1969) as manifesting the excesses of liberal judicial activism.[23] Attorney General Edward Levi's memorandum to President Ford that provided evaluations of potential candidates said of Stevens, "He is generally a moderate conservative in his approach to judicial problems, and in cases involving attempted expansion of constitutional rights and remedies."[24] Thus the *New York Times* reported that Stevens "is described as a centrist who tends to side with the prosecution in criminal cases."[25] Ultimately, Justice Stevens was approved by a 98 to 0 vote in the U.S. Senate and subsequently sworn in on December 19, 1975.

At the time of Stevens's appointment to the Supreme Court, some observers' assumptions about what to expect from a Republican appointee may have been shaped by the four appointments by President Richard Nixon that preceded the appointment of Stevens. Nixon turned the Warren Court's liberalism into a political campaign issue in 1968 by claiming that the Supreme Court's decisions helped criminals and hampered law enforcement. Moreover, in his cultivation of southern white voters to draw them away from the soon-to-be-defunct segregationist wing of the Democratic Party, Nixon used his criticism of the Supreme Court to signal his opposition to proactive remedies for school desegregation, such as judicially ordered busing plans. Nixon openly vowed to appoint a southerner to the Supreme Court as an additional signal to conservative white voters, although the Senate ultimately blocked both of his southern nominees, Haynsworth and Carswell.[26] Thus, Nixon nominated Warren Burger, Harry Blackmun, William Rehnquist, and

Lewis Powell with the specific expectation that they would be law-and-order justices who would turn the Supreme Court away from the liberal, rights-protective path of the Warren Court era. Yet the context of Stevens's appointment, albeit by a Republican president, was quite different from the historical moment and presidential motivations of the nominations that immediately preceded him—as well as those that came later. It is possible that some observers' initial predictions and characterizations about Stevens erroneously assumed that he would be similar to the other Republicans appointed to the Court in the 1970s.

Because of the particular appointing president and historical moment in which he was nominated for the Supreme Court, Stevens did not face the same partisan scrutiny and opposition that would become common in the 1980s and thereafter. Gerald Ford was an accidental president, voted into public office only by the voters of Grand Rapids, Michigan, and not by the national electorate. The accidental nature of Ford's elevation to the presidency upon Nixon's Watergate-driven resignation seemed even more remarkable in light of a comment by Ford's Yale Law School classmate, Justice Potter Stewart. Justice Stewart told an interviewer that if someone had told his law school class that one of them was destined to be president and told each of them to write down the name of who that would be, then, in Stewart's words: "[E]veryone would have gotten at least one vote except our classmate Jerry Ford. At least each of us would have voted for himself, but Jerry Ford and the rest of us all knew that he was going to return to Grand Rapids and practice law."[27] Instead, history created a different path as President Nixon selected Ford, the Republican leader in the House of Representatives, to become vice president after the resignation of Vice President Spiro Agnew. Agnew resigned in 1973 during a criminal investigation into his prior activities as governor of Maryland. When Nixon subsequently resigned in the aftermath of the Watergate scandal in 1974, Ford, who unexpectedly inherited the presidency, felt obligated to restore the public's confidence in the national government. Thus, as described by David O'Brien, Ford "departed from the practices and priorities of other recent Presidents" by choosing Stevens based on professional considerations rather than partisanship or ideology.[28]

Stevens did not face the rigorous, partisan, litmus-test-oriented confirmation hearings that have become standard since 1987. As Joyce Baugh has documented, the failed nomination of Judge Robert Bork in 1987 initiated an era of heightened partisanship that motivated many opposing-party senators to vigorously challenge subsequent Supreme Court nominees.[29] By contrast, although Stevens was asked questions about various matters during the confirmation hearings, his nomination predated the partisan politicization of the abortion issue. Thus, Stevens wrote later that he was not asked any questions about the then two-year-old decision in *Roe v. Wade* (1973).[30] When Senator

Strom Thurmond of South Carolina wanted to talk to nominee Stevens about the issue of capital punishment, according to Stevens, Thurmond said, "I am not going to ask you for your opinion—for that would be improper—but I want to tell you how I feel about it."[31] Such kid-glove treatment is difficult to imagine for observers familiar with Supreme Court nominations in the three decades that followed. In essence, Stevens may not have received sufficient critical scrutiny to fully illuminate the judicial values evident in his court of appeals decisions.

More importantly, because Stevens was a Republican nominee, he was nearly assured of support from Republican senators who would not have wanted President Ford, a fellow Republican, to face the embarrassment and political diminution experienced by President Nixon when his nominees—Haynsworth and Carswell—were blocked from confirmation. Thus the questions directed at Stevens during his hearings came from Democratic senators, such as Edward Kennedy of Massachusetts and John Tunney of California, who were concerned about whether he might be too conservative. Observers perhaps saw Stevens's answers to questions from liberal senators as predictably reassuring by necessity in the confirmation context rather than as evidence that a closer and more comprehensive examination of his appellate court record would show him to be more liberal than expected. In addition, his sterling reputation for nonpartisan professionalism both as an attorney and as an appellate judge reduced potential concerns that might otherwise have led senators to vigorously test or challenge his viewpoints.

EXPLAINING THE LIBERALISM OF STEVENS

Analysts have put forth several speculative theories to explain why Republican appointees Stevens, Blackmun, and Souter ultimately defied original predictions and were more liberal and protective of rights over the course of their careers than other Republican appointees of their era. One hypothesis about Republican appointees to the Supreme Court in recent decades concerns the differences between the justices depending on whether or not they had to move to Washington, D.C., in order to assume a seat on the Court.[32] For those already located in or near the heart of American politics, the District of Columbia, by virtue of their prior service in presidential administrations or service on the U.S. Court of Appeals for the District of Columbia Circuit (e.g., Burger, Rehnquist, Scalia, and Thomas), there appeared to be more consistent conservatism in their voting patterns. By contrast, the Republican appointees who moved to Washington, D.C., from elsewhere in the country (e.g., Blackmun, Stevens, O'Connor, Kennedy, and Souter) to assume a seat on the Supreme Court were the ones whose decisions were more liberal than originally anticipated. As Linda Greenhouse described with respect to Justice Blackmun,

> Both Blackmun and O'Connor experienced the personal disruption of a mid-life move to a distant city and culture with which they were almost entirely unfamiliar. This mind-bending experience, and their lack of a personal agenda, left each of these Justices open to new and unexpected influences in a way that Clarence Thomas, for example, has not been. The world of Clarence Thomas, a product of bureaucratic Washington by the time he was named to the Court at the age of forty-three, has become more insular and self-reinforcing, while the worlds of Harry Blackmun and Sandra O'Connor became ever more open.[33]

If this speculative explanation for justices' decision-making behavior has validity, then it could hypothetically apply to Justice Stevens, who had lived in Chicago for all but a few years of his life when he moved to Washington, D.C., at age fifty-five to join the Supreme Court. However, this explanation focuses primarily on why justices change their views during their service on the Court. Although there is evidence that Stevens changed his position on some issues, as the chapters of this book will describe, there is also clear evidence that he arrived at the Court in 1975 with judicial values and approaches to certain legal issues that were more liberal and rights-protective than observers had anticipated.

Michael Dorf employed a slightly different approach by examining whether prior experience in the federal executive branch explained why certain Republican justices, such as Rehnquist, Scalia, and Thomas, did not "evolve" during their service on the Supreme Court.[34] Although this hypothesis holds true in contrasting the liberalism of Stevens and Souter with the consistent conservatism of the aforementioned justices, even Professor Dorf did not conclude that federal executive service explained subsequent judicial decision making. Instead, Dorf said that "[t]he answer appears to be that when Republican Presidents chose nominees from outside the Beltway [of Washington, D.C.], they were not looking for staunch conservatives."[35] In considering the case of Stevens, Dorf asserted that "[b]y nominating the highly regarded Stevens, Ford eliminated any doubt about his commitment to an independent judiciary" and thereby advanced the president's goal of making the choice based on professional qualifications rather than ideology.[36] As a result, the key to understanding Justice Stevens's divergence from initial expectations based on his political party affiliation and reputation as a business lawyer is the recognition that Stevens already possessed rights-protective judicial values prior to his Supreme Court appointment.

Perhaps more relevant to understanding Justice Stevens's liberal judicial values is Mark Tushnet's observation about the changes in the Republican Party over the course of Stevens's career. Professor Tushnet's description of

Justice Souter fits Justice Stevens equally well. In Tushnet's words, "[Souter] was a Republican, but a northeastern Republican, representative of the party before its transformation by Goldwater and Reagan."[37] Obviously, Stevens was from Illinois rather than New England, but northern Republicans from the Great Lakes region were similarly moderate prior to the transformation of their party. By the 1990s, the Republican Party was dominated by social issue conservatives and corporate interests. Party activists enforced ideological orthodoxy on political candidates and officeholders, including requirements to oppose abortion, reduce taxes, and cut social programs and income support for the poor. The Republican Party of the late 1940s and 1950s, when Stevens completed his legal training and began his career, had a broader membership base, including social policy liberals. The mainstream Republicans of the Eisenhower era did not feel obligated to be ideological purists and ardent conservatives. Thus Stevens's moderate wing of the Republican Party was nearly extinct by the final two decades of his career on the Court. It was no surprise then that he, like Souter, timed his retirement to permit a Democratic president, Barack Obama, to select his replacement. Justice Stevens presumably recognized that any new appointee from a contemporary Republican president would likely contribute to the Court's move away from the rights-protective judicial philosophy and decisions that he espoused.

As will be presented in chapter 4's discussion of prisoners' rights, Stevens revealed very liberal positions on the rights of convicted offenders during his very first months on the Supreme Court. His dissenting opinions in *Meachum v. Fano* (1976) and *Estelle v. Gamble* (1976) advocated a remarkably broad and protective vision of constitutional rights. These initial prisoners' rights opinions provide strong evidence that Stevens brought to the Supreme Court with him a well-formed judicial philosophy and rights-oriented approach to constitutional interpretation that were the products of his values, education, and life experiences. His important formative experiences included his service as a Supreme Court law clerk in the 1947 Term, his experience as a volunteer attorney for convicted offenders, and his judicial decision making during five years as a federal appellate judge. These experiences contributed to his performance from the outset of his Supreme Court career as one of the leading defenders of rights in criminal justice. Justice Stevens's development of a strongly rights-protective orientation toward criminal justice issues prior to his appointment to the Court differentiated him from the other relatively liberal Republican appointees of his era, Justices Blackmun and Souter, who became markedly more liberal in criminal justice cases while serving on the Supreme Court.

ELEMENTS OF JUSTICE STEVENS'S JUDICIAL PHILOSOPHY

A judge's judicial philosophy contains many elements, including values and policy preferences, approaches to interpretation of constitutional provisions and statutes, and views about the appropriate role of judges in the governing system. Because Justice Stevens was such an independent thinker and prolific opinion writer, the analysis of his judicial philosophy is especially challenging. By contrast, a number of his colleagues, both liberal and conservative, appeared to be guided by discernible ideological leanings and predictable preferred outcomes. At the time of his retirement, Stevens was typically described as the "liberal wing's leader" for his final two decades on the Court.[38] However, because of Stevens's independence of thought and case-by-case approach to decision making, even his liberal colleague Justice Brennan had never considered him entirely predictable. In an interview with his biographer, Brennan said of Stevens, "It has to be trial and error. . . . I just have to write the damn thing [i.e., draft of an opinion] and wait. And if John reacts against something, he very quickly lets me know."[39]

Because of Stevens's case-by-case approach to judicial decision making, he did not espouse a general theory of constitutional interpretation. By contrast, his originalist colleagues, Scalia and Thomas, became magnets for scholarly analyses that explored their fidelity to, consistent application of, and deviations from the original intent theory of interpretation that they trumpeted in judicial opinions and public speeches. Yet, specific values and themes were evident in Stevens's approach and these can be illuminated by an examination of his opinions in the realm of criminal justice. Thus an analysis of Stevens's role in policy-shaping debates about constitutional rights reveals the judicial philosophy that guided his decision making for a variety of issues.

The Concept of Liberty

In his final term on the Supreme Court, Stevens and his colleagues considered a monumental case addressing whether the Second Amendment right involving firearms applied as a limitation on regulatory actions by states and cities (*McDonald v. City of Chicago*, 2010). Two years earlier, the justices narrowly voted, 5 to 4, to declare that the Second Amendment provides a right for law-abiding individuals to keep handguns in their homes for self-protection (*District of Columbia v. Heller*, 2008). Justice Stevens wrote a lengthy dissenting opinion in *Heller* that confronted Justice Scalia's originalist majority opinion on its own terms by providing substantial historical evidence for the alternative argument that the Second Amendment was intended to permit states to arm their militias rather than to provide a personal constitutional right for individuals. Because the case concerned a law in the

District of Columbia, the Second Amendment precedent only clearly applied to federal jurisdictions. When the issue reached the Court again in *McDonald* to decide whether the Second Amendment should be incorporated and applied against states and cities, the deeply divided justices split into the same voting coalitions as in *Heller*. Justice Samuel Alito wrote the majority opinion invalidating city ordinances in Chicago and Oak Park, Illinois, that had barred private handgun ownership within city limits. In response, Justice Stevens wrote a detailed opinion that challenged the judicial philosophy, analysis of history, and conclusions embodied in Alito's majority opinion.[40]

When asked during an interview whether his *McDonald* dissent was like a retiring professor's last lecture that summarizes and emphasizes the most important teachings or research conclusions of the professor's career, Stevens did not resist the analogy.[41] As he said, "I guess it was [like a last lecture] in some respects. . . . It all sort of struck me in that particular case that the Court had not thought through the issues very carefully."[42] In describing the opinion, he acknowledged, in his words, that "I thought I should put some things in my last shot" prior to retirement.[43] The *McDonald* dissent was limited in scope because the Court was looking at a specific legal issue. However, Stevens used the opportunity to discuss concepts that were especially important to his judicial decision making: liberty and substantive due process. A former Stevens law clerk, Jamal Greene, described *McDonald* as "the case in which Justice Stevens offered the most complete articulation of his judicial philosophy."[44]

The word "liberty" appears in the Due Process Clauses of both the Fifth and Fourteenth Amendments. The familiar phrase of the Fourteenth Amendment, ". . . nor shall any State deprive any person of life, liberty, or property, without due process of law," expresses a lofty ideal but lacks specific guidance on meaning, especially with respect to the ambiguous words "liberty" and "due process." Not surprisingly, the interpretation of these words has been a significant source of disagreement among the Supreme Court's justices in the decades since the ratification of the Fourteenth Amendment in 1868. In the modern era, the debate surrounding the recognition of rights under substantive due process has involved political conservatives accusing liberal Supreme Court justices of exceeding their authority by creating new rights and invalidating legislative enactments. For example, these critics point to such Supreme Court decisions as *Lawrence v. Texas* (2003) that recognized a violation of individuals' right to liberty when a state statute criminalized consensual, non-commercial, private sexual behavior of gays and lesbians. Those who adopt a limited view of due process often argue that the phrase refers only to "procedural due process," namely an entitlement to a hearing or procedural steps before the government can take away one's life, liberty, or property. Indeed, Justice Stevens wrote that he originally interpreted the Due Process Clause that way: "When I became a federal judge in

1970, I thought that the text of the Due Process Clause defined the limits of its coverage. A literal reading of that text provides procedural safeguards, but has no substantive conduct."[45] However, Stevens also described how, prior to his appointment to the Supreme Court in 1975, he came to interpret the Due Process Clause as a source of substantive rights through the protection of the concept of individual liberty.[46]

In describing his recognition of substantive due process, Justice Stevens noted that Justice Louis Brandeis similarly changed his views about the Due Process Clause after becoming a judge.[47] In discussing his own change in perspective Stevens quoted key language from Brandeis's opinion in *Whitney v. California* (1927), an opinion that Stevens described as "stirring":[48]

> Despite arguments to the contrary which had seemed persuasive to me, it is [now] settled that the due process clause of the Fourteenth Amendment applies to matters of substantive law as well as to matter of procedure. Thus all fundamental rights comprised within the term liberty are protected by the Federal Constitution from invasion by the states.[49]

Moreover, Justice Stevens admitted that he had always assumed that Justice Oliver Wendell Holmes opposed recognition of substantive due process because the famous jurist dissented against the majority's decision to enforce a right to economic liberty in *Lochner v. New York* (1905). In *Lochner*, the Supreme Court majority struck down a state occupational health law that limited working hours in bakeries. However, Stevens later wrote that a closer examination of opinions revealed that Holmes actually endorsed substantive due process but only for "fundamental principles as they have been understood by the traditions of our people and our law."[50]

In a speech after his retirement, Justice Stevens praised Justice John Harlan's dissent in *Poe v. Ullman* (1961) as "one of the Court's greatest opinions."[51] The *Poe* case concerned a challenge by two married couples to Connecticut's law banning the use of contraceptives. A majority of justices rejected the challenge by concluding that the controversy was not yet ripe because no one had been arrested and prosecuted under the Connecticut law. In dissent, Harlan disagreed with the conclusion that the Court should not yet address the constitutional issues raised in the case. In addition, he articulated the basis for applying substantive due process in order to conclude that the Connecticut statute should be invalidated because, in his words: it "violates the Fourteenth Amendment. I believe that a statute making it a criminal offense for *married couples* to use contraceptives is an intolerable and unjustifiable invasion of privacy in the conduct of the most intimate concerns of an individual's personal life" (emphasis in original).[52] Elsewhere in the opinion, Harlan argued that the "liberty" protected by the Fourteenth Amendment is not limited to the list of specific rights enumerated in the Bill of Rights, but instead "is a rational continuum which, broadly speaking, includes a freedom from all substantial arbitrary impositions and purposeless restraints."[53]

In his speech, Justice Stevens quoted Harlan's language that anticipated and rejected critics' claims that the use of substantive due process is merely a license for judges to create new rights and thereby place their own values and policy preferences into constitutional law. According to Harlan's *Poe* dissent, it is not the case that "judges have felt free to roam where unguided speculation might take them."[54] Instead, judges must strike a balance between "liberty of the individual"[55] and the "demands of organized society."[56] In Harlan's words, "The balance of which I speak is the balance struck by this country, having regard to what history teaches are the traditions from which it developed as well as the traditions from which it broke."[57]

Justice Stevens's praise for Harlan's opinion as "one of the Court's greatest" and the material from the opinion that he chose to highlight in his speech demonstrated Stevens's commitment to substantive due process. Moreover, he sought to show that judges do not have untethered discretion in interpreting the word "liberty" and deciding what rights are protected through the Due Process Clause. Instead, he clearly endorsed the viewpoint shared by Harlan and Holmes that the liberty protected by the Due Process Clause is defined by fundamental rights that are discernible from the nation's traditions.

Justice Stevens also saw his approach to judicial decision making as similar to that of his colleague Justice Potter Stewart. Among Stewart's notable opinions was his concurring opinion in the landmark abortion-rights precedent, *Roe v. Wade* (1973), two years prior to Stevens's appointment to the Supreme Court. In referring to the Supreme Court's prior precedent in *Griswold v. Connecticut* (1965) that established a right for married couples to obtain contraceptives, Stewart emphasized that the right was based on the substantive due process protection of "liberty" rather than "privacy." According to Stewart,

> So it was clear to me then, and it is equally clear to me now, that the *Griswold* decision can be rationally understood only as a holding that the Connecticut statute substantively invaded the "liberty" that is protected by the Due Process Clause of the Fourteenth Amendment. As so understood, *Griswold* stands as one in a long line of . . . cases decided under the doctrine of substantive due process, and I now accept it as such.[58]

By contrast, Justice Harry Blackmun's majority opinion in *Roe v. Wade* (1973) establishing a woman's right of choice to terminate a pregnancy relied on the "right to privacy . . . founded in the Fourteenth Amendment's concept of personal liberty and restrictions upon state action."[59] Justice Stevens later said in an interview that the right of choice regarding abortion would have been established on much firmer legal ground "if [Blackmun's majority] opinion had said what Potter Stewart said very briefly."[60] In Stevens's view, basing the abortion right on liberty, a word that is actually in the text of the Constitution, rather than privacy, which is not, "might have been much more acceptable, instead of trying to create a new doctrine that really didn't make sense."[61]

In an interview, Justice Stevens said, "There's some background to my being particularly close to Stewart and then indirectly to Harlan,"[62] a justice who served with Stewart but had passed away before Stevens was appointed to the Supreme Court. According to Stevens,

> I did take the time once to compare my votes on the court of appeals with votes in cases where the Supreme Court had passed [judgment] on the same issues. The only justice on the Court who agreed with me on every case was Potter Stewart. I thought about that. Our reasoning wasn't always the same but I always thought that my thinking was basically pretty close to Potter's. And I felt that way when we were here [on the Supreme Court] together.[63]

The shared endorsement of substantive due process and the focus on the protection of liberty were key elements in common for Stewart and Stevens, as well as for Harlan.

Justice Stevens found himself dissenting in various cases when advocating on behalf of the substantive due process rights embodied in the liberty concept. As chapter 4 will discuss, for example, Stevens argued for broad recognition of liberty interests in prisoners' rights cases. In addition, Stevens used liberty interests as the basis for his unsuccessful argument for convicted offenders to have a constitutional right for the testing of preserved evidence when new DNA testing methods may establish their innocence (*District Attorney's Office for the Third Judicial District v. Osborne,* 2009).

Contesting Originalism and Empowering Judges

Justice Stevens was unique among Supreme Court justices in referring to the Due Process Clause as the "liberty clause."[64] His use of this term reflected his emphasis on the concept and its importance for the definition and judicial protection of rights. Justice Scalia, who wrote his concurring opinion in *McDonald* for the sole purpose of refuting Stevens's dissent, referred to Stevens's phraseology by saying "never mind that the 'liberty clause' is really a Due Process Clause."[65] Justice Scalia also articulated the most pointed criticism of Stevens's advocacy of a vague test that identifies as constitutional rights those protections for individuals that are so fundamental that they are, in the words of Justice Benjamin Cardozo's test in *Palko v. Connecticut* (1937) upon which Stevens relied, "implicit in the concept of ordered liberty." In Scalia's words, Stevens's "approach therefore does nothing to stop a judge from arriving at any conclusion he sets out to reach."[66]

While acknowledging that the *Palko* test "undeniably requires judges to apply their own reasoned judgment,"[67] Stevens disagreed with Scalia's assertion and explained how judges are constrained in their decisions about what rights exist under the apparently open-ended concept of liberty in the Due Process Clause. According to Stevens,

> [H]istorical and empirical data of various kinds ground the analysis. Textual commitments laid down elsewhere in the Constitution, judicial precedents, English common law, legislative and social facts, scientific and professional developments, practices of other civilized societies, and, above all else, the "traditions and conscience of our people," . . . are critical variables. They can provide evidence about which rights really are vital to ordered liberty, as well as a spur to judicial action.[68]

Justice Stevens's explanation of the appropriate approach described it as "not an exact methodology, but rather a framework for decision making."[69] Thus his discussion of the judge's task emphasized the importance of "historical experience and reasoned judgment" and the avoidance of relying on "merely personal and private notions."[70] Stevens identified the importance of the "conceptual core" of protected liberty as "[s]elf-determination, bodily integrity, freedom of conscience, intimate relationships, political equality, dignity, and respect."[71] He emphasized that the constraints on judges in interpreting liberty and defining associated rights are precedent, "respect for the democratic process,"[72] and "the need to approach our work with humility and caution."[73] Especially important for Stevens and his approach to judicial decision making was, in his description, "the common-law method—taking cases and controversies as they present themselves, proceeding slowly and incrementally, building on what came before."[74] In his view, "[t]his piecemeal approach allowed the Court to scrutinize more closely the right at issue in any given dispute, reducing both the risk and the cost of error."[75]

Justice Stevens's description in his *McDonald* dissent of the various factors that guided and restrained his interpretation of the protections provided by the "Liberty Clause" of the Fourteenth Amendment could never provide reassurance to originalist justices, such as Scalia and Thomas, who purport to interpret the Constitution according to the original intentions of the framers. They would never believe that Stevens did not insert his values into such decisions. As Jeffrey Shaman has noted, however, there is no doubt that the originalists themselves place their values into decisions through the selective evidentiary choices and interpretations of history that they use to rationalize their conclusions about what the Constitution's framers intended as the meaning of a particular provision.[76] Yet, the originalists, unlike Stevens, claim that they are aspiring to obediently follow an authoritative source. Stevens, by contrast, was quite open about the inevitable fact that "judges [must] apply their own reasoned judgment."[77] For example, in describing his approach to determining the current state of evolving social values concerning Eighth Amendment violations of the Cruel and Unusual Punishments Clause, Stevens said, "[B]ut in the last analysis, . . . the judges really have to make the crucial decision themselves. . . . I really think it is your appraisal of whether or not society has changed in its attitude."[78]

His frankness concerning the propriety and necessity of judges making judgments about liberty, substantive due process, and other issues was an inevitable consequence of two additional aspects of his views about constitutional interpretation. First, unlike the originalists who claim, albeit inconsistently, that the Constitution's meaning is static and fixed by history, Stevens argued that liberty is a "'dynamic concept' . . . [and] [i]ts dynamism provides a central means through which the Framers enabled the Constitution to 'endure for the ages to come.'"[79] Justice Stevens also wrote, "For history, like the law and life itself, involves a process of change, of growth, and of improvement."[80] He quoted approvingly from an article by Chief Justice William Rehnquist that said "[t]he framers of the Constitution wisely spoke in general language and left to succeeding generations the task of applying that language to the unceasingly changing environment in which they would live."[81] In Stevens's conception of the Constitution and law, it was inevitable that judges must make reasoned judgments to keep interpretations reflective of the needs and values of contemporary society. In a speech at the University of Chicago Law School in 1991, Stevens pointed approvingly to Supreme Court decisions in the mid-twentieth century that expanded the right to counsel for criminal defendants as examples of appropriate judgments through which the "rule[s] of law . . . unquestionably changed while the text of those amendments has remained the same."[82]

Second, as a closely related point, Stevens argued in his *McDonald* dissent that judges abdicated their responsibility to make judgments when they relied on a rigid, historical approach to provide the meaning of constitutional provisions. As Stevens said, in a statement that was certainly aimed at his colleagues Scalia and Thomas, "The judge who would outsource the interpretation of 'liberty' to historical sentiment has turned his back on a task the Constitution assigned to him and drained the document of its intended vitality."[83] Justice Stevens reinforced the same point in his memoir of the Supreme Court when he compared his colleagues Justices Thurgood Marshall and Clarence Thomas:

> While Thurgood's jurisprudence reflected an understanding that the Constitution was drafted "to form a more perfect Union"—and thus to accommodate unforeseen changes in society—Justice Thomas's repeated emphasis on historical analysis seems to assume that we should view the Union as perfect at the beginning and subject to improvement only by following the cumbersome process of amending the Constitution.[84]

Learning on the Bench

Justice Stevens emphasized the importance of a judge continuing to learn on the bench and acknowledged that his analysis of specific issues was affected by what he learned through judicial experience.[85] Thus Stevens's liberal judicial values and approach to decision making, while substantially developed by the time of his appointment to the Supreme Court in 1975, were not fixed or static. For example, Linda Greenhouse observed with respect to the evolution of his opinions on abortion, "As Justice Stevens would show throughout his career on the Court, he was never willing to take for granted that he had been right in the past without thinking the problem through in each subsequent iteration."[86]

Justice Stevens was open to the possibility of changing his mind as a reflection of his fact-based, case-by-case approach. Justices who follow a rigid, rule-based approach to deciding cases seem much less likely to be open to analyzing, evaluating, and questioning their own reasoning through the opinion-writing process. Justice Stevens's inclusion of his law clerks in a give-and-take exchange of ideas and arguments provided him with additional information to consider as part of his willingness to question his own views. As described by Stevens,

> I always talk to my law clerks. I don't have them write bench memos, but I always review the cases and my thinking about the case both before and after argument. I ask them to come in, and we sit down and talk about what happened at the argument. Then I'll talk to them again before and after conference. I have a lot of conversation with my clerks to get their reaction to a case.[87]

A documentary film on the Supreme Court included an on-camera conversation between Stevens and a law clerk with the following exchange:

> *Justice Stevens*: [pointing to the law clerk] "One [case] that you convinced me to change my mind on, you remember? You convinced me once, but then I think I got unconvinced."
>
> *Law Clerk*: "Then you got reconvinced again."
>
> *Justice Stevens*: "Reconvinced. . . . We went back and forth on it several times."[88]

There is no doubt that Justice Stevens was very knowledgeable and confident about his own judicial values and his approach to judicial decision making. The foregoing examples are not inconsistent with the argument that Stevens's education and experiences helped to shape a well-formed judicial philosophy prior to his appointment to the Supreme Court in 1975. They merely illustrate his willingness to listen and learn, consistent with his acknowledgment that judges should always keep learning on the bench and eschew decision-making approaches that purport to be static or rule-based.[89]

Federalism

One of the important debates within the Supreme Court during Justice Stevens's tenure concerned the issue of federalism, especially the authority of Congress to enact certain laws. After the Supreme Court's composition changed during the 1930s with the infusion of President Franklin Roosevelt's appointees, the Court consistently adopted a broad and deferential view of the constitutionality of federal legislation enacted under the congressional commerce power. Changes to the Court's composition prior to and during Justice Stevens's tenure led to further debates over this issue and other matters of federalism, including cases that affected criminal justice, as new appointees sought to redefine and limit congressional power and thereby give greater authority to states to handle their own affairs.

A case argued before the Supreme Court less than two months after Justice Stevens's arrival gave him his first exposure to the debate within the Court. In *National League of Cities v. Usery* (1976), then-Associate Justice Rehnquist, one of the advocates of states' authority, wrote for a five-member majority in concluding that state and local governments were not subject to the minimum wage and maximum hour provisions of the federal Fair Labor Standards Act (FLSA). Justice Brennan, joined by his fellow Warren Court holdovers, Justices Marshall and White, wrote a vigorous dissent against the diminution of federal legislative authority. Years later, Stevens acknowledged that, in retrospect, he came to the conclusion that he agreed with Brennan's powerful language, including characterizing the majority's decision as a "catastrophic body blow" to the power of Congress.[90] At the time, however, Brennan's use of such strong language led newcomer Stevens to write his own separate dissenting opinion. It was a very early reflection of the independent thinking and inclination to explain his own views that would characterize Stevens's judicial behavior throughout his entire Supreme Court career. Consistent with his concern for the practical consequences of judicial decisions, Stevens opened his dissent with a striking illustration of the effects of the majority's decision: "The Court holds that the Federal Government may not interfere with a sovereign State's inherent right to pay a substandard wage to the janitor at the state capitol. The principle on which the holding rests is difficult to perceive."[91] Speaking from what appeared to be the perspective of an attorney knowledgeable about economic issues through antitrust work, Stevens expressed skepticism about the wisdom of minimum wage laws such as the FLSA. However, he acknowledged that his personal views about the statute had no bearing on its constitutionality. Instead, he gave examples of a variety of other federal laws that he believed "unquestionably" applied to state and local governments, such as tax laws, employment discrimination laws, and environmental protection laws, to make the point that the majority was incorrect in limiting the reach of the FLSA. This initial opinion did not establish Stevens as a strong advocate of national power in relation to state power, but it gave an early indication that Stevens was not among those on the Court who would actively seek to limit federal authority in favor of state autonomy.

The direct impact of the *National League of Cities* decision lasted less than a decade as Justice Blackmun shifted his views on the issue. Thus the decision was overturned by Blackmun and the four *National League of Cities* dissenters who formed a new five-member majority in *Garcia v. San Antonio Metropolitan Transit Authority* (1985). The debate over the applicability of the FLSA foreshadowed larger debates that would emerge after additional changes in the Court's composition.

For legal observers, the blockbuster decision that reopened the battle was *United States v. Lopez* (1995). Although the *National League of Cities* decision had limited the applicability of a federal law, the *Lopez* decision actually struck down an enactment by Congress as unconstitutional. In *Lopez*, a five-member majority struck down the Gun-Free School Zones Act of 1990 as exceeding congressional authority to legislate under the commerce power. The law, like other federal enactments related to criminal justice, reflected an effort by members of Congress to demonstrate that they were taking action against a problem that they perceived to be of great concern to the public: the danger to children from guns in or near schools. A high school senior was arrested on school property carrying a concealed handgun. He was charged under the Gun-Free School Zones Act with committing a federal crime. After he was convicted of the crime, his attorney challenged the constitutionality of the law on appeal. When the case reached the Supreme Court, Chief Justice Rehnquist's majority opinion declared that the Commerce Clause did not authorize Congress to enact a federal criminal statute directed at an individual carrying a handgun at a local school. In essence, Rehnquist and the majority concluded that this activity was not part of "interstate commerce" and therefore was under the exclusive authority of state and local laws. In dissent, Justice Stephen Breyer argued for a broad interpretation of congressional commerce power, consistent with Court precedents stretching back to the late 1930s. Justice Stevens was one of the three justices who joined Breyer's dissent endorsing broad federal power. Several years later, he joined similar dissenting opinions by Justices Breyer and Souter that contested the majority's invalidation of a portion of the federal Violence Against Women Act as an excessive exercise of congressional commerce power (*Morrison v. United States*, 2000).

Justice Stevens took the opportunity to give voice to his views in *Printz v. United States* (1997), a case concerning the congressional authority to command state and local officials to take specific actions. In *Printz*, local sheriffs challenged congressional authority to require them to conduct background checks on handgun purchasers in their jurisdiction as specified in the federal Brady Handgun Violence Prevention Act. This was not a case concerning congressional commerce power. Instead, as noted by Justice Scalia in the majority opinion, it concerned the federal authority to command action by other levels of government: "Because there is no constitutional text speaking to this precise question, the answer to the [local chief law enforcement officers'] challenge must be sought in historical understanding and practice, in the structure of the Constitution, and in the jurisprudence of this Court."[92] On behalf of the majority, Scalia's opinion sided with the local sheriffs by concluding, "The Federal Government may neither issue directives requiring the States to address particular problems, nor command the States' officers, or those of their political subdivisions, to administer or enforce a federal regulatory program."[93]

Speaking for the four dissenters, Stevens disagreed with Scalia's interpretation of history and conceptualization of government powers. In sum, Stevens declared,

> When Congress exercises the powers delegated to it by the Constitution, it may impose affirmative obligations on executive and judicial officers of state and local governments as well as ordinary citizens. This conclusion is firmly supported by the text of the Constitution, the early history of the Nation, decisions of this Court, and a correct understanding of the basic structure of the Federal Government.[94]

Among the specific points made by Stevens to refute Scalia's analysis were the recognized federal power to direct actions to address national emergencies and the fact that the Brady Act requirements were created and imposed by the national legislature that included elected representatives from across the nation. With respect to the issue of national emergencies, he pointed to the legislative history of the Brady Act as demonstrating an intention to deal with the nation's epidemic of handgun violence and cited statistics on the thousands of homicides committed by people using handguns.

Justice Stevens also argued that the Brady Act reflected an exercise of the congressional commerce power, reiterating Justice Breyer's *Lopez* argument about handguns as purchased-and-sold products, along with their constituent manufactured components, that move through interstate commerce. He rejected any assertion that the Tenth Amendment's reservation of powers for the states served as a bar to this statute and its command to state and local officials. Having argued that congressional power clearly existed under the Commerce Clause in Article I, section 8 of the Constitution, Stevens stated emphatically, "There is not a clause, sentence, or paragraph in the entire text of the Constitution of the United States that supports the proposition that a local police officer can ignore a command contained in a statute enacted by Congress pursuant to an express delegation of power enumerated in Article I."[95] Justice Stevens had previously written an opinion expressing a similar viewpoint when the majority had limited federal authority to command states to dispose of radioactive waste materials (*New York v. United States*, 1992).

Justice Stevens subsequently wrote an important majority opinion on federalism in *Gonzales v. Raich* (2005). The case examined the applicability of federal drug laws after California enacted state laws to permit the medicinal use of marijuana. The case arose when federal officers seized and destroyed marijuana plants being grown by two individuals who, with doctors' approval, used marijuana to treat their medical conditions. His majority opinion limited the applicability of the *Lopez* and *Morrison* precedents as he reaffirmed the Court's commerce power precedents from the 1930s to the mid-1990s that granted broad congressional power even as to products, such as homegrown marijuana for personal use, that did not necessarily move through interstate commerce. Justice Stevens said, "[W]e have no difficulty concluding that Congress had a rational basis for believing that failure to regulate the intrastate manufacture and possession of marijuana would leave a gaping hole in the [Controlled Substances Act]."[96] Commentators regarded Stevens's opinion in *Gonzales v. Raich* as putting a stop to the efforts of his conservative colleagues to sharply limit federal power in favor of greater state autonomy. In the aftermath of the Court's decision, Linda Greenhouse wrote "But what had seemed until very recently to be legacy in the making now appears evanescent, perhaps even illusory. Those who thought they were witnessing a [states' rights] revolution [from the Supreme Court] were . . . using very different words" after seeing Stevens's majority opinion.[97] Moreover, she wrote specifically of Stevens's role: "For the eighty-five-year-old Stevens, a vigorous dissenter from the Rehnquist [era] federalism decisions, it was a moment to savor . . . [as he] managed to pull together and hold a majority" for this case and several decisions on other major issues.[98]

Even after he retired from the Supreme Court, Stevens continued to criticize the Court's federalism decision in *Printz*. In light of the demonstrated risk of terror attacks, based on actual experience from September 11, 2001, as well as other forms of national emergencies, Stevens saw grave practical problems from the Court's decisions that limited federal authority. In his memoir about the Supreme Court, Stevens wrote: "I often wonder whether the tragic events of 9/11 have given members of the majority any second thoughts about the wisdom of their decision. I find it hard to believe that they would adhere to their flawed historical analysis today."[99] Moreover, in a speech in October 2012, Stevens said,

> Before foreseeable catastrophes actually occur it would make sense to amend the Constitution to eliminate the unfortunate judge-made rule that never should have been adopted in the first place and can only impede the efficient implementation of federal programs. A rule that prohibits the federal government from requiring state officials to take action to help locate missing children, to apprehend violent offenders, and to forestall terrorist attacks and the spread of communicable diseases, cannot be wise.[100]

Justice Stevens advocated correcting what he saw as shortsighted errors by the Court through amending the Constitution to add four words to Article VI. Thus the language that says "This Constitution, and the Laws of the United States . . . shall be the supreme Law of the Land; and the Judges in every State shall be bound thereby" would instead say that "the Judges *and other public officials*" would be bound by federal law.[101]

The foregoing examples indicated that Stevens endorsed strong national government power for domestic policy matters and resisted efforts to turn back the clock on constitutional doctrine in order to give states greater autonomy.

Human Consequences and Fairness

In his memoir, Justice Stevens's description of Chief Justice Rehnquist included one sentence that seemed to characterize Rehnquist's orientation toward fairness as the antithesis of that espoused by Stevens: "[Rehnquist] often described the harsh consequences of his strict enforcement of a rule that seemed inequitable to some of us as 'tough tacos.'"[102] Such a dismissive attitude about issues of fairness and justice was unthinkable for Stevens. As will be evident through numerous examples in the chapters of this book, Stevens stood in stark contrast to Rehnquist in criminal justice cases. He consistently evinced both great sensitivity to the human consequences of the Court's decisions and a keen awareness of unfairness or bias in legal processes and judicial decisions. As Stevens noted in an interview, "You can't talk about an issue without thinking about its actual impact on the world."[103]

The chapters that follow describe Stevens's votes and opinions on various criminal justice issues, including prisoners' rights, *Miranda* warnings, and capital punishment. Over time in the 1980s and 1990s, there was an increase in the number of justices appointed to serve with Stevens who regularly agreed with Rehnquist's views on criminal justice issues. When Rehnquist, an appointee of President Richard Nixon, began his service on the Court in January 1972, there were cases in which Rehnquist stood out as the lone dissenter and the most conservative member of the Court. As described by Nina Totenberg, "Once on the [C]ourt, Rehnquist became known for his single-vote dissents. . . . Indeed, so frequently was he the lone dissenter that at one point, his law clerks presented him with a small Lone Ranger doll."[104]

Justice Stevens often pointed out that seven of the nine justices appointed during his tenure on the Court were more conservative than the justice that he or she replaced. The only exceptions were Ruth Bader Ginsburg, who replaced Byron White in 1993, and perhaps Sonia Sotomayor, who replaced David Souter in 2009. This compositional change in the Court meant that Rehnquist gained like-minded colleagues, especially those with rule-based approaches to interpretation, such as Scalia and Thomas, who could support the sentiment expressed in his "tough tacos" retort to complaints about inequitable results in cases. Thus Stevens's emphasis on human consequences and fairness often placed him in the role of dissenter for a variety of criminal justice issues.

There were many examples of opinions in which Stevens demonstrated that his concerns about fairness and human consequences were an important element in his judicial philosophy. As will be discussed in chapter 8 concerning capital punishment, Stevens repeatedly expressed dismay about the Court's approval of jury selection processes that excluded potential jurors who were opposed to the death penalty. This process created grave risks that capital juries would be biased in favor of the prosecution. After his retirement, he told Nina Totenberg that he believed that the Court's decisions concerning capital punishment over the years tended to "load the dice in favor of the prosecution and against the defendant."[105]

Within this concern about fairness, as indicated by the capital jury selection issue, Stevens complained that the Court too frequently seemed to see itself as an institutional component of the government's crime control efforts. For Stevens, that orientation produced unfairness to individuals when the Court went out of its way to assist and support prosecutors. Instead, he saw the Court's role as operating independently to impartially protect rights for individuals and interpret challenged aspects of constitutional, statutory, and case law. In *Florida v. Meyers* (1984), Stevens spoke out strongly about the Court's slanted use of its power to issue summary decisions:

> Since the beginning of the October 1981 Term, the Court has decided in summary fashion nineteen cases, including this one, concerning the constitutional rights of persons accused or convicted of crimes. All nineteen were decided on the petition of a warden or prosecutor, and in all he was successful in obtaining reversal of a decision upholding a claim of constitutional right. I am not saying that none of these cases should have been decided summarily. But I am saying that this pattern of results, and in particular the fact that in its last two and one-half Terms the Court has been unwilling in even a single criminal case to employ its discretionary power of summary disposition in order to uphold a claim of constitutional right, is quite striking.[106]

In another case, Justice Stevens made the same critical observation that "we have most frequently come to the aid of a prosecutor or warden who has been rebuffed by another court."[107] However, he added a touch of sarcasm to his criticism by noting that "[t]oday we exercise our majestic power to enforce a School Board's suspension of a tenth-grade student who consumed too much alcohol."[108] He wondered if the Court would have considered it a matter of equal "national importance" to correct an outcome in favor of a student who had been unjustly suspended.[109] Justice Stevens also complained about the unfair impact on prisoners in the aftermath of congressional legislation to tighten procedural rules for habeas corpus petitions and the Court majority's inclination to favor criminal justice officials in such cases. In Stevens's words, "The text of the Antiterrorism and Effective Death Penalty Act of 1996 itself provides sufficient obstacles to obtaining habeas relief without placing a judicial thumb on the warden's side of the scales."[110]

Despite his emphasis on the human consequences of judicial decisions, Stevens certainly made specific decisions that disappointed individuals, declined to vindicate rights claims, and imposed burdens on individuals. For example, his federalism opinion in *Gonzales v. Raich* (2005) had adverse impacts on individuals who, with the approval of their doctors, used medical marijuana to relieve pain and other difficult symptoms of various health conditions. As in other cases, Stevens did not necessarily place the interests of individuals first as he sought the proper analysis of legal principles and likely consequences of decisions in various fact situations. However, individuals' interests, fairness, and human consequences were neither ignored nor summarily dismissed. They were considered among the many factors that he evaluated in seeking to reach the proper conclusion in a case. In *Gonzales*, for example, Stevens specifically acknowledged the human dimension of the case by saying, "The case is made difficult by respondents' strong arguments that they will suffer irreparable harm because, despite a congressional finding to the contrary, marijuana does have valid therapeutic purposes."[111] He emphasized, however that the legal issue to be decided by the Court in the case concerned an important matter about the extent of federal legislative power. Rather than dismiss the interests of the medical patients involved in the case, he turned his attention to them at the end of the opinion and made suggestions about alternative paths of policy change. Justice Stevens wrote, "As the Solicitor General confirmed during oral argument, the statute authorizes procedures for the reclassification of Schedule I drugs. But perhaps even more important than these legal avenues is the democratic process, in which the voices of voters allied with these respondents may one day be heard in the halls of Congress."[112]

Scholars' Characterizations of Justice Stevens

In light of the approach to judicial decision making evident in Stevens's opinions, speeches, and writings, scholars assessing the first two decades of his career on the Supreme Court described him as a jurist "who eschews theory in favor of practical reason . . . [and who] deliberately makes decisions that would create the most reasonable results on the facts as he understood them."[113] In the view of Robert Judd Sickels, Stevens could be praised for his "love of fairness in each individual case," but also criticized because "his jurisprudence . . . will be associated with doctrinal unpredictability [and] a certain ad hoc quality."[114] Frederick Schauer argued that Stevens avoided the creation of doctrinal rules that will give clear guidance to judges in future cases because he preferred to develop standards that would assist with case-by-case evaluation of the various situations that may give rise to legal disputes.[115]

Consistent with these other analyses, William Popkin saw three key elements in what he characterized as Stevens's "coherent judicial philosophy" during the first half of Stevens's Supreme Court career.[116] First, Stevens sought to identify appropriate decision makers and defer to their decisions using such devices as state courts' independent state grounds for decisions and limiting grants of certiorari. Second, according to Popkin, "Justice Stevens extols the virtues of case-by-case deliberation and warns against the hazards of hypothetical rulemaking."[117] Third, Popkin saw Stevens's decisions as demonstrating his view that "the Court should protect *individual dignity* . . . [through] creative application of constitutional principles, such as due process and equal protection."[118] In adding together these elements, Popkin applied a label to Stevens for the first half of his Supreme Court career: "Common Law Lawyer on the Supreme Court."[119] In later evaluating Stevens's entire career, Rodger Citron endorsed that label by concluding that "[n]o other justice is as committed to the common law approach as Stevens."[120] For Citron, this conclusion was based on Stevens's commitment to "the common law notion that the law develops on a case-by-case basis over time" as well as Stevens's willingness to exercise judicial power, albeit "in moderation, deferring to other legal decision makers where appropriate."[121]

The foregoing description of Stevens's decision-making methods as a "common law" approach was supplemented by other scholars' various labels to describe Stevens and his judicial philosophy. Pamela Karlan said his "opinions reflect a tough-minded realism."[122] Professor Sickels used the term "judicial pragmatism."[123] Because Stevens's decisions were not reflexively or consistently liberal—or conservative—across a variety of issues, his early Supreme Court career was most memorably described in tongue-in-cheek fashion by Bradley Canon as "the Lone Ranger in a Black Robe."[124]

Later, looking back at Justice Stevens's entire career, Diane Marie Amann argued that the complexity of Stevens's approach and the wide range of issues about which he wrote opinions made it impossible to pigeonhole his interpretive approach into a single descriptive category. As Amann noted,

> Commentators who attempted to label Justice Stevens during his three-decade tenure frequently opted for a version of "pragmatism." In Justice Stevens's last fifteen Terms on the bench, during which he served as senior Associate Justice, commentary shifted to monikers more akin to "legal realism." The Justice himself often embraced "judicial restraint" as a watchword. No one of these three labels could encompass the Justice's entire jurisprudence, however.[125]

Professor Amann argued that Stevens's interpretive approach should be understood as drawing from other approaches, including looking to originalist historical sources, but then selectively applying the most appropriate approach to the case at hand. As described by Amann, "Justice Stevens's technique begins with flexible exploration of all the othe[r] [methodologies], selects those useful to the matter at hand, and then proceeds to a decision that is not only comprehensive in its analysis, but also just in its application."[126] Thus she characterized Stevens as manifesting "a constitutional jurisprudence grounded in values of liberty and equality"[127] with an interpretive approach that employed "a flexible and synthetic exploration of options"[128] to produce "constitutional interpretation . . . that accommodates a contemporary sense of justice."[129] Moreover, she saw the same approach in many of the opinions of Justice Wiley Rutledge and Rutledge's contemporary Justice Frank Murphy, thus linking the development of Stevens's overall approach to constitutional interpretation with his experience and learning as a Supreme Court law clerk for Justice Rutledge during the 1947 term.

CONCLUSION

The foregoing elements of Stevens's judicial philosophy will be evident in many of his criminal justice opinions that illuminate his role and influence in the chapters that follow. Justice Stevens was well-positioned to assume a leading role on the Supreme Court by virtue of arriving at the high court with well-formed, rather than still-developing, liberal judicial values at a moment when the Court's changing composition steered its docket and decisions toward the diminution of rights in criminal justice. With the retirements of liberal Warren Court holdovers Justices Brennan and Marshall as well as the departure of the increasingly liberal Justice Blackmun, Stevens became the most senior and influential defender of constitutional rights on the Court for nearly two decades. Although the context in which Stevens served on the Supreme Court often placed him in the role of a dissenter defending the preservation rights developed by the Warren Court's decisions, he had opportunities to shape the law through influencing or writing majority opinions and through the body of opinions that he created to educate and influence future judicial officers.

The influence of Stevens's life experiences on the development of his judicial values and decision making are explored in chapters 2 and 3 concerning, respectively, his life experiences prior to becoming a judge and his five years of service as a judge on the U.S. Court of Appeals for the Seventh Circuit in Chicago. Chapter 4 presents his Supreme Court opinions and votes in prisoners' rights cases, the area in which Stevens most quickly established himself as a uniquely outspoken advocate of constitutional rights in the realm of criminal justice. The discussions of *Miranda* rights, the right to counsel, and trial rights in chapters 5 and 6 similarly illuminate topics for which Stevens was a consistently strong advocate of protecting rights based on judicial values that he brought with him to the Supreme Court. The examination of search and seizure cases in chapter 7 shows how Stevens's case-by-case approach to judicial decision making could produce a mixed record of support for rights claims for certain criminal justice issues, albeit with strong support for several rights-protecting precedents. Chapter 8 analyzes Justice Stevens's record on capital punishment issues, the criminal justice subject for which commentators claim that he most clearly changed his views and decisions over the course of his career. The book concludes with an overall assessment of his role, influence, and impact in chapter 9.

NOTES

1. The opinion-counting methods, including reliance on data from the Supreme Court Data Base, http://scdb.wustl.edu/about.php (Harold J. Spaeth, originator and lead contributor), are described in Ross E. Davis, Craig D. Rust, and Adam Aft, "Supreme Court Sluggers: John Paul Stevens Is No Stephen J. Field," *Green Bag* 13 (2010): 475–80. The opinion totals are from an updated count as of October 2010 by Davis, Rust, and Aft available at www.greenbag.org/sluggers/sluggers_cards_and_stats.html, accessed July 2, 2015.

2. Adam Liptak, "A Justice Slows His Hiring, and Some Wonder About His Future," *New York Times*, September 3, 2009, A14.

3. Ibid.

4. Jeff Bleich, Daniel Powell, Aimee Feinberg, and Michelle Friedland, "Justice John Paul Stevens: A Maverick, Liberal Libertarian, Conservative Statesman on the Court," *Oregon State Bar Bulletin* 67 (October 2007): 27.

5. Joan Biskupic, "Supreme Court's Stevens Keeps Cards Close to Robe," *USA Today*, October 18, 2009, accessed May 19, 2015, http://usatoday30.usatoday.com/news/washington/judicial/2009-10-18-stevens-supreme-court-justice_N.htm.

6. Tinsley E. Yarbrough, *David Hackett Souter: Traditional Republican on the Rehnquist Court* (New York: Oxford University Press, 2005), 258.

7. Jennifer Senior, "In Conversation: Antonin Scalia," *New York Magazine*, October 6, 2013, accessed May 19, 2015, http://nymag.com/news/features/antonin-scalia-2013-10/.

8. Jeffrey A. Segal and Harold J. Spaeth, "Decisional Trends in the Warren and Burger Courts: Results from the Supreme Court Judicial Database Project," *Judicature* 73 (1989): 103.

9. Voting percentages calculated from data in Lee Epstein, Jeffrey A. Segal, Harold J. Spaeth, and Thomas G. Walker, *The Supreme Court Compendium: Data, Decisions and Developments*, 5th ed. (Washington, D.C.: Congressional Quarterly Press, 2012), 561–64.

10. Ibid.

11. Jeffrey Rosen, "The Dissenter," *New York Times Magazine*, September 23, 2007, 52, accessed May 19, 2015, http://www.nytimes.com/2007/09/23/magazine/23stevens-t.html?pagewanted=all.

12. Lee Epstein, Andrew D. Martin, Kevin M. Quinn, and Jeffrey A. Segal, "Ideological Drift Among Supreme Court Justices: Who, When, and How Important?" *Northwestern University Law Review* 101 (2007): 1508–9.

13. Ibid., 1504.

14. Linda Greenhouse, *Becoming Justice Blackmun* (New York: Times Books, 2005), 138, 251.

15. Yarbrough, *David Hackett Souter*, 195–96.

16. Robert D. McFadden, "The President's Choice: John Paul Stevens," *New York Times*, November 29, 1975, 1, 14.

17. Ward Farnsworth, "Realism, Pragmatism, and John Paul Stevens," in *Rehnquist Justice: Understanding the Court Dynamic*, ed. Earl M. Maltz (Lawrence: University Press of Kansas, 2003), 157.

18. "Court Nominee Is Hard to Label," *New York Times*, November 30, 1975, sec. 4, 1.

19. Robert S. Boyd, "Judge Stevens—His Views on Law," *Chicago Tribune*, November 30, 1975, 6.

20. David M. O'Brien, "The Politics of Professionalism: President Gerald R. Ford's Appointment of Justice John Paul Stevens," *Presidential Studies Quarterly* 21 (1991): 106.

21. Ibid., 103–7.

22. Ibid., 112.

23. Anthony Lewis, "The Stevens Nomination," *New York Times*, December 4, 1975, 41.

24. O'Brien, "The Politics of Professionalism," 117.

25. Lesley Oelsner, "Factors in Court Choice: Ford Seems to Have Followed Tradition and Political Aims in Naming Stevens," *New York Times*, November 30, 1975, 31.

26. John Anthony Maltese, *The Selling of Supreme Court Nominees* (Baltimore: Johns Hopkins University Press, 1998), 12–17, 70–85.

27. Robert Bendiner, "The Law and Potter Stewart: An Interview with Justice Potter Stewart," *American Heritage*, vol. 35 [1] (December 1983), accessed May 19, 2015, http://www.americanheritage.com/content/law-and-potter-stewart-interview-justice-potter-stewart.

28. O'Brien, "The Politics of Professionalism," 103.

29. Joyce A. Baugh, *Supreme Court Justices in the Post-Bork Era: Confirmation Politics and Judicial Performance* (New York: Peter Lang, 2002), 1–5.

30. John Paul Stevens, *Five Chiefs: A Supreme Court Memoir* (Boston: Little, Brown, 2011), 143.

31. Ibid., 127.

32. Lawrence Baum, *Judges and Their Audiences: A Perspective on Judicial Behavior* (Princeton, N.J.: Princeton University Press, 2006), 150–51.

33. Linda Greenhouse, "Change and Continuity on the Supreme Court," *Washington University Journal of Law and Policy* 25 (2007): 53.

34. Michael C. Dorf, "Does Federal Executive Branch Experience Explain Why Some Republican Supreme Court Justices 'Evolve' and Others Don't?" *Harvard Law and Policy Review* 1 (2007): 457.

35. Ibid., 470.

36. Ibid., 471.

37. Mark Tushnet, *A Court Divided: The Rehnquist Court and the Future of Constitutional Law* (New York: W.W. Norton, 2005), 61.

38. Jess Bravin, "Stevens Evolved From Court Loner to Liberal Wing's Leader," *Wall Street Journal Online*, June 30, 2010, accessed May 19, 2015, http://www.wsj.com/articles/SB10001424052748703374104575337264290709470.

39. Seth Stern and Stephen Wermiel, *Justice Brennan: Liberal Champion* (Boston: Houghton Mifflin Harcourt, 2010), 495.

40. Justice John Paul Stevens, interview with author, U.S. Supreme Court, Washington, D.C., July 29, 2010.

41. Ibid.

42. Ibid.
43. Ibid.
44. Jamal Greene, "The Rule of Law as a Law of Standards," *Georgetown Law Journal* 99 (2011): 1298.
45. John Paul Stevens, "Learning on the Job," *Fordham Law Review* 74 (2006): 1561.
46. Stevens, *Five Chiefs*, 25–26.
47. Stevens, "Learning on the Job," 1561.
48. Ibid., 1562.
49. Ibid., quoting *Whitney v. California*, 274 U.S. 357, 373 (1927) (Brandeis, J., concurring).
50. Ibid., 1561, quoting *Lochner v. New York*, 198 U.S. 45, 76 (1905) (Holmes, J., dissenting).
51. Justice John Paul Stevens (ret.), speech at Federal Bar Council Annual Law Day Dinner, New York City, May 3, 2011, accessed May 19, 2015, http://www.supremecourt.gov/publicinfo/speeches/Federal%20Bar%20Council%20Annual%20Law%20Day%20Dinner(1613_001).pdf.
52. *Poe v. Ullman*, 367 U.S. 497, 539 (Harlan, J., dissenting).
53. Ibid., 543 (Harlan, J., dissenting).
54. Stevens, speech to Federal Bar Council, quoting *Poe v. Ullman*, 367 U.S. at 542 (Harlan, J., dissenting).
55. Ibid.
56. Ibid.
57. Ibid.
58. *Roe v. Wade*, 410 U.S. 110, 167-68 (1973) (Stewart, J., concurring).
59. *Roe v. Wade*, 410 U.S. 113, 153 (1973).
60. Rosen, "The Dissenter," 76.
61. Ibid.
62. Stevens, interview with author, U.S. Supreme Court, Washington, D.C., July 29, 2010.
63. Ibid.
64. *McDonald v. City of Chicago*, 130 S.Ct. at 3092 (Stevens, J., dissenting); see also John Paul Stevens, "The Bill of Rights: A Century of Progress," *University of Chicago Law Review* 59 (1992): 20.
65. *McDonald v. City of Chicago*, 130 S.Ct. at 3055 n. 6 (Scalia, J., concurring).
66. *McDonald v. City of Chicago*, 130 S.Ct. at 3054 (Scalia, J., concurring).
67. *McDonald v. City of Chicago*, 130 S.Ct. at 3096 (Stevens, J., dissenting).
68. Ibid.
69. Ibid.
70. Ibid., 3100 (Stevens, J., dissenting).
71. Ibid., 3101 (Stevens, J., dissenting).
72. Ibid., 3102 (Stevens, J., dissenting).
73. Ibid., 3101 (Stevens, J., dissenting).
74. Ibid., 3102 (Stevens, J., dissenting).
75. Ibid.
76. Jeffrey M. Shaman, "The End of Originalism," *San Diego Law Review* 47 (2010): 83–108.
77. *McDonald v. City of Chicago*, 130 S.Ct. at 3096 (Stevens, J., dissenting).
78. Stevens, interview with author, U.S. Supreme Court, Washington, D.C., July 29, 2010.
79. *McDonald v. City of Chicago*, 130 S.Ct. at 3099 (Stevens, J., dissenting).
80. John Paul Stevens, "A Judge's Use of History—Thomas E. Fairchild Inaugural Lecture," *Wisconsin Law Review* (1989): 235.
81. John Paul Stevens, "Judicial Restraint," *San Diego Law Review* 22 (1985): 451–52, quoting William Rehnquist, "The Notion of a Living Constitution," *Texas Law Review* 54 (1976): 694.
82. Stevens, "The Bill of Rights," 27.
83. *McDonald v. City of Chicago*, 130 S.Ct. at 3099 (Stevens, J., dissenting).
84. Stevens, *Five Chiefs*, 187–88.

85. Stevens, "Learning on the Job," 1561–67.
86. Linda Greenhouse, "John Paul Stevens as Abortion-Rights Strategist," *UC Davis Law Review* 43 (2010): 763.
87. Bryan A. Garner, "Interview with Justice John Paul Stevens," *The Scribes Journal of Legal Writing* (2010): 47.
88. *This Honorable Court: Inside the Marble Temple* (documentary film), Public Broadcasting System (PBS), television broadcast September 12, 1989.
89. Stevens, "Learning on the Job," 1561–67.
90. Stevens, *Five Chiefs*, 140.
91. *National League of Cities v. Usery*, 426 U.S. 833, 880 (1976) (Stevens, J., dissenting).
92. *Printz v. United States*, 521 U.S. 989, 905 (1997).
93. Ibid., 935.
94. *Printz v. United States*, 521 U.S. 989, 939 (1997) (Stevens, J., dissenting).
95. Ibid., 944 (Stevens, J., dissenting).
96. *Gonzales v. Raich*, 545 U.S. 1, 22 (2005).
97. Linda Greenhouse, "The Rehnquist Court and Its Imperiled States' Rights Legacy," *New York Times*, June 12, 2005, accessed May 19, 2015, http://www.nytimes.com/2005/06/12/weekinreview/12green.html?oref=login.
98. Ibid.
99. Stevens, *Five Chiefs*, 190.
100. John Paul Stevens, Speech to Chicago Bar Association, John Paul Stevens Awards Luncheon, Chicago, Ill., October 2, 2012, accessed May 19, 2015, http://www.supremecourt.gov/publicinfo/speeches/JPS%20Speech(Chicago)_10-02-2012.pdf .
101. Ibid.
102. Stevens, *Five Chiefs*, 178.
103. Stevens, interview with author, U.S. Supreme Court, Washington, D.C., July 29, 2010.
104. Nina Totenberg, "Rehnquist: From Lone Dissenter to Consensus Builder," *All Things Considered* news program, National Public Radio, September 4, 2005, accessed May 19, 2015, http://www.npr.org/templates/story/story.php?storyId=4832353.
105. Nina Totenberg, "Justice Stevens: An Open Mind On a Changed Court," *Morning Edition* news program, National Public Radio, October 4, 2010, accessed May 19, 2015, http://www.npr.org/templates/story/story.php?storyId=130198344.
106. *Florida v. Meyers*, 466 U.S. 380, 386-387 (1984) (Stevens, J., dissenting).
107. *Board of Education of Rogers v. McCluskey*, 458 U.S. 966, 972-73 (1982) (Stevens, J., dissenting).
108. Ibid., 973.
109. Ibid.
110. *Carey v. Musladin*, 127 S.Ct. 649, 655-56 (2006) (Stevens, J., concurring in the judgment).
111. *Gonzales v. Raich*, 545 U.S. 1, 9 (2005).
112. Ibid., 33.
113. Farnsworth, "Realism, Pragmatism, and John Paul Stevens," 178.
114. Robert Judd Sickels, *John Paul Stevens and the Constitution: The Search for Balance* (University Park, Penn.: Pennsylvania State University Press, 1988), 179.
115. Frederick Schauer, "Justice Stevens and the Size of Constitutional Decisions," *Rutgers Law Journal* 27 (1996): 556–58.
116. William Popkin, "A Common Law Lawyer on the Supreme Court: The Opinions of Justice Stevens," *Duke Law Journal* (1989): 1090.
117. Ibid., 1105.
118. Ibid., 1090.
119. Ibid., 1087.
120. Rodger D. Citron, "The Last Common Law Justice?" SCOTUS BLOG, May 6, 2010, accessed on May 19, 2015, http://www.scotusblog.com/2010/05/the-last-common-law-justice/.
121. Ibid.
122. Pamela S. Karlan, "Cousins' Kin: Justice Stevens and Voting Rights," *Rutgers Law Journal* 27 (1996): 522.

123. Sickels, *John Paul Stevens and the Constitution*, 1.
124. Bradley C. Canon, "Justice John Paul Stevens: The Lone Ranger in a Black Robe," in *The Burger Court: Political and Judicial Profiles*, eds. Charles M. Lamb and Stephen C. Halpern (Urbana: University of Illinois Press, 1991), 343.
125. Diane Marie Amann, "John Paul Stevens, Originalist," *Northwestern University Law Review* 106 (2012): 748–49.
126. Ibid., 751.
127. Ibid., 750.
128. Ibid., 765.
129. Ibid., 766.

Chapter Two

Family Background and Life Experiences

As many biographers have persuasively demonstrated, Supreme Court justices, like other Americans, learn values from their parents and teachers. They are influenced by their religious beliefs. They gain an understanding of American society through their schooling and personal observations. Thus justices' life experiences, including familial influences, political socialization, formal education, and initial professional careers, undoubtedly help to shape the personal values, judicial attitudes, and policy preferences that affect judicial decisions.[1] Scholars often scrutinize political party affiliations,[2] socioeconomic and religious backgrounds,[3] and prior professional experiences[4] as potential indicators of judicial nominees' values, policy priorities, and preferred interpretive approaches.[5] Specific background attributes and experiences do not necessarily affect individuals in precisely the same manner. However, these factors contribute to the acquisition of values and attitudes as well as both practical and normative understandings about the nature and operation of American government and society.

Supreme Court justices themselves acknowledge the impact of life experiences. According to Justice Sandra Day O'Connor:

> We're all creatures of our upbringing. We bring whatever we are as people to a job like the Supreme Court. We have our life experiences. For example, for me it was growing up on a remote ranch in the West. If something broke, you'd have to fix it yourself. The solution didn't always have to look beautiful, but it had to work. So that made me a little more pragmatic than some other justices.
>
> I liked to find solutions that would work. . . . It's important for the Supreme Court to have a broader set of life experiences than just people who have served as judges.[6]

In a similar fashion, Justice Stevens explicitly acknowledged the impact of life experiences on his performance as a judge. Thus he said in a 2010 interview, "I've confessed to many people that I think my personal experience has had an impact on what I've done. . . . Time and time again, not only for myself but for other people on the [C]ourt, during discussions of cases you bring up experiences that you are familiar with."[7] In a separate interview, he reinforced this point by saying, "You can relate to a case if you have had a similar experience or even if you have just read about it."[8] Thus any understanding of Stevens's opinions and legacy must include consideration of the ways in which his life experience helped to shape his judicial philosophy, understanding of society, and, ultimately, his participation and influence in the Supreme Court's cases. The biographical discussion that follows focuses on the social background and life experiences that presumably shaped Justice Stevens's values, judicial philosophy, and viewpoints related to criminal justice issues.

FAMILY BACKGROUND

John Paul Stevens spent his childhood in family circumstances that appear to be significantly more affluent and privileged than those of any other recent justice. The family's history included the elements of westward migration, a transition from farming to big city commerce, and the substantial financial rewards of successful risk-taking, initiative, and hard work in business enterprises. Colchester, Illinois, a town in McDonough County on the western side of the state, was the birthplace of Justice Stevens's father, Ernest J. Stevens (1884–1972) and the place where the family's financial fortune began to develop. In 1844, Justice Stevens's great-grandfather, Socrates Stevens, a schoolteacher and farmer, moved from Indiana to McDonough County. At that time, the area was not far removed from being frontier territory. The state had established the county just fourteen years earlier in 1830 when it concluded that the population was growing enough to justify the development of local governing institutions within that area. Moreover, the county was not far south of the skirmishes and battle sites of the 1832 Blackhawk War in Illinois and Wisconsin in which Illinois militia men, including a future president, Abraham Lincoln, joined federal troops in fighting Native Americans who were understandably unhappy about their land being taken by white settlers.

Socrates Stevens was prominent in the community as, for example, a founding officer of the Christian Church in Colchester and the unsuccessful Republican candidate for county treasurer in 1863. Although it was very unusual for that era, he sent two of his sons to college, including Justice Stevens's grandfather, James Stevens, who attended Abingdon College in

Illinois for one academic term.[9] Abingdon College closed in the later years of the nineteenth century and was later absorbed into Eureka College, the eventual twentieth-century alma mater of President Ronald Reagan.[10] The sons of Socrates Stevens, including the two who had attended Abingdon College, began to develop business enterprises in Colchester as their careers moved from teaching and farming into the more lucrative world of commerce.

James Stevens and his brothers started a dry goods store in Colchester which was described in 1885 as "the largest business of the kind in the county."[11] In 1881, they established and owned the only bank in Colchester. They were also partners in a "fire-clay works" business in nearby Bardolph, Illinois, that manufactured bricks, drain tile, and sewer pipe.[12] In 1888, James moved to Chicago where his brother Charles was already successfully established in the clothing and dry goods business. James joined that business and then subsequently established his own identity and substantial fortune by developing the Illinois Life Insurance Company, for which he was president and chairman of the board. James and his sons also built and ran the LaSalle Hotel in Chicago.[13] A profile of Chicago leaders published in 1912 said that the insurance company, hotel, and other business enterprises were "monuments to the perseverance and intelligence of Mr. Stevens, who has built up vast enterprises as the city has builded . . . [and he] contribut[ed] to the material welfare of his adopted city."[14]

Ernest Stevens, the father of the future Supreme Court justice, was a graduate of Northwestern University Law School but he chose a career in hotel management over a career in law. He managed his family's LaSalle Hotel and later developed his own ambitious business enterprise. After two years of construction, in 1927 he opened the Stevens Hotel (now the Chicago Hilton and Towers) on South Michigan Avenue in Chicago. At the time of its opening, it was the largest hotel in the world and the first to have a bathroom in every guest room. It was a grand, ornate hotel with ballrooms, a theater, a rooftop miniature golf course, and a landing area for amphibious planes immediately in front of the hotel on Lake Michigan.[15]

Born in 1920, John Paul Stevens was the youngest of Ernest Stevens's four sons. As a result of the financial success of his grandfather and father, he spent his childhood in affluent circumstances in Chicago's Hyde Park neighborhood with vacations at the family's Lake Michigan summer house in Lakeside, Michigan. One indicator of the family's affluence was evident in the presence of household staff in his childhood home, as indicated by the household's listing in the 1930 U.S. Census:

Ernest Stevens, age 46, President-Hotel
Elizabeth Stevens, age 46
Ernest Stevens, age 20, general work about office, Hotel

Richard Stevens, age 15
William Stevens, age 12
John Stevens, age 9
Sarah Orre, age 42, Norwegian, Cook
Hannah Olson, age 63, Norwegian, Maid
Sarah Johnson, age 24, Swedish, Maid[16]

This snapshot of the Stevens household conveys an image of affluence that is beyond the understanding and experience of all but the wealthiest Americans. In addition, his elite education at the University of Chicago Lab Schools from elementary grades through high school followed by his undergraduate years at the University of Chicago placed him in school environments with peers who were predominantly from affluent segments of society.

Despite family circumstances that could easily have insulated him from knowledge and understanding of other Americans' lives, including those affected by the criminal justice system, Stevens had life experiences that contributed to his awareness of issues related to criminal justice. For example, when asked during an interview about his exposure to and awareness of discrimination issues during his early life, Stevens described two memorable experiences.[17] First, as a schoolboy during the 1920s and 1930s, he visited Gulf Coast towns in segregated Mississippi and Alabama. He remembered seeing the pervasive manifestations of racial discrimination and segregation, such as the separate drinking fountains, restrooms, and other facilities. As he noted in an interview, "During spring vacation, my parents took me down to Biloxi, Mississippi, and I spent three or four spring vacations down there and another time in Fairhope, Alabama, and you were aware there of the black and white restroom facilities and that sort of thing. I saw enough of it to know that it really existed."[18] Historian Leon Litwack described this era in the South as an especially severe period of subordination, mistreatment, and racial violence directed at African Americans.[19] Thus Stevens may have seen particular scenes and events that ultimately helped to shape his strong sensitivity and objections to discrimination.

Second, Stevens retained indelible memories of unequal treatment of his Jewish classmates during his undergraduate years at the University of Chicago in the late 1930s, especially with respect to being blocked from joining fraternities at the college. In an interview, he recalled, "I was very conscious of discrimination against Jews. . . . When I went to college that was the discrimination issue that was talked about back in those days."[20] Justice Stevens had Jewish friends who were affected by discrimination and he recalled thinking at the time how terribly unfair it was to treat people in a discriminatory fashion. As described by Stevens, "So I think I grew up as a youngster really realizing that there were members of society who were treated differently—and it was irrational because I knew them as friends."[21]

A journalist's article in *Chicago Magazine* in 2006 detailed the experience in Justice Stevens's life that was widely perceived to be the most striking and memorable event that would shape his view about criminal justice.[22] Many sources repeated the story thereafter, especially in discussions of his life and career at the time of his retirement. Questions remain about how, if at all, to link this memorable experience to the formation of his judicial philosophy and his decision making in criminal justice cases.

When the Great Depression hit, Ernest Stevens, like other hotel operators, encountered financial difficulties due to Americans' reduced business and personal travel. In order to help pay his business debts and avoid the risk of losing the grand Stevens Hotel, he borrowed money from his father's Illinois Life Insurance Company, where he himself served on the board of directors. As the world's largest hotel, its construction cost nearly $30 million, which would be $330 million in today's dollars. Ernest needed the funds in order to pay the financial obligations of his hotel company.[23] As the company's financial situation deteriorated, leading the family to eventually lose the hotel, Ernest, his brother Raymond, who was the president of the insurance company, and their father James, the chairman of the board of the insurance company, were all charged with embezzlement from the transactions that used the insurance company's resources in the unsuccessful attempt to save the hotel. Raymond Stevens died after the indictment was issued, apparently by suicide. The prosecutor did not proceed against James Stevens because of his poor health. Thus Ernest, the father of the future Supreme Court justice, was the only defendant prosecuted and convicted of the crime.[24]

Ernest Stevens filed an appeal and the Illinois Supreme Court overturned his conviction. The state high court found that "[i]n this whole record there is not a scintilla of evidence of any concealment or fraud attempted."[25] The Illinois Supreme Court noted that it may have been unwise for the insurance company to expend its capital on the hotel, but the court concluded that no evidence was ever presented to show that anyone in the Stevens family ever pocketed any money from these transactions or that these transactions were done in any secret manner. In essence, the appellate court concluded that

> It is a far cry from a mistake in investment made in good faith to a felonious, fraudulent investment made for the purpose of converting the funds of the lender to the use of the accused. There is here no evidence of fraudulent intent. We are of the opinion that the record does not justify the verdict of guilty. . . . The judgment is reversed.[26]

The trial itself was covered by newspapers in a sensational and inflammatory manner, reflecting both the nature of that era's journalists and the public's Depression-era mood that relished the downfall of the rich.[27] One might naturally presume that a teenager whose father faced a long prison sentence in a trial with front-page news coverage would be deeply affected by the experience. When initially asked during a 2007 interview about whether his father's trial affected his later views as a Supreme Court justice, Stevens replied, "I'm sure it did. . . . You can't forget that."[28] He added that the experience taught him the "very important lesson" that "the criminal justice system can misfire sometimes" because "it seriously misfired in that case."[29]

Later, however, Stevens reconsidered the nature of his actual memories and feelings from that part of his life. He was deeply troubled by published accounts that resurrected newspapers' inaccurate reports from 1933 that described the teenaged Stevens as present in the courtroom and visibly upset by the verdict.[30] According to Stevens, in fact, he was not in the courtroom at all during the trial. In later interviews, he made a point of asserting that his parents had protected him from exposure to the trial and they made sure that he continued to live a normal, happy teenager's life, even during the highly publicized trial.[31] Nina Totenberg described how Stevens conveyed his reconsideration of the issue in her 2010 interview with the justice:

> Justice Stevens disavows the notion that his concern for the rights of criminal defendants might stem from his own family's experience. . . . Stevens acknowledges that he has thought about whether [his father's trial] experience affected his views. But, he adds, "I don't really think it had any impact whatsoever on me, to tell the truth."[32]

Totenberg then described how the justice's voice "crack[ed] with emotion" as he stated emphatically that he was unaffected by the trial because he knew that his father was such a good man that the teenaged Stevens "never really considered it being a realistic possibility that he would ever go to jail."[33]

In a 2010 interview for this book, Stevens's presentation of his memories and the trial's lack of influence on his judicial decision making were virtually identical to Totenberg's description from her interview. Indeed, at the conclusion of the interview, Justice Stevens asked this author to turn the tape recorder back on so that he could make "one more point" and he then sought to correct the misimpression from earlier interviews that he had been affected by the trial.[34] As described by Stevens,

> It never even crossed my mind that he would go to jail because I knew what kind of guy he was. If I had thought my father was going to go to prison, that would have made a bigger impression—but actually it just never seemed to me to be a possible outcome. Life was really kind of normal, which it would not be if this was something hanging over your everyday life. I never went to the courthouse at all. I had a very normal, happy year at that time—maybe I was totally naïve—but he was a very decent man and it was just totally out of character [to conceive of him as guilty of a crime].[35]

It was evidently very important to Stevens to retract his earlier off-the-cuff comment, "I'm sure it did," when first asked about whether his father's trial had affected his own judicial decision making on criminal justice issues.

Notwithstanding Stevens's reconsideration and clarification of his memories concerning his actual feelings and reactions to his father's trial, he did not disavow this author's suggestion that there could be some influence on his thinking as a judge, even if the influence was only modest. When presented with the possibility that his retrospective awareness about his father's trial could reinforce his later recognition as a judge that trials can reach incorrect results and that access to appeals and post-convictions reviews are essential for correcting such errors, Stevens acknowledged that was indeed possible.[36] Stevens said, "I would not quarrel with the idea that in retrospect it was an example [that made] you realize that the system makes mistakes . . . and the importance of appellate process. But it's not because of the trauma of what happened at that time."[37]

In the interview exchange about this topic, Stevens seemed most concerned about refuting any possible inference that his father's experience had led him to choose a career in law or that it had led him to reflexively support broad rights for criminal defendants. In fact, he intended to teach literature and he entered graduate school at the University of Chicago to study English prior to leaving for service in the U.S. Navy in December 1941. He did not decide to attend law school until encouraged to do so by an older brother when he returned to Chicago after World War II. Moreover, he took great pride in his careful fact-based, case-by-case common law approach to judicial decision making. Thus he appeared to resent any misinformation that might lead to simplistic, pop-psychology conclusions attributing his decisions endorsing rights in the criminal justice process to his memories of his father's trial. However, as a thoughtful individual who endorsed the notion that people, including judges, learn from their experiences, he was open to the suggestion that his knowledge about the trial could serve as an example to heighten his awareness about the need for access to appeals. As a lawyer and a judge, Stevens saw plenty of other examples of errors in criminal justice processes, so his father's case was not necessarily the experience that had an especially profound impact on his awareness, thought processes, and decisions.

MILITARY SERVICE

One of the most significant experiences of Stevens's life was his service as a U.S. Navy officer during World War II. This experience presents an intriguing, albeit highly speculative, possibility of influence on his opinions in specific cases. After graduating from the University of Chicago in 1941 and initially beginning work on a graduate degree in literature, Stevens decided to join the navy without knowing that his country was on the verge of being attacked by a foreign power. Indeed, he had his induction physical on December 6, 1941—the day before the Japanese attack on Pearl Harbor precipitated American mobilization and full military engagement.[38] Justice Stevens spent the war working as an officer in a communications intelligence unit in Hawaii involved in "traffic analysis and in the decryption of enemy call signs."[39] Although he was sometimes erroneously characterized as assigned to break Japanese communication codes, Stevens never made that claim and described the actual nature of his wartime work as follows:

> [W]hen I was on active duty I served as a traffic analyst, rather than a decoder or cryptographer. The job of the traffic analyst was to obtain intelligence about enemy activities by monitoring his communications without reading their text—what today is often called "metadata" analysis. That skill is critically different from actually reading the intercepted messages. Knowledge about the volume of the traffic in certain locations, identities of senders and addressees, their choice of codes, and the length and timing of their messages may enable the analyst to draw useful inferences.[40]

As described by Eugene Fidell, a leading expert on military law and a former U.S. Coast Guard officer, "Those who have served in uniform can attest that military service is a vivid experience. . . . It is tempting to speculate that the approach apparent in Justice Stevens's votes and writing in military-related cases reflect the three years he served in Hawaii [during the war]."[41] Thus, like others who served in the war and who inevitably knew personally other men of his generation who were killed or wounded in action, military experience appeared to shape Stevens's views about specific issues.

The most widely noted and discussed link between Stevens's military experience and his judicial opinions appeared in *Texas v. Johnson* (1989), the highly publicized and controversial case concerning Texas's prosecution of a political protester for burning an American flag. An unusual combination of liberal and conservative justices issued a 5 to 4 decision declaring that flag-burning is a form of symbolic speech that is protected by the First Amendment. Justice Stevens parted company with Brennan and Marshall, two justices with whom he regularly agreed on many constitutional rights issues. He declined to join the dissenting opinion by Chief Justice Rehnquist that was endorsed by Justices White and O'Connor, and instead wrote his own solo dissent. Professor Fidell speculated that "Perhaps it was because Justice Stevens found the matter so profoundly disturbing that it was essential that the voice be his own."[42] The case elicited rhetoric about patriotism and the flag's important symbolism and it was not about military matters. Yet Stevens made reference to the sacrifices of military personnel in connection with the flag's importance. After reciting a list of American heroes, including Patrick

Henry, Nathan Hale, Susan B. Anthony, Abraham Lincoln, and Booker T. Washington, who were motivated by American "ideas of liberty and equality," he described the same motivation in wartime service. In Stevens's words, these ideas motivated:

> the Philippine scouts who fought at Bataan [and] the soldiers who scaled the bluff at Omaha Beach. If those ideas are worth fighting for—and our history demonstrates that they are—it cannot be true that the flag that uniquely symbolizes their power is not itself worthy of protection from unnecessary desecration.[43]

Justice Stevens also chose to read his dissent from the bench when the Court announced its decision, a practice that accentuates the intensity of a justice's disagreement and one that Stevens used only two dozen times in his thirty-five-year career on the Court.[44] According to one law clerk's description, Stevens was visibly angry when he read his dissent in the quiet courtroom,[45] although other eyewitness accounts did not make note of any unusual emotion expressed by Stevens.[46] The following year Stevens wrote another strong dissent in a parallel case, *United States v. Eichman* (1990), which struck down the federal flag-burning statute on First Amendment grounds.

According to Professor Fidell, when Justice Stevens addressed military issues, he had a "determinedly independent perspective not easily pigeonholed as liberal, conservative, or 'activist.'"[47] In criminal justice cases that involved military veterans, however, it appeared that Stevens and other justices may have manifested special empathy toward veterans; an empathy that Linda Greenhouse questioned as "selective" and not applied equally to other similarly situated defendants.[48] For example, in *Porter v. McCollum* (2009), the Court considered an ineffective assistance of counsel claim by a death-row inmate named George Porter. In a per curiam opinion, an unsigned statement from the Court without any particular justice identified as the author, the opinion recounted with an unusually descriptive degree of sympathetic detail the traumatizing experiences in Porter's life, especially child abuse and later horrific hand-to-hand combat as a teenaged marine in Korean War battles. Similarly, in *Rita v. United States* (2007), concerning federal sentencing guidelines, Stevens wrote a concurring opinion that specifically called attention to the defendant's status as a veteran and labeled as "a serious omission" the trial judge's failure to include consideration of this military service when determining the criminal sentence. Whether or not these cases provide evidence that Stevens's military experience affected certain decisions, Stevens acknowledged the effect of military service on his views about a specific issue: capital punishment.

In several interviews, Stevens repeated a story from his military service that he said led him to think deeply about the death penalty.[49] On April 18, 1943, American forces used information from intercepted messages to target Admiral Isoroku Yamamoto and shoot down the plane on which he was a passenger. Although Stevens had no role in breaking the particular code that led the United States to know about Admiral Yamamoto's travel plans in the war zone, he was on duty when the message was received in Hawaii about the success of the mission in eliminating an important commander of Japanese naval forces. Justice Stevens said, "Even at the time, it seemed to me kind of strange that you had a mission to kill a particular individual. . . . And it was an individual who was a friend of some of the [U.S.] Navy officers,"[50] as Yamamoto had studied at Harvard and spent time in the United States in the decades before the war.[51] According to Stevens, "[t]he targeting of a particular individual with the intent to kill him was a lot different than killing a soldier in battle and dealing with a statistic."[52] He eventually translated his discomfort about this episode into his assessment of the extremely difficult decision that jurors must make in deciding whether a specific defendant should be executed for committing a murder.

Interviewers who have heard Stevens talk about this experience presented it as a matter of enduring significance for his thoughts about the death penalty, using such characterizations as "a moral dilemma that had haunted him for decades"[53] and an "event . . . [that] would stay with him for the rest of his life."[54] Another interviewer wrote that "Stevens said that, partly as a result of his World War II experience, he has tried on the [C]ourt to narrow the category of offenders who are eligible for the death penalty and to ensure that it is imposed fairly and accurately."[55] The experience apparently contributed to the sense of uneasiness about capital punishment that was evident in Stevens's opinions throughout his judicial career.

LAW SCHOOL EDUCATION

After the war, at his brother's suggestion, Stevens abandoned his original plan to earn a graduate degree in literature and instead enrolled in law school at Northwestern University, his father's alma mater. He graduated at the top of his class and was an editor of the law review. In speeches and interviews, his references to the impact of his legal education pointed to both specific influential professors and Northwestern's particular approach to teaching law.

Justice Stevens contrasted the approach to legal education at his alma mater with that at Harvard, which he characterized as a "rule-oriented approach."[56] He described Northwestern's approach as fact-based and case-focused.[57] Justice Stevens pointed to this difference in law school education as one basis for his analytical disagreements in many cases with Harvard-educated Antonin Scalia. Indeed, Justice Scalia wrote an article entitled "The Rule of Law as a Law of Rules."[58] The article did not discuss Stevens, as Scalia was relatively new to the Supreme Court at the time and the scope of his disagreements with Stevens had not yet been revealed. However, Scalia's characterization about the choice of perspectives could readily serve to contrast his approach from that employed by Stevens. As Scalia said, "by making the mode of analysis relatively principled or relatively fact-specific, the courts can either establish general rules or leave ample discretion for the future."[59] Justice Scalia described an approach that might apply to Stevens by saying, "That is one image of how justice is done—one case at a time, taking into account all the circumstances, and identifying within that context the 'fair' result."[60] However, he then disparaged that approach by equating it with the judging methodology on the then-popular television show, "People's Court," involving televised small claims cases. Justice Scalia admitted that as a law student he was "a great enthusiast for this approach—an advocate of both writing and reading the 'holding' of a decision narrowly, thereby leaving greater discretion to future."[61] As a lawyer, law professor, and judge, however, Scalia said that he learned to value a rule-based approach to law.

By contrast, Stevens explicitly expressed wariness about the creation of firm rules. Thus, in *McDonald v. City of Chicago* (2010), concerning the application of the Second Amendment to cities and states, he rejected the thought of seeking to formulate "any all-purpose, top-down, totalizing theory of 'liberty.'"[62] In Stevens's view, "That project is bound to end in failure or worse."[63] Legal scholars described Stevens as preferring to create and apply standards rather than rules. In Jamal Greene's description, "Ever the common law judge, facts matter to Justice Stevens; for him, a single standard might be applied differently in different factual contexts in order to further the underlying purpose of a given constitutional or statutory text."[64] The straightjacket imposed by a rule-based approach can preclude careful examination of the facts as an aid to reaching conclusions that advance the underlying purposes of law in individual cases. As described by Joseph Thai, "Out of principle as well as pragmatism, Stevens left room for future judges to consider unforeseen facts and unintended consequences."[65]

Justice Stevens wrote that he learned from his law professor and mentor Nathaniel Nathanson to recognize the benefit of avoiding the impulse to create a rule when the first opportunity arises in addressing an issue. Stevens advocated, in his words, a "doctrine of judicial restraint . . . [that] teaches judges to focus their attention on the issue that must be addressed in order to decide the case or controversy between the specific litigants before the Court."[66] The rule-based approach, in comparison, according to Stevens, "provides [judges] with the opportunity to state controlling propositions of law in large black letters and to formulate the glittering generalities that law students can memorize and computers can readily store in their data banks."[67] However, Stevens drew from the lessons of Professor Nathanson to argue that the rule-based approach thereby created dangers that "glittering generality will turn out to be an overstatement that fails to anticipate the contemporary garb in which a basic theme will appear in future cases."[68] Justice Stevens credited his Northwestern education with contributing to his awareness that living in a changing world required judges to apply legal interpretations to new situations. As a Supreme Court justice, Stevens argued that resisting the temptation to create rigid rules leaves open the opportunity for judges, as well as legislators and other elected officials, to learn more over time about the existence and changing nature of issues. Thus they can work toward developing law that fits society's needs better than a flat rule created in the first instance.[69]

In retirement, Stevens reiterated this viewpoint when asked in 2013 to comment on retrospective criticisms of a majority opinion he had written in *Crawford v. Marion County Election Board* (2008). On behalf of the Court, Stevens had rejected a challenge to Indiana's law imposing new photographic identification requirements for voting, despite assertions that the law was unnecessary to prevent voter fraud and would effectively interfere with the ability of many less-affluent people to participate in elections. Justice Stevens acknowledged that he was not "a fan of voter ID" laws but claimed that the law's opponents had failed to provide enough evidence to support their claim that the law would suppress voting.[70] He pointed to the case-based, rather than rule-based, focus of his opinion by saying, "My opinion should not be taken as authority that voter-ID laws are always OK. . . . The decision in the case is state-specific and record-specific."[71]

SUPREME COURT CLERKSHIP

John Paul Stevens's experience as a Supreme Court law clerk for Justice Wiley Rutledge during the 1947 term profoundly affected his thinking about law, including legal issues in criminal justice. He came to admire greatly the interpretive approach and conclusions of Rutledge, a mentor who influenced Stevens's eventual development as a judge.[72] Justice Stevens has described Rutledge as "one of my heroes."[73] It is not mere happenstance that visitors to Justice Stevens's chambers could not avoid noticing the prominently displayed photos of two men admired and respected by Stevens who played special roles in his life and career: Justice Rutledge, a judicial role model and mentor, and President Ford, the man who appointed Stevens to the high court.[74] When asked about what he learned from Rutledge that he applied in his own career as a Supreme Court justice, Stevens focused on an element of judicial role and the judge's responsibility to the public:

> I learned an awful lot, I have to tell you. I learned to take the time to write out your own draft opinion so you're sure you understand the case before you turn it over to someone else to work on. I learned that every case is important, and not just where there's a lot of money involved and important public issues involved. Every case is important to the people who are involved in it.[75]

When he eventually became a federal court of appeals judge and later a Supreme Court justice, Stevens emulated Rutledge in the practice of writing his own first drafts of his opinions in order to keep himself closely connected to the facts and issues in each case. Justice Rutledge permitted each law clerk to write the first draft for only one opinion each year. In Stevens's clerkship year, he wrote the first draft of Rutledge's opinion for an antitrust case, *Mandeville Island Farms, Inc. v. American Crystal Sugar Co.* (1948).[76] Justice Stevens acknowledged his own limited impact on the opinion for which he wrote the first draft. As described by Stevens, "I remember drafting that opinion—seven or eight pages long. And then when I got the draft back, it was about thirty pages long and [Justice Rutledge] took the opportunity to overrule the old [*United States v.*] *E. C. Knight* [(1895)] case. . . . So I had maybe four or five paragraphs in the middle of that opinion."[77]

Other Supreme Court justices routinely delegate to law clerks the task of writing first drafts of opinions, based on the justices' instructions about the preferred outcome and reasoning. For example, Scalia said to an interviewer in 2013, "I almost never do the first draft. . . . I edit [my opinions] considerably between the first and last [drafts]."[78] By contrast, even as he was the Court's most prolific opinion writer, Stevens sat down and drafted each opinion himself before handing the draft to the law clerks to check facts and make suggestions for revisions. When asked why he adopted this practice, Stevens noted how the opinion-drafting process helped him gain a deeper understanding of each case and thereby test his own reasoning and conclusions. According to Stevens,

> I think a judge learns more about a case if he has to put his thoughts down on paper. It helps you think through a case, and when you write it out yourself, you often learn things about the case that you hadn't realized. It's part of the learning process and decisional process that I think is really quite important.[79]

In explaining the benefits of personally thinking deeply about the first draft while it is in progress, Stevens said, "your reasoning will either make sense or it won't. And if it doesn't, you change your vote, or you change your whole approach."[80]

In addition to influencing Stevens's process for evaluating cases and writing opinions, the clerkship with Justice Rutledge also exposed Stevens to a wide range of legal issues, including many criminal justice matters that he would later confront as a judicial officer. He clerked for Rutledge during a term in which the Supreme Court faced a number of cases that called into question the fairness of practices and procedures in the criminal justice system. As Stevens noted in an interview, "you get pretty deeply involved when you work on particular cases [as a law clerk]."[81] Justice Rutledge was known, in Laura Krugman Ray's words, as a jurist concerned about "the law in terms of its effects on people . . . [and] doing justice rather than following precedent."[82] Justice Stevens's experiences while working closely with and learning from Rutledge appeared to contribute to his close attention to issues of fairness, a consideration that loomed large in many cases he addressed as Supreme Court justice.

During the 1947 term, issues concerning custodial questioning and the right to counsel arose in a number of cases at the U.S. Supreme Court as Stevens researched legal issues and wrote memos for Justice Rutledge. Three cases during that term directly raised *Miranda*-type situations involving African American teenagers whose confessions may have been coerced. One case arose in Ohio (*Haley v. Ohio*, 1948), one in Mississippi (*Lee v. Mississippi*, 1948), and one in Alabama (*Taylor v. Alabama*, 1948). In the Alabama case, in which National Association for the Advancement of Colored People (NAACP) attorney and future Supreme Court Justice Thurgood Marshall presented the defendant's case to the Supreme Court, Rutledge joined Justice Frank Murphy's dissent against the majority's endorsement of the state supreme court's affirmation of the conviction. In the other two cases, Rutledge was a member of the majority that identified a problem concerning the voluntariness of the confessions and thereby reversed lower court decisions that had sustained the convictions. The description by Justice William O. Douglas of the majority's conclusions in the Ohio case, *Haley v. Ohio* (1948), demonstrated that Rutledge and like-minded justices during that term were concerned about the very issues that the Warren Court would seek to prevent with its bright-line rule in *Miranda v. Arizona* (1966) eighteen years later:

> The age of petitioner, the hours when he was grilled, the duration of his quizzing, the fact that he had no friend or counsel to advise him, the callous attitude of the police towards his rights combine to convince us that this was a confession wrung from a child by means which the law should not sanction. Neither man nor child can be allowed to stand condemned by methods which flout constitutional requirements of due process of law. . . .
>
> . . . The Fourteenth Amendment prohibits the police from using the private, secret custody of either man or child as a device for wringing confessions from them.[83]

At that moment in history, the Sixth Amendment right to counsel cases were guided by *Betts v. Brady* (1942), which required appointment of counsel for indigents in state cases only when special circumstances prevented them from representing themselves in court.[84] Under this standard, defendants who could read and write and who appeared to have normal intelligence, whether or not they were even high school graduates, were typically treated as if they were capable of serving as their own defense attorneys. The Court was still nearly fifteen years away from making a uniform rule in *Gideon v. Wainwright* (1963) requiring appointment of counsel for all indigent defendants facing serious charges. As a result, many petitioners brought claims in the 1947 term when they did not receive the benefit of counsel. Stevens had intimate exposure to the issues and the lawyers' briefs as he watched his mentor, Justice Rutledge, consistently support efforts to broaden the definition of the right to counsel. John Ferren, Rutledge's biographer, described Stevens's mentor during this era by saying, "Beginning in the 1945 Term, Rutledge began what eventually became a campaign to assure criminal defendants a truly effective right to counsel in state as well as federal courts."[85] Thus Stevens gained knowledge and experience in the chambers of a justice whose concern for the representation of criminal suspects and defendants was quite evident.

For example, Diane Marie Amann's research from the Rutledge Papers at the Library of Congress revealed that a memo written by Stevens provided key language used by Rutledge in *Marino v. Ragen* (1947) to criticize the post-conviction judicial processes in Illinois.[86] The case concerned an Italian immigrant teenager who spoke no English and had no attorney, but was convicted of murder and given a life sentence. In *Townsend v. Burke* (1948), Rutledge joined the majority opinion that concluded representation by counsel was essential to a fair proceeding in order to avoid the use of erroneous records for sentencing. Justice Rutledge also joined an opinion by Justice Murphy in *Wade v. Mayo* (1948), a habeas corpus case declaring that when an individual has an "incapacity" that impedes his ability to represent himself in court, "the refusal to appoint counsel is a denial of due process of law."[87] In another example from that term, Rutledge joined Justice Hugo Black's opinion in *Von Moltke v. Gillies* (1948) declaring that a Detroit housewife accused of being a German spy during World War II "was entitled to counsel other than that given her by Government [law enforcement] agents . . . [and] [s]he [was] still entitled to that counsel before her life or her liberty can be taken from her."[88] In addition, Rutledge's dissenting opinion in *Gryger v. Burke* (1948), on behalf of himself and Justices Black, Douglas, and Murphy, expressed his dissatisfaction with the then-existing rule that limited the requirement of appointed counsel to indigents determined by trial judges to have a special inability to represent themselves in court. In Rutledge's words,

> Perhaps the difference serves only to illustrate how capricious are the results when the right to counsel is made to depend not upon the mandate of the Constitution, but upon the vagaries of whether judges, the same or different,

> will regard this incident or that in the course of particular criminal proceedings as prejudicial.[89]

In his post-retirement memoir about the Supreme Court, Justice Stevens highlighted the fact that a right to counsel case was one of the two Supreme Court decisions that bothered him most during his clerkship year. In Stevens's words, "The cases in which Rutledge dissented that troubled me most were *Bute v. Illinois* (1948), holding that Illinois did not have to appoint counsel for a defendant charged with a felony carrying a twenty-year sentence" as well as the case of *Ahrens v. Clark* (1948).[90] In *Ahrens*, Stevens made important contributions to a controversial dissenting opinion by Rutledge that advocated the importance of access to habeas corpus, even for Germans residing in the United States who were in government custody and facing deportation in the aftermath of World War II.[91] Eventually, Justice Stevens's own Supreme Court opinions, like those of his mentor Justice Rutledge in the 1947 term, advocated broader availability of defense counsel for indigent criminal defendants.

At the time that Stevens served as Justice Rutledge's law clerk during the 1947 term, the right to trial by jury had not yet been incorporated for application to state criminal justice systems. The Sixth Amendment's right to trial by jury applied only to federal criminal trials until the Supreme Court incorporated the right for application to the states in *Duncan v. Louisiana* (1968). Until 1968, states administered their own laws that determined whether criminal defendants were entitled to jury trials.

Law clerk Stevens was at the Court when Thurgood Marshall argued the case of *Patton v. Mississippi* in November 1947. Subsequently, the Supreme Court issued a unanimous opinion by Justice Black supporting a defendant's claim that Lauderdale County, Mississippi, had systematically excluded African Americans from juries for thirty years in violation of the Equal Protection Clause.[92] The issue of a defendant's entitlement to a public trial and complete judicial processes arose in the challenge to Michigan's system of secret, one-man grand jury proceedings in *In re Oliver* (1948). After hearing testimony in secret from a witness in a gambling investigation, the judge who served as the one-man grand jury declared that he did not believe the witness. The judge immediately sentenced the witness to sixty days in jail for contempt of court. Justice Black's opinion invalidated the Michigan procedure by declaring that "[i]t is 'the law of the land' that no man's life, liberty or property be forfeited as a punishment until there has been a charge fairly made and fairly tried in a public tribunal."[93] Observers have described the case as incorporating the Sixth Amendment right to a public trial and applying that right as an obligation in state courts,[94] albeit with the later clarification that the right is not absolute and cannot necessarily be asserted successfully in all circumstances.[95]

The *Oliver* case reinforced the significance of full trial processes as both essential elements of due process and a reflection of important Anglo-American traditions. The importance of the criminal jury lurked, at least implicitly, in the analysis of the case. Moreover, Rutledge, who joined Black's opinion, wrote his own concurring opinion that advocated the complete application of the Bill of Rights to state justice systems. Justice Rutledge criticized his colleagues and prior justices by saying, "The case demonstrates how far this Court departed from our constitutional plan when, after the Fourteenth Amendment's adoption, it permitted selective departure by the states from the scheme of ordered personal liberty established by the Bill of Rights."[96] Thus Stevens was certainly well aware that Justice Rutledge strongly advocated that the right to trial by jury be guaranteed in state criminal trials as part of the universal application of all Sixth Amendment rights to court systems throughout the entire country.

In all three Fourth Amendment search and seizure cases decided in the 1947 term, Justice Rutledge joined majority opinions that identified rights violations by federal officials who conducted improper searches.[97] For example, in *United States v. Di Re* (1948),[98] seven justices rejected the warrantless search of an individual who was sitting in a car with a criminal suspect. Both individuals were found to be in possession of counterfeit gasoline rationing coupons. Justice Jackson's majority opinion emphasized the broad purposes of the Fourth Amendment and the importance of limiting police authority. In Jackson's words,

> It is said that if such arrests and searches cannot be made, law enforcement will be more difficult and uncertain. But the forefathers, after consulting the lessons of history, designed our Constitution to place obstacles in the way of a too permeating police surveillance, which they seemed to think was a greater danger to a free people than the escape of some criminals from punishment.[99]

In his later opinions as a Supreme Court justice, Stevens asserted both of the central points presented by Jackson. Justice Stevens often took note of the underlying purposes of the Fourth Amendment and, especially in his support for the exclusionary rule, Stevens accepted the possibility that some criminals will go free as the price for limiting police authority. If Rutledge influenced Stevens's views on the Fourth Amendment, that influence was in the direction of emphasizing skepticism about warrantless searches and highlighting the need to exclude improperly obtained evidence, elements that were both very evident in Stevens's later opinions.

Several cases decided by the Court in the 1947 term gave Stevens exposure to issues of racial discrimination. This exposure was shaped by Rutledge's role as one of the most liberal justices of his era and one who voiced strong concerns about racial discrimination. With respect to the justice system, in addition to the previously mentioned Mississippi case concerning systematic exclusion of African Americans from juries,[100] Rutledge also objected to the use of "blue ribbon" juries in New York that excluded African Americans and women.[101] As previously discussed, Rutledge and other justices also objected to the treatment of African American teenagers by police in Ohio, Mississippi, and Alabama who obtained confessions through high-pressure, incommunicado interrogation practices that were common at the time.[102]

Law clerk Stevens worked for Justice Rutledge during an era in which the NAACP under Thurgood Marshall pursued its litigation strategy that would ultimately lead to the landmark decision in *Brown v. Board of Education* (1954). From the late 1930s to the early 1950s, Marshall set the stage for *Brown* through a series of cases that tested various aspects of racial discrimination. As a law clerk, Stevens watched in January 1948 as Thurgood Marshall argued the case of *Sipuel v. Board of Regents* (1948), concerning the University of Oklahoma's exclusion from admission to its law school of an otherwise qualified African American woman solely on account of her race.[103] It was one of five cases that Marshall argued before the Court that term.[104] The Supreme Court unanimously ruled in Ms. Sipuel's favor and her victory served as one of the stepping-stone decisions on the road to *Brown*. In February 1948, when Marshall subsequently unsuccessfully requested an order from the Supreme Court to compel Oklahoma to comply with the *Sipuel* decision, Rutledge was the lone justice to argue that Oklahoma's courts were delaying and evading the Supreme Court's decision and therefore they should be ordered to comply.[105]

There were other cases that raised issues of race during that term for which Stevens likely did research and memos while observing close at hand Justice Rutledge's contributions to diminishing legal and public acceptance of racial discrimination. Reflecting his sensitivity to issues of race and the unfairly adverse impact on human lives from racial discrimination, in retrospect Justice Stevens wrote that *Shelley v. Kraemer* (1948) and *Hurd v. Hodge* (1948), famous cases concerning restrictions on the sale of property to African Americans, were "the two most important cases of the term."[106] In *Bob-Lo Excursion Company v. Michigan* (1948), Justice Rutledge wrote the majority opinion for the Supreme Court that upheld the validity of a prosecution under the Michigan Civil Rights Act when boat operators refused to accept an African American high school student as a passenger during a class trip to an island amusement park. In another example during Stevens's clerkship, the Court decided an additional case with implications for racial discrimination concerning a state statute depriving a Japanese-American man of his ownership interest in real estate.[107]

Robert Schapiro has documented how Stevens's approach to federalism issues followed from the opinions and viewpoints of his mentor Justice Rutledge from whom he learned so much during his year as a law clerk.[108] Professor Schapiro noted that Stevens "frequently has cited Justice Rutledge as setting forth the definitive account of the Commerce Clause."[109] Furthermore, Schapiro concluded that Stevens shared Rutledge's conception of the Commerce Clause as a "doctrine of empowerment, rather than one of limitation" for Congress.[110] In identifying the connections between Stevens's approach and that of Rutledge, Schapiro argued that,

> For Justice Stevens, as for Justice Rutledge, the Commerce Clause provided the solution to the primary problem faced by the framers . . . , how to bring the nation together. Justice Stevens has argued that the nationalizing purpose of the Commerce Clause should lead to a broad interpretation of congressional power. . . . Further following from Justice Rutledge, Justice Stevens generally has embraced the concurrent exercise of state and federal power.[111]

In addition to learning about constitutional law and judicial decision making through his daily contact with and supervision by Rutledge, Stevens also had the opportunity to see close at hand the interactions and decision making of President Franklin Roosevelt's other liberal appointees. Rutledge's frequent allies in Supreme Court decisions during the 1947 term—Hugo Black, William O. Douglas, and Frank Murphy—played central roles in turning the Court's attention toward issues of constitutional rights and endeavored to expand legal protections for individuals.

To what extent was the work of Supreme Court Justice Stevens influenced by the year he spent as a law clerk for Justice Rutledge? Justice Stevens clearly developed his values and judicial philosophy through familial influences, formal education, and a life's worth of experiences that extended far beyond his single year as a Supreme Court law clerk. Yet his clerkship experience was also unquestionably important. In his writings, speeches, and interviews, Stevens openly acknowledged how much he learned from Rutledge. In addition, several scholars have examined specific links between the cases that the young law clerk observed and researched for Justice Rutledge during the 1947 term and their influence on his own later opinions as a Supreme Court justice. Joseph Thai carefully studied Stevens's research and drafting for Justice Rutledge's dissenting opinion in *Ahrens v. Clark* (1948).[112] Professor Thai found that this case concerning the right of access to the courts for 120 Germans detained for deportation on Ellis Island in the aftermath of World War II later shaped Justice Stevens's opinion in *Rasul v. Bush* (2004), concerning access to the courts for terrorism suspects held at Guantanamo Bay, Cuba. Professor Ray evaluated various similarities between Rutledge and Stevens, and gave examples, such as First Amendment Establishment Clause cases, in which their dissents were similar.[113] Professor Amann analyzed his clerkship with Justice Rutledge as well as his service as a U.S. Navy officer in World War II to make broader points about Stevens's jurisprudence on equality[114] and her characterization of Stevens as "a human rights judge."[115]

Justice Stevens often told the story of how a coin flip with another editor of *Northwestern University Law Review* determined that Stevens would accept a clerkship with Justice Rutledge rather than with Chief Justice Fred Vinson.[116] In light of Stevens's acknowledgment of Rutledge's influence over his understanding of legal issues and judicial decision making, it raises an interesting question about whether and how Justice Stevens and his decisions might have been different if that historic coin flip had gone the other way.

EXPERIENCE AS A PRACTICING ATTORNEY

After his clerkship year with Justice Rutledge, Stevens declined an opportunity to be considered for a faculty position at Yale Law School because he was intent on becoming a practicing attorney. He returned to Chicago and joined the law firm of Poppenhusen, Johnston, Thompson, Raymond, and Mayer. The firm was considered large for its time because it had more than two dozen lawyers. A few years later, he formed his own law firm with other young attorneys who had joined the Poppenhusen firm with him in 1948.[117]

As much as any other justice in recent decades, except perhaps Thurgood Marshall, Stevens gained significant expertise as a practicing attorney whose varied experiences included courtroom advocacy on a range of issues. Most of his career was spent at the small firm that he co-founded, Rothschild, Stevens, Barry, and Myers. The founding partners were described by the lawyer-son of one partner as "generalists" who welcomed any client "no matter what the nature of their problem."[118] Their general law practice gave Stevens many opportunities to engage in client advocacy. His cases ranged from his *pro bono* representation of criminal offenders seeking to appeal their convictions to a nationally prominent trial representing the Oakland Athletics baseball team owner Charlie Finley in a contract case[119] to Stevens's lone oral argument before the U.S. Supreme Court representing Bowman Dairy Company in a 1962 antitrust case.[120] In addition to experiences with *pro bono* representation of convicted offenders, Stevens also gained experience in criminal law from a limited number of other cases in the earliest years of his career. As he described in an interview, "I was involved in a number of criminal antitrust cases. . . . One of the major trials that I worked on was an indictment . . . under the Sherman Act, the *National City Lines* case."[121] Justice Stevens's significant previous experience as a practicing attorney presumably contributed to his belief in and advocacy for the adversary system of justice in his judicial opinions concerning Sixth Amendment rights and other aspects of judicial process.

Justice Stevens grew up in Chicago, which was known for a long history of abusive police practices spanning many decades, including incidents in the 1980s and 1990s, when officers used either physical or psychological pressure to force arrestees to confess to crimes that they did not commit.[122] For example, in December 2012 the CBS News program *Sixty Minutes* broadcast a story concerning nine young men who as teenagers were pressured by Chicago police in the 1990s to admit to rapes and murders, thus sending them to prison for two decades before DNA testing years later indicated that they were not guilty.[123] Justice Stevens was asked during an interview about the possibility that growing up in Chicago, with its long history of abusive police behavior and corruption, informed and affected his sensitivity to certain issues in criminal justice. He agreed that it was possible and quickly noted that, by contrast, Chief Justice William Rehnquist, who manifested much greater trust in criminal justice officials, grew up in Milwaukee, a city with reform-minded police chiefs and early professionalization efforts.[124]

In his public speeches, Justice Stevens alluded to his knowledge of police brutality in Chicago. In one speech referring to the 1930s in Chicago, Stevens said, "At that time, less prosperous criminals were sometimes treated brutally by Chicago police officers seeking confessions of guilt,"[125] a declaration that was directly connected to underlying risks in *Miranda*-related cases. In another speech, Stevens spoke of police misconduct in a case in which he represented a convicted offender.[126] In yet another speech, he provided a few details about the case: "It was a few years after my graduation [from law school], in the course of *pro bono* representation of an inmate who had been in prison since 1937, that I learned that some of those interrogations did, in fact, involve brutal and indefensible police conduct."[127]

In the speech about his personal experience, Stevens referred to *People v. LaFrana* (1954), an Illinois Supreme Court case in which he helped free a client who was imprisoned for seventeen years after being tortured by Chicago police into confessing to a murder that he did not commit. As described by Stevens, his constitutional law professor from Northwestern, Nathaniel Nathanson, was appointed by the U.S. Supreme Court to represent Arthur LaFrana. LaFrana had confessed to the murder of a theater cashier in 1937, but later pursued a *pro se* claim that his confession had been involuntary. In arguing before the U.S. Supreme Court in 1951, Nathanson also represented two other Illinois prisoners who sought to raise claims about coerced confessions. In *Jennings v. Illinois* (1951), a 7-to-2 decision authored by Chief Justice Fred Vinson, the U.S. Supreme Court remanded the cases to the Illinois courts to determine whether the petitioners' claims could be examined under the state's Post-Conviction Hearing Act. If not, then the U.S. Supreme Court said that the petitioners could present their claims in a U.S. district court.

According to Stevens, "[b]ecause Nat's extensive experience in litigation had primarily involved appellate advocacy, he asked me to handle the investigation and trial of the confession issue [in LaFrana's case]."[128] Stevens represented LaFrana in an evidentiary hearing before an Illinois trial court and the case was subsequently examined by the Illinois Supreme Court. In *People v. LaFrana*, the Illinois Supreme Court described the evidence presented in the case:

> According to defendant's testimony, when he refused to confess the captain hit him repeatedly with fists and with a night stick. His hands were then handcuffed behind him and he was blindfolded. A rope was put in between the handcuffs and he was suspended from a door with his hands behind him and his feet almost off the floor. While he was hanging from the door, he was repeatedly struck until he lapsed into unconsciousness. When he lost consciousness he was taken down from the door and when he regained consciousness he would be hung back up on the door and again questioned and struck. After about fifteen minutes of this treatment he agreed to sign a confession. He was taken downstairs to the captain's office where he signed a confession.[129]

The Illinois Supreme Court regarded LaFrana's version of events as corroborated by a newspaper photograph taken the day after his interrogation that showed cuts and bruises on his face as well as swelling around his eye. In addition, the physician who examined him at the jail the following week testified that the abrasions on LaFrana's wrists could have been caused by hanging him over a door, but could not have been caused by any normal use of handcuffs. Stevens was appalled that the police falsely claimed that LaFrana's injuries were caused when he fell down the stairs while going to use the men's room, a claim that was completely inconsistent with the nature of the injuries.[130]

In light of the number of brief references to this case in his speeches, it seems clear that LaFrana's victimization at the hands of the police was an important, unforgettable memory that came to mind for Justice Stevens when he confronted *Miranda*-related questions about protecting suspects from improper coercion by police. Indeed, when describing the event during an interview, Stevens reflexively placed his own hands behind his back and lifted them into an awkward position as he said he could never forget what the Chicago police had done to LaFrana.[131]

Justice Stevens's general experience as an attorney also informed his view on an issue that arose in several cases addressed by the Supreme Court. It would be an understatement to say that he felt very strongly about both the importance of the adversary system and the need for the police and prosecutor to respect that system by refraining from communicating with defendants who are represented by an attorney. The emphatic words in his judicial opinions reflected the sentiments that he expressed in an interview:

> My experience in trial situations made me sensitive. . . . [I] think it is just not fair procedure to send an investigator out to talk to the opposing party without them knowing what is going on and so forth. You just don't do those things. And I think that particular rule is—and my experiences in practice—had a huge impact on my reaction to that. I'm just really terribly offended at the notion that this guy has had a lawyer appointed for him—and the police can go off on their own when they know what is going on—You just don't do that. I attribute my strong feelings about that to the fact that I had some experience in private practice.[132]

INVESTIGATIVE COMMISSION

During the 1950s and 1960s, Stevens was an active attorney in Chicago and had little reason to be known and recognized outside of the legal community, except perhaps for being mentioned in national news articles as the attorney representing major league baseball owner Charles O. Finley.[133] In 1969, however, Stevens came into the public eye through his role as the appointed chief investigator for a special commission established to examine allegations of conflicts of interest among Illinois Supreme Court justices, specifically financial links between certain justices and entities, such as banks, with cases before the court.[134] After highly publicized commission hearings in which Stevens played a quasi-prosecutorial role, two justices resigned from the Illinois Supreme Court.[135] Stevens's public visibility from the hearings subsequently contributed to his appointment as a judge on the U.S. Court of Appeals for the Seventh Circuit in 1970, the judgeship which subsequently led to his appointment to the U.S. Supreme Court in 1975.[136] Justice Stevens pointed to this investigative experience as the source of several lessons that apparently shaped his consideration of cases and his path to becoming a prolific opinion writer.

The investigation began with allegations circulated by a gadfly crusader against corruption in the courts named Sherman Skolnick. Skolnick, a man of modest means who suffered from paralysis due to polio, devoted himself to a mission as a self-taught litigator in the aftermath of an unsuccessful lawsuit filed by his parents. The parents had sued over the mishandling of a $14,000 stock fund that had been set up to provide for the care of Sherman and they lost in the Illinois Supreme Court. Skolnick said afterward, "We went all the way to the state Supreme Court . . . and lost. I vowed to my parents that I would devote my life to helping others in the courts."[137]

Because Skolnick did not have formal education in law, affluence, social status, or political connections and because he constantly filed lawsuits and made accusations against public officials, he was the type of person that news reporters and government officials could easily dismiss as a misguided crackpot. Indeed, Skolnick's accusations in this case only moved forward to reveal improper conduct on the state supreme court because a few newspaper reporters took an interest in his claims and pursued their own investigations.[138]

As it turned out, Skolnick's greatest impact on history may be the effect that his efforts had on a man who eventually gained an appointment to the U.S. Supreme Court. In the foreword that he wrote for Kenneth Manaster's book about the investigative commission, *Illinois Justice*, Stevens acknowledged that the example of Skolnick provided an important lifelong lesson about the need to keep channels of communication and access open in order to permit people to raise their claims to courts and other authorities. According to Stevens, in the case of imprisoned criminal offenders, this lesson was particularly important because of the Supreme Court's tendency to effectively prohibit future petition filings from specific prisoners if those individuals are perceived as abusing the legal process by filing too many unsubstantiated claims.[139] The method used by the Court to block such filings is to deny specific individuals the opportunity to have the Court's filing fees waived. Most self-prepared petitions, known as *pro se* cases because individuals are representing themselves without an attorney, are accompanied by an *in forma pauperis* petition that requests the waiver of filing fees based on the claim that the litigant is too poor to pay. Because prisoners typically have little or no money, they usually file such petitions seeking fee waivers. Thus the Supreme Court can effectively block future filings from specific individuals by simply declaring that they will have to pay filing fees for all future actions filed with the Court. Because this poses an impossible burden on penniless prisoners, it effectively closes the courthouse door on any future claims. As described by Justice Stevens,

> [M]y reaction to so-called *pro se* petitions—those filed by lay litigants without the assistance of counsel—is also markedly different from that of any of my colleagues. . . . My memory of the unexpected merit that we found in the allegations made by Sherman Skolnick has remained a powerful reminder that categorical prohibitions against repetitive filings can create a real risk of injustice. . . . [A]t virtually every Court conference I find myself dissenting from three or four orders imposing special burdens on this disfavored class of litigants.[140]

Because convicted offenders file such a significant portion of the several thousand *pro se* petitions filed with the Supreme Court each year, prisoners are the primary members of the "disfavored class of litigants" to whom Stevens referred.

In the foreword to *Illinois Justice*, Stevens also declared that his examination of practices within the Illinois Supreme Court convinced him of the importance of ensuring that dissenting viewpoints are publicly reported and not voluntarily suppressed. He acknowledged that it was the practice in many appellate courts for dissenting judges to avoid presenting their views or even reporting the fact that they disagreed with a decision. Some judges, according to Stevens, saw dissenting opinions as "a threat to the collegiality of the appellate court" and a practice that "undermine[d] the illusion that the law is a seamless web of certain, definite, and harmonious rules."[141] Justice Stevens objected to appellate courts creating the illusion of unanimity when there was actually disagreement within a court. He came to believe that the public was entitled to know about disagreements among judges on an appellate court. According to Stevens, "This experience is what persuaded me, when I became an appellate judge, that it's not for me to decide [about recording my disagreement]: If I don't agree, I should record that fact, and that's what I've always done."[142]

One of the other issues of concern for Stevens in the investigation was the practice on the Illinois Supreme Court of assigning opinion-writing responsibilities before the case was heard by the court. This created risks that if a case was assigned in advance to a judge with biases or susceptibility to outside influence, that judge would be in a position to exert extra influence over the reasoning and conclusions contained in the court's opinion. Moreover, it could make other members of the appellate court less careful and diligent in preparing for and analyzing such cases because they know in advance that they will not be writing the opinion for the court. As Stevens observed, "Any procedure that elevates the role of a single judge above that of his or her colleagues before the court addresses the merits of a case tends to undermine the central purpose of a multijudge panel."[143]

Although the U.S. Supreme Court operates under a system in which opinion-writing assignments are made after the case is heard and discussed by the justices, Stevens's observation of the assignment-timing issues in the Illinois Supreme Court influenced his judicial behavior in a specific way. Unlike most other justices on the U.S. Supreme Court, Stevens declined to participate in the "cert pool," in which a single law clerk working for one justice writes a memo for all of the justices characterizing the issues in a petition and making a recommendation about whether or not the Court should accept the case for decision. For Stevens, the "cert pool" process presented a parallel problem of not enough people looking carefully and diligently at each petition before the justices decided which cases to accept. Thus Stevens had one of his own law clerks analyze each petition and write a memo specifically for him. He did not want to rely solely on the advice and recommendations of a single law clerk elsewhere in the Court whom he did not hire, train, or supervise himself. As Stevens said, "My abstention from my current colleagues' process of assessing petitions for review on the basis of a single memorandum prepared for a 'pool' of justices is, in part, a product of my work for the Special Commission."[144] Justice Stevens said that his decision to decline the use of the "pool" memo was also based on his prior experience as a law clerk for Justice Rutledge. That experience led him to conclude he could more quickly make an accurate judgment about whether to grant or deny the petition by glancing at the original papers himself, rather than reading a law clerk's detailed arguments for each side.[145] Justice Stevens was more interested than most other justices in being personally involved in evaluating certiorari petitions. Late in his career, he noted that he remained personally involved by saying, "I tend to read the cert petition before I vote to grant."[146] However, he also acknowledged the importance of his own law clerks' role by conceding that "unless one of my clerks had identified [a petition] as a potential grant, I usually will not read the original papers myself."[147] Thus, his experiences with the investigative commission, as well as his clerkship with Justice Rutledge, taught Stevens to be personally and closely engaged in evaluating cases and drafting his own opinions.

PERSONAL EXPERIENCE AND JUDICIAL OPINIONS

Although the influence of personal experience is typically hidden from public view as it shapes the justice's thinking and discussions with other justices, it can occasionally be explicitly evident in a judicial opinion. For example, in *Smith v. Robbins* (2000), Stevens objected to the majority's acceptance of a procedure through which an indigent defendant's appointed attorney concluded that an appeal would be frivolous and filed a form to that effect at the state appellate court without delineating the reasons for the conclusion. In his dissenting opinion, Stevens openly relied on his own experience:

> To make my second point I shall draw on my own experience as a practicing lawyer and as a judge. On a good many occasions I have found that the task of writing out the reasons that support an initial opinion on a question of law—whether for the purpose of giving advice to my client or for the purpose of explaining my vote as an appellate judge—leads to the conclusion that was not previously apparent. . . . Because counsel may discover previously unrecognized aspects of the law in the process of preparing a written explanation for his or her conclusion, the discussion requirement provides an additional safeguard against mistaken conclusions by counsel.[148]

In *Scott v. Harris* (2007), Stevens was the lone dissenter when he objected to a summary judgment that dismissed a driver's lawsuit against the police officers who caused his permanent paralysis by ramming his car when trying to stop him on a roadway. After watching the video from the police cruiser's dash-mounted camera that recorded the driver's failure to stop when the pursuing police car used its lights and siren, the majority of justices concluded that the driver was responsible for his own catastrophic injuries. Justice Stevens, by contrast, believed that the driver's actions were less obviously dangerous than presumed by the majority and therefore a jury should have decided the case. As the oldest justice on the Court at that time, Stevens based his conclusion, in part, on his own experiences in learning to drive before the nation's interstate highway system was constructed:

> I can only conclude that my colleagues were unduly frightened by two or three images on the tape that looked like bursts of lightning or explosions, but were in fact merely the headlights of vehicles zooming by in the opposite lane. Had they learned to drive when most high-speed driving took place on two-lane roads rather than on superhighways—when split-second judgments about the risk of passing a slowpoke in the face of oncoming traffic were routine—they might well have reacted to the videotape more dispassionately.[149]

CONCLUSION

Several important points need to be highlighted about this book's argument that the life experiences that helped to shape Justice Stevens's judicial values differentiated him from other liberal Republican appointees of his era. In essence, unlike Justices Blackmun and Souter, Justice Stevens brought a well-formed, rights-protective judicial philosophy with him to the Supreme Court at the time of his appointment. First, there is no simple or definitive causal arrow that can be drawn from a particular life experience to a particular decision by a judge. Any discussions of linkages between life experiences and judicial decisions are necessarily speculative. Yet, Justice Stevens himself has pointed to specific life experiences as shaping his views on particular issues. Thus, although discussions of life experiences might be dismissed as unproven when examined according to the rigorous standards of social science analysis, there is value in understanding a judge's social background, education, and experiences. These elements undoubtedly contribute, albeit in unmeasurable ways, to the development of every judge's judicial philosophy, understanding of American society, political values, and policy preferences. As demonstrated by numerous judicial biographies, the illumination of a judge's life experiences helps to provide a richer understanding of the factors that contributed to that judicial decision maker's ultimate influence and impact on law and policy.

Moreover, this book's inclusion of life experiences as an influence on the development of Stevens's values and judicial philosophy concerning specific issues does not imply that his judicial opinions in each case were solely or even primarily the result of these factors. Judicial decisions are also shaped by the institutional context of a court and the interactions between judges in the court's decision-making processes. On multi-judge appellate courts, such as the U.S. Supreme Court, judges must engage in persuasion while they also compromise and accommodate the viewpoints of colleagues in order to develop judicial opinions that will garner majority support. Thus judicial opinions cannot automatically be viewed as pure, unadulterated expressions of a judge's philosophy and values, especially in a majority opinion that was developed to both represent a viewpoint and simultaneously retain the support of other justices. Dissenting opinions may create freer opportunities for Supreme Court justices to present their truest analyses and viewpoints about issues. If so, Stevens's opinions are especially intriguing both because he was the Supreme Court's most prolific author of dissenting opinions and because he spent much of his career writing rights-protective dissents in criminal justice cases as the Court's majorities frequently diminished the scope of constitutional rights. However, analysts must always bear in mind that many dissents are also written with strategic considerations in mind. Justices may craft dissents in a calculated manner to cultivate the support of specific colleagues for decisions in the near future or to lay the groundwork for affecting the development of legal precedents farther into the future.

In addition, the argument that Stevens brought a well-formed judicial philosophy to the Supreme Court at the time of his appointment does not mean that his approach to decision making and his judicial decisions never changed. As chapter 8 will discuss with respect to capital punishment, Stevens clearly changed his views about this issue over the course of his career. As other scholars have discussed, Stevens's approach to the issues of abortion and affirmative action also changed during his years on the Supreme Court.[150] Although Stevens immediately demonstrated in 1976 the rights-protective nature of his approach to many issues in his first Supreme Court opinions, he later emphasized the importance of a judge continuing to learn on the bench and acknowledged that his analysis of specific issues was affected by what he learned through judicial experience.[151]

NOTES

1. Justin Wedeking, "Why Do Policy-Motivated Justices Conform to Unfavorable Precedents? The Role of Social-Legal Backgrounds and Precedential Characteristics," *Justice System Journal* 33 (2012): 69–95.

2. Christopher E. Smith, "Polarization and Change in the Federal Courts: En Banc Decisions in the U.S. Court of Appeals," *Judicature* 74 (1990): 133–37.

3. George Kannar, "The Constitutional Catechism of Antonin Scalia," *Yale Law Journal* 99 (1990): 1297–1357.

4. C. Neal Tate, "Personal Attribute Models of the Voting Behavior of U.S. Supreme Court Justices: Liberalism in Civil Liberties and Economics Decisions," *American Political Science Review* 75 (1981): 355–67.

5. Kannar, "The Constitutional Catechism of Antonin Scalia," 1297–1320.

6. Walter Isaacson, "A Justice Reflects," *The Daily Beast* website, June 29, 2009, accessed May 21, 2015, http://www.thedailybeast.com/articles/2009/06/29/a-justice-reflects.html.

7. Adam Liptak, "At 89, Stevens Contemplates Law, and How to Leave It," *New York Times*, April 3, 2010, accessed May 21, 2015, http://www.nytimes.com/2010/04/04/us/04stevens.html?_r=0.

8. Justice John Paul Stevens, interview with author, U.S. Supreme Court, Washington, D.C., July 29, 2010.

9. *History of McDonough County, Illinois* (Springfield, Ill.: Continental Historical Co., 1885), 259, 477, 601–16.

10. Terry Hogan, "The Birth and Death of Abingdon College," *The* (Galesburg, Ill.) *Zephyr*, February 13, 2006, accessed May 21, 2015, http://www.thezephyr.com/backtrack/abingdoncollege.htm.

11. *History of McDonough County*, 60.

12. Josiah Seymour Currey, *Chicago: Its History and Its Builders*, vol. V (Chicago: The S.J. Publishing Co., 1912), 600–2, 612, 1002–3.

13. Ibid., 611–12.

14. Ibid., 612.

15. Robert V. Allegrini and Geraldine Hempel Davis, *Chicago's Grand Hotel: A History of the Hilton Chicago* (Lafayette, Colo.: Moonlight Publishing, 2002), 1–12.

16. U.S. Bureau of Census, *Fifteenth Census of the United States: 1930,* Chicago, Cook County, Illinois, Sheet No. 5A, April 1930.

17. Justice John Paul Stevens, interview with author, U.S. Supreme Court, Washington, D.C., July 29, 2010.

18. Ibid.

19. Leon F. Litwack, *Trouble in Mind: Black Southerners in the Age of Jim Crow* (New York: Knopf, 1998), xiv–xvi.

20. Justice John Paul Stevens, interview with author, U.S. Supreme Court, Washington, D.C., July 29, 2010.

21. Ibid.

22. Charles Lane, "Heartbreak Hotel," *Chicago Magazine*, August 2006, accessed May 21, 2015, http://www.chicagomag.com/Chicago-Magazine/August-2006/Heartbreak-Hotel/.

23. Ibid.

24. Ibid.

25. *People v. Stevens*, 193 N.E. 154, 160 (1934).

26. Ibid.

27. Bill Barnhart, "Justice Stevens and the News Media: An Exercise in Exposition," *Northwestern Law Review* 106 (2012): 663.

28. Jeffrey Rosen, "The Dissenter," *New York Times Magazine*, September 23, 2007, 54.

29. Ibid.

30. Bill Barnhart and Gene Schlickman, *John Paul Stevens: An Independent Life* (DeKalb, Ill.: Northern Illinois University Press, 2010), 34.

31. Justice John Paul Stevens, interview with author, U.S. Supreme Court, Washington, D.C., July 29, 2010.

32. Nina Totenberg, "Justice Stevens: An Open Mind on A Changed Court," *Morning Edition* news program, National Public Radio, October 4, 2010, accessed May 21, 2015, http://www.npr.org/templates/story/story.php?storyId=130198344.

33. Ibid.

34. Justice John Paul Stevens, interview with author, U.S. Supreme Court, Washington, D.C., July 29, 2010.

35. Ibid.

36. Ibid.

37. Ibid.

38. Kenneth Manaster, *Illinois Justice: The Scandal of 1969 and the Rise of John Paul Stevens* (Chicago: University of Chicago Press, 2001), 38.

39. John Paul Stevens, "Letter to the Editor," *New York Times*, November 4, 2007, accessed May 21, 2015, http://query.nytimes.com/gst/fullpage.html?res=9903E0DF153DF937A35752C1A9619C8B63.

40. John Paul Stevens, speech at Georgia State University College of Law, Atlanta, Georgia, April 16, 2014, accessed May 20, 2015, http://www.supremecourt.gov/publicinfo/speeches/JPS%20Speech_Atlanta_04-16-2014.pdf.

41. Eugene Fidell, "Justice John Paul Stevens and Judicial Deference in Military Matters," *UC Davis Law Review* 43 (2010): 1001.

42. Ibid., 1003.

43. *Texas v. Johnson*, 491 U.S. 397, 439 (1989) (Stevens, J., dissenting).

44. Jill Duffy and Elizabeth Lambert, "Dissents from the Bench: A Compilation of Oral Dissents by U.S. Supreme Court Justices," *Law Library Journal* 102 (2010): 24–37.

45. Edward Lazarus, *Closed Chamber* (New York: Times Books, 1998), 36.

46. Glen Elsasser, "Constitution Protects Burning Flag As Protest, Court Rules," *Chicago Tribune*, June 22, 1989, 1; Al Kamen, "Court Nullifies Flag-Desecration Laws," *Washington Post,* June 22, 1989, A1; Linda Greenhouse, "Justices, 5–4, Back Protesters' Right to Burn the Flag," *New York Times,* June 22, 1989, A1; Stephen Wermeil, "Justices Say First Amendment Protects Burning of Flag—Another Decision Allows Publishing Certain Data Even If Laws Are Broken," *Wall Street Journal*, June 22, 1989, 1.

47. Fidell, 1000.

48. Linda Greenhouse, "Selective Empathy," *New York Times*, December 3, 2009, accessed May 21, 2015, http://opinionator.blogs.nytimes.com/2009/12/03/selective-empathy/.

49. Jeffrey Toobin, "After Stevens: What Will the Supreme Court Be Like Without Its Liberal Leader?" *The New Yorker*, March 22, 2010, 43; Rosen, "The Dissenter," 55; Diane Marie Amann, "John Paul Stevens, Human Rights Judge," *Fordham Law Review* 74 (2006): 1582–83.

50. Toobin, "After Stevens," 43.

51. Ibid.

52. Amann, "John Paul Stevens, Human Rights Judge," 1583.

53. Toobin, "After Stevens," 43.

54. Amann, "John Paul Stevens, Human Rights Judge," 1582.

55. Rosen, "The Dissenter," 55.

56. John Paul Stevens, "Northwestern University School of Law's 151st Commencement Address," *Northwestern Law Review* 106 (2012): 852.

57. Justice John Paul Stevens, interview with author, U.S. Supreme Court, Washington, D.C., July 12, 2006.

58. Antonin Scalia, "The Rule of Law as a Law of Rules," *University of Chicago Law Review* 56 (1989): 1175–88.

59. Ibid., 1177.

60. Ibid., 1176.

61. Ibid., 1178.

62. *McDonald v. City of Chicago*, 130 S.Ct. 3020, 3100 (Stevens, J., dissenting).

63. Ibid.

64. Jamal Greene, "The Rule of Law as a Law of Standards," *Georgetown Law Journal* 99 (2011): 1290–91.

65. Joseph Thai, "Did Justice Stevens Change?" SCOTUSblog, April 29, 2010, accessed May 21, 2015, http://www.scotusblog.com/2010/04/did-justice-stevens-change/.

66. John Paul Stevens, "Judicial Restraint," *San Diego Law Review* 22 (1985): 446.

67. Ibid., 447.

68. Ibid., 448.

69. Ibid.

70. Jess Bravin, "Voter-ID Laws Worry Jurist," *Wall Street Journal*, October 17, 2013, accessed May 21, 2015, http://www.wsj.com/articles/SB10001424052702304384104579141701228734132.

71. Ibid.

72. Laura Krugman Ray, "Clerk and Justice: The Ties That Bind John Paul Stevens and Wiley B. Rutledge," *Connecticut Law Review* 41 (2008): 214–15.

73. Brian Lamb, Susan Swain, and Mark Farkas, eds., *The Supreme Court: A C-Span Book Featuring the Justices in Their Own Words* (New York: Public Affairs, 2010), 37.

74. Ibid., 41.

75. Ibid., 38.

76. John Paul Stevens, *Five Chiefs: A Supreme Court Memoir* (Boston: Little, Brown, 2011), 188–89.
77. Justice John Paul Stevens, interview with author, U.S. Supreme Court, Washington, D.C., July 29, 2010.
78. Jennifer Senior, "In Conversation: Antonin Scalia," *New York Magazine*, October 6, 2013, accessed May 21, 2015, http://nymag.com/news/features/antonin-scalia-2013-10/.
79. Bryan A. Garner, "Interview with Justice John Paul Stevens," *The Scribes Journal of Legal Writing* (2010): 42.
80. Totenberg, "Justice Stevens: An Open Mind on a Changed Court," accessed on May 21, 2015, http://www.npr.org/templates/story/story.php?storyId=130198344.
81. Justice John Paul Stevens, interview with author, U.S. Supreme Court, Washington, D.C., July 29, 2010.
82. Ray, "Clerk and Justice," 219–20.
83. *Haley v. Ohio*, 332 U.S. 596, 600–1 (1948).
84. *Betts v. Brady*, 316 U.S. 455 (1942).
85. John M. Ferren, *Salt of the Earth, Conscience of the Court: The Story of Justice Wiley Rutledge* (Chapel Hill, N.C.: University of North Carolina Press, 2004), 352.
86. Amann, "John Paul Stevens, Human Rights Judge," 1590.
87. *Wade v. Mayo*, 334 U.S. 672, 684 (1948).
88. *Von Moltke v. Gillies*, 332 U.S. 708, 726 (1948).
89. *Gryger vs. Burke*, 334 U.S. 728, 736 (1948) (Rutledge, J. dissertation).
90. Stevens, *Five Chiefs*, 68.
91. Amann, "John Paul Stevens, Human Rights Judge," 1591–92; Craig Green, "Wiley Rutledge, Executive Detention, and Judicial Conscience at War," *Washington University Law Review* 84 (2006): 115–19.
92. *Patton v. Mississippi*, 332 U.S. 463 (1947).
93. *In re Oliver*, 333 U.S. 257, 278 (1948).
94. Henry J. Abraham, *Freedom and the Court*, 5th ed. (New York: Oxford University Press, 1988), 78.
95. *Globe Newspaper Co. v. Superior Court*, 457 U.S. 596, 606 (1982).
96. *In re Oliver*, 333 U.S. at 280 (Rutledge, J., concurring).
97. *Johnson v. United States*, 333 U.S. 10 (1948); *United States v. Di Re*, 332 U.S. 581 (1948); *Trupiano v. United States*, 334 U.S. 699 (1948).
98. *United States v. Di Re*, 332 U.S. 581 (1948).
99. Ibid., 595.
100. *Patton v. Mississippi*, 332 U.S. 463 (1947).
101. *Moore v. New York*, 333 U.S. 565 (1948).
102. *Haley v. Ohio*, 332 U.S. 596 (1948); *Lee v. Mississippi*, 332 U.S. 742 (1948); *Taylor v. Alabama*, 335 U.S. 252 (1948).
103. John Paul Stevens, "Address to the American Bar Association Thurgood Marshall Awards Dinner." Chicago, Ill., August 6, 2005, accessed May 21, 2015, http://www.supremecourt.gov/publicinfo/speeches/viewspeech/sp_08-06-05.
104. Stevens, *Five Chiefs*, 69.
105. *Fisher v. Hurst*, 333 U.S. 147 (1948).
106. Stevens, *Five Chiefs*, 68.
107. *Oyama v. California*, 332 U.S. 633 (1948).
108. Robert A. Schapiro, "Justice Stevens's Theory of Interactive Federalism," *Fordham Law Review* 74 (2006): 2144–47.
109. Ibid., 2146.
110. Ibid., 2147.
111. Ibid., 2146–47.
112. Joseph Thai, "The Law Clerk Who Wrote *Rasul v. Bush*," *Virginia Law Review* 92 (2006): 501–32.
113. Ray, "Clerk and Justice," 211–63.
114. Diane Marie Amann, "John Paul Stevens and Equally Impartial Government," *UC Davis Law Review* 43 (2010): 885–925.

115. Amann, "John Paul Stevens, Human Rights Judge," 1569–1605.
116. John Paul Stevens, "A Personal History of the Law Review," *Northwestern University Law Review* 100 (2006): 26.
117. Stevens, *Five Chiefs*, 86–87.
118. Rosemary Simota Thompson, "Justice John Paul Stevens: Chicago's Native Son," *Chicago Bar Association Record* 24 (September 2010): 32.
119. Alan L. Unikel, "A Supremely Memorable Case," *Chicago Bar Association Record*, 24 (September 2010): 48–51.
120. *United States v. Borden Company et al*, 370 U.S. 460 (1962).
121. Justice John Paul Stevens, interview with author, U.S. Supreme Court, Washington, D.C., July 29, 2010.
122. Jodi Rudoren, "Inquiry Finds Police Abuse, but Says Law Bars Trials," *New York Times*, July 20, 2006, accessed May 21, 2015, http://www.nytimes.com/2006/07/20/us/20chicago.html?pagewanted=all; Susan Saulny and Eric Ferkenhoff, "Ex-Officer Linked to Brutality Is Arrested," *New York Times*, October 22, 2008, accessed May 21, 2015, http://www.nytimes.com/2008/10/22/us/22chicago.html.
123. CBS News, *Sixty Minutes*, "Chicago: The False Confession Capital," December 9, 2012, accessed May 21, 2015, http://www.cbsnews.com/videos/chicago-the-false-confession-capital/.
124. Justice John Paul Stevens, interview with author, U.S. Supreme Court, Washington, D.C., July 12, 2006.
125. John Paul Stevens, "The Bill of Rights: A Century of Progress," *University of Chicago Law Review* 59 (1992): 13, 15n.7.
126. John Paul Stevens, "Random Recollections," *San Diego Law Review* 42 (2005): 269.
127. John Paul Stevens, "Judicial Activism: Ensuring the Powers and Freedoms Conceived by the Framers for Today's World," *Chicago Bar Association Record* 16 (2002): 25.
128. Stevens, "Random Recollections," 270.
129. *People v. LaFrana*, 122 N.E.2d 583, 585 (Ill. 1954).
130. Stevens, *Five Chiefs*, 80.
131. Justice John Paul Stevens, interview with author, U.S. Supreme Court, Washington, D.C., July 12, 2006.
132. Justice John Paul Stevens, interview with author, U.S. Supreme Court, Washington, D.C., July 29, 2010.
133. Manaster, *Illinois Justice*, 39.
134. Ibid., 237–42.
135. Ibid., 238–41.
136. Ibid., 264–69.
137. Ibid., 3–4.
138. Ibid., 5–6.
139. John Paul Stevens, "Foreword," in Kenneth A. Manaster, *Illinois Justice: The Scandal of 1969 and the Rise of John Paul Stevens* (Chicago: University of Chicago Press, 2001), xi.
140. Ibid.
141. Ibid., xii.
142. Manaster, *Illinois Justice*, 273.
143. Stevens, "Foreword," xi.
144. Ibid.
145. Stevens, *Five Chiefs*, 139.
146. Garner, "Interview with Justice John Paul Stevens," 45.
147. Ibid.
148. *Smith v. Robbins*, 528 U.S. 259, 290-91 (Stevens, J., dissenting).
149. *Scott v. Harris*, 550 U.S. 372, 390 n. 1 (Stevens, J., dissenting).
150. Linda Greenhouse, "Justice John Paul Stevens as Abortion-Rights Strategist," *UC Davis Law Review* 43: 749–82; Amann, "John Paul Stevens and Equally Impartial Government," 885–925.
151. Stevens, "Learning on the Job," 1561–67.

Chapter Three

Judge Stevens on the U.S. Court of Appeals

The newspaper coverage of the Illinois Supreme Court investigation in 1969 propelled John Paul Stevens into the public eye. His role in the investigation enhanced his already prominent reputation in the legal community as an outstanding trial attorney and civic-minded participant in bar association projects. He caught the attention of the staff of Senator Charles Percy as they brought suggestions to their boss about potential nominees for an open judgeship on the Chicago-based U.S. Court of Appeals for the Seventh Circuit. When Percy met with Stevens to discuss the open judgeship, he was happy to discover that it was the same John Stevens that he remembered as an acquaintance among other top students during their overlapping undergraduate years at the University of Chicago.[1]

With the endorsement of Percy, Stevens was nominated by President Nixon and confirmed by the U.S. Senate. Upon being sworn in as a federal appellate judge on November 2, 1970, Stevens began his five years of service as a Seventh Circuit judge.[2] This experience provided important preparation for his later career as a Supreme Court justice. Justice Stevens began his judicial career on the Seventh Circuit just one year after the close of the Warren Court era (1953–1969) during which the Supreme Court significantly expanded and strengthened the constitutional rights of criminal suspects and defendants. Thus he joined the federal judiciary at the moment when the Supreme Court's composition began to change in a direction that led to numerous challenges to Warren Court precedents as new justices, beginning with new Chief Justice Warren Burger, sought to diminish or eliminate rights-protecting precedents from the 1960s.

During his service on the Seventh Circuit, Stevens developed his judicial philosophy and approach to decision making. While aspects of his decision making continued to evolve during his years on the Supreme Court, many elements of his approach to deciding cases were well-developed by the time he arrived in Washington in 1975. Years later, Justice Stevens said in interviews that his service on the Seventh Circuit exposed him to many of the same legal issues that he would subsequently address again in Supreme Court cases.[3] He pointed specifically to his service on a special three-judge district court in *Hartke v. Roudebush* (1970), a case concerning the 1970 vote-counting dispute for the Indiana senate race, as educating him in advance about the issues that arose for the 2000 presidential election controversy in *Bush v. Gore* (2000).[4] Prisoners' rights and other criminal justice matters were also among those issues with which he gained familiarity from his Seventh Circuit service.

THE GENESIS OF A JUDICIAL CAREER: *GROPPI V. LESLIE*

Among Stevens's earliest Seventh Circuit opinions, issued just two months after he was sworn into office, was a dissent he wrote after the *en banc* rehearing of *Groppi v. Leslie* (1971). The dissenting opinion demonstrated that Stevens had developed his conception of the importance of procedural protections for "liberty" in the Fourteenth Amendment by the earliest moment in his judicial career.

James Groppi was a Catholic priest from Milwaukee who was well known for organizing protest marches on a variety of civil rights issues. He had participated in the famous March on Washington in 1963 as well as other civil rights protests in the South. Father Groppi was very active in organizing antidiscrimination protests in Milwaukee concerning such matters as fair housing.[5] His legal case arose when he led a "Mothers March on Madison" to protest cuts in public assistance. After he and other protestors occupied the Wisconsin state legislature's chambers for eleven hours as part of the protest, he was arrested. The Wisconsin legislature quickly enacted a measure declaring that Groppi had engaged in disorderly conduct and therefore was guilty of contempt of the legislature. The legislature ordered that he be jailed for the offense without any prior notice of the charge or proceedings to permit him to contest the charge.[6] Groppi's habeas corpus action challenging his confinement in jail was rejected by the state circuit court and the Wisconsin Supreme Court. Subsequently, a U.S. district judge granted his petition and ordered him to be released based on the absence of due process in the imposition of the punishment. However, the district judge's decision was reversed by a three-judge panel of the Seventh Circuit five days prior to Stevens's swearing-in ceremony as a judge on that court. Thus, as an inexperienced new judge, Stevens found himself immediately serving as a member of an *en banc* panel of seven appellate judges who reheard Groppi's case. Indeed,

Stevens's memoir of the Supreme Court reported that he had been among the judges to vote in favor of rehearing the case.[7]

In a 4 to 3 decision, the *en banc* panel upheld the three-judge panel's earlier decision endorsing the state legislature's power to order Groppi jailed for contempt. The majority opinion declared, "We hold . . . that the basic public need for inviolability of the legislative process of our government dictates the availability of the power of summary contempt punishment to the legislative branch."[8] In writing on behalf of the three dissenters, Stevens focused on the deprivation of Groppi's liberty without granting him the protections of the Fourteenth Amendment's Due Process Clause. According to Stevens, the protection of liberty by that clause includes "[o]ne of the oldest and most consistently accepted maxims in our legal tradition[:] . . . the proposition that 'no man shall be punished before he has had an opportunity of being heard.'"[9] The opinion also clearly stated the dissenters' conclusion that "[t]he procedure which Wisconsin employed to deprive the petitioner of his liberty violated that ancient maxim."[10]

In his memoir, Stevens recalled that a senior judge on the Seventh Circuit had characterized the *Groppi* case as a high-visibility legal dispute. The senior judge declared that the case presented the opportunity for an appellate judge to write a law-and-order opinion of the sort that might catch the attention of the Nixon administration and lead Nixon to elevate that judge to the Supreme Court.[11] Indeed, Judge John Hastings told Stevens that he assigned the majority opinion to Judge Wilbur Pell for the very reason that it was the kind of case that could lead Pell to be noticed by Nixon's advisors.[12] As a result, Stevens recalled that he wrote his dissent while being highly conscious of the fact that it would be regarded as excessively liberal and objectionable by the Republican political establishment. According to Stevens, "That dissent may well have been my most significant court of appeals opinion because I thought that it put an end to any possibility that I might be considered for appointment to the Supreme Court."[13]

In light of Stevens's description of the circumstances of the case, why did the *Groppi* case not raise concerns among conservative senators during his later Supreme Court confirmation process in 1975? While Stevens's dissent was certainly liberal in its defense of due process rights, even at the expense of a legislature's power to protect the integrity of its own operations, the opinion did not eventually stand out as unusually or improperly liberal in the eyes of Republicans in the 1970s. The U.S. Supreme Court subsequently heard *Groppi v. Leslie* in November 1971 and issued a 7 to 0 ruling overturning the decision of Stevens's court of appeals colleagues in January 1972. At the time of the Court's consideration of the case, future Justices Lewis Powell and William Rehnquist were still undergoing their confirmation processes so the high court was operating with only seven justices. The majority opinion, written by President Nixon's first law-and-order appointee, Chief Justice

Warren Burger, declared that "we conclude that petitioner was denied due process of law by the procedures employed in punishing him for contempt."[14] Thus, the dissenting opinion that Stevens regarded as potentially defining him as too liberal for the political tastes and preferences of the Republican establishment was, in effect, fully endorsed by Nixon's handpicked Chief Justice. The opinion illuminated Stevens's protective orientation toward procedural due process but, in the context of the times, it reflected a perspective shared by the most prominent Republican law-and-order jurist, too.

PRISONERS' RIGHTS

When Stevens became a federal judge in 1970, the Supreme Court had given only limited attention to the issue of prisoners' constitutional rights. In *Cooper v. Pate* (1964), the Supreme Court declared that incarcerated convicted offenders could use a federal civil rights statute (Title 42, section 1983 of the U.S. Code) to file civil lawsuits concerning their constitutional rights. This decision opened the doors of federal courthouses to lawsuits by prisoners seeking remedial judicial orders and compensation for rights violations by corrections officials. In *Lee v. Washington* (1968), the Supreme Court ruled against the rigid use of racial segregation throughout prisons. Subsequently, in *Johnson v. Avery* (1969) the Supreme Court barred corrections officials from preventing a prisoner from receiving another prisoner's help with legal research for preparation of a petition unless corrections officials provided an alternative form of legal assistance to ensure that prisoners have access to the courts. Other than these decisions, the Supreme Court had not done much to define the constitutional rights of prisoners. By contrast, however, during the 1960s federal judges in the lower courts had become increasingly active in issuing decisions and remedial orders affecting the administration of and conditions within prisons.[15] Thus appeals concerning prisoners' rights cases were reaching the courts of appeals at the time that Stevens became a judge in 1970. Federal appellate judges, including Stevens, had the opportunity to define aspects of prisoners' rights because there were very few guiding Supreme Court precedents yet in existence.

Because of the timing and length of his tenure as a Seventh Circuit judge, it is likely that Stevens gained more experience in deciding prisoners' rights cases prior to his appointment to the Supreme Court than did any other justices with whom he later served. The one exception might be Justice Harry Blackmun, who had served on the U.S. Court of Appeals for the Eighth Circuit prior to his appointment to the Supreme Court in 1970 and therefore also had previous experience deciding prisoners' cases during this formative era. As an Eighth Circuit judge, within the area of prisoners' rights Blackmun was well-known for his court of appeals opinion that prohibited whipping as an impermissibly cruel and unusual form of punishment in Arkansas prisons in *Jackson v. Bishop* (1968). The case is regarded as the precedent that outlawed this form of corporal punishment in prisons. Moreover, Blackmun later said in a memo to Stevens during the drafting process for a 1978 prisoners' rights case, "[*Jackson*] broke the ice in what theretofore had been a reluctance on the part of federal courts at the appellate level to interfere with state prison administration."[16]

The other justices on the Supreme Court at the time of Stevens's appointment in 1975 who also had lower court judicial experience were not similarly situated to have gained prior experience in deciding prisoners' rights cases. Justice Potter Stewart's service on the Sixth Circuit in the 1950s was prior to the initiation of active prisoners' rights litigation in the 1960s. Justice Thurgood Marshall's service on the Second Circuit was too brief—only twenty-four months—to match the experience that Justice Stevens gained during five years on the Court of Appeals. Chief Justice Warren Burger served on an appellate court—the District of Columbia Circuit—that did not have jurisdiction over federal prisoners' cases from multiple states, as was true in the other circuits.

Among the justices appointed during Stevens's tenure on the Court, four previously served on the District of Columbia Circuit (Ruth Bader Ginsburg, Antonin Scalia, Clarence Thomas, and John Roberts) and had limited exposure to prisoners' cases. While several of the other later-appointed justices had experience in other circuits' courts of appeals (David Souter, Stephen Breyer, Samuel Alito, Sonia Sotomayor), their tenures on the federal appellate courts occurred after many aspects of prisoners' rights legal doctrines had been established by Supreme Court precedents produced in the 1970s and 1980s. By contrast, Stevens heard and decided cases on the Seventh Circuit in the early 1970s while the definitions of prisoners' rights were still being developed. Unlike those later colleagues whose decisions in the 1980s and 1990s were significantly guided by established precedents, Stevens was considering prisoners' rights cases at a time when lower court judges were deeply involved in interpreting the Constitution to develop these rights.

In his memoir about the Supreme Court, Stevens credited Chief Justice Warren Burger with writing an especially important majority opinion in *Morrissey v. Brewer* (1972) that laid the groundwork for later expansions of constitutional protections for prisoners.[17] *Morrissey* concerned whether the Due Process Clause gave a parolee the right to be heard or other procedural rights prior to having his parole revoked and being sent back to prison for an alleged violation of parole rules or conditions. Chief Justice Burger's opinion made a clear declaration that parolees, although still under criminal sanction and state supervision, retain a liberty interest protected by the Due Process Clause. In Burger's words,

> We see, therefore, that the liberty of a parolee, although indeterminate, includes many of the core values of unqualified liberty and its termination inflicts a "grievous loss" on the parolee and often on others. It is hardly useful any longer to try to deal with this problem in terms of whether the parolee's liberty is a "right" or a "privilege." By whatever, name, the liberty is valuable and must be seen as within the protection of the Fourteenth Amendment. Its termination calls for some orderly process, however informal.[18]

Justice Stevens later said that Chief Justice Burger's opinion "effectively repudiated the old rule that a prisoner could be treated as a slave."[19] Stevens also said that Burger's opinion provided the basis for his own Seventh Circuit majority opinion in *United States ex rel. Miller v. Twomey* (1973), the case which reinforced Stevens's protective view of liberty interests under the Due Process Clause. Much like his characterization of the *Groppi* opinion as his "most significant court of appeals opinion,"[20] Stevens described *United States ex rel. Miller* as "one of the most important opinions that I had written as a circuit judge."[21] Stevens regularly cited and quoted his *United States ex rel. Miller* opinion when he wrote rights-protective decisions concerning prisoners' cases while serving on the Supreme Court.

Just as with the *Groppi* opinion, Stevens's *United States ex rel. Miller* opinion was not out of step with the approaches of prominent law-and-order jurists in 1975. In fact, the Supreme Court's *Morrissey* decision recognizing liberty interests and due process rights for convicted offenders on parole was written by Chief Justice Burger on behalf of the entire Court, including Justice Rehnquist. In *Morrissey*, Justice William O. Douglas dissented in part only because he would have granted more extensive procedural rights, such as the right to counsel, than those recognized by other justices as part of due process.

The *United States ex rel. Miller* case was actually the consolidation of several prisoners' cases from Illinois and Wisconsin. The consolidated cases each raised different claims, including a demand for procedural due process in disciplinary actions that remove earned "good time" or that send prisoners to punitive segregation. There was also a claim against prison officials in one of the cases for serious injuries suffered by one prisoner that were caused by another prisoner who had repeatedly assaulted different prisoners with a baseball bat without being punished or controlled by prison officials. In his opinion, Stevens characterized the consolidated cases as requiring the appellate court to determine, in light of the Supreme Court's new precedent in *Morrissey v. Brewer*, the extent to which prisoners had specific recognizable rights that would effectively limit the discretionary decision-making authority of corrections officials.

The Supreme Court's precedent in *Morrissey* specifically recognized a retained liberty interest for *parolees* since the issue in the case concerned procedural rights for parole revocation. Stevens applied the liberty concept from *Morrissey* to conclude that *incarcerated offenders* also retained liberty interests that were protected by the Constitution. His opinion was, in effect, an expansion of the Burger's reasoning to recognize broader rights protections for offenders held in prisons. The key language used by Stevens reflected the emphasis on the concept of liberty and the importance of protecting human dignity that would later be characteristic of his opinions as a Supreme Court justice. Indeed, the language of his opinion appeared to be quite consistent with the emphasis on liberty evident in his "last lecture" dissenting opinion thirty-seven years later in the gun rights case of *McDonald v City of Chicago* (2010). With the following words, Stevens made his central point in *United States ex rel. Miller v. Twomey* (1973):

> In view of the fact that physical confinement is merely one species of legal custody, we are persuaded that *Morrissey* actually portends a more basic conceptual holding: liberty protected by the due process clause may—indeed must to some extent—coexist with legal custody pursuant to a conviction. The deprivation of liberty following an adjudication of guilt is partial, not total. A residuum of constitutionally protected rights remain.
>
> As we noted in *Morales v. Schmidt* [(1973)], the view once held that an inmate is a mere slave is now totally rejected. The restraints and the punishment which a criminal conviction entails do not place the citizen beyond the ethical tradition that accords respect to the dignity and intrinsic worth of every individual. "Liberty" and "custody" are not mutually exclusive concepts.[22]

Judge Stevens applied his reasoning to the consolidated cases to recognize violations of procedural due process for the claims concerning disciplinary actions. The opinion required written notice of charges and an opportunity to be heard before an impartial tribunal when any disciplinary deprivation rose to the level of a "grievous loss" of liberty. However, his opinion rejected the Eighth Amendment claim of the prisoner seriously injured by the baseball bat attack. He did not view prison officials as having violated any constitutional rights and instead indicated that the appropriate legal action would be a personal injury lawsuit against the attacker.

Interestingly, Stevens was not the most liberal judge on the appellate panel with respect to support for prisoners' rights. Chief Judge Luther Swygert wrote a dissenting opinion because he believed the Stevens majority opinion should have recognized additional specific due process rights for prison disciplinary proceedings claims. Moreover, he disagreed with Stevens's rejection of the Eighth Amendment claim for the baseball bat assault because he concluded that prison officials had recklessly permitted access to a weapon for a prisoner with a record of committing violent assaults against other prisoners. Thus Swygert believed that prison officials should be subject to a lawsuit for violating the injured prisoner's constitutional protection against cruel and unusual punishments.

Other cases heard by the Seventh Circuit gave Stevens additional experience with prisoners' rights issues. For example, in *Haines v. Kerner* (1974) he was a member of a three-judge panel that included retired Supreme Court Justice Tom Clark. The panel considered and rejected due process and Eighth Amendment claims by a prisoner who spent fifteen days in disciplinary segregation for assaulting another prisoner. The panel issued an unsigned per curiam opinion so Stevens's precise contribution to the opinion is unknown although he clearly agreed with the unanimous decision. Similarly, in *Thomas v. Pate* (1974), Stevens was a member of a panel that heard a variety of claims concerning medical treatment, disciplinary proceedings, and other issues. The panel upheld the lower court's dismissal of most issues, but remanded for a new trial on claims of racial segregation in cell assignments and racial discrimination in prison job assignments. The appellate court indicated that prison officials bore a significant burden in presenting justifications for any decisions that appeared to violate the Supreme Court's prohibition on racial segregation in prisons in *Lee v. Washington* (1968).

In *Chapman v. Kleindienst* (1973), Stevens served on a panel that ruled in the prisoner's favor when a trial judge prematurely terminated a Black Muslim prisoner's presentation of evidence concerning free exercise of religion and Eighth Amendment claims. Such cases that raised a variety of prisoners' rights claims served to give Stevens significant experience in examining existing law, specific fact situations, and the application of his own judicial philosophy to these issues.

As a Seventh Circuit judge, Stevens was the author of additional opinions that favored prisoners' rights. In *Morales v. Schmidt* (1973), a prisoner was prevented from corresponding with his wife's sister because a letter intercepted and retained by prison officials indicated that the prisoner, unbeknownst to his wife, fathered her sister's child. Prison officials believed it was inappropriate for him to correspond with a woman with whom he had an illicit relationship. They also asserted that they possessed nearly complete authority under a Wisconsin statute to limit prisoners' correspondence. The majority decision reversed the lower court's ruling that required prison officials to demonstrate a compelling interest to justify the prohibition on the correspondence in question. The majority viewed that standard as too demanding and therefore showed more deference to prison officials by requiring only a rational basis to justify the prohibition on remand. Stevens wrote a dissenting opinion in which he stated that it is "clear that plaintiff's incarceration has not completely extinguished his First Amendment rights."[23] He noted the existence under the First Amendment of "the prisoner's right to communicate with others" as well as "society's right to know what is happening in a penal institution."[24] Stevens argued that corrections officials' ad hoc actions in limiting prisoners' communications required greater justification than if they had clear guidelines to follow.[25]

In *Bonner v. Coughlin* (1975), Stevens wrote the majority opinion recognizing Fourth Amendment protections against unreasonable searches and seizures of prisoners' cells. Bonner claimed that a "shake down" search of his cell resulted in the loss of the trial transcript for his case. In criminal cases, a trial transcript can be essential for the prisoner's preparation of an appeal or a habeas corpus petition. The district court issued a summary judgment in favor of corrections officials, but Stevens's majority opinion reversed that decision. The Stevens majority opinion rejected prison officials' claims that prisoners have no reasonable expectation of privacy in their cells and possessions, and therefore, in their view, the Fourth Amendment did not apply to searches of cells. By contrast, according to Stevens,

> Respect for the dignity of the individual compels a comparable conclusion with respect to his interest in privacy. Unquestionably, entry into a controlled environment entails a dramatic loss of privacy. Moreover, the justifiable reasons for invading an inmate's privacy are both obvious and easily established. We are persuaded, however, that the surrender of privacy is not total and that some residuum meriting the protection of the Fourth Amendment survives the transfer into custody.[26]

Thus Stevens's frequent emphasis on the underlying constitutional value of protecting human dignity served as a basis for the announced holding in the case: "We hold that a prisoner enjoys the protection of the Fourth Amendment against unreasonable searches, at least to some minimal extent."[27] On behalf of the panel, Stevens ordered that the case be remanded to permit further proceedings to examine Bonner's claims concerning the Fourth Amendment and right of access to the courts.

The preceding cases provide examples of Stevens's experience with prisoners' rights issues prior to his appointment to the Supreme Court. For Stevens, his opinion recognizing expanded liberty interests for incarcerated offenders in *United States ex rel. Miller v. Twomey* (1973) was especially important. Justice Stevens described his *United States ex rel. Miller* opinion as helping him in his confirmation hearings for the Supreme Court when Senator Edward Kennedy asked him to provide evidence that he would treat underprivileged citizens fairly. According to Stevens, the *United States ex rel. Miller* opinion enabled him to produce two letters from incarcerated offenders in Illinois state prisons who expressed their support for him.[28]

SUSPECTS AND DEFENDANTS

Many of the Warren Court justices had personal knowledge of or experience with abusive, unfair practices in the justice system by coming into adulthood before the professionalization of policing and the diminution of discrimination by prosecutors and judges.[29] Thus specific decisions, such as *Mapp v. Ohio* (1961) and *Miranda v. Arizona* (1966), can be seen as creating clear, strong rules to limit the discretionary authority of police and prosecutors in order to reduce the risk of abusive actions. Simultaneously, these decisions defined broader constitutional rights for criminal suspects and defendants. Justice Stevens had his own awareness of the risks of officials' abusive behavior, particularly through his experience representing LaFrana, the man tortured into confessing by the Chicago police. Presumably, this knowledge contributed to Stevens's judicial philosophy and approach for issues under the Fourth, Fifth, and Sixth Amendments as he stood out throughout his Supreme Court career for emphasizing the importance of legal protections for suspects and defendants. In addition, his judicial experiences on the Seventh Circuit appellate court gave him additional exposure to such issues and the opportunity to further develop his judicial philosophy concerning constitutional rights in criminal justice.

During his service as a judge on the Seventh Circuit, Stevens wrote an opinion in *Hampton v. City of Chicago* (1973). This was a highly publicized civil rights lawsuit in which Chicago police officers were accused of intentionally shooting and killing in a hail of gunfire the leaders of the local Black Panther Party as they slept in their beds. In a predawn raid in 1969, more than a dozen police officers entered the apartment where the Black Panthers were sleeping and fired more than eighty rounds, killing Fred Hampton and Mark Clark. They arrested others present at the apartment and charged them with attempted murder for allegedly firing at the police, although subsequent investigations indicated that only one shot was fired by someone in the apartment in response to the police gunfire. In the civil lawsuit that eventually followed, the U.S. district judge dismissed claims against various defendants, including Mayor Richard Daley and the prosecutors who allegedly helped to plan the raid. On behalf of a unanimous Seventh Circuit panel, the opinion by Judge Stevens reversed the district court decision with respect to several defendants and permitted the lawsuit to proceed against the prosecutors and the police officers who investigated the raid, in addition to the fourteen officers who had been at the scene of the raid—the only defendants who had failed to convince the district court to dismiss the claims against them. Nearly a decade later, the case concluded when the government paid a settlement of nearly $2 million to the survivors.[30] In light of such experiences, it is clear that for Stevens, like his later colleagues from the Warren Court era, Justices Brennan and Marshall, the risk of abusive police behavior was real and not merely a remote, hypothetical possibility.

Judge Stevens served on panels that considered *Miranda* and right to counsel issues. His decisions in these cases indicated that Stevens possessed significant concerns about protecting the rights of suspects questioned while in custody and was more inclined than some of his Seventh Circuit colleagues to find that police officers had violated a suspect's rights. In *United States v. Springer* (1972), for example, a bank robbery suspect challenged the admissibility of his confession because, after an attorney had been appointed to represent him at his preliminary appearance in court, FBI agents questioned him and induced him to sign a waiver of rights without notifying his attorney. The two-member majority on the appellate court panel ruled against the defendant and held that the defendant had failed "to present some facts tending to show that the waiver was not voluntary or knowledgeable."[31] By contrast, Stevens wrote a dissenting opinion in which he asserted that the FBI agents had violated the important principles of the right to counsel during custodial questioning, notwithstanding the existence of a waiver of rights signed by the defendant. Indeed, while the majority considered the signed waiver "sufficient to raise a presumption of validity and shift the burden of going forward to the accused,"[32] Stevens regarded that same waiver signed by the defendant without counsel present as evidence that the defendant did not understand that he was waiving his rights. According to Stevens, "The fact that the agents had defendant sign a waiver of rights form on May 18 after counsel had been appointed provides affirmative evidence that he did not fully grasp the significance of the procedural situation in which he found himself."[33] Stevens's dissenting opinion strongly asserted his view about the importance of the defense attorney as an essential actor for ensuring the fairness of criminal justice processes:

> After counsel had been appointed to represent him, and while he was in custody, the defendant was visited by two agents of the prosecutor. Defense counsel was not present and received no advance notice of their proposed visit. The sole purpose of the visit was to obtain evidence for use at trial. . . . In the civil context I would consider this behavior as unethical and unfair. In a criminal context I regard it as such a departure from "procedural regularity" as to violate the due process clause of the Fifth Amendment. If the evidence of guilt is as strong as the prosecutor contends, such direct communication is all the more offensive because it was unnecessary. If there is doubt about defendant's guilt, it should not be overcome by a procedure such as this.[34]

The opinion by Stevens indicated that his view of fairness was closely tied to his expectations about the operation of the adversarial system of justice. As he would later demonstrate in his opinions as a Supreme Court justice, Stevens was a strong advocate of the adversarial process. Without a defense attorney involved, not only are the suspect's rights placed at risk, but the adversarial process is less able to serve its truth-seeking function by challenging factual claims by the police and prosecutor. During his career on the Supreme Court, Stevens was especially outspoken when he perceived his colleagues to tilt the balance in favor of police and prosecutors by accepting situations in which the defense attorney was bypassed or excluded by law enforcement officials.

In *United States v. Fowler* (1973), Stevens was a member of an appellate panel that examined the case of a post office burglary and the teenage suspect who was arrested and questioned by a postal inspector at the police station. Although Stevens did not write the court's opinion, he was one of the two judges constituting the panel majority that concluded that the teenager had a right to be given *Miranda* warnings under the principles of *In re Gault* (1967), the landmark Supreme Court decision that extended constitutional rights to juveniles in delinquency cases. Over the dissent of one panel member, Stevens and his colleague concluded that the youth's confession should not have been admitted into evidence because it appeared that, although he was given limited warnings, he had not been fully and properly apprised of his *Miranda* rights. For example, the postal inspector's trial testimony indicated that he did not warn the teenager that any responses to questions could be used as evidence of guilt. The interrogation context as described in Judge Roger Kiley's majority opinion in *Fowler* appeared to fit precisely with the concerns Stevens had seen expressed by liberal Supreme Court justices during the 1947 term in which he served as Justice Rutledge's law clerk:

> When his confession was made Fowler was sixteen years of age. So far as the record shows he had not previously been arrested, had not previously been in jail, nor had he ever been interrogated by law enforcement officials. One need only recall his own adolescence to appreciate the impact upon this boy, alone in a jail room, in custody of a postal inspector, being warned of his constitutional rights. . . . In these circumstances it is difficult to accept the notion that defendant fully comprehended what he was being told.[35]

It is especially noteworthy that in this empathetic description of an inexperienced, frightened teenager in the disorienting context of custodial questioning, Judge Kiley cited and quoted the Supreme Court's decision in *Haley v. Ohio* (1948). This case involving a teenage suspect was presumably quite familiar to Stevens because, as noted previously, *Haley* was one of the three cases concerning police questioning of teenage suspects decided by the Court during Stevens's year as a law clerk. In his judicial opinions and speeches over the years, Stevens demonstrated a penchant for citing cases with which he had personal familiarity through direct involvement. Thus Judge Kiley's prominent use of the *Haley* case may be evidence of input by Stevens into the content of the majority opinion.

Judge Stevens wrote the majority opinion for a unanimous Seventh Circuit panel in *United States v. Oliver* (1974). Oliver was under investigation by the Internal Revenue Service for understating his income on his tax returns. Having learned that Oliver was present in the Milwaukee Federal Building, IRS agents asked him to come to their offices and proceeded to interview him. They provided him with a limited warning about his rights, but as Stevens concluded in the opinion, "the warnings did not include advice that Oliver could remain silent or that he could have a lawyer present during the interview."[36] During the interview, "a person who purported to have a message for the defendant from his attorney was not permitted to communicate with the defendant."[37] The case hinged on the issue of whether Oliver was free to leave during the interview or whether he was being subjected to in-custody questioning for purposes of *Miranda*. In the hands of another jurist, the suspect would have lost if the judge simply declared that Oliver was free to leave. Such a judge could have concluded that *Miranda* warnings were not required because Oliver had come to the office voluntarily, was not placed under arrest, and, was presumed to know, like other citizens of average knowledge and intelligence, that people are entitled to walk away from law enforcement officers during questioning when not legally confined to that location. Instead, Stevens evaluated the factual context and applied the law to conclude that "[t]he incriminating evidence obtained from [Oliver's] interrogation was inadmissible."[38] According to Stevens:

> In this case it is plain that the purpose of the agents' interrogation of the defendant was to develop evidence which would secure his conviction of a crime. The criminal investigation of Oliver had commenced several months before he was questioned, and there was no ambiguity about the agents' mission. No doubt . . . Oliver was free to leave at any time, and therefore not strictly in custody. But since the agents were in a position to intercept a message from his attorney, and actually did so, it is appropriate, for the purpose of applying the Miranda test, to characterize the situation as one in which defendant's liberty was significantly restrained.[39]

These three Seventh Circuit cases, *Springer*, *Fowler*, and *Oliver*, in which Stevens defended *Miranda* protections and the right to counsel, do not indicate that he reflexively or ideologically supported claims by defendants in every context. Indeed, he did not. In the *Oliver* case, Stevens rejected the defendant's second claim that his conviction should be reversed because the Fifth Amendment protected him from compelled disclosure of his illegal activities, which he asserted would have occurred if he had reported his income accurately in light of evidence that he was involved in narcotics trafficking. In another example during his time on the Seventh Circuit bench, Stevens was the lone dissenter against the decision in *United States v. Smith* (1971) that found a violation of Rule 11 of the Federal Rules of Criminal Procedure when a defendant was not fully advised that his guilty plea to the specific charge would make him ineligible for parole. However, with respect to Stevens's concerns about the risk of improper police conduct while questioning suspects and the importance of defense counsel in the adversary system, these three cases show that Stevens brought with him to the Supreme

Court strong, well-developed viewpoints about the importance of *Miranda* and the right to counsel.

TRIAL RIGHTS

During an interview in 2010, when asked why his Supreme Court opinions defined him as an especially strong advocate of the jury's role in the adversary system, Stevens revealed a little-known, key experience in his life that gave him great confidence in the jury system: "Not only my own trial experience [as an attorney] but I sat as a trial judge for a while when the docket was really behind in the Northern District of Indiana. I sat for a couple of weeks. I only tried two cases but I had a docket of about a dozen or so [cases], but most of them settled."[40] As indicated by this statement, during his tenure as a Seventh Circuit appellate judge in Chicago, he volunteered to sit as a U.S. district judge at the nearby Hammond, Indiana, courthouse to handle trial-level cases for a brief period when the district court was shorthanded. Justice Stevens described his experience in the following way:

> A couple . . . both of them teachers and exemplary representatives of the community, were the plaintiffs. And the defendant was a hotshot teenager who [allegedly] smashed his car into their car. And they sued him [in federal court as a diversity of citizenship lawsuit between residents of two different states]. . . . If you just wanted to get background and appearances, they were the perfect witnesses, and perfect citizens and so on and so forth. But the kid was telling the truth. And the jury figured it out. . . . And I've had other experiences—where the juries really are a very reliable method of finding the facts. You get common experience and common judgment together [in the jury room] and it gets the right answer. I have a lot of faith in juries, notwithstanding the fact that I recognize the risk of prejudice and so on and so forth, if they are inflamed improperly with victim impact testimony and that sort of stuff.[41]

Justice Stevens summarized and reiterated the impact of this experience by saying, "My limited experience as a trial judge added to my conviction that juries make a lot of sense."[42] Moreover, he expressed a mild regret that there were not larger numbers of experienced trial attorneys appointed to the Supreme Court whose experiences might have given them greater understanding and appreciation of the jury's role in the trial process. As Stevens said, "Each particular nominee that has come along I have thought to be fully qualified. . . . But I do think it is unfortunate that there aren't more Lewis Powells, and Bill Rehnquists, and Byron Whites who have had some experience in the courtroom."[43] In sum, his experience as a trial attorney and his brief experience as a trial judge cemented and reinforced his favorable view of the jury system's capability and importance in the American adversarial system of justice. His Supreme Court opinions later reflected this perspective as he resisted limitations on the jury's role, advocated for fair jury processes, and generally sought to protect other trial-related constitutional rights.

By the time Stevens became a judge on the U.S. Court of Appeals in 1970, the Sixth Amendment right to trial by jury had been incorporated and applied to all states two years earlier by the Supreme Court in *Duncan v. Louisiana* (1968). Thus there were more possibilities for such issues to be raised on appeal in federal courts as convicted offenders sought vindication of their rights under the U.S. Constitution. As an appellate judge, Stevens sat on panels that heard a variety of issues, but not necessarily the same mix of issues that he would later see as a Supreme Court justice. The Supreme Court chooses which cases it will hear. It typically seeks to reserve its time and attention for major issues that reflect disagreements between the U.S. courts of appeals or that seek the expansion or reconsideration of the definition of a right. By contrast, as a Seventh Circuit judge, Stevens heard routine appeals that asked the appellate judges to conclude that a trial judge had failed to follow proper precedents or procedures. Moreover, courts of appeals judges feel obligated to follow Supreme Court precedents while the Supreme Court has greater freedom to refine or reverse existing doctrine. Appellate judges can certainly apply their reasoning in interpreting and applying precedents, yet their subordinate place in the hierarchy of the court system limits their freedom to follow the logical dictates of their judicial philosophy and values. Thus, while Stevens was less likely to face groundbreaking issues or freely articulate his viewpoints on the Seventh Circuit, his five years of experience as an appellate judge gave him exposure to issues concerning the jury's role in the trial process.

The Seventh Circuit jury cases did not provide a clear indication that Stevens would later emerge as a strong advocate for this Sixth Amendment right on the Supreme Court. Several jury cases showed that Stevens distinguished himself from his colleagues by favoring individuals' claims when other judges disagreed. However, for specific issues, Stevens turned aside individuals' claims. In considering his Seventh Circuit record on jury issues, one can legitimately ask whether his views changed over time to make him more supportive of individuals' Sixth Amendment jury-related claims during his career on the Supreme Court. It is possible, however, that any perceived differences in his conclusions about juries in Seventh Circuit cases and Supreme Court cases reflected differences in the nature of the issues and the constraints of precedent that he faced at each court.

In *United States v. Catalano* (1971), Stevens joined a unanimous opinion that rejected a variety of claims, including a defendant's assertion that two specific jurors should have been excused for bias during the jury selection process. In *Chase v. United States* (1972), concerning four individuals charged with stealing and burning records from a Selective Service office during the Vietnam War, Stevens wrote the majority opinion for a panel that rejected various claims on appeal after the individuals were convicted at trial. The appellants alleged that the trial court failed to ensure that the jury was drawn from a fair cross-section of the community because young adults were insufficiently represented. Judge Stevens, on behalf of the panel, followed existing Supreme Court precedents by concluding that "a claim of discrimination against young adults is insufficient unless 'intentional and systematic' exclusion is established."[44]

The case of *United States v. Thomas* (1972) led Stevens to write a dissenting opinion with which he might not have agreed in his later years on the Supreme Court. During their deliberations, jurors in a criminal case had access to a newspaper article about the case that several jurors reportedly used to try to persuade other jurors to issue a guilty verdict. On appeal, the majority opinion concluded that the jurors' exposure to prejudicial information meant that the defendant was entitled to a new trial. Judge Stevens, by contrast, dissented. He concluded that the appellate court should defer to the trial judge's conclusion that the jury's exposure to the news article did not require a new trial. In Stevens's words, "I am persuaded, however, that the probability of significant prejudice is not plain enough to warrant disagreement with the contemporaneous evaluation made by an experienced trial judge."[45] In the conclusion of the opinion, Stevens stated a truism that seems striking in light of its emphasis on the toleration of errors; an emphasis that is less evident in his Supreme Court opinions on jury issues. As stated by Stevens, "Almost every trial requires some compromise with standards of absolute perfection; such deviations must be tolerated if the jury system is to function effectively."[46]

In other cases, by contrast, Stevens's careful consideration of issues led him to favor individuals' claims concerning jury issues presented to the Seventh Circuit. In *United States v. Greene* (1974), for example, Stevens dissented in support of an individual who objected to jury instructions concerning the insanity defense in his trial for an attempted hijacking of a commercial airliner. Judge Stevens concluded there was "a substantial likelihood that the outcome of the jury's deliberations was affected" by the judge's failure to advise the jurors that the defendant would not automatically be set free if they acquitted him by reason of insanity.[47]

In *United States v. Booker* (1974), a case that was a precursor to issues that he would later examine as a Supreme Court justice, Stevens wrote the majority opinion concerning the risk of racial bias in the jury selection process for the trial of an African American defendant. On behalf of the panel, despite the fact that there were five African Americans on the twelve-member jury. Stevens found that "the trial judge committed error by refusing to interrogate prospective jurors on the subject of possible racial prejudice."[48] He cited both Supreme Court and Seventh Circuit precedents as guiding the panel's conclusion that the presence of African American jurors did not render the error harmless. As Stevens said, "We think it equally plain that the presence of some black jurors does not cure the error committed during the voir dire [jury selection process]. For if even one member of the jury harbors racial prejudice against the accused, his right to trial by an impartial jury is impaired."[49]

In a case concerning the Seventh Amendment right to a civil jury trial, Stevens wrote a majority opinion that emphasized the historical importance of jury trial. Although not a criminal case, the presentation of Stevens's reasoning in *Rogers v. Loether* (1972) included language emphasizing the importance of the jury in the Anglo-American tradition of using an adversarial justice system. In the case, an African American woman filed a civil rights lawsuit alleging that the defendant-landlords refused to rent an apartment to her because of her race. The trial judge denied the defendant-landlords' request for a jury trial and, instead, presided over a bench trial that awarded the prospective renter $250 in punitive damages. The defendant-landlords raised several issues on appeal to the Seventh Circuit. In his opinion, Judge Stevens found no basis to disturb the trial judge's finding of discrimination or the award of punitive damages. However, Stevens and the two other judges on the panel found a violation of the Seventh Amendment right to trial by jury "[i]n suits at common law, where the value in controversy shall exceed twenty dollars."[50] The majority opinion analyzed both the Seventh Amendment as well as the federal civil rights statute under which the lawsuit was filed. The latter was analyzed to determine if Congress had intended for such cases to be outside of the scope of the Seventh Amendment's coverage of "suits at common law." The Stevens majority opinion concluded that "in view of our grave doubts as to constitutionality of a denial of the right to a jury trial and the failure of Congress expressly to indicate that the traditional procedure for litigating damage claims should not be followed, the statute should be construed to authorize trial by jury."[51]

Judge Stevens's majority opinion in *Rogers v. Loether* included language that emphasized the importance of the jury in the justice system, an ideal that presumably applied with more force to criminal cases because an individual's liberty is at risk in criminal trials. Early in his opinion, Stevens included an exceptionally long quotation from an 1830 opinion[52] by the notable early legal scholar and Supreme Court justice Joseph Story that, in Stevens's characterization, "eloquently described the purpose of the [Seventh] amendment."[53] The quotation selected by Stevens began with the following words: "The trial by jury is justly dear to the American people. It has always been an object of deep interest and solicitude, and every encroachment upon it has been watched with great jealousy."[54] Later in the opinion, Stevens characterized existing precedents by declaring that "[i]n an unbroken line of cases involving enforcement of statutory rights, the Supreme Court has treated the right to a jury trial as a matter too obvious to be doubted."[55] While the reasoning in Stevens's opinion rested on an examination of history and precedent, as if to show that the court of appeals was obligated to reach this result regarding the Seventh Amendment, the choice of language by Stevens seemed to reflect reverence for the role and importance of the jury.

It is difficult to draw firm conclusions about how Justice Stevens's experience on the Seventh Circuit may have influenced his later Supreme Court opinions on jury issues. Because judges on U.S. courts of appeals bear a responsibility to comply with the Supreme Court's precedents, their opinions cannot necessarily be regarded as the truest expressions of their own interpretive approaches and judicial philosophies. In dissenting opinions, in particular, appellate judges serving on three-judge panels can distinguish themselves from their colleagues and explain their individual conclusions as lone dissenters. However, even in dissent, these judges may see themselves as following precedent rather than enjoying an opportunity to express their own analysis and conclusions. What can be said with respect to Stevens and his Seventh Circuit jury-issue cases? Clearly, his Seventh Circuit experiences gave him familiarity with issues related to the adversarial process and the Sixth Amendment right. He demonstrated concern about fairness in jury trials through the opinions examining the issue of racial bias during jury selection and the need for careful jury instructions. He used language that reflected an emphasis on the importance of the jury in the trial process. Yet for some issues he also indicated a pragmatic tolerance for less-than-perfect proceedings, an approach that called upon judges to make decisions about which errors are harmless and which require a remand for a new trial.

SEARCH AND SEIZURE

In 1975, if one had attempted to predict Justice Stevens's future decisions on Fourth Amendment issues based on the search and seizure cases in which he participated as a Seventh Circuit judge, one would likely have predicted a conservative orientation toward such issues. In fifteen search and seizure cases, Stevens voted to reject individuals' rights claims eleven times[56] and supported individuals in only four cases.[57] For several reasons, however, the mere tally of votes in intermediate appellate court cases did not necessarily provide a good basis for predicting later judicial behavior on a court of last resort, such as the U.S. Supreme Court. As with other issues, Judge Stevens was obligated to follow the Supreme Court's precedents, applying rules and producing outcomes with which he would not necessarily agree if he had been deciding the cases as a matter of first impression. The voting record produced by Stevens on the Seventh Circuit was also driven by the particular mix of cases and issues that were presented to panels on which Stevens served. The small number of search and seizure cases decided by Stevens did not reflect an examination of the complete range of issues that can arise under the Fourth Amendment. In addition, the possibility exists that Stevens changed his orientation toward search and seizure issues over the course of his years on the Supreme Court. Justice Stevens later said in remarks at a Fordham Law School symposium in 2006, "I know that I, like most of my colleagues, have continued to participate in a learning process while serving on the bench."[58] Moreover, he may have felt a greater responsibility to be outspoken and assertive in defense of Fourth Amendment rights on the Supreme Court from the early 1990s and thereafter. The retirements in 1990 and 1991 of two key Fourth Amendment defenders, the liberal holdovers from the Warren Court era, Justices Brennan and Marshall, left Stevens as one of the primary remaining advocates of the exclusionary rule and clear limits on police officers' discretionary authority to undertake investigative actions.

As a Seventh Circuit judge, Stevens wrote few opinions on search and seizure issues and several of them provided little insight into his thinking about the Fourth Amendment. For example, he followed established precedents in two opinions rejecting standing claims by defendants who sought suppression of evidence found in the possession of other people.[59] He also wrote opinions rejecting claims about insufficient specificity in search warrants and judicial wiretap orders.[60] These cases gave him experience with issues that he later addressed on the Supreme Court.

A few Seventh Circuit opinions by Stevens showed his approach to search and seizures issues, but they did not necessarily provide a basis for predicting his future votes and opinions. In his majority opinion in *United States v. Jeffers* (1975), Judge Stevens supported the admissibility of incriminating evidence found during a search of a woman's purse and calf-length boots. The woman had entered a police station to request the return of a purse that she dropped when fleeing the nearby scene of gunfire that occurred in the early hours of the prior morning. The Supreme Court's precedent in *Terry v. Ohio* (1968) established that officers could conduct a brief, carefully limited frisk of the outer clothing of individuals whose behavior the officers observed and, from those observations, reasonably concluded that the individuals were possibly armed and intending to commit a crime. The precedent was carefully written by Chief Justice Earl Warren to prohibit officers from conducting intrusive discretionary searches of individuals based on mere hunches and curiosity about what might be found. Yet, the factual circumstances in which Stevens endorsed the legality of the *Terry* search did not readily fit the facts and rule described in the *Terry* precedent. The officer apparently did not spend time observing the woman for suspicious behavior before conducting the search. The search of the purse was arguably more intrusive than the Warren Court's authorization of "a carefully limited search of the outer clothing of such persons in an attempt to discover weapons which might be used to assault him."[61] However, one might readily conclude that a purse is a convenient and accessible container for a gun or a knife and therefore eligible for such a search.

By contrast, the order to remove the calf-length boot, which led to the discovery of "a capsule possibly containing a narcotic drug,"[62] seemed more clearly to exceed the scope of a limited *Terry* search. If examination of the boot was justified by reasonable suspicions about possible weapons, the officer presumably could have detected any accessible knife, gun, or other weapon by frisking the woman's pant leg and boot. As it turned out the removal of the boot and discovery therein of the suspicious capsule led to the woman's immediate arrest and consequently resulted in a more careful examination of the purse's contents, as a search incident to a lawful arrest under the Supreme Court's precedent in *Chimel v. California* (1969). The closer inspection of the purse revealed notebooks containing records of drug transactions by a criminal gang targeted for investigation by the Gary, Indiana, police department. The Stevens opinion rejected assertions that these notebooks should be excluded from evidence as the product of an illegal search.

The *Jeffers* opinion seemed to stretch the Supreme Court's original justification for stop-and-frisk searches, as described in *Terry v. Ohio,* well beyond its original intentions. Such deference to law enforcement interests and acceptance of expanded police authority was not present in Stevens's subsequent Supreme Court decisions on frisk searches. This initial opinion on *Terry* searches did not reflect the skepticism about excessive intrusions imposed by police evident in Stevens's rights-protective approach to stop-and-frisk cases that emerged during his later service on the nation's highest court.

The Seventh Circuit opinions by Stevens demonstrated that commitment to the exclusionary rule was a component of his judicial philosophy prior to his appointment to the Supreme Court. In *United States v. Pratter* (1972), Judge Stevens wrote a majority opinion requiring the exclusion of evidence when federal customs officers violated a federal statute that defined when they could "break open" the door to a house in order to execute a search warrant. The analysis in the opinion articulated the importance of excluding improperly obtained evidence, despite the cost to society's interest in crime control and the punishment of lawbreakers. In Stevens's words:

> The price which society must pay to forestall the repetition of such blunders [by law enforcement officers] is that the accused shall go free, or at least at his trial the evidence seized as a result of that invasion of his home may not be used against him. Otherwise the congressional requirement of professionalism in the execution of search warrants might not accomplish its dual purpose of protecting the privacy of the home and ensuring a high degree of expertise in the performance of a vital police function.[63]

The opinion also emphasized the importance that Stevens placed on recognizing the need to protect citizens' homes from intrusion by police officials. According to Stevens, emphasis must be placed on "the Anglo-American tradition of respect for the privacy of the home and the dignity of the citizen even when suspected of criminal behavior."[64]

In his majority opinion for the Seventh Circuit in *United States v. Rosselli* (1974), Stevens provided a precursor to later decisions that demonstrated his skepticism of warrantless searches of homes. An arrestee's admission about a recent delivery of marijuana led officers to make a warrantless entry into Rosselli's apartment, where the delivery had been made, based on the claim that exigent circumstances required an immediate entry to prevent the destruction of evidence. Judge Stevens's majority opinion took the government to task for failing to "adequately explain why no attempt to obtain a warrant was made, or why no consideration was given to placing the . . . apartment under surveillance while an attempt to secure a warrant was made."[65] Stevens acknowledged that emergency situations could exist to justify a warrantless entry in some cases. However, the facts of the particular case led him, in his words, to attach "importance to the character of the defendant's expectation of privacy, [and] his unquestioned right to refuse admittance to his home unless a demand was supported by a warrant."[66]

The underlying considerations and priorities in the *Rosselli* opinion appeared in Stevens's later Supreme Court opinions on warrantless searches. In *Payton v. New York* (1980), for example, Justice Stevens's opinion on behalf of a six-justice majority barred warrantless entry into homes by police for purposes of making routine felony arrests. Justice Stevens pointed to the purposes, history, and specific language of the Fourth Amendment to emphasize the protection against warrantless entry into homes except under exigent circumstances. As Stevens noted,

> The Fourth Amendment protects the individual's privacy in a variety of settings. In none is the zone of privacy more clearly defined than when bounded by the unambiguous physical dimensions of an individual's home—a zone that finds its roots in clear and specific constitutional terms: "The right of the people to be secure in their . . . houses . . . shall not be violated."[67]

Similarly, in *Griffin v. Wisconsin* (1987), concerning a state regulation that authorized warrantless searches of probationers' homes, Stevens said in dissent, "Mere speculation by a police officer that a probationer 'may have had' contraband in his possession is not a constitutionally sufficient basis for a warrantless, nonconsensual search of a private home. I simply do not understand how five Members of this Court can reach a contrary conclusion."[68]

THE DEVELOPMENT OF A JUDICIAL PHILOSOPHY

Stefanie Lindquist's systematic examination of the Seventh Circuit's cases during Stevens's tenure as a judge led her to conclude that he was a centrist judge "on a court whose judges championed constitutional and civil liberties and rendered decisions that reflected an expansive interpretation of those rights."[69] In examining Stevens's record in all of his Seventh Circuit cases, Lindquist said, "The portrait of his voting behavior on the circuit is thus of an iconoclast—neither predictably liberal nor conservative."[70] In comparison to other judges on the Seventh Circuit during that era, according to Lindquist's analysis, Stevens did not stand out as a liberal jurist despite regularly supporting individuals' rights claims for that court's decisions on certain issues. Professor Lindquist speculated that Stevens's five-year experience working with very liberal judges on the Seventh Circuit may have contributed to his openness to considering different ideas and approaches. In her words, "Although we have no direct evidence that his interaction with Democratic appointees on the Seventh Circuit influenced Justice Stevens ideologically, it is certainly possible that his respect for his more liberal colleagues on the circuit caused him to be open to alternative viewpoints and ideas."[71] While it seems clear that Stevens's earlier experience as a law clerk for Justice Rutledge influenced the development of his judicial philosophy, the influence of his interactions with Seventh Circuit colleagues was admittedly uncertain. However, it seems plausible to think that his interactions with Seventh Circuit judges and his close reading of their opinions in the deliberative appellate process may have contributed to his development. This seems especially plausible in the case of a judge who acknowledged and endorsed the importance of judges continuing to learn as they served on the bench.[72]

The Seventh Circuit experience had a clearer influence with respect to a specific aspect of Stevens's judicial philosophy and approach to decision making. The elements of liberty and substantive due process that were central to Stevens's judicial philosophy were shaped by his experience on the court of appeals. According to Stevens, a Seventh Circuit case concerning the asserted right of a father to be present in the delivery room for the birth of his child led him to reconsider his original limited view of due process after reading more closely opinions written by Justices Oliver Wendell Holmes and Louis Brandeis.[73] Originally, Stevens had thought of the right to due process as being focused on procedural rights rather than the substantive rights that became embodied in his broad conception of liberty. Judge Stevens wrote the appellate panel's majority opinion ruling against the father's claim in *Fitzgerald v. Porter Memorial Hospital* (1975). Yet, his opinion acknowledged various Supreme Court precedents that recognized substantive rights through the Due Process Clause, including parents' control over their children's education, married couples' access to contraceptives, and the right of choice concerning abortion.[74]

In this Seventh Circuit opinion, just as he did in later opinions on the Supreme Court, Stevens expressed regret that these rights were typically labeled as part of a right to "privacy." Instead, Stevens saw these rights as flowing from the constitutional protection for liberty expressed in the Due Process Clause. In Stevens's words, "The character of the Court's language in these cases brings to mind the origins of the American heritage of freedom—the abiding interest in individual liberty that makes certain state intrusions on the citizen's right to decide how he will live his own life intolerable."[75] Thus, just prior to his appointment to the Supreme Court, Stevens's experience of learning from the cases that he heard as a Seventh Circuit judge led him to adopt an expansive view of the substantive rights protections provided by the Due Process Clause. By adopting this perspective, Stevens placed himself in opposition to future Supreme Court colleagues, such as Antonin Scalia, who criticized decisions based on substantive due process as improperly expanding the role of judges and facilitating judicial intrusions into law and policy decisions that should be left to elected officials.

NOTES

1. Kenneth Manaster, *Illinois Justice: The Scandal of 1969 and the Rise of John Paul Stevens* (Chicago: University of Chicago Press, 2001), 264–67.
2. Ibid., 267.
3. Justice John Paul Stevens, interview with author, U.S. Supreme Court, Washington, D.C., July 12, 2006.
4. Jeffrey Rosen, "The Dissenter," *New York Times Magazine*, September 23, 2007, 81.
5. "James Groppi Dead at 54; Ex-Priest Led Rights Fight," *New York Times,* November 5, 1985, accessed May 23, 2015, http://www.nytimes.com/1985/11/05/us/james-e-groppi-dead-at-54-ex-priest-led-rights-fight.html.
6. *Groppi v. Leslie*, 436 F.2d 326, 327 (7th Cir. 1970).
7. John Paul Stevens, *Five Chiefs: A Supreme Court Memoir* (New York: Little, Brown, 2011), 124.
8. *Groppi v. Leslie*, 436 F.2d at 332.
9. *Groppi v. Leslie*, 436 F.2d at 332–33 (Stevens, J., dissenting).
10. Ibid., 333 (Stevens, J., dissenting).
11. Stevens, *Five Chiefs*, 123–24.
12. Ibid., 123.
13. Ibid., 124.
14. *Groppi v. Leslie*, 404 U.S. 496, 499 (1972).
15. Malcolm M. Feeley and Edward L. Rubin, *Judicial Policy Making and the Modern State: How the Courts Reformed America's Prisons* (New York: Cambridge University Press, 1998), 39–40.
16. Memo from Justice Harry Blackmun to Justice John Paul Stevens, June 15, 1978, *Hutto v. Finney*, 437 U.S. 678 (1978), Box 268, Harry A. Blackmun Papers, Manuscript Division, Library of Congress, Washington, D.C.
17. Stevens, *Five Chiefs*, 115–16.
18. *Morrissey v. Brewer*, 408 U.S. 471, 482 (1972).

19. Stevens, *Five Chiefs*, 115.
20. Ibid., 124.
21. Ibid., 133.
22. *United States ex rel. Miller v. Twomey*, 479 F.2d, 701, 712 (7th Cir. 1973).
23. *Morales v. Schmidt*, 489 F.2d 1335, 1346 (7th Cir. 1973) (Stevens, J., dissenting).
24. Ibid.
25. Ibid., 1348 (Stevens, J., dissenting).
26. *Bonner v. Coughlin*, 517 F.2d 1311, 1316 (7th Cir. 1975).
27. Ibid., 1317.
28. Stevens, *Five Justices*, 132–33.
29. Christopher E. Smith, *The Rehnquist Court and Criminal Punishment* (New York: Garland, 1997), 34–37.
30. "Settlement Near in Panther Suit," *New York Times*, October 26, 1982, accessed May 23, 2015, http://www.nytimes.com/1982/10/26/us/settlement-near-in-a-panther-suit.html.
31. *United States v. Springer*, 460 F.2d 1344, 1349 (7th Cir. 1972).
32. Ibid.
33. *United States v. Springer*, 460 F.2d at 1355 (Stevens, J., dissenting).
34. Ibid., 1354–55 (Stevens, J., dissenting).
35. *United States v. Fowler*, 476 F.2d 1091, 1093 (7th Cir. 1973).
36. *United States v. Oliver*, 505 F.2d 301, 306 (7th Cir. 1974).
37. Ibid., 304.
38. Ibid., 306.
39. Ibid., 305–6.
40. Justice John Paul Stevens, interview with author, U.S. Supreme Court, Washington, D.C., July 29, 2010.
41. Ibid.
42. Ibid.
43. Ibid.
44. *Chase v. United States*, 468 F.2d 141, 146 (7th Cir. 1972).
45. *United States v. Thomas*, 463 F.2d, 1061, 1066 (7th Cir. 1972) (Stevens, J., dissenting).
46. Ibid.
47. *United States v. Greene*, 497 F.2d 1069, 1092 (7th Cir. 1974) (Stevens, J., dissenting).
48. *United States v. Booker*, 480 F.2d 1310, 1310 (7th Cir. 1974).
49. Ibid., 1311.
50. U.S. Constitution, Amendment VII.
51. *Rogers v. Loether*, 467 F.2d 1110, 1113 (7th Cir. 1972).
52. *Parsons v. Bedford*, 28 U.S. (3 Pet.) 433 (1830).
53. *Rogers v. Loether*, 467 F.2d at 1113.
54. Ibid.
55. Ibid., 1114.
56. *United States v. Dichiarinte*, 445 F.2d 126 (7th Cir. 1971); *United States v. Lee*, 448 F.2d 604 (7th Cir. 1971); *United States v. Mayfield*, 451 F.2d 1381 (7th Circuit 1971); *United States v. Ware*, 457 F.2d 828 (7th Cir. 1972); *United States v. Kahn*, 471 F.2d 191 (1972); *United States v. Wilson*, 479 F.2d 936 (7th Cir. 1973); *United States v. Fern*, 484 F.2d 666 (1973); *United States v. Bolin*, 514 F.2d 554 (1975); *Mabra v. Gray*, 518 F.2d 512 (1975); *United States v. Jeffers*, 520 F.2d 1256 (1975); *United States v. Lisk*, 522 F.2d 228 (7th Cir. 1975).
57. *United States v. Fullmer*, 457 F.2d 447 (7th Cir. 1972); *United States v. Pratter*, 465 F.2d 227 (7th Cir. 1972); *United States v. Gardner*, 467 F.2d 205 (1972); *United States v. Rosselli*, 506 F.2d 627 (7th Cir. 1974).
58. John Paul Stevens, "Learning on the Job," *Fordham Law Review* 74 (2006): 1562.
59. *United States v. Lisk*, 522 F.2d 228 (7th Cir. 1975); *Mabra v. Gray*, 518 F.2d 512 (7th Cir. 1975).
60. *United States v. Lee*, 448 F.2d 604 (7th Cir. 1971); *United States v. Kahn*, 471 F.2d 191 (7th Cir. 1972) (Stevens, J., concurring in part and dissenting in part).
61. *Terry v. Ohio*, 392 U.S. 1, 30 (1968).

62. *United States v. Jeffers*, 520 F.2d at 1267.
63. *United States v. Pratter*, 465 F.2d at 233 (7th Cir. 1972).
64. Ibid., 230.
65. *United States v. Rosselli*, 506 F.2d at 630 (1974).
66. Ibid., 631.
67. *Payton v. New York*, 445 U.S. 573, 589 (1980).
68. *Griffin v. Wisconsin*, 483 U.S. 868, 890 (1987) (Stevens, J., dissenting).
69. Stefanie A. Lindquist, “Supreme Court Prequel: Justice Stevens on the Seventh Circuit,” *Northwestern University Law Review* 106 (2012): 720.
70. Ibid., 727–28.
71. Lindquist, “Supreme Court Prequel,” 741.
72. Stevens, “Learning on the Job,” 1562.
73. Ibid., 1561.
74. *Fitzgerald v. Porter Memorial Hospital*, 523 F.2d 716, 723 (7th Cir. 1975).
75. Ibid., 719–20.

Chapter Four

Prisoners' Rights

After his nomination was confirmed by a 98 to 0 vote in the U.S. Senate, Stevens was sworn in as an Associate Justice of the U.S. Supreme Court on December 19, 1975. On April 21, 1976, after just four months on the Supreme Court, Stevens and the other justices heard oral arguments in *Meacham v. Fano* (1976). The case concerned whether prisoners are entitled to a hearing before being transferred to a prison with less favorable living conditions. After a series of fires were set inside a medium-security prison, several prisoners were ordered transferred to a maximum-security institution or confinement in segregation based on secret information provided to prison officials by informants within the prison. The prisoners denied involvement in the fires at a hearing to reclassify their security status, but they were not allowed to hear the evidence against them. Thus they claimed that their due process rights were violated.

On behalf of a six-justice majority, Justice Byron White's opinion concluded that the Due Process Clause does not provide any such due process rights for prisoners who are being transferred. According to White,

> [W]e cannot agree that any change in the conditions of confinement having a substantial adverse impact on the prisoner involved is sufficient to invoke the protections of the Due Process Clause. The Due Process Clause, by its own force, forbids the State from convicting any person of crime and depriving him of his liberty without complying fully with the requirements of the Clause. But, given a valid conviction, the criminal defendant has been constitutionally deprived of his liberty to the extent that the State may confine him and subject him to the rules of its prison system so long as the conditions of confinement do not otherwise violate the Constitution. [1]

Observers of the increasingly conservative Supreme Court of Chief Justice Warren Burger's era (1969–1986) likely expected that if anyone dissented against White's ruling, it would be Justices Marshall and Brennan, the holdover stalwart liberals of the Warren Court era. Justice Marshall's long career as a legendary civil rights attorney had provided a basis for accurately anticipating his continued advocacy for broad constitutional rights during his service as an Associate Justice. Justice Brennan was a key participant in the Warren Court's expansion of constitutional rights in criminal justice. Yet, it was the newcomer Stevens who wrote a strongly worded dissenting opinion in favor of prisoners' rights on behalf of himself and Justices Marshall and Brennan.

The former antitrust attorney, who only a few months earlier had been widely described by politicians and journalists alike as a conservative-leaning centrist, wrote an opinion that was striking for its outspoken advocacy of broad constitutional rights for incarcerated criminal offenders. Justice Stevens described the majority opinion's rationale as "disturbing"[2] and concluded that it "demeans the concept of liberty itself."[3] He argued that the majority's rationale effectively made a prisoner "little more than the slave described in the nineteenth-century [judicial] cases [that rejected the concept of prisoners' rights]."[4] According to Stevens, "I think it clear that even the inmate retains an unalienable interest in liberty—at the very minimum the right to be treated with dignity—which the Constitution may never ignore."[5]

A few months later, Stevens again asserted his strong advocacy of prisoners' rights. In a case argued on October 5, 1976, at the very start of the Supreme Court's next term and less than ten months after he became an associate justice, Stevens wrote a unique dissenting opinion in support of broader rights. This time, however, he not only spoke out strongly for recognizing a right to medical care for prisoners in *Estelle v. Gamble* (1976), but he did so as the author of a solo dissent criticizing a majority opinion written by Justice Marshall and joined by Brennan and every other justice. In Stevens's view, the majority opinion by the Supreme Court's most noted and rights-protective liberal justice did not go far enough in recognizing and protecting a medical care right for prisoners.

These prisoners' rights cases were not the only examples of Stevens asserting himself during his first months on the Court as one of the most liberal justices for specific issues. In *Mathews v. Lucas* (1976), a case that was argued less than one month after Stevens took his seat on the Court, a six-justice majority endorsed a law that discriminated against children born out of wedlock in determining eligibility for social security survivor benefits after the death of a parent. Justice Stevens wrote a dissenting opinion on behalf of Brennan and Marshall that began with a strong statement against the majority's acceptance of such discrimination: "The reason why the United States Government should not add to the burdens that illegitimate children inevitably acquire at birth is radiantly clear: we are committed to the proposition that all persons are created equal."[6]

These examples provide striking evidence that Stevens arrived at the Supreme Court with well-formed judicial values and he was willing to assert his judicial philosophy on behalf of constitutional rights immediately, even when addressing controversial issues and, as in *Estelle*, disagreeing with all of his colleagues. Moreover, he immediately emphasized the importance of liberty and equality as these initial opinions provided him with the opportunity to highlight for a national audience the centrality of these concepts to the judicial philosophy that he had developed through prior experience on the Seventh Circuit. Indeed, as described in earlier chapters, Stevens brought to the Court a familiarity with prisoners' issues that was probably unmatched by any of his colleagues, other than possibly Justice Marshall.

Analyses of Justice Stevens's first decade on the Supreme Court characterized him as a "maverick" who was the Court's "least predictable member."[7] Yet, with respect to one set of issues, Stevens was surprisingly predictable. As Bradley Canon concluded in his study of Stevens's decision making during the Burger Court era, "In no other area of criminal justice did Stevens differentiate himself so much from the Burger Court majority as in prisoners' rights. He supported the prisoner in sixteen of seventeen cases considered [from 1975 through 1986, Stevens's years of service on the Burger Court]."[8]

During the subsequent Rehnquist Court era (1986–2005), Stevens supported prisoners' claims in 80 percent of the Supreme Court's fifty-six cases concerning constitutional and statutory protections for prisoners, a percentage exceeded only by those of the most consistently liberal justices, Brennan and Marshall.[9] However, because they retired early in the Rehnquist era, they participated in only twelve and thirteen cases, respectively, from among the fifty-six total cases.[10] Thus Stevens was the justice who was notably consistent in supporting prisoners' claims in the largest number of cases throughout this era and, indeed, throughout his lengthy career on the Supreme Court. As indicated by his 80 percent rate of support, there are certainly examples of cases in which Stevens did not support prisoners' claims, such as *Parratt v. Taylor* (1981), concerning the negligent loss of a prisoner's property, and *Overton v. Bazzetta* (2003), concerning an asserted constitutional right to see family visitors. Overall, however, Justice Stevens's consistent record and outspokenness on prisoners' rights issues made him a historically unique voice on the Court.

SUPREME COURT DECISIONS PRIOR TO *TURNER V. SAFLEY* (1987)

Liberty, as a key concept in Stevens's judicial philosophy, ran as a consistent theme in his opinions throughout his entire judicial career and was the centerpiece of his first prisoners' rights opinion in *Meachum v. Fano* (1976). From the outset of his career on the Supreme Court, he made clear his view that even incarcerated offenders retain liberty interests, despite being members of a political minority that had earned its despised status and was regarded historically as undeserving of all but the most limited constitutional protections. In *Meachum*, Stevens found most "disturbing" Justice White's assertion that protected liberty interests find their source either in the Constitution or in state law. If neither of those sources provided a liberty interest in a specific context, then, according to White, there is no liberty interest to be protected in that context. In sharp contrast to White's analysis, Stevens described a natural law conception of liberty possessed by human beings that was not dependent on the language of constitutions, statutes, or judicial decisions. According to Stevens,

> If man were a creature of the State, the analysis would be correct. But neither the Bill of Rights nor the laws of sovereign States create the liberty which the Due Process Clause protects. The relevant constitutional provisions are limitations on the power of the sovereign to infringe on the liberty of the citizen. The relevant state laws either create property rights, or they curtail the freedom of the citizen who must live in an ordered society. Of course, law is essential to the exercise and enjoyment of individual liberty in a complex society. But it is not the source of liberty, and surely not the exclusive source.
>
> I had thought it self-evident that all men were endowed by their Creator with liberty as one of the cardinal unalienable rights. It is that basic freedom which the Due Process Clause protects, rather than the particular rights and privileges conferred by specific laws or regulations.[11]

This was an exceptionally broad conception of liberty and one that was perfectly consistent with Stevens's presentation decades later in the Second Amendment incorporation case, *McDonald v. City of Chicago* (2010), concerning the viewpoint he shared with Justice Harlan about the definition of protected liberty not being dependent on any specific provision of the Bill of Rights.

In the case at hand, Stevens noted that he would not necessarily recognize procedural rights for every prison transfer. However, he emphasized that liberty interests are implicated and must be protected whenever there is a "grievous loss" of liberty.[12] In this case, his assessment of the facts led him to observe, "I am unable to identify a principled basis for differentiating between a transfer from the general prison population to solitary confinement and a transfer involving equally disparate conditions between one physical facility and another."[13] Because the prisoners were transferred to higher security institutions with more spartan conditions and fewer privileges, Stevens recognized a "grievous loss" of liberty that should have triggered the provision of procedural rights.

Justice Stevens quoted at length from his own Seventh Circuit opinion in *United States ex rel. Miller v. Twomey* (1973) and he accused the majority of demeaning the Supreme Court's own protection of liberty in *Morrissey v. Brewer* (1972). Stevens then wrote the words which arguably provided the underlying basis for all of his subsequent opinions that advocated the protection of rights for convicted offenders. For Stevens, the fundamental basis for prisoners' rights rested on a lofty ideal that he described in dramatic fashion with the following words: "For if the inmate's protected liberty interests are no greater than the State chooses to allow, he is really little more than the slave described in the nineteenth-century cases. I think it clear that even the inmate retains an unalienable interest in liberty—at the very minimum the right to be treated with dignity—which the Constitution may never ignore."[14]

Justice Stevens had the opportunity to reiterate the judicial philosophy and reasoning evident in *Meachum* just a few years later in *Hewitt v. Helms* (1983). The majority recognized a limited liberty interest, based on state laws and regulations, possessed by a prisoner sent into a lengthy period of solitary confinement after a violent disturbance. By contrast, Stevens reiterated a natural law view that all prisoners, as human beings, inherently retain an interest in liberty during imprisonment that is not granted by the Constitution or any law. Thus he dissented against the majority's approval of minimal procedural protections for prisoners sent into solitary confinement. To Stevens, such a transfer involved a significant imposition on liberty that required higher standards of due process in order to make it more difficult for officials to place a prisoner in such conditions for a lengthy time period without demonstrated justification.

Justice Stevens wrote an important majority opinion in *Hutto v. Finney* (1978), a case argued two years after he joined the Supreme Court. The case concerned a challenge to conditions in punishment cells in an Arkansas prison. A U.S. district court concluded that the conditions violated the Eighth Amendment prohibition on cruel and unusual punishments and therefore ordered the state to take remedial action. The case came to the Supreme Court because Arkansas challenged the judge's orders with respect to a thirty-day maximum limit on confinement in punitive isolation and the state's obligation to pay attorneys' fees to the prisoners' lawyers under the federal Civil Rights Attorney's Fees Awards Act. In the Supreme Court, the representation of the prisoners, including the list of attorneys "on brief," consisted of a roster of prominent civil rights attorneys from the NAACP Legal Defense Fund. For the State of Arkansas, an assistant attorney general argued the case and future Democratic President Bill Clinton, who was then the Arkansas Attorney General, was listed as one of the two state attorneys "on brief" who contributed to the preparation of the state's arguments. The administration of Democratic President Jimmy Carter was represented by Solicitor General Wade McCree, who joined the American Civil Liberties Union and other civil rights advocates to support the prisoners' position.

The Supreme Court's decision was regarded as providing an important endorsement for the authority of lower court federal judges to issue remedial orders regarding prison conditions, even though such orders clashed with states' traditional autonomy in running their own prison systems. Moreover, such orders also imposed significant expenses on prison systems, especially in southern states that were required to build new prisons and hire professional staff. In effect, southern states were forced to move away from what Malcolm Feeley and Edward Rubin called the "plantation model" that used prisoners as quasi-slave laborers who were supervised, often violently, by other prisoners instead of trained staff.[15] In *Hutto*, only Justice Rehnquist disagreed with the district court's authority to issue remedial orders in the case, although Chief Justice Burger and Justice Powell parted company with the majority on the specific issue of awarding attorneys' fees to the prisoners' lawyers. As discussed in detail by Professors Feeley and Rubin, federal judges issued remedial orders that altered prisons' policies and practices in virtually every state during the prison litigation reform era from the 1960s through the 1980s.[16] The *Hutto* ruling confirmed the legitimacy of federal judges' actions in scrutinizing and remedying substandard conditions in state prisons. It endorsed court-ordered changes in prison operations and thereby helped to upgrade conditions, institutionalize bureaucratic practices, and professionalize the management of correctional institutions nationwide.

The *Hutto* opinion gave Stevens the opportunity to describe the kinds of conditions that led federal judges to intervene. Such descriptions moved the debates about judicial action from abstract discussions of the Eighth Amendment to vivid depictions of inhumane conditions. As described by Stevens,

> Confinement in punitive isolation was for an indeterminate period of time. An average of four, and sometimes as many as ten or eleven, prisoners were crowded into windowless 8' by 10' cells containing no furniture other than a source of water and a toilet that could only be flushed from outside the cell. . . . At night the prisoners were given mattresses to spread on the floor. Although some prisoners suffered from infectious diseases such as hepatitis and venereal disease, mattresses were removed and jumbled together each morning, then returned to the cells at random in the evening. . . . Prisoners in isolation received fewer than 1,000 calories a day; their meals consisted primarily of four-inch squares of "grue," a substance created by mashing meat, potatoes, oleo, syrup, vegetables, eggs, and seasoning into a paste and baking the mixture in a pan. . . .

> Because of their inadequate numbers, guards assigned to the punitive isolation cells frequently resorted to physical violence, using nightsticks and Mace in their efforts to maintain order. Prisoners were sometimes left in isolation for months, their release depending on "their attitudes as appraised by prison personnel."[17]

In footnotes in the opinion, Stevens added further details about the problems of the Arkansas prison system, including prisoners being forced to work in the prison's agricultural fields sixty hours per week without proper clothing, the uncontrolled sexual victimization of weaker prisoners, and the lack of adequate medical care. He also described the prison's practice of issuing guns to "trusty" inmates who brutalized the other inmates with impunity as the prison employed only eight nonconvict guards to supervise one thousand prisoners.

Many justices appointed to the Court in later years had little exposure to cases with findings of fact illuminating the brutal treatment and inhumane conditions that affected all facets of the environment and practices in certain prison systems prior to judicially-imposed reforms. By contrast, Stevens became a judge early enough in the 1970s to know the horrors imposed on imprisoned offenders in certain states. His knowledge of both the risks and realities of abuses when prisoners were unprotected by the recognition and enforcement of constitutional rights undoubtedly contributed to his consistent advocacy of, in his words, "the right to be treated with dignity—which the Constitution may never ignore."[18]

The descriptive aspects of Stevens's opinion in *Hutto* clashed directly with Justice Rehnquist's dissenting opinion that said "The Court's affirmance of a District Court's injunction against a prison practice which has not been shown to violate the Constitution can only be considered an aberration."[19] At that moment, Rehnquist appeared to adopt a uniquely extreme position that was resistant to the recognition of prisoners' rights. No one knew at that time that years later Rehnquist would be joined by other justices—Scalia and Thomas—whose judicial philosophies made them even more strongly opposed to recognizing and protecting rights for people in correctional settings.

Justice Stevens had another opportunity to write a majority opinion in a corrections law case in 1978, but the strength of his advocacy for transparency in the operations of such institutions went too far to retain the support that he needed among his colleagues. The case of *Houchins v. KQED, Inc.* (1978) raised issues about freedom of the press under the First Amendment that Stevens saw as having important implications for the protection of prisoners' and pretrial detainees' rights. A sheriff in California denied a broadcast news organization's request to permit a reporter and cameraman to enter a county jail to visit a section where a suicide had occurred. Additional requests were denied when news reporters sought to investigate other incidents at the jail. After the lawsuit was filed, the sheriff initiated limited public tours at the jail and said that reporters could go on the tours, albeit without their cameras. At the same time, the sheriff also modified a policy that had required inspection of all outgoing, non-legal mail sent by jail inmates. In effect, the sheriff reacted to the lawsuit by abandoning the previous prohibition on prisoners mentioning any officers' names or describing their actions in the jail. Materials in the Blackmun Papers at the Library of Congress indicate that the justices voted 4 to 3 to support the news organization's claimed right of access. Only seven justices participated because Justices Blackmun and Marshall recused themselves from the case.

According to the opinion assignment sheet for December 10, 1977, Justice Brennan, who was the senior justice in the majority, assigned the majority opinion to Stevens.[20] Justices Powell and Stewart also voted with the majority while Chief Justice Burger and Justices White and Rehnquist were the three justices who disagreed and planned to dissent.

Justice Stevens circulated a first draft on March 15, 1978, that began with the words "MR. JUSTICE STEVENS delivered the opinion of the Court," reflecting the draft's status as the initial opinion for the majority.[21] As typically happens in the Supreme Court's decision-making process, the first draft attracted comments and suggestions as well as expressions of agreement and disagreement. On March 16, Justice Brennan circulated a memo saying simply, "I agree,"[22] and on March 23, Justice Powell followed suit with a memo saying only, "Please join me,"[23] the usual phrasing justices used to indicate that they are joining an opinion. On March 28, Chief Justice Burger circulated a memo indicating that he would draft a dissent. He also commented that "If my position does not cover the views of [the other dissenters] Byron [White] and Bill Rehnquist, they, too, may have something to say [in their own dissenting opinions]."[24]

These initial memos among the justices followed predictably from the vote in conference on the case. However, the next memo moved the decision-making process in a new direction. On April 24, Justice Potter Stewart circulated a memo that said,

> Try as I may, I cannot bring myself to agree that a county sheriff is constitutionally required to open up a jail that he runs to the press and public. Accordingly, I shall not be able to subscribe to the opinion you have circulated, affirming the judgment of the Court of Appeals.
>
> My tentative view, which may not stand up, is that it would be permissible in this case to issue an injunction assuring press access equivalent to existing public access, but not the much broader injunction actually issued by the District Court. I shall in due course circulate an expression of these views.[25]

Because Stewart had originally been among the four justices in the majority, his reaction to the first draft of the majority opinion meant that Stevens had lost his majority by writing an opinion that was, in effect, too liberal and too protective of rights. When such changes or refinements in positions happen during the process of drafting and circulating opinions, there may be an opportunity for the original author of the majority's first draft to recapture the decisive voter by toning down the opinion, altering the reasoning, or otherwise accommodating the views of the wavering justice. In this case, however, Stewart appeared to express fundamental disagreement with Stevens's view on the right that needed to be vindicated in the context of a correctional institution. At the end of his career, Stevens stated in interviews that, when he was the senior justice in the majority for a close case, he often assigned the opinion to the justice who was most likely to waver. According to Stevens, "Sometimes . . . in all candor, if you think somebody might not be solid, . . . it might be wiser to let that person write the opinion" because people "tend to become even more convinced" when they have the job of articulating the justifications for a position.[26] Thus, in this case, if Stewart revealed himself to be the least committed member of the majority during the discussion in conference, then Brennan may have made a mistake by assigning the opinion to Stevens, a justice who had already written strong opinions about rights in correctional settings.

The following day, Chief Justice Burger immediately pounced on the opportunity to potentially capture Stewart's vote and form a majority opposed to the position held by Stevens, Brennan, and Powell. Burger's memo noted that he had spent "a substantial amount of time on a dissent in this case," thus implying that he had put a great deal of thought into these issues. Moreover, his memo declared "I agree with Potter's view that media have a right of access but not beyond that of the public generally."[27] In a series of subsequent memos, Burger expressed agreement with ideas in the draft of Stewart's concurrence and even noted that he would include in his opinion a long quotation from a law review article that Stewart had written. When Justice White circulated his memo indicating that he joined Burger's opinion, he did not merely note "please join me," as is typical. Instead, White wrote two paragraphs that appeared aimed at persuading Stewart to join the Burger opinion and closed with "I join your opinion and hope that it commands a majority."[28]

Ultimately, Burger gained Stewart's vote on the outcome, but Stewart did not join Burger's opinion. Thus Burger wrote a plurality opinion announcing the judgment of the Court and therefore the opinion did not have the same precedential value as a majority opinion. Justice Stewart wrote a concurring opinion and Stevens's draft majority opinion was ultimately issued as a dissenting opinion. In addition, because Stewart decided that he would announce his concurrence orally from the bench, Stevens decided that he, too, would announce his opinion. As he said in his memo to Burger, "Although I previously indicated that I would not say anything orally in this case, since both you and Potter are announcing your positions, I will take about a minute."[29] In this instance, it appeared that Stevens simply concluded that his position should be announced, albeit very briefly, simply to avoid having it obscured by the fact that the other two opinions in the case were being announced. In other oral dissents in his career, it was much clearer that it was based on very strong feelings about the decision. In *Houchins,* Stevens merely announced,

> This Court has never squarely answered the question whether a state may pursue a policy of entirely excluding both the public and the press from any access to information about prison conditions. I think that question must be answered in order to decide this case properly. For reasons stated at length in an opinion which Mr. Justice Brennan, Mr. Justice Powell and I have joined, we would hold that such a policy of total exclusion is unconstitutional.[30]

Although the focus of the legal issue in question was a First Amendment issue about freedom of the press and the public's access to information about governmental institutions, Stevens's opinion made it very clear that he saw the protection of prisoners and pretrial detainees as a central consideration in the case. He discussed at length his view that "there is no legitimate penological justification for concealing from citizens the conditions in which their fellow citizens are being confined."[31] Justice Stevens asserted that there are important benefits from transparency in correctional institutions. In his words, "While a ward of the State and subject to its stern discipline, [a prisoner] retains constitutional protections against cruel and unusual punishment, . . . protection which may derive more practical support from access to information about prisons by the public than by occasional litigation in a busy court."[32] He also emphasized the importance of safeguarding presumptively innocent pretrial detainees who are housed under tough conditions in jails but are constitutionally protected against the imposition of punishment unless and until they are convicted of a crime.

It seems clear that Stevens did not seek to compromise his conclusions in order to persuade Stewart to stay as the decisive fourth vote to create a majority. The strength of Stevens's opinion in supporting the rights at issue had an impact on the outcome of the case, but not in the way that Stevens would have preferred. Thus Stevens's role as an outspoken protector of prisoners' rights had the effect of shifting a case outcome away from his preferred position.

Many commentators see the Court's decision in *Bell v. Wolfish* (1979) as the first clear sign of the high court's move toward advocating deference to corrections officials and stopping the expansion of rights in correctional institutions.[33] Justice Rehnquist's majority opinion mandated the subordination of unconvicted pretrial detainees' rights claims to the purported security concerns of jail officials. Justice Stevens, joined by Brennan, and with Marshall dissenting separately, protested that the majority's "withdrawal of fundamental rights is not limited to those for whom punishment is proper [i.e., convicted offenders], or to those detainees posing special security risks."[34] He concluded that the failure to protect rights went too far by imposing unnecessary deprivations on presumptively innocent pretrial detainees who posed no special security risks. Stevens argued that the challenged policies and procedures at the jail, concerning such issues as body-cavity searches and access to books, were all unconstitutional. The right to due process forbids the government from punishing people who have not yet been found guilty through proper judicial procedures. As acknowledged in Rehnquist's majority opinion, "[W]hat *is* at issue when an aspect of pretrial detention that is not alleged to violate any express guarantee of the Constitution is challenged, is the detainee's right to be free from punishment."[35] In light of the core focus of his judicial philosophy, Stevens saw this principle as intimately connected to his view of liberty and substantive due process rights. He wrote in his dissent:

> This right to be free of punishment is not expressly embodied in any provision in the Bill of Rights. Nor is the source of this right found in any statute. The source of this fundamental freedom is the word "liberty" itself as used in the Due Process Clause, and as informed by "history, reason, the past course of decisions," and the judgment and experience of "those whom the Constitution entrusted" with interpreting that word.[36]

Thus Stevens justified his disagreement with the majority's approval of restrictive jail policies and procedures by identifying the existence of punishment produced by those policies and procedures. According to Stevens, the pretrial detainees' constitutional rights were violated because, in his words:

> I think it is unquestionably a form of punishment to deny an innocent person the right to read a book loaned to him by a friend or relative while he is temporarily confined, to deny him the right to receive gifts or packages, to search his private possessions out of his presence, or to compel him to exhibit his private body cavities to the visual inspection of a guard.[37]

In sum, Stevens's greater sensitivity to burdens and deprivations imposed on pretrial detainees led him to define the concept of punishment more broadly than the majority and thereby view the policies and procedures as violating the Due Process Clause.

In *Hudson v. Palmer* (1984), the majority opinion effectively barred Fourth Amendment protection for prisoners' private possessions and thus made such items freely subject to searches and seizures. By contrast, Stevens's dissent, joined by Justices Brennan, Marshall, and Blackmun, argued that prisoners enjoy protected possessory interests to various items under the First, Fourth, Eighth, and Fourteenth Amendments.[38] The *Hudson* case appeared to be one of the examples to which Justice Stevens may have been referring when he said years later in several interviews that his experience on the court of appeals had already given him exposure to many of the issues that he faced on the Supreme Court. The factual circumstances and issue in the case were parallel to the Seventh Circuit case *Bonner v. Coughlin* (1975) in which then Judge Stevens wrote a majority opinion diametrically opposed to Chief Justice Burger's later rejection of Fourth Amendment protection for prison cells in *Hudson*.

In *Hudson*, Justice Stevens's incredulity at Chief Justice Burger's assertion that prisoners possess no reasonable expectation of privacy in their cells and their property was evident in his response to Burger's opinion. In Stevens's words, "Are all of these items subject to unrestrained perusal, confiscation, or mutilation at the hands of a possibly hostile guard? Is the Court correct in its perception that 'society' is not prepared to recognize *any* privacy or possessory interest of the prison inmate—not matter how remote the threat to prison security may be?"[39] Stevens referred to the Eighth Amendment standard, established in *Trop v. Dulles* (1958), that defines violations of the prohibition on "cruel and unusual punishments" according to the evolving values of our civilized society. In Stevens's words, "To hold that a prisoner's possession of a letter from his wife, or a picture of his baby, has no protection against arbitrary or malicious perusal, seizure, or destruction would not, in my judgment, comport with any civilized standard of decency."[40]

As in many other opinions, Stevens made a strong statement in *Hudson* concerning prisoner's rights and, moreover, his statement in *Hudson* reiterated a prior declaration that he had made as a Seventh Circuit judge. A decade earlier in his majority opinion for the court of appeals in *Bonner v. Coughlin* (1975), Stevens had examined the search of a prisoner's cell and declared "We hold that a prisoner enjoys the protection of the Fourth Amendment against unreasonable searches, at least to some minimal extent."[41] Stevens had brought with him to the Supreme Court a well-formed view that prisoners retain an element of Fourth Amendment interests and protections in their cells and possession. However, he found that the majority of justices on the Court did not share his view when the high court examined the issue amid its move toward the diminution of prisoners' rights.

Justice Stevens's concern for preserving Fourth Amendment protections for convicted offenders later carried over into other correctional contexts as he dissented against warrantless searches of probationers' homes (*Griffin v. Wisconsin*, 1987). He also dissented against suspicionless searches of parolees and characterized the Court's approval of such searches in *Samson v. California* (2006) as "an unprecedented curtailment of liberty."[42]

TURNER V. SAFLEY AND ITS AFTERMATH

The Supreme Court made a major decision with far-reaching consequences in *Turner v. Safley* (1987) and Justice Stevens had a major role in the expression of an opposing viewpoint for the new precedent itself as well as for later majority decisions that followed this precedent. The case raised two rights claims by prisoners. First, there was a claimed rights violation when prison policies limited the ability of prisoners to correspond with prisoners incarcerated in other facilities. Second, Missouri prison regulations limited prisoners' ability to get married. The regulation said that prisoners could only marry with the permission of the prison superintendent and such permission would only be granted for "compelling reasons." Prison officials admitted that they would only accept one justification as compelling: a pregnancy or birth of a child. When the justices discussed the case at conference and took their initial vote, they were as deeply divided as they could possibly be. Four justices—Rehnquist, Scalia, White, and Powell—rejected both rights claims and four justices—Brennan, Marshall, Stevens, and Blackmun—supported both rights claims. Thus the deciding vote was cast by Justice O'Connor, who rejected the rights claim concerning prisoner-to-prisoner correspondence but supported the claim concerning a broader entitlement to marry while in prison. As a result, O'Connor was assigned the majority opinion because she was the only justice who represented the majority perspective on both issues.

After the vote, Brennan circulated a memo to Marshall, Stevens, and Blackmun that said, "We four are in dissent in No. 85-1384, *Turner v. Safley*. Would you, John, mind trying the dissent?"[43] In a memo circulated among these justices later on the same day, Stevens said that he would be happy to write the dissent concerning the prisoner correspondence issue. When Stevens eventually circulated the first draft of his dissent, he received suggestions for changes. Based on a clear example of the law clerk to law clerk intelligence-gathering activities that occur behind the scenes at the Supreme Court, a memo to Justice Blackmun from one of his law clerks revealed:

> I recommend that you wait for the second draft of JUSTICE STEVENS' concurring/dissenting opinion in this case before joining it. His law clerk has indicated that JUSTICE STEVENS has agreed to modify his statement on the first page concerning the reasons for agreeing with JUSTICE O'CONNOR's finding that the marriage regulation is invalid. JUSTICE BRENNAN sent JUSTICE STEVENS a private note asking that he modify it somewhat to indicate that JUSTICE O'CONNOR applies a too lenient standard but even

> under that standard the regulation is invalid. . . . JUSTICE STEVENS has agreed to change the sentence on the first page and add a footnote.[44]

The law clerk also endorsed Justice Stevens's approach of "point[ing] to the majority's inconsistent approach to [judicial] deference [to corrections officials' decisions] depending on whether the majority is addressing the mail regulation or the marriage regulation."[45] When Stevens circulated a second draft of his opinion three days later, Justice Blackmun wrote "Wow!" in the top left corner of his copy, apparently in reaction to the strong language that Stevens used to oppose the deferential standard articulated by O'Connor's opinion.[46]

In her majority opinion, O'Connor announced a four-part test for examining these prisoners' rights issues. The first prong of the test was "there must be a 'valid, rational connection' between the prison regulation and the legitimate governmental interest put forward to justify it."[47] The other prongs examined whether there were alternative ways for the prisoner to exercise the right in question, the potential impact on staff and prisoners if the prison accommodated the right, and the possible existence of an easy alternative option to make the right available to prisoners. After the behind-the-scenes suggestion from Brennan, Stevens's opinion spoke out sharply against O'Connor's application of a rational basis test. In the view of Stevens, as well as Brennan, Marshall, and Blackmun, this approach was insufficiently protective of prisoners' rights because it would lead judges to defer to corrections officials' unsubstantiated claims that a wide array of rights-limiting policies and practices were necessary in order to protect safety and security. Justice Stevens and his like-minded colleagues wanted corrections officials to be required to actually demonstrate a substantial or compelling reason for any policies and practices that collided with prisoners' constitutional rights. Instead, O'Connor's standard created the risk of unquestioning and automatic judicial acceptance of the denial of rights as long as corrections officials claimed that a policy or practice advanced institutional security or promoted another legitimate goal. Thus Stevens wrote a paragraph—that elicited the "Wow!" response in Blackmun's notes—which said the following:

> But if the standard can be satisfied by nothing more than "a *logical* connection" between the regulation and any legitimate penological concern perceived by a cautious warden, . . . it is virtually meaningless. Application of the standard would seem to permit disregard for inmates' constitutional rights whenever the imagination of the warden produces a plausible security concern and a deferential trial court is able to discern a logical connection between that concern and the challenged regulation. Indeed, there is a logical connection between prison discipline and the use of bullwhips on prisoners; and security is logically furthered by a total ban on inmate communication, not only with

> other inmates but also with outsiders who conceivably might be interested in arranging an attack within the prison or an escape from it.[48]

As characterized by Stevens, O'Connor's test opened the door to the wholesale disregard of prisoners' rights based on imaginary or pretextual justifications asserted by corrections officials. To dramatize his position, he observed that O'Connor's approach could be used to justify the use of bullwhips on prisoners, a practice that was almost universally acknowledged to be a violation of the Eighth Amendment ever since a court of appeals opinion by then Judge Blackmun outlawed the practice in Arkansas prisons in *Jackson v. Bishop* (1968). Indeed, even Justice Scalia, who recognized very few rights for prisoners, initially acknowledged in the 1980s that he would be unlikely to endorse the use of whips in prisons, despite the practice's apparent acceptability under his originalist theory of constitutional interpretation.[49] Years later, however, Scalia backtracked and claimed that his fidelity to originalism would lead him to endorse flogging as a constitutionally permissible punishment.[50]

Surprisingly, O'Connor's formulation of the deferential *Turner* test led her four colleagues who had voted "no" on both rights issues to change their votes and endorse her position completely, including her support of a marriage right for prisoners. As described to Justice Blackmun by a memo from one of his law clerks on April 13, 1987:

> She has, however, received join memos from Justice Powell and Chief Justice Rehnquist who initially voted to reverse [and reject the rights claims] on both issues. Apparently, she has done such an effective job of establishing a "lesser standard of scrutiny . . . for determining the constitutionality of prison rules" that they have decided to go along with the invalidation of the marriage rule. Her opinion effectively states that courts should defer to any rational prison rule.[51]

One month later, Justice Scalia, the justice least likely to support prisoners' rights at that moment in Supreme Court history, sent a join memo to O'Connor and the other justices that said, "I would be pleased to join your revised opinion, and am withdrawing my separate concurrence."[52] Justice White's join memo a few days later was more revealing. White said, "Although I have doubts on the marriage issue, show me as joining."[53] Thus all nine justices unanimously endorsed a limited right of prisoners to marry unless corrections officials have a specific reason to prohibit the marriage, a right with relatively little impact on correctional administration or the discretionary authority of corrections officials. Given that four justices initially voted against recognizing the right as well as White's revealing comment, it is difficult to believe that all four justices switched sides on the issue simply because O'Connor's opinion persuaded them to change their views. In light of their general reluctance to recognize rights for prisoners, especially by Scalia and Rehnquist, it seems plausible that at least some of the four position-changers accommodated recognition of a marriage right with little impact on the operations of corrections institutions in order to show strong support for O'Connor's deferential test; a test that had obvious potential for significantly impacting judicial consideration of subsequent prisoners' rights claims concerning a variety of issues. If they had continued to argue against recognition of the marriage right that O'Connor endorsed, they would, in effect, have produced criticisms of either the creation or the application of the new *Turner* test. By contrast, accommodating O'Connor's views on the marriage right resulted in a strong endorsement of the *Turner* test by all four position-changing justices.

The *Turner* test, with its deferential posture toward the justifications presented by corrections officials for limitations on rights, had impact well beyond the specific decision in that case. Courts, including the Supreme Court, used the deferential four-part test to evaluate a variety of prisoners' rights claims. For example, the Court immediately applied the test to reject a First Amendment free exercise of religion claim by minimum-security Muslim prisoners who were barred from leaving their outside work assignments to re-enter their correctional facility for Friday prayer services. The Court majority endorsed this denial of access while simultaneously acknowledging that these prayer services were a central element of the prisoners' religious practices. In *O'Lone v. Estate of Shabazz* (1987), Justice Blackmun's notes on the justices' discussion of the case in conference showed that both O'Connor and Powell explicitly indicated that the *Turner* standard should be applied in this case, a sign that some justices anticipated *Turner*'s influence and applicability for other issues even before the Court had officially announced its decision in *Turner*.[54]

Chief Justice Rehnquist wrote the Court's opinion for a five-member majority in *O'Lone*. The majority opinion applied the *Turner* test and permitted prison officials' security concerns and administrative-convenience claims to override the prisoners' exercise of religion. Justice Brennan wrote the dissent on behalf of Stevens, Marshall, and Blackmun. His dissent complained about the *Turner* test's inadequacy for properly protecting prisoners' rights. For example, Brennan said, "If the Court's standard of review is to represent anything more than reflexive deference to prison officials, any finding of reasonableness must rest on firmer ground than the record now presents."[55]

As the Supreme Court applied the deferential *Turner* test to various prisoners' rights claims in subsequent years, Stevens spent the final two decades of his career criticizing the standard as excessively deferential to corrections officials and resisting the application of the test. In addition, he argued that the test was not being applied in accordance with its original articulation. In one majority opinion concerning an asserted First Amendment right for a prisoner to assist another prisoner with legal research, Justice Thomas implied that the *Turner* test had been established as the sole standard for evaluating all prisoners' rights claims. According to Thomas, the *Turner* test was "a unitary, deferential standard for reviewing prisoners' constitutional claims."[56] Justice Stevens consistently resisted such efforts to expand the influence of the deferential standard which was created in the context of two specific First Amendment rights concerning freedom of expression in prisoner-to-prisoner correspondence and freedom of association in prisoners' opportunities to get married.

Justice O'Connor, the creator of the *Turner* test, also ended up resisting the expansion of the test's application to a wider array of rights issues, albeit without agreeing with Stevens's continuous criticism of the test itself. As we will see in the next section's discussion of *Johnson v. California* (2005), O'Connor resisted the efforts of Thomas and Scalia to apply the deferential test to an Equal Protection Clause case concerning racial segregation in a prison. After her retirement from the Supreme Court, O'Connor served as a member of a three-judge panel in an Eighth Circuit case that unanimously rejected the application of the *Turner* test to a First Amendment Establishment Clause case concerning religion-based rehabilitation programs for prisoners that were administered by a Christian organization (*Americans United for Separation of Church and State v. Prison Fellowship Ministries*, 2007).

Justice Stevens's objections to the deferential *Turner* test were evident in *Thornburgh v. Abbott* (1989), a case challenging federal prison officials' prohibition on prisoners receiving certain magazines. One magazine was prohibited because it published an article about a prisoner who died from an asthma attack as a result of allegedly inadequate medical care in a federal prison. In a dissenting opinion, joined by Marshall and Brennan, Stevens voiced his objection to the *Turner* test itself through such statements as "[t]he feeble protection provided by [*Turner*'s] 'reasonableness standard' applied within the framework of these regulations is apparent in this record."[57] Justice Stevens also objected to the expanding application of the *Turner* test. In *Thornburgh*, he accused the majority of improperly applying the *Turner* test to the issue of outsiders' First Amendment rights, here the magazine publishers' freedom-of-the-press interests in communicating to prisoners, even though prior precedents demanded a higher standard of justification by prison officials before interfering with such interests.

In the Supreme Court's original decision related to outsiders' First Amendment rights in communicating with prisoners, *Procunier v. Martinez* (1974), the Court demanded that prison officials show "an important or substantial governmental interest unrelated to the suppression of expression" and that "the limitation of First Amendment freedoms [was] no greater than [was] necessary or essential."[58] Justice Stevens complained about the *Thorn-*

burgh majority's failure to adhere to this precedent by saying, "In lieu of *Martinez*'s rationale, which properly takes into consideration the effects that prison regulations have on the First Amendment rights of nonprisoners, the Court applies a manipulable 'reasonableness' standard to a set of regulations that too easily may be interpreted to authorize arbitrary rejections of literature addressed to inmates."[59]

In *Washington v. Harper* (1990), a six-justice majority applied the *Turner* test to endorse the Washington prison system's application of limited due process rights in conjunction with seeking to forcibly medicate a prisoner who was suffering from mental illness. Justice Stevens wrote the dissent on behalf of Brennan and Marshall. The first lines of the dissent summarized Stevens's position by saying, "The Court has undervalued respondent's liberty interest; has misread the Washington involuntary medication Policy and misapplied our decision in *Turner v. Safley*. . . ; and has concluded that a mock trial before an institutionally biased tribunal constitutes 'due process of law.'"[60] As was true in other prisoners' rights cases, this case triggered a core element of Stevens's judicial philosophy by implicating the concept of liberty under the Due Process Clause. In addition, Stevens criticized the majority's application of the *Turner* test because he concluded that the Court did not carefully evaluate the individual justifications put forward by corrections officials to ensure that they were, indeed, rationally related to a legitimate purpose. Instead, according to Stevens:

> The State, and arguably the Court, allows the [Special Offender Center] to blend the state interests in responding to emergencies and in convenient prison administration with the individual's interest in receiving beneficial medical treatment. The result is a muddled rationale that allows the "exaggerated response" of forced psychotropic medication on the basis of purely institutional concerns. So serving institutional convenience eviscerates the inmate's substantive liberty interest in the integrity of his body and mind.[61]

As in other cases implicating liberty interests going back to his first Supreme Court opinion on prisoners' rights in *Meachum v. Fano* (1976), Stevens's vision of the protections required by the Due Process Clause was much more protective of rights than the approaches applied by a majority of his colleagues.

In another example, Stevens offered an additional critique of the Court's application of the *Turner* test in *Beard v. Banks* (2006). Prison officials denied prisoners in a high-security disciplinary unit access to newspapers, magazines, and personal photographs. The case illuminated how far the *Turner* test had been stretched. Justice Breyer's plurality opinion purported to apply the deferential rational basis test as the first part of *Turner*'s requirements. However, he also admitted that the other components of the four-part test could not actually be applied to these circumstances in accordance with the requirements of the original *Turner* precedent as articulated by Justice O'Connor's seminal opinion in 1987. Justice Thomas, whose extremely limited view of prisoners' rights was drastically different than that of Justice Stevens, wrote a concurring opinion, joined by Scalia, endorsing deference to prison officials. Yet, Thomas's opinion also explained why this case demonstrated that the actual *Turner* test was unworkable in some circumstances. Stevens and Thomas both viewed the *Turner* test as flawed, although they had different visions of the implications of the flaws, with Stevens seeking stronger rights and less deference to corrections officials and Thomas advocating the opposite approach and results.

In *Beard*, the prison officials' justifications for the regulations included security concerns about the use of magazines, newspapers, and family photographs as weapons or for starting fires. They also justified the regulations with a deprivation theory of rehabilitation. The prison officials sought to withhold access to these items as an incentive for good behavior that could lead the prisoners to regain access. In dissent, Stevens obliterated the purported security justification that had been accepted by the majority of justices as he noted that these prisoners were allowed access to Bibles, toilet paper, religious newspapers, law books, and related legal periodicals—items that are equally susceptible to being used as weapons or for starting fires. He also harshly criticized what he saw as the inhumanity of depriving prisoners of access to reading material and family photographs under these circumstances. According to Stevens,

> What is perhaps most troubling about the prison regulation at issue in this case is that the rule comes perilously close to a state-sponsored effort at mind control. . . . In this case, the complete prohibition on secular, nonlegal newspapers, newsletters, and magazines prevents prisoners from "receiv[ing] suitable access to social, political, esthetic, moral, and other ideas," which are central to the development and preservation of individual identity, and are clearly protected by the First Amendment. . . . Similarly, the ban on personal photographs, for at least some inmates, interferes with the capacity to remember loved ones, which is undoubtedly a core part of a person's "sphere of intellect and spirit." Moreover, it is difficult to imagine a context in which these First Amendment infringements could be more severe; LTSU-2 inmates are in solitary confinement for twenty-three hours a day with no access to radio or television, are not permitted to make phone calls except in cases of emergency, and may only have one visitor per month. They are essentially isolated from any meaningful contact with the outside world. The severity of the constitutional deprivations at issue in this case should give us serious pause before concluding, as a matter of law, that the challenged regulation is consistent with the sovereign's duty to treat prisoners in accordance with "the ethical tradition that accords respect to the dignity and intrinsic worth of every individual."[62]

Even in a rare case in which he agreed with the Court's rejection of a rights claim under the *Turner* test, albeit without endorsing the majority's application of the test itself, Stevens sought to express a reminder about the underlying importance of prisoners' rights. When the majority in *Overton v. Bazzetta* (2003) rejected a challenge to visiting policies in the Michigan prison system, Stevens filed a concurring opinion, joined by Justices Ginsburg, Breyer, and Souter. Despite turning aside this particular rights claim, Stevens wanted to remind everyone that, in his words,

> [N]othing in the Court's opinion today signals a resurrection of any such approach [that treats prisoners as slaves without rights] in cases of this kind. To the contrary, it remains true that the "restraints and the punishment which a criminal conviction entails do not place the citizen beyond the ethical tradition that accords respect to the dignity and intrinsic worth of every individual."[63]

The quotation upon which Stevens relied was from his very own Seventh Circuit opinion in *United States ex rel. Miller v. Twomey* (1973). He used that decision as a frequent touchstone in his Supreme Court opinions as he implicitly highlighted the importance of the prior experiences that enabled him to arrive at the Supreme Court with well-developed views about prisoners' rights.

ACCESS TO THE COURTS

One especially important issue for prisoners is access to the courts. The Sixth Amendment right to counsel focuses on providing defense attorneys to represent criminal defendants at the investigatory and trial stages of prosecution processes. In *Ross v. Moffitt* (1974), the Supreme Court made clear that the constitutional right to counsel extended beyond the trial stage only to the initial appeal after conviction, but not to later post-conviction legal processes. Because there is no constitutional right to assistance of counsel beyond the first appeal of right, prisoners must usually struggle to prepare their own habeas corpus petitions and civil rights lawsuits concerning alleged violations of constitutional rights in correctional settings. Obviously, anyone who has not been trained in law would have difficulty preparing and presenting legal claims according to proper legal procedures. The task is all the more challenging in the prison context because so many convicted offenders lack formal education and literacy skills.[64] With an awareness of this context, Justice Stevens demonstrated special concern about keeping courts open and available for the claims submitted by convicted offenders. As described in chapter 2, Stevens specifically attributed his sensitivity to issues of court access to his experience with the Illinois investigative commission that had its origins in a single citizen's persistent complaints about conflicts of interest among justices on the Illinois Supreme Court. In Stevens's words, "My memory of the unexpected merit that we found in the allegations made by Sherman Skolnick has remained a powerful reminder that categorical prohibitions against repetitive filings can create a real risk of injustice."[65] Thus Stevens objected when other justices approved orders to block prisoners from filing petitions in court merely because they had filed numerous unsuccessful claims in the past.[66]

An example of one such order that Stevens found to be objectionable was among the U.S. Supreme Court's Orders issued on February 26, 2007:

> 06-8547 WOODBERRY, THOMAS V. BRUCE, WARDEN ET AL.
> The motion of petitioner for leave to proceed *in forma pauperis* is denied, and the petition for a writ of certiorari is dismissed. See Rule 39.8. As the petitioner has repeatedly abused this Court's process, the Clerk is directed not to accept any further petitions in noncriminal matters from petitioner unless the docketing fee required by Rule 38(a) is paid and the petition is submitted in compliance with Rule 33.1. See *Martin v. District of Columbia Court of Appeals*, 506 U.S. 1 (1992) (*per curiam*). Justice Stevens dissents. See *id.*, at 4, and cases cited therein.[67]

When the Supreme Court previously issued a similar order in *In re McDonald* (1989), Stevens was among four dissenters in what Justice Brennan's dissenting opinion called "the first such act in its almost two-hundred-year history [in which] the Court today bars its doors to a litigant prospectively."[68] By the time that the Court issued a similar order in *In re Sindram* (1991), Brennan had retired, so only Justices Marshall, Blackmun, and Stevens dissented from the decision. Four months later, these same three justices dissented against the Court's decision to amend Rule 39 in order to purportedly protect the institution against "those who would abuse the integrity of our process by frivolous filings."[69] The amended Rule 39.8 permitted the Court to deny a motion for leave to proceed *in forma pauperis* when a petition is found to be "frivolous or malicious."[70] Litigants who proceed *in forma pauperis* are those granted permission by a court to file and pursue their claims without paying court fees. Because the rule only applied to petitioners—such as prisoners—who are too poor to pay the $300 filing fee, Justice Marshall's dissent complained that "This Court once had a great tradition: 'All men and women are entitled to their day in Court.' That guarantee has now been conditioned on monetary worth. It now will read: 'All men and women are entitled to their day in Court only if they have the means and the money.'"[71]

Justice Stevens also filed a dissenting opinion against the rule change. He presented a strong, clear statement in opposition to the Court's action that limited access to the courts for certain poor litigants:

> I have not detected any significant burden on the Court, or threat to the integrity of its processes by the filing of frivolous petitions. . . . Transcending the clerical interest that supports the Rule is the symbolic interest in preserving equal access to the Court for both the rich and the poor. I believe the Court makes a serious mistake when it discounts the importance of that interest.[72]

Thus Stevens was concerned not only about the human consequences of shutting out litigants who may have valid claims, but also about how the image of courts would suffer. In effect, the rule blocked selected individuals' access to the branch of government responsible for ensuring, as the words engraved in marble above the Supreme Court's own entry doors say, "Equal Justice Under Law." Unlike several other justices, Stevens did not treat efficiency and court administration as paramount priorities when considering criminal justice-related claims about rights violations.

Later that same year, when the Court applied the new Rule 39.8 to bar petitions from two petitioners in *Zatko v. California* (1991), Thurgood Marshall had retired and been replaced by Clarence Thomas. Thus Justices Stevens and Blackmun were the only dissenters. In his dissenting opinion, Stevens criticized his colleagues by saying, "Although the Court may have intended to send a message about the need for the orderly administration of justice and respect for the judicial process, the message that it actually conveys is that the Court does not have an overriding concern about equal access to justice for the rich and the poor."[73]

As indicated by the aforementioned Supreme Court order in *Woodberry v. Bruce* (2007), retirements on the Court left Stevens as the only remaining member from the original four-justice group that consistently dissented against such bars to petitions beginning in 1989. Justice Stevens remained consistent in his opposition to such orders as an enduring reflection of the lesson he learned from Sherman Skolnick's efforts to call attention to improper behavior by Illinois Supreme Court justices in 1969.

In the aftermath of Stevens's retirement in 2010, the Court contained four Democratic appointees who were often labeled as the Court's liberals. President Bill Clinton's two appointees, Justice Ginsburg and Justice Breyer, had both served with Stevens for more than fifteen years but they did not join him in consistently objecting to these orders by the Court. The two new appointees by Democratic President Barack Obama, Justice Sotomayor and Justice Kagan, immediately demonstrated liberal voting records and an inclination to protect rights in criminal justice. Yet, they, too, declined to assume the role of Stevens in speaking out against orders that effectively excluded specific incarcerated litigants. For example, on November 4, 2013, the Court issued orders in a variety of cases, including *Robinson v. United States*[74] and *Jeffus v. United States*.[75] In both of these cases, the Court declined to accept the cases for hearing, denied the requests to waive filing fees, and, in addition, announced: "As the petitioner has repeatedly abused this Court's process, the Clerk is directed not to accept any further petitions in noncriminal matters from petitioner unless the docketing fee required by Rule 38(a) is paid."[76] Unlike when Stevens served on the Court, not a single justice dissented from these orders. Unless a future justice emerges to reactivate Stevens's role, the justices' uniform silence in the face of the closing of the courthouse door may indicate that such orders have become routine and universally accepted by both conservatives and liberals. If the retirement of Stevens ultimately represents the final loss of a voice on the Court against such orders, idealistic conceptions of access to the courts will have no visible defenders on the high court. Moreover, specific individuals may experience unremedied rights violations through the exclusion of potentially valid claims.

THE LONE DISSENTER IN PRO-RIGHTS CASES

A particularly striking way to illuminate Stevens's unique role as the foremost advocate of prisoners' rights is to examine situations in which the Court favored prisoners' arguments, yet Stevens was the lone dissenter because he concluded that the Court did not go far enough in protecting prisoners' rights. One might expect a consistent advocate of prisoners' rights to accept and appreciate those moments when a majority of justices recognized and protected constitutional rights of convicted offenders. After all, in the controversial realm of prisoners' rights, even incremental steps toward strengthening constitutional protections could be seen as deserving endorsement and support for potentially laying the groundwork toward broader protections. However, Stevens showed a willingness to push for his broader vision of the Constitution's protections for prisoners, even when that push required him to criticize decisions in which prisoners' advocates had won victories in the Supreme Court.

As mentioned at the beginning of the chapter, the second prisoners' rights opinion that Stevens wrote at the beginning of his Supreme Court career was a key example of his uniquely protective advocacy for prisoners' rights. In *Estelle v. Gamble* (1976), the justices agreed that prisoners possess a limited right to medical care as a component of the Eighth Amendment protection against cruel and unusual punishments. The case had historical importance because it was the first Supreme Court decision to apply the Eighth Amendment to conditions of confinement in prisons. According to Malcolm Feeley and Edward Rubin, at that moment in history the case "can be regarded as a *sotto voce* signal to the lower courts that they could continue on their course" of reforming prison conditions nationwide through remedial judicial orders produced by constitutional litigation.[77] A Stevens-authored majority opinion two years later in *Hutto v. Finney* (1978) explicitly confirmed the Supreme

Court's endorsement of lower court orders to remedy unconstitutional conditions confinement in prisons. That case concerned the horrific living conditions and inadequate nutrition inside overcrowded punishment cells in an Arkansas prison.

According to Mark Tushnet's examination of the Thurgood Marshall Papers in the Library of Congress, when Marshall was assigned to write the majority opinion in *Estelle*, he "got annoyed at a flurry of memoranda from his colleagues insisting on limiting the right [to medical care for prisoners] fairly severely."[78] Justice Marshall endeavored to produce an opinion that would satisfy as many colleagues as possible without, in his words, "abandoning my position in toto."[79] By accommodating suggestions from colleagues, Marshall was able to win the support of Justices Rehnquist and Powell, two colleagues who initially planned to dissent from the decision. Marshall's majority opinion ultimately established a limited right to medical care for prisoners, defined merely as a right to be protected against officials' "deliberate indifference to serious medical needs."[80]

As the lone dissenter, Stevens complained that "by its repeated references to 'deliberate indifference' and the 'intentional' denial of adequate medical care, I believe the Court improperly attaches significance to the subjective motivation of the [corrections official] as a criterion for determining whether cruel and unusual punishment has been inflicted."[81] In Stevens's view, rights violations should be identified by examining the specific conditions and practices that were alleged to be "cruel and unusual" rather than seeking evidence about "the motivation of the individual" responsible for the conditions and practices.[82] Thus he believed that an improper deprivation of medical care should be judged objectively by the nature of the prisoner's need and the nature of the care provided. He was deeply skeptical of the majority's approach of having the violation of a constitutional right depend not on the nature of the medical care provided, but on the thoughts and motives of corrections officials. Under such an approach, two similarly situated prisoners who are denied treatment for the same serious medical condition could be judged differently with respect to fulfillment of the constitutional right. According to the majority's analysis, a conclusion about whether a rights violation occurred would depend on whether a deprivation of care was caused by a corrections official's evident lack of concern and action. The identical deprivation of care for another prisoner would apparently be perfectly acceptable if a corrections official claimed that she wanted to help the prisoner but lacked the funds to do so. Justice Stevens concluded his dissenting opinion with a historical reference to horrific conditions of confinement in a notorious Civil War-era prisoner of war camp where thousands of Union troops died from malnutrition and disease: "Whether the conditions at Andersonville were the product of design, negligence, or mere poverty, they were cruel and inhuman."[83] In other words, the conditions at the prison camp, like the medical care needs and treatment of contemporary incarcerated offenders, should be judged by their adequacy and appropriateness and not evaluated solely on the intentions of officials who made decisions about the policies and practices that created those conditions.

The fears that Justice Stevens expressed in his 1976 dissenting opinion about the consequences of linking a subjective-intent test to the identification of Eighth Amendment medical care violations were later validated. In *Wilson v. Seiter* (1991), Justice Scalia seized Marshall's *Estelle* formulation that was narrowly applied to medical care and expanded the subjective test to all conditions-of-confinement claims alleging any Eighth Amendment violations. Justice Scalia's majority opinion ignored the Court's prior decisions on conditions of confinement for general living conditions in prisons, including the Stevens-authored majority opinion in *Hutto v. Finney* (1978), that used an objective assessment to identify Eighth Amendment violations. Instead, Scalia relied on the Court's Eighth Amendment precedents focusing on the specific conditions of medical care (*Estelle v. Gamble*, 1976) and use of force to quell a disturbance (*Whitley v. Albers*, 1986) to claim that these narrow precedents employing subjective-intent tests should actually govern *all* Eighth Amendment evaluations of general living conditions.[84]

Echoing Stevens's earlier warning in *Estelle v. Gamble*, Justice White, joined by Justices Marshall, Blackmun, and Stevens, complained in *Wilson* about Scalia's approach by saying, "It leaves open the possibility, for example, that prison officials will be able to defeat a [constitutional rights lawsuit] challenging inhumane prison conditions simply by showing that the conditions are caused by insufficient funding from the state legislature, rather than by any deliberate indifference on the part of prison officials."[85] White also noted that "[i]nhumane prison conditions are often the result of cumulative actions and inactions, by numerous officials" which makes it impossible to evaluate how subjective intent produced inhumane conditions of confinement.[86] When Justices White, Marshall, and Blackmun protested against Scalia's application of the subjective intent test to Eighth Amendment claims concerning general living conditions in prisons, they were belatedly adopting the concerns raised solely by Stevens fifteen years earlier in *Estelle v. Gamble*.

Another striking example of Stevens's unique outspokenness on behalf of prisoners' rights arose in *Johnson v. California* (2005). The Supreme Court was presented with a challenge to California's practice of enforcing strict racial segregation in cells in the prison system's processing center. For up to sixty days, new prisoners entering the system and prisoners being transferred between institutions were held in double cells with prisoners who shared their racial or ethnic classification. The segregation was not based on general classifications such as Asian-Americans and Latinos. The ethnic segregation was so strict that, for example, it housed Japanese-American prisoners with other Japanese-American prisoners and Chinese-American prisoners with other Chinese-American prisoners. California claimed strict racial and ethnic segregation in cells was necessary to prevent violence between members of race-based gangs, even though officials simultaneously permitted these prisoners to mix together with those from other ethnic and racial groups during the day outside of the segregated double cells in which they slept at night.

When faced with an equal protection challenge to these cell segregation practices, California argued that the Supreme Court should not apply the "strict scrutiny" test that is usually applicable in racial discrimination cases under the Fourteenth Amendment's Equal Protection Clause. That test would have required California to demonstrate a "compelling" need to engage in segregation and governments rarely can prevail when required to meet that standard to justify differential treatment by race or ethnicity. Instead, California wanted the Court to apply the deferential "rational basis" test from *Turner v. Safley* because, in its view, this was a special corrections context in which prison security concerns should have precedence over prisoners' rights claims. As a practical matter, California may also have been concerned about the difficulty they would face in showing a compelling justification for racial segregation under strict scrutiny analysis because the other forty-nine states managed to run their prison processing centers without engaging in such race-based separation in living quarters. Ultimately, in the Court's majority opinion, Justice O'Connor, the creator of the *Turner* test, rejected California's arguments and remanded the case with instructions to apply the "strict scrutiny" test.

The three dissenters in the case were Justices Thomas, Scalia, and Stevens. In the context of a prisoners' rights case, this is an odd combination of dissenters because Stevens was the Court's foremost advocate of prisoners' rights while Scalia and Thomas consistently advocated the diminution and, indeed, elimination of most prisoners' rights. Because of their claimed philosophical deference to other branches of government as well as their originalist approach to constitutional interpretation, Thomas and Scalia argued, for example, that the framers of the Constitution "simply did not conceive of the Eighth Amendment as protecting inmates from harsh treatment."[87] Indeed, the only right for prisoners that Thomas and Scalia explicitly endorsed appeared to be a very limited right of access to the courts that merely forbade prison officials from blocking access to a mailbox where prisoners could place letters that they wished to mail to a courthouse.[88]

Of course, the fact that these three justices were the dissenters in *Johnson* did not mean that they agreed on the outcome of the case. Justice Thomas's dissenting opinion, joined by Scalia, endorsed California's argument and advocated the application of *Turner* and its deferential "rational basis" test to the issue of racial segregation in prison processing centers. The opinion argued in favor of deferring to corrections' official judgment about the need for segregation and warned of the threat of violence from race-based gangs in prisons.

By contrast, Stevens dissented separately and alone because he concluded that Justice O'Connor's majority opinion did not go far enough to protect prisoners' rights against racial segregation. Stevens agreed with the majority that the "strict scrutiny" test should apply, but he wanted the Court to go even further by immediately declaring that California had committed an Equal Protection violation. Thus he objected to the order by O'Connor and the majority that the case be remanded to the lower courts for further consideration of how the cell segregation practices should be evaluated under the "strict scrutiny" test. Justice Stevens noted "the inherent indignity of segregation and its shameful historical connotations" and indicated that he found it "distressin[g]" that California had never experimented with race-neutral methods of addressing the perceived risks of prison gang problems in processing centers.[89] In his view, "[t]he California Department of Corrections (CDC) has had ample opportunity to justify its policy during the course of this litigation, but has utterly failed to do so whether judged under strict scrutiny or the more deferential standard set out in *Turner v. Safley*."[90] In evaluating the anecdotal testimony of prison officials about their perceptions concerning a need to divide prisoners by race and ethnicity, Stevens declared, "this comment supports the suspicion that the policy is based on racial stereotypes and outmoded fears about the dangers of racial integration. This Court should give no credence to such cynical, reflexive conclusions about race."[91]

As indicated by the dates of decision evident in the examples of *Estelle v. Gamble* (1976) and *Johnson v. California* (2005), Stevens was uniquely outspoken on prisoners' rights issues from the very beginning of his career through his final terms prior to his retirement in 2010. In *Estelle*, the nation's highest court gave its first endorsement to the recognition of a limited right to medical care for prisoners under the Eighth Amendment. In *Johnson*, the Court rejected the expansion of the deferential *Turner* standard into Equal Protection Clause racial discrimination cases in prisons. Yet, in both cases Stevens dissented because the Court did not go far enough to protect prisoners' constitutional rights. Justice Stevens's opinions in these cases, as well as the cases on prisoners' rights decided in the years between these bookend moments of his career, helped to establish and consistently reaffirm his continuous role as a leading advocate for prisoners' rights.

THE FOREMOST ADVOCATE OF PRISONERS' RIGHTS

Within months after his appointment to the Supreme Court, Justice Stevens produced outspoken opinions advocating broad protections for incarcerated criminal offenders. As described in this chapter, Stevens asserted himself through his dissent on behalf of prisoners' retained liberty interests in *Meachum v. Fano* (1976) and his prescient objection to using a subjective-intent standard to limit the recognition of Eighth Amendment violations in *Estelle v. Gamble* (1976). These opinions provide especially strong evidence that Stevens arrived at the Supreme Court with a well-formed judicial philosophy, partly born of his prior experiences with prisoners' issues when he was a lawyer and a judge on the court of appeals. In this legal realm, his opinions concerning the importance of constitutional rights in the context of corrections reflected the emphasis on the concept of liberty that was a core element of his judicial philosophy.

As subsequent chapters will describe, Stevens's role for many criminal justice issues was as an advocate for the maintenance and strengthening of precedents established by the Warren Court prior to Stevens's appointment early in the Burger Court era. By contrast, Stevens was already on the Court for several of its most far-reaching, rights-protective decisions concerning prisoners' rights. These included rights concerning medical care and constitutional conditions of confinement (*Estelle v. Gamble*, 1976), access to legal research materials (*Bounds v. Smith*, 1977), and remedial judicial orders (*Hutto v. Finney*, 1978). Thus, when Stevens sought to preserve and expand the protections from these cases, he spoke out on behalf of precedents whose original formulations included his input.

Justice Stevens's opinion in *Hutto* was one of only a few opportunities that he enjoyed for writing majority opinions in prisoners' rights cases. During Stevens's tenure on the Supreme Court, in John Fliter's characterization, the high court moved from a "mixed record on prisoners' rights"[92] during the Burger Court era to, during the Rehnquist Court era, "only a handful of decisions . . . that favored the claims of the individual prisoner, and most of these were decided on narrow grounds."[93] Overall, political pressure, legislative action, and Supreme Court decisions during these eras moved in the direction of narrower definitions of prisoners' legal protections and increased judicial deference to corrections officials.[94] Because the Court's decision making tended to move away from the protection of broad rights for prisoners, Stevens frequently disagreed with the majority of his colleagues. Thus he wrote notable dissents against many of the most significant decisions that diminished prisoners' rights, mandated deference to corrections officials, and limited the remedial authority of federal judges in corrections law cases.

Ultimately, Stevens may stand out in history as the Court's foremost advocate of prisoners' rights. For example, as materials in the Blackmun Papers at the Library of Congress indicate, Stevens was quite willing to follow Brennan's suggestion to sharpen his criticism of O'Connor's rights-diminishing majority opinion in *Turner v. Safley*. Moreover, his uncompromising advocacy for prisoners' rights apparently prevented him from accommodating Stewart in order to retain majority support in *Houchins v. KQED*. In the 1970s, Stevens was able to contribute to seminal, rights-protecting decisions prior to the curtailment of judicial supervision and reform of prison operations. His continuing presence on the Court as it refined and narrowed prisoners' rights in the 1980s and thereafter gave him a platform to raise objections against the specific decisions that ultimately made it much more difficult for prisoners to succeed in strengthening and gaining judicial protection for constitutional rights. With the exception of the rare later case based on prison conditions starkly out of step with national standards, such as the Supreme Court's decision concerning medical and mental health care in California's significantly overcrowded prisons in *Brown v. Plata* (2011),[95] the era of prison reform litigation and the development of prisoners' rights appears to be over. Thus it seems unlikely that another Supreme Court justice will have the opportunity to address the range of issues decided during Stevens's long career and thereby match his unique historic role as an especially strong advocate for rights in the context of corrections.

NOTES

1. *Meachum v. Fano*, 427 U.S. 215, 224 (1976).
2. *Meachum v. Fano*, 427 U.S. at 229 (Stevens, J., dissenting).
3. Ibid., 233 (Stevens, J., dissenting).
4. Ibid.
5. Ibid.
6. *Mathews v. Lucas*, 427 U.S. 495, 516 (1976) (Stevens, J., dissenting).
7. Robert Judd Sickels, *John Paul Stevens and the Constitution* (University Park, PA: Pennsylvania State University Press, 1988), 1.
8. Bradley C. Canon, "Justice John Paul Stevens: The Lone Ranger in a Black Robe," in *The Burger Court: Political and Judicial Profiles*, eds. Charles M. Lamb and Stephen C. Halpern (Urbana, IL: University of Illinois Press, 1991), 370–71.
9. Christopher E. Smith and Anne Corbin, "The Rehnquist Court and Corrections Law: An Empirical Assessment," *Criminal Justice Studies* 21 (2008): 186.
10. Ibid.
11. *Meachum v. Fano*, 417 U.S. 215, 230 (1976) (Stevens, J., dissenting).
12. Ibid., 235.
13. Ibid.
14. Ibid., 233.
15. Malcolm M. Feeley, and Edward L. Rubin, *Judicial Policy Making and the Modern State: How the Courts Reformed America's Prisons* (New York: Cambridge University Press, 1998), 166–70.
16. Ibid., 39–46.
17. *Hutto v. Finney*, 637 U.S. 678, 682-84 (1978).
18. *Meachum v. Fano*, 417 U.S. at 233 (Stevens, J., dissenting).
19. *Hutto v. Finney*, 637 U.S. at 710 (Rehnquist, J., dissenting).
20. Justice William Brennan's copy of Chief Justice Warren Burger's assignment sheets, December 10, 1977, Box I: 449, William J. Brennan Papers, Manuscript Division, Library of Congress, Washington, D.C. [accessed July 2, 2015 from website of Professor Paul Wahlbeck, George Washington University, http://home.gwu.edu/~wahlbeck/Personal_Homepage/Home.html].

21. Justice John Paul Stevens's First Draft of Majority opinion in *Houchins v. KQED, Inc.*, 438 U.S. 1 (1978), March 15, 1978, Box 266, Harry A. Blackmun Papers, Manuscript Division, Library of Congress, Washington, D.C.

22. Memo from Justice William Brennan to the Court, March 16, 1978, *Houchins v. KQED, Inc.*, 438 U.S. 1 (1978), Box 266, Harry A. Blackmun Papers, Manuscript Division, Library of Congress, Washington, D.C.

23. Memo from Justice Lewis Powell to the Court, March 23, 1978, *Houchins v. KQED, Inc.*, 438 U.S. 1 (1978), Box 266, Harry A. Blackmun Papers, Manuscript Division, Library of Congress, Washington, D.C.

24. Memo from Chief Justice Warren Burger to the Court, March 28, 1978, *Houchins v. KQED, Inc.*, 438 U.S. 1 (1978), Box 266, Harry A. Blackmun Papers, Manuscript Division, Library of Congress, Washington, D.C.

25. Memo from Justice Potter Stewart to the Court, April 24, 1978, *Houchins v. KQED, Inc.*, 438 U.S. 1 (1978), Box 266, Harry A. Blackmun Papers, Manuscript Division, Library of Congress, Washington, D.C.

26. Jeffrey Rosen, "The Dissenter" *New York Times Magazine*, September 23, 2007, 53.

27. Memo from Chief Justice Warren Burger to the Court, April 25, 1978, *Houchins v. KQED, Inc.*, 438 U.S. 1 (1978), Box 266, Harry A. Blackmun Papers, Manuscript Division, Library of Congress, Washington, D.C.

28. Memo from Justice Byron White to the Court, June 12, 1978, *Houchins v. KQED, Inc.*, 438 U.S. 1 (1978), Box 266, Harry A. Blackmun Papers, Manuscript Division, Library of Congress, Washington, D.C.

29. Memo from Justice John Paul Stevens to the Court, June 22, 1978, *Houchins v. KQED, Inc.*, 438 U.S. 1 (1978), Box 266, Harry A. Blackmun Papers, Manuscript Division, Library of Congress, Washington, D.C.

30. Audio Recording of Supreme Court opinions announcements, *Houchins v. KQED, Inc.*, 438 U.S. 1 (1978), on June 26, 1978, OYEZ website, accessed on July 2, 2015, http://www.oyez.org/cases/1970-1979/1977/1977_76_1310.

31. *Houchins v. KQED, Inc.*, 438 U.S. at 36 (Stevens, J., dissenting).

32. Ibid., 37 (Stevens, J., dissenting).

33. Ira P. Robbins, "The Cry of *Wolfish* in the Federal Courts: The Future of Federal Judicial Intervention in Prison Administration," *Journal of Criminal Law and Criminology* 71 (1980): 211–25; Christopher E. Smith, "The Governance of Corrections: Implications of the Changing Interface of Courts and Corrections," in *Boundary Changes in Criminal Justice Organizations*, ed. Charles M. Friel, Vol. 2 of *CRIMINAL JUSTICE 2000* (Washington, D.C.: National Institute of Justice, 2000), 113–66.

34. *Bell v. Wolfish*, 441 U.S. 520, 590 (1979) (Stevens, J., dissenting).

35. *Bell v. Wolfish*, 441 U.S. at 534.

36. *Bell v. Wolfish*, 441 U.S. at 580 (Stevens, J., dissenting).

37. Ibid., 595 (Stevens, J., dissenting).

38. *Hudson v. Palmer*, 468 U.S. 517, 541-49 (Stevens, J., concurring in part and dissenting in part).

39. Ibid., 542–43 (Stevens, J., concurring in part and dissenting in part).

40. Ibid., 558 (Stevens, J., concurring in part and dissenting in part).

41. *Bonner v. Coughlin*, 517 F.2 1311, 1317 (7th Cir. 1975).

42. *Samson v. California*, 547 U.S. 843, 857 (Stevens, J., dissenting).

43. Memo from Justice William Brennan to Justices Thurgood Marshall, John Paul Stevens, and Harry Blackmun, January 23, 1987, *Turner v. Safley*, 482 U.S. 78 (1987), Box 472, Harry A. Blackmun Papers, Manuscript Division, Library of Congress, Washington, D.C.

44. Memo from law clerk to Justice Harry Blackmun, May 23, 1987, *Turner v. Safley*, 482 U.S. 78 (1987), Box 472, Harry A. Blackmun Papers, Manuscript Division, Library of Congress, Washington, D.C.

45. Ibid.

46. Circulated second draft of Justice John Paul Stevens's opinion concurring in part and dissenting in part, May 26, 1987, *Turner v. Safley*, 482 U.S. 78 (1987), Box 472, Harry A. Blackmun Papers, Manuscript Division, Library of Congress, Washington, D.C.

47. *Turner v. Safley*, 482 U.S. 78, 89 (1987).
48. *Turner v. Safley*, 482 U.S. at 100-1 (Stevens, J., concurring in part and dissenting in part).
49. Antonin Scalia, "Originalism: The Lesser Evil," *University of Cincinnati Law Review* 57 (1986): 849–65.
50. Jennifer Senior, "In Conversation: Antonin Scalia," *New York Magazine*, October 6, 2013, accessed May 19, 2015, http://nymag.com/news/features/antonin-scalia-2013-10/index3.html.
51. Memo from law clerk Beth B. to Justice Harry Blackmun, April 13, 1987, *Turner v. Safley*, 482 U.S. 78 (1987), Box 472, Harry A. Blackmun Papers, Manuscript Division, Library of Congress, Washington, D.C.
52. Memo from Justice Antonin Scalia to the Court, May 14, 1987, *Turner v. Safley*, 482 U.S. 78 (1987), Box 472, Harry A. Blackmun Papers, Manuscript Division, Library of Congress, Washington, D.C.
53. Memo from Justice Byron White to the Court, May 19, 1987, *Turner v. Safley*, 482 U.S. 78 (1987), Box 472, Harry A. Blackmun Papers, Manuscript Division, Library of Congress, Washington, D.C.
54. Conference discussion notes of Justice Harry Blackmun, March 27, 1987, *O'Lone v. Estate of Shabazz*, 482 U.S. 342 (1987), Box 472, Harry A. Blackmun Papers, Manuscript Division, Library of Congress, Washington, D.C.
55. *O'Lone v. Estate of Shabazz*, 482 U.S. 342, 367–68 (1987) (Brennan, J., dissenting).
56. *Shaw v. Murphy*, 532 U.S. 223, 229 (2001).
57. *Thornburgh v. Abbott*, 490 U.S. 401, 429 (1989) (Stevens, J., concurring in part and dissenting in part).
58. *Procunier v. Martinez*, 416 U.S. 396, 413 (1974).
59. *Thornburgh v. Abbott*, 490 U.S. 401, 427 (1989) (Stevens, J., concurring in part and dissenting in part).
60. *Washington v. Harper*, 494 U.S. 210, 237 (1990) (Stevens, J., concurring in part and dissenting in part).
61. Ibid., 249–50 (Stevens, J., concurring in part and dissenting in part).
62. *Beard v. Banks*, 548 U.S. 521, 552–53 (2006) (Stevens, J., dissenting).
63. *Overton v. Bazzetta*, 539 U.S. 126, 138 (2003) (Stevens, J., concurring).
64. Christopher E. Smith, "Examining the Boundaries of *Bounds*: Prison Law Libraries and Access to the Courts," *Howard Law Journal* 30 (1987): 34–36.
65. John Paul Stevens, "Foreword," in Kenneth A. Manaster, *Illinois Justice: The Scandal of 1969 and the Rise of John Paul Stevens* (Chicago: University of Chicago Press, 2001), xi.
66. Ibid.
67. *Woodberry v. Bruce*, 127 S.Ct. 1376 (2007).
68. *In re McDonald*, 489 U.S. 180, 185 (1989) (Brennan, J., dissenting).
69. *In re Amendment to Rule 39*, 500 U.S. 13 (1991).
70. Ibid.
71. Ibid., 15 (Marshall, J., dissenting).
72. Ibid., (Stevens, J., dissenting).
73. *Zatko v. California*, 502 U.S. 16, 19-20 (Stevens, J., dissenting).
74. *Robinson v. United States*, No. 13-6545 (2013).
75. *Jeffus v. United States*, No. 13-6717 (2013).
76. Ibid.
77. Feeley and Rubin, 44.
78. Mark Tushnet, *Making Constitutional Law: Thurgood Marshall and the Supreme Court, 1961–1991* (New York: Oxford University Press, 1997), 64.
79. Ibid, 63.
80. *Estelle v. Gamble*, 429 U.S. 97, 104 (1976).
81. Ibid., 116 (Stevens, J., dissenting).
82. Ibid.
83. Ibid., 117 (Stevens, J. dissenting).

84. Christopher E. Smith, "The Malleability of Constitutional Doctrine and Its Ironic Impact on Prisoners' Rights," *Boston University Public Interest Law Journal* 11 (2001): 84–85.
85. *Wilson v. Seiter*, 501 U.S. 294, 311 (1991) (White, J., concurring in judgment).
86. Ibid., 310 (White, J., concurring in judgment).
87. *Hudson v. McMillian*, 468 U.S. 1, 19 (1992) (Thomas, J., dissenting).
88. Christopher E. Smith and Joyce A. Baugh, *The Real Clarence Thomas: Confirmation Veracity Meets Performance Reality* (New York: Peter Lang, 2000), 98.
89. *Johnson v. California*, 543 U.S. 499, 521 (Stevens, J., dissenting).
90. Ibid., 517 (Stevens, J., dissenting).
91. Ibid., 519 (Stevens, J., dissenting).
92. John A. Fliter, *Prisoners' Rights: The Supreme Court and Evolving Standards of Decency* (Westport, Conn.: Greenwood Press, 2001), 136.
93. Ibid., 184.
94. Smith, "The Governance of Corrections," 159.
95. Margo Schlanger, "*Plata v. Brown* and Realignment: Jails, Prisons, Courts, and Politics," *Harvard Civil Rights-Civil Liberties Law Review* 48 (2013): 174.

Chapter Five

Miranda and Right to Counsel

Throughout his judicial career, Justice Stevens was a strong advocate for the adversary system of justice. He was especially outspoken in emphasizing the importance of the criminal defense attorney's essential role and the value of empowering juries as decision makers. Adversarial elements of the American legal tradition are relevant in the criminal justice process from police officers' interactions with suspects in custody through post-trial sentencing proceedings. Rights under the Fifth and Sixth Amendments serve to limit officials' actions in these stages of the justice process and Stevens's opinions about these rights evinced concerns consistent with the elements of his judicial philosophy. He saw the criminal defense attorney, jury, and other aspects of the adversary system as important mechanisms for advancing fairness and diminishing the risks of undesirable human consequences in criminal cases. As the Court's composition changed, Stevens frequently criticized his colleagues' failure to uphold the ideals of the country's adversarial system and their apparent eagerness to increase the discretionary authority of police and trial judges at the expense of individuals' rights.

As described in chapters 2 and 3, Stevens's personal experience as a lawyer, Supreme Court law clerk, and court of appeals judge made him keenly aware of the risks of abusive police behavior if there were no opportunities for suspects to have counsel present during questioning. As a Supreme Court law clerk in the 1947 Term, he saw several cases of African American teenagers pressured to confess to crimes after hours of incommunicado interrogation. His mentor, Justice Rutledge, objected to police practices in each of these cases.[1] Stevens alluded repeatedly to his unforgettable memory of the Chicago police beating a confession out of Arthur LaFrana, the wrongly convicted man who gained his freedom in the 1950s when Stevens served as his attorney in post-conviction legal processes.[2] In his service on the court of appeals, Stevens had the opportunity to consider *Miranda* and right to counsel issues as a judge.[3] Thus Stevens was well-positioned to bring with him to the Supreme Court already developed views about the importance of constitutional rights protections for criminal suspects and defendants.

In his memoir about the Supreme Court, Stevens characterized Chief Justice Earl Warren's majority opinion in *Miranda* as one of three Warren opinions that "represented giant strides forward on the road to the formation of a more perfect union."[4] The other two cases Stevens cited were the society-altering decisions concerning school desegregation in *Brown v. Board of Education* (1954) and the requirement of fairly drawn legislative districts in *Reynolds v. Sims* (1964). Justice Stevens said of all three that "[e]ach of those opinions was a principled application of constitutional law that correctly rejected earlier precedent."[5] Data from the Supreme Court Judicial Database indicate that Justice Stevens was second only to Justice Thurgood Marshall in his consistent support for assertions of *Miranda* rights by suspects in cases from 1975 through 2010. The protections established by the Warren Court's decision sought to prevent abusive and coercive actions by police during the questioning of suspects as well as to enable the defense attorney to ensure that rights are respected. Justice Marshall supported rights claims in more than 90 percent of the cases that concerned police practices in questioning criminal suspects. Stevens, along with Justice Brennan, were the only other justices to support rights claims in more than 80 percent of such cases.[6]

As this chapter will discuss, although Stevens consistently defended *Miranda* rights, he differed from Marshall in a number of cases concerning right to counsel issues in the later stages of the justice process. Marshall seemed to adhere to a defendant-centered view that led to reflexive support for assertions of the Sixth Amendment right. By contrast, Stevens's lawyer-centered view and case-by-case approach treated attorneys' decisions more respectfully, even at the expense of certain defendants' expectations and interests.

THE IMPORTANCE OF REPRESENTATION BY COUNSEL

Miranda and right to counsel issues related directly to Stevens's emphasis on the importance of the adversary process as a central component of the judicial values evident in his court opinions. A core element of *Miranda* warnings is notice to suspects in custody that they have a right to be represented by counsel during questioning and to have counsel appointed for that purpose if they are too poor to retain their own counsel. Legal scholars often distinguish the Fifth Amendment right to counsel in *Miranda*, designed to help protect the privilege against compelled self-incrimination, from the right to counsel in the Sixth Amendment, which is considered an element of the pretrial and trial stages of the justice process after prosecution has been initiated. However, one underlying function of these distinguishable rights is the same: application of the principles of the adversary system to protect the rights and interests of an individual who is facing the investigatory, accusatory, and prosecutorial powers of the government.

The role of the defense counsel as a key actor in the adversarial system of justice had special importance to Justice Stevens. In the later years of the Rehnquist Court era and early years of the Roberts Court era, he stood out as the foremost advocate of the adversary system, including the right to counsel. Many of his opinions contained strong advocacy for the adversary system and representation by legal counsel. With respect to the Fifth Amendment right to counsel relevant to *Miranda* rights and police questioning, Stevens insisted that "[t]he pretrial right to counsel is not ancillary to, or of lesser importance than, the right to rely on counsel at trial."[7] This protective, expansive conception of right to counsel and its importance at the early stage of custodial questioning by police distinguished Stevens from most of his colleagues on the Court.

During his confirmation hearings before the Senate Judiciary Committee in 1975, Supreme Court nominee Stevens spoke with great clarity about his view of the importance of legal representation in criminal justice cases:

> SENATOR [JOHN] TUNNEY [(D-Calif)]: Do you have anything that you would care to express on the general subject of right to counsel that might help the committee in any future action?
>
> JUDGE STEVENS: Yes. I don't hesitate to say that I think one of the most important aspects of procedural fairness is availability of counsel to the litigant on either side. I could not overemphasize the importance of the lawyer's role in the adversary process and it is unquestionably a matter of major importance in all litigation.[8]

The subsequent judicial opinions written by Stevens reinforced this statement from his confirmation testimony. For example, in *Penson v. Ohio* (1988), a Stevens-authored majority opinion found that a convicted offender had been denied adequate representation when his attorney ignored potentially arguable claims and asserted that there was no basis for an appeal. Justice Stevens wrote that "[i]t bears emphasis that the right to be represented by counsel is among the most fundamental rights. We have long recognized that 'lawyers in criminal courts are necessities, not luxuries.' . . . As a general matter, it is through counsel that all other rights of the accused are protected."[9] He also declared that "[t]he paramount importance of vigorous representation follows from the nature of our adversarial system of justice. This system is premised on the well-tested principle that truth—as well as fairness—is 'best discovered by powerful statements on both sides of the question.'"[10]

As indicated by his words in *Penson*, Stevens strongly advocated fulfillment of the requirements of the nation's adversary system of justice. He was critical of his colleagues when he saw their decisions diminish the elements of the adversary system and permit actions by police and prosecutors in the absence of the defense counsel. In *United States v. Cronic* (1984), a case that established standards for evaluating ineffective assistance of counsel, Stevens wrote,

> An accused's right to be represented by counsel is a fundamental component of our criminal justice system. Lawyers in criminal cases "are necessities, not luxuries." Their presence is essential because they are the means through which the other rights of the person on trial are secured. Without counsel, the right to a trial itself would be "of little avail," as this Court has recognized repeatedly, "Of all the rights that an accused person has, the right to be represented by counsel is by far the most pervasive, for it affects his ability to assert any other rights he may have."[11] [citations omitted]

Outside of the realm of criminal justice, Stevens insisted that representation by counsel was essential elsewhere in the American adversary system of justice. In *Lassiter v. Department of Social Services* (1981), a case concerning an indigent woman seeking a right to representation when fighting the termination of parental rights, Stevens emphatically asserted this view. Stevens characterized representation by counsel as a matter of "fundamental fairness"[12] and as essential to the protection of the "priceless" right to liberty that is safeguarded by the Due Process Clause.[13]

> In my opinion, the reasons supporting the conclusion that the Due Process Clause of the Fourteenth Amendment entitles the defendant in a criminal case to representation by counsel apply with equal force to a case of this kind. The issue is one of fundamental fairness, not of weighing the pecuniary costs against societal benefits. Accordingly, even if the costs to the State were not relatively insignificant, but rather were just as great as the costs of providing prosecutors, judges, and defense counsel to ensure the fairness of criminal proceedings, I would reach the same result in this category of cases. For the value of protecting our liberty from deprivation by the State without due process of law is priceless.[14]

In *Walters v. Radiation Survivors* (1985), he described "the function of the independent lawyer as a guardian of our freedom" in a case about opportunities to retain private counsel in disputes concerning veterans' benefits.[15] He reiterated this point by writing that "the citizen's right to consult with an independent lawyer and to retain a lawyer to speak on his or her behalf is an aspect of liberty that is priceless."[16] By characterizing representation by counsel as a "priceless" aspect of the most fundamental of all rights—liberty, he demonstrated the strength of his belief in the counsel's essential role. Moreover, by linking the right to counsel to a core concept of his judicial philosophy, Stevens highlighted the role of the attorney in the adversary system. In his *Walters* opinion, he used Shakespeare to highlight the necessity of legal counsel. Stevens referred to the source and motives for the famous line from the play *Henry VI, part II* (Act IV), "The first thing we do, let's kill all the lawyers." Stevens emphasized, "As a careful reading of that text will reveal, Shakespeare insightfully realized that disposing of lawyers is a step in the direction of a totalitarian form of government."[17]

As indicated by the foregoing examples, Stevens's strong support for the adversary system of justice and his view of counsel as essential to the protection of individual liberty led him to be an outspoken advocate for the necessity of counsel during police questioning as well as later stages of the pretrial and trial processes in criminal cases.

SUPREME COURT CASES ON *MIRANDA* AND RIGHT TO COUNSEL

As noted in the discussion of his *Miranda*-related decisions as a court of appeals judge on the Seventh Circuit in chapter 3, Stevens sided with the government in specific situations. He did not reflexively support individuals' claims in *Miranda* and right to counsel cases. For example, in *Colorado v. Spring* (1987), Stevens joined a majority opinion that declared, over the dissents of Justices Marshall and Brennan, that no *Miranda* violation occurred when federal agents did not inform a suspect of exactly which crimes would be the subject of questioning when they informed him of his *Miranda* rights. In *Illinois v. Perkins* (1990), Stevens joined a majority opinion that, over the dissent of Justice Marshall, found no *Miranda* violation when an undercover police officer posing as a jail inmate asked questions of a fellow inmate that elicited incriminating responses.

These examples serve as reminders that Justice Stevens was regarded by scholars as a jurist who looked closely at the facts of individual cases in seeking to serve the ends of justice and who thereby earned the label of "pragmatist" rather than ideologue. As described by Ward Farnsworth, "Stevens's judicial style reflect[ed] a preference for complexity, subtlety, and accuracy in individual cases. . . . Stevens is indeed more likely than his colleagues to pore over the facts in the record of the case and tie his proposed resolution to them snugly."[18] Although Stevens was more consistently supportive of *Miranda* claims than any justice other than Thurgood Marshall, his assessment of the facts in a particular case could lead him to endorse actions by the police or the prosecutor. By contrast, Marshall's thoroughgoing skepticism about the risks of abuse by police and unfairness by prosecutors appeared to lead him to almost automatically endorse the claims of individuals for certain criminal justice issues, including *Miranda*, right to counsel, and search and seizure.

Relatively few *Miranda*-related cases during Stevens's career on the Supreme Court produced decisions in support of individuals' claims. During his career, the increasingly conservative Supreme Court produced a prolonged shift toward limiting and modifying the rights-enforcing rules of the Warren Court era. For example, Charles Ogletree complained that "[u]nder Chief Justice Rehnquist, the Court has evinced a deep skepticism about the validity of the *Miranda* decision itself. It has, for example, virtually eliminated the requirement that the *Miranda* waiver be given knowingly and intelligently."[19] Justice Stevens only had one opportunity to use the opinion-assigning authority as senior justice in the majority to assign a justice to write on behalf of the Court in a *Miranda* case (*Missouri v. Seibert,* 2004). He also wrote only one pro-*Miranda* majority opinion, an opinion that was assigned to him by then senior Associate Justice William Brennan (*Arizona v. Roberson*, 1988).

Thus Stevens's legacy for Fifth Amendment *Miranda* cases was based largely on his dissenting opinions that sought to defend these rights during the investigatory phase of criminal cases against the efforts of his conservative colleagues to, in the words of Charles Lamb, "whittle away at it or to construe it narrowly."[20] These dissenting opinions, while not numerous, enabled Stevens to lay out strong arguments that by virtue of publication will remain available to potentially influence and guide future judges and Supreme Court justices.

In *Rhode Island v. Innis* (1980), the Burger Court majority found no *Miranda* violation when, after giving the suspect the required warnings and hearing the suspect request an attorney, an officer commented to another officer that he hoped no children at a nearby school for the disabled would find the gun discarded by a robber and thereby hurt themselves. In response to hearing the officer's comment, the suspect stated that he was willing to show the officers where the gun was hidden. The majority said that *Miranda* issues did not apply because the officer's statement did not constitute interrogation as it was not a question directed at the suspect. In his dissenting opinion, Stevens strongly disagreed because he believed that any statements, whether directed at the suspect or stated between officers in the suspect's presence, "should be considered interrogation . . . [when they] appear designed to elicit a response from anyone who in fact knew where the gun was located."[21] Stevens saw the majority's decision as creating an incentive for police officers to undermine the fundamental purpose of *Miranda* and ignore the requirement that requests for counsel be respected:

> [T]he Court's test creates an incentive for police to ignore a suspect's invocation of his rights in order to make continued attempts to extract information from him. If a suspect does not appear to be susceptible to a particular type of psychological pressure, the police are apparently free to exert that pressure on him despite his request for counsel, so long as they are careful not to punctuate their statements with question marks. . . . The Court thus turns *Miranda*'s unequivocal rule against any interrogation at all into a trap in which unwary suspects may be caught by police deception.[22]

In another example, *Moran v. Burbine* (1986), the majority declined to require police officers to inform a suspect that a specific attorney had already notified the police that he was representing the suspect and wanted to be present for any questioning. Indeed, a police official inaccurately, or possibly dishonestly, told the attorney that the suspect would not be questioned until the following day. Instead, the police read the suspect his *Miranda* rights, obtained his waiver of rights, and proceeded to question him without telling him that he was already represented by an attorney. Justice Stevens wrote a lengthy, indignant dissent that castigated the majority for its disregard of the importance of the adversary system and for its insensitivity to the risks of improper police behavior. Stevens asserted that "[u]ntil today, incommunicado questioning has been viewed with the strictest scrutiny by this Court; today, incommunicado questioning is embraced as a societal goal of the highest order that justifies police deception of the shabbiest kind."[23] Stevens further asserted that "[t]he possible reach of the Court's opinion is stunning. For the majority seems to suggest that police may deny counsel all access to a client who is being held."[24]

Justice Stevens made it very clear that the application of the right to counsel did not hinge on technical distinctions about whether the right exists in some circumstances but not others. To him the right's existence did not depend on whether it falls under the Fifth Amendment, when the attorney has not yet met with the suspect, or falls under the Sixth Amendment, when representation has begun, or falls under the Due Process Clause, when an issue of fundamental fairness arises. As Stevens said in *Oregon v. Elstad* (1985), the right to counsel is of paramount "importance [as] one of the core constitutional rights that protects every American citizen from the kind of tyranny that has flourished in other societies."[25] When criminal suspects were not given access to counsel, Stevens argued for the recognition of a clear rights violation, whether seen as under one provision of the Constitution or another:

> In my view, as a matter of law, the police deception of [the attorney] was tantamount to a deception of [the suspect] himself. It constituted a violation of [the suspect's] right to have an attorney present during questioning that began shortly thereafter. The existence of that right is undisputed. Whether the

> source of that right is the Sixth Amendment, the Fifth Amendment, or a combination of the two is of no special importance, for I do not understand the Court to deny the existence of the right.[26]

Moreover, Stevens advocated, as he said in *Moran v. Burbine* (1986), "the principle that due process requires fairness, integrity, and honor in the operation of the criminal justice system, and in its treatment of the citizen's cardinal constitutional protections."[27] Thus Stevens believed that police actions could violate not only the counsel right in the Fifth Amendment's privilege against compelled self-incrimination and the Sixth Amendment right to counsel, but also the right to due process: "In my judgment, police interference in the attorney-client relationship is the type of governmental misconduct on a matter of central importance to the administration of justice that the Due Process Clause prohibits."[28]

THE PRIMACY OF THE ATTORNEY AND THE INTEGRITY OF THE JUSTICE PROCESS

At the heart of Stevens's outrage about the police deception and exclusion of the defense attorney in *Moran v. Burbine* (1986) was his view of the attorney's important role in the adversary system. Stevens's opinions in the *Miranda* and right to counsel cases did not merely emphasize the protection of rights; they also rested on his determination to fulfill the ideals and functions of the adversary system by respecting the necessity of the defense attorney's presence and participation. As stated by Stevens in his *Moran* dissent:

> This case turns on a proper appraisal of the role of the lawyer in our society. If a lawyer is seen as a nettlesome obstacle to the pursuit of wrongdoers—as in an inquisitorial society—then the Court's decision today makes a good deal of sense. If a lawyer is seen as an aid to the understanding and protection of constitutional rights—as in an accusatorial society—then today's decision makes no sense at all.[29]

As an advocate of *Miranda* rights and right to counsel, this perspective on lawyers distinguished Stevens from the Court's other strongest advocate of his era, Thurgood Marshall. Marshall's perspective appeared to be much more suspect- and defendant-centered and essentially driven by his skepticism about the risks of police abuse and prosecutorial unfairness. Thus one is hard-pressed to find examples of cases in which Marshall did not support the individual's claim of a rights violation for these issues. By contrast, Stevens, although very concerned about the protection of defendant's rights, especially in *Miranda* cases, filtered his view of some right-to-counsel issues through the lens of his idealized aspirations for the important role of attorneys in the adversary system. In many cases, such as *Moran v. Burbine,* this placed

Stevens and Marshall in agreement about the violation of the defendant's rights, whether from merely emphasizing the rights of the individual or the denigration of the lawyer's role in the adversary system. In other cases, however, a difference in emphasis could lead Stevens and Marshall to disagree.

For example, in *McKaskle v. Wiggins* (1984), Stevens supported O'Connor's majority opinion declaring that no right was violated when a judge appointed a standby attorney to support a defendant who had chosen to assert his right to represent himself at trial. By contrast, Marshall joined White's dissenting opinion that supported the defendant's claim that the imposition of a standby defense attorney who injected himself into the proceedings during trial violated the defendant's right to dispense with representation by an attorney. The divergent viewpoints in such cases may rest on Stevens's long-standing belief in—and high expectations for—the professionalism of lawyers. For example, after serving as the very first law clerk for newly appointed Judge Stevens on the Seventh Circuit in 1970, Gary Senner recalled that "one of the things that impressed me then, which I think was evident during his service on the Supreme Court, was his high regard for lawyers and the legal profession."[30]

In cases raising issues about whether an attorney's performance was so deficient as to constitute ineffective assistance of counsel and therefore a violation of the Sixth Amendment right to counsel, Marshall's defendant-centered approach could separate him from Stevens's focus on the need to be respectful of the primacy of the attorney's role and judgments. The two justices were on opposite sides of the precedent-setting decision in *Strickland v. Washington* (1984) in which O'Connor's majority opinion, endorsed by Stevens, articulated difficult-to-prove elements for establishing ineffective assistance of counsel. The standard presented by O'Connor required that defendants prove that their attorneys made such serious errors that the defendants were deprived of a fair trial and reliable result. This standard was criticized as tolerating halfhearted and patently deficient efforts by defense attorneys as judges sought to avoid second-guessing attorneys' strategies.[31] In its most disturbing manifestation, one that required several appellate reviews before it was finally reversed, the standard led Texas judges in *Burdine v. Johnson* (2000) to conclude initially that a defense attorney who fell asleep in court during a death penalty trial did not provide ineffective assistance of counsel. Although sleeping was an obvious error, the defendant could not prove that the attorney was asleep at specific critical moments during the trial that would have made the trial unfair and unreliable. By contrast, Marshall's dissenting opinion in *Strickland* strongly expressed a defendant-centered approach by objecting to the burden of proof imposed on defendants who assert a violation of right to counsel and by viewing more broadly the nature of defendants' right to counsel.

In *Strickland*'s companion case, *United States v. Cronic* (1984), Marshall merely concurred in the judgment and declined to join in Stevens's majority opinion. The Court rejected lower court findings about ineffective assistance of counsel by an inexperienced replacement attorney who was given only twenty-five days to prepare for trial in a mail fraud case that the government had investigated and prepared for more than four years. Marshall agreed that the attorney in this case did not violate the Sixth Amendment right to counsel. However, he was unwilling to join Stevens's majority opinion that generally precluded judges from presuming ineffective assistance of counsel based on the circumstances of a case, such as an attorney's inexperience and relative lack of time to prepare. Presumably, as expressed in the *Strickland* dissent, Marshall's perspective on right to counsel was focused on protecting the defendant from adverse impacts while Stevens favored respecting defense attorneys' judgments about strategy, even when those judgments turned out to provide a less-than-optimal presentation of the defendant's case.

This difference in perspective may also have influenced the disagreements between Stevens and Marshall in *Burger v. Kemp* (1987) and *United States v. Gouveia* (1984). In *Burger*, a majority opinion by Stevens rejected an ineffective assistance of counsel claim based on an alleged conflict of interest when a defendant's attorney assisted his law partner in the representation of a co-defendant in a murder case. Justice Marshall joined Blackmun's dissenting opinion, also joined by Brennan and Powell, which argued for finding a rights violation because the defendants' interests were at odds with respect to the determination of relative culpability for the murder and therefore the joint representation reflected an unacceptable conflict of interest. In *Gouveia*, Stevens and Marshall disagreed about whether the accusatory process that triggers appointment of counsel was initiated in the circumstances of a case. Several prisoners who were to be charged with the murder of a fellow inmate were placed in solitary confinement for a period of eight months without the appointment of defense counsel. In his defendant-centered approach, Marshall was the lone justice to conclude that the circumstances surrounding the lengthy pretrial segregation constituted the beginning of the accusatory process that requires appointment of counsel.

Justices Stevens and Marshall squared off directly in *Perry v. Leeke* (1989). The case concerned the issue of whether a criminal defendant could be forbidden by the trial judge from consulting with his defense attorney when there was a fifteen-minute recess at the conclusion of the defendant's direct testimony and just prior to the start of cross-examination by the prosecutor. The majority opinion by Stevens found no violation of the right to counsel because he placed the highest value on the integrity of the truth-seeking function of the trial process. He emphasized that the need to make sure that the attorney did not coach the defendant-witness outweighed the defendant's claimed right to consult with the attorney during a brief recess. Marshall's dissent, joined by Brennan and Blackmun, strongly disagreed with Stevens's opinion. Marshall objected to the interference with attorney-client communications and rejected the assumption that consultations in this context would adversely affect the truth-seeking process. Marshall's defendant-centered perspective led to strong advocacy for the defendant's right to consult with the attorney without impediments.

Related disagreements between Stevens and Marshall based on this divergence in their perspectives affected cases concerning other trial rights. For example, *Taylor v. Illinois* (1988), a case concerning the Sixth Amendment Compulsory Process Clause, also illuminated the difference between a defendant-centered analysis and one that looks to the integrity of the system or the primacy of the attorney. In an attempted-murder trial, a defense attorney violated court rules by failing to list a witness that he intended to call to the witness stand. After the trial already started and it was too late for the prosecutor to interview the defense witness prior to the presentation of testimony, the defense attorney dishonestly claimed that he had just located the witness. Therefore the attorney said he was not able to give the prosecutor and judge proper notice prior to the trial about the impending testimony. Under questioning from the judge, the surprise witness revealed that the defense attorney had actually contacted him prior to the start of the trial. The trial judge responded to this action by barring any testimony from the surprise witness, despite the fact that the witness's testimony could help support a potential self-defense claim by the defendant. Stevens wrote the majority opinion endorsing the trial judge's punitive action by arguing that:

> [T]he lawyer has—and must have—full authority to manage the conduct of the trial. The adversary process could not function effectively if every tactical decision required client approval. . . . Putting to one side the exceptional cases in which counsel is ineffective, the client must accept the consequences of the lawyer's decision to forgo cross-examination, to decide not to put certain witnesses on the stand, or to decide not to disclose the identity of certain witnesses in advance of trial.[32]

Stevens's majority opinion emphasized the integrity of court rules, the lawyer's role in an adversary system, and the need to rely on attorneys' professional judgments, including those that impose adverse consequences upon the defendant. By contrast, Marshall's defendant-centered approach led him to join Justice Brennan's dissenting opinion that asserted "where a criminal defendant is not personally responsible for the discovery violation, alternative sanctions are not only adequate to correct and deter discovery violations, but are far superior to the arbitrary and disproportionate penalty imposed by the preclusion [of potentially exculpatory evidence]."[33] Brennan's opinion argued that the integrity of the justice process could be adequately protected by granting the prosecution a continuance to prepare for the witness's testimony or informing the jury about the violation of court rules. Moreover, Brennan argued that the attorney who violated the court rule could be punished for his conduct rather than disadvantage the interests of a defendant who did not participate in the misconduct but lost a chance to present a full defense as a result:

> In the absence of any evidence that a defendant played any part in an attorney's willful discovery violation, directly sanctioning the attorney is not only fairer but more effective in deterring violations than excluding defense evidence. . . . The threat of disciplinary proceedings, fines, or imprisonment will likely influence attorney behavior to a far greater extent than the rather indirect penalty threatened by evidentiary exclusion.[34]

Although Stevens and Marshall were the two most accomplished trial attorneys on the Supreme Court during the era in which they served together, their substantial courtroom experience did not lead them to view trial rights in a similar fashion for all situations. As illustrated by the preceding examples, unlike Marshall, Stevens did not adopt a defendant-centered perspective in analyzing all claims related to right to counsel and other trial rights. Marshall's extraordinary level of support for individuals' claims of rights violations concerning counsel and other criminal justice issues, such as his 100 percent support for individuals in one analysis of twenty-five Sixth Amendment cases from 1986 through 1991,[35] invited criticism of his judicial decisions as reflexive or ideological. By contrast, Stevens evinced a mix of priorities and values, depending on the type of case and the specific circumstances of claims regarding representation by counsel.

Although Stevens did not share Marshall's defendant-centered approach across the full range of right to counsel cases, he was still one of the Court's strongest advocates of the Sixth Amendment right. Several cases confronted the justices with the issue of whether the right to counsel was triggered in a specific situation. Justice Stevens generally advocated a broad scope of the right that would encompass more situations than several of his colleagues were willing to recognize. In *Scott v. Illinois* (1979), Stevens was among four dissenters who objected to a Rehnquist-authored majority opinion declaring that counsel was not required in a shoplifting case for which the defendant was not sentenced to serve any time in jail. Justice Stevens joined Brennan's dissenting opinion that emphasized the importance of defense counsel for a fair proceeding as well as the Sixth Amendment's words declaring that the right to counsel and other trial rights must be available "[i]n all criminal prosecutions."[36] In *Alabama v. Shelton* (2002), Stevens was in the five-member majority that forbade the imposition of suspended jail sentences without the offer or provision of counsel for an indigent defendant. Similarly, in *Halbert v. Michigan* (2005), Stevens joined the six-member majority to declare that Michigan must provide counsel for indigent defendants convicted by plea who sought to file an appeal.

Despite endorsing a standard that was deferential to attorneys' decisions in determining the existence of ineffective assistance of counsel, Stevens was willing to identify constitutionally deficient performances by attorneys in specific situations. For example, Stevens wrote the majority opinion in *Padilla v. Kentucky* (2010) declaring that a defendant was deprived of adequate representation by counsel when the defense attorney failed to advise him that his guilty plea would, by virtue of his status as a non-citizen, subject him to deportation. In *Roe v. Flores-Ortega* (2000), Stevens joined the justices who concluded that an attorney must consult with the defendant before deciding not to file an appeal after conviction and, in *Smith v. Robbins* (2000), he dissented against the majority's acceptance of an attorney's summary declaration that no grounds for appeal existed.

As indicated by the foregoing discussion, Stevens can be described as a strong supporter of a broad conception of right to counsel. However, his endorsement of defendants' Sixth Amendment claims concerning defense attorneys' trial performance included consideration of the need to defer to certain decisions by attorneys due to their important role in the adversary process. Thus there could be circumstances in which defendants felt dissatisfied with attorneys' actions but Stevens was unwilling to agree that a constitutional rights violation occurred. By contrast, the pretrial investigatory stages of the criminal justice process that involve the questioning of suspects by police embody a merger of the suspects' interests and the key role of the defense attorney in the adversary system. As a result, Stevens was especially outspoken and consistent in advocating a protective application of the defense attorney's role in Fifth Amendment *Miranda* cases as well as in the Sixth Amendment early stage right-to-counsel cases involving police efforts to question suspects who were already represented by counsel.

RESPONDING TO THE DIMINUTION OF RIGHTS FOR SUSPECTS AND EARLY-STAGE DEFENDANTS

Nearly all of Stevens's opinions on *Miranda* issues were written during the 1980s. This decade included the later years of the Burger Court era and the first years of the Rehnquist Court era when a divided Court struggled with whether and how to limit or refine the Warren Court's rights-protecting decisions. More than twenty years later, at the very end of his career, Stevens asserted himself again to express his strong views on *Miranda* and related right-to-counsel issues.

In 2009, Stevens encountered the Roberts Court majority's aggressive intention to whittle away aspects of rights for criminal suspects and defendants in its decision in *Montejo v. Louisiana*. The path to *Montejo* began with an important precedential opinion by Justice Stevens twenty-three years earlier in *Michigan v. Jackson* (1986). The *Montejo* case concerned the *Miranda*-related aspect of the Sixth Amendment right to counsel when police question suspects who have already been charged with a crime. Justice Stevens was a key figure in writing opinions that sought to defend the original principle protected in his *Michigan v. Jackson* opinion.

In the Michigan case, a murder suspect requested representation by an attorney at his arraignment. A notice of appointment was promptly mailed by the court to an attorney. However, before the attorney received the mailed notice, police officers went to the jail to question the suspect. They informed him of his *Miranda* rights and gained incriminating statements from him during questioning. The Supreme Court faced the question whether the suspect's request for an attorney at the arraignment served to bar the police from initiating questioning outside of the presence of an attorney. Previously, in *Edwards v. Arizona* (1981), the Court had held that police violate the Fifth Amendment privilege against compelled self-incrimination if they re-initiate questioning of a suspect who had previously indicated during questioning that he wanted the appointment and presence of counsel for any communications with the police. The Michigan case considered whether a request for representation by counsel under the Sixth Amendment that is made by a charged defendant at an arraignment has the same preclusive effect on police-initiated-questioning as the Fifth Amendment assertion of right to counsel under *Miranda* by a not-yet-charged suspect during custodial questioning. The counterargument for both contexts focused on the assertion that when suspects voluntarily waive their *Miranda* rights and speak to the police, their incriminating statements can be used against them even if police had initiated questioning while knowing that the suspect had previously requested representation by counsel.

In his majority opinion in *Michigan v. Jackson*, Stevens concluded that "the reasons for prohibiting the interrogation of an uncounseled prisoner who has asked for the help of a lawyer are even stronger after he has been formally charged with an offense than before."[37] Over the objections of three dissenters, Stevens argued that because the arraignment changes the individual from a "suspect" to an "accused," it is important to provide protections against police efforts to elicit information that might have been permissible earlier in the investigatory process. Thus Stevens announced the rule of the case by saying, "We thus hold that, if police initiate interrogation after a defendant's assertion, at an arraignment or similar proceeding, of his right to counsel, any waiver of the defendant's right to counsel for that police-initiated interrogation is invalid."[38] Stevens's opinion reinforced his consistently expressed view that police and prosecutors should not be permitted to find ways to cut defense attorneys out of the justice process. Moreover, in many contexts, he complained about the ethical impropriety and rejection of the ideals of the adversary process that were evident when one side in a legal proceeding seeks information from the opposing party without respecting that party's entitlement to representation by counsel.

In subsequent terms, as the Court majority weakened the application of the rule, Stevens wrote dissenting opinions to defend the principle that he had articulated in *Michigan v. Jackson*. For example, in *Patterson v. Illinois* (1988), Stevens dissented against the majority's approval of the introduction of incriminating statements obtained by police in post-indictment questioning of the defendant outside of the presence of counsel. While the majority concluded the defendant had knowingly and intelligently waived his rights after being given *Miranda* warnings, Stevens, as the strong defender of the adversary process, argued that the actions of police were unethical as well as improper under the Sixth Amendment. As indicated by the words of Stevens's dissent, this situation embodied a merger of his strong concerns about the risks of police abuse and his advocacy for the attorney's essential role in the adversary process:

> The Court should not condone unethical forms of trial preparation by prosecutors or their investigators. In civil litigation it is improper for a lawyer to communicate with his or her adversary's client without either notice to opposing counsel or the permission of the court. An attempt to obtain evidence for use at trial by going behind the back of one's adversary would be not only a serious breach of professional ethics, but also a manifestly unfair form of trial practice. In the criminal context, the same ethical rules apply and, in my opinion, notions of fairness that are at least as demanding should also be enforced.[39]

In *Michigan v. Harvey* (1990), Stevens objected when the majority permitted the use for impeachment purposes of incriminating statements obtained through a post-arraignment police interview with a suspect outside of the presence of defense counsel. The strength of Stevens's opposition to what he viewed as the erosion and "manipulat[ion]" of the *Michigan v. Jackson* principle was evident in his scathing characterization of the majority's reasoning as "nothing more than an argument against the rule of law itself."[40] Drawing upon his long-standing concerns about the risks of deceptive and improper police conduct, Stevens further declared that "[t]he tragedy of today's decision is not merely its denigration of the constitutional right at stake; it also undermines the principle that those who are entrusted with the power of government have the same duty to respect and obey the law as the ordinary citizen."[41]

Justice Stevens again found himself arguing against the Court's diminution of the right to counsel in *McNeil v. Wisconsin* (1991). The majority permitted the police to question a jailed defendant, who was already represented by a public defender on a robbery charge, about other crimes in a different city. When the defendant waived his *Miranda* rights and made incriminating statements, the Court permitted those statements to be used against him. Justice Stevens began his dissenting opinion by forthrightly declaring, "The Court's opinion demeans the importance of right to counsel."[42] He predicted that the Court's decision would give "leeway [to] . . . the police to file charges selectively in order to preserve opportunities for custodial interrogation" for separate offenses, even when "the investigations were concurrent and conducted by overlapping personnel."[43] This sensitivity to the risk of deceptive, manipulative law enforcement practices was reiterated later in the opinion when he chastised the majority for its failure to acknowledge the "danger of 'subtle compulsion.'"[44]

The majority's decision in *McNeil* also elicited a strong statement from Stevens about the importance of counsel in the adversary system that forms the foundation for truth seeking and the protection of rights in American judicial processes. Justice Stevens was very troubled that "the Court's decision is explained by its fear that making counsel available to persons held in custody would 'seriously impede effective law enforcement,'" thereby treating the lawyer as a "nettlesome obstacle to the pursuit of wrongdoers."[45] Stevens complained that the Court's decision "evidences an inability to recognize the difference between an inquisitorial and an adversarial system of justice."[46] What he described as the Court's "preference for an inquisitorial system of justice" clashed directly with Stevens's own steadfast advocacy for the American "tradition" of defense lawyers and the adversary system.[47] According to Stevens,

> Undergirding our entire line of cases requiring the police to follow fair procedures when they interrogate presumptively innocent citizens suspected of criminal wrongdoing is the long-standing recognition that an adversarial system of justice can function effectively only when the adversaries communicate with one another through counsel and when laypersons are protected from overreaching by more experienced and skilled professionals.[48]

He explicitly cited himself in quoting from the identical arguments that he had raised in *Moran v. Burbine* (1986): "If a lawyer is seen as an aid to the understanding and protection of constitutional rights—as in an accusatorial society [i.e., adversarial system]—then today's decision makes no sense at all."[49]

In *Michigan v. Jackson* (1986), Stevens's opinion established important protections against the questioning of charged defendants outside of the presence of counsel and he subsequently defended that principle against the Court's expansion of police authority in *Patterson v. Illinois* (1988), *Michigan v. Harvey* (1990), and *McNeil v. Wisconsin* (1991). Thus Stevens must have been disheartened when, during oral arguments for *Montejo v. Louisia-*

na in 2009, Justice Samuel Alito suggested from the bench that the Court should consider overruling *Michigan v. Jackson*, a possibility that had not been raised or sought by the parties as an issue in the case. This suggestion led to the unusual circumstance of the Court ordering the parties to submit additional post-argument written briefs on the issue of whether Stevens's majority opinion in *Michigan v. Jackson* should be overruled.[50]

The issue divided interested observers and experts as the Obama administration and eleven states advocated overruling *Jackson* while a number of former judges and prosecutors claimed that the *Jackson* holding had provided a workable, bright-line rule to guide police.[51] Some experts argued that "the protection offered by the [C]ourt in Stevens'[s] 1986 opinion [in *Michigan v. Jackson*] is especially important for vulnerable defendants, including the mentally and developmentally disabled, addicts, juveniles, and the poor."[52] Ultimately, the majority opinion in *Montejo* was assigned by Chief Justice Roberts to Scalia, a justice who literally never supported the protection of individuals' rights in any *Miranda*-related cases[53] and who actively advocated abolishing *Miranda* warnings.[54] Justice Scalia wrote for the five-member majority that overruled *Michigan v. Jackson*. References to *Miranda* warnings appeared in the *Montejo* majority opinion as Scalia claimed that *Miranda* warnings alone provide sufficient protection for already-charged defendants who are deciding whether to waive their Sixth Amendment right to counsel during questioning. Justice Stevens vigorously contested this assertion by Scalia. According to Stevens, *Miranda* warnings are adequate for informing an arrested suspect of the right to remain silent, but are inadequate for informing already charged and represented defendants about "the ways in which a lawyer might assist her client during conversations with the police."[55]

Justice Scalia's opinion was pointedly critical of Stevens's majority opinion in *Jackson* as well as Stevens's dissenting opinion in *Montejo*. In the oral announcement of the Court's *Montejo* decision, Scalia was quite harsh in summarizing his criticisms of Stevens's *Jackson* opinion. He said that the Stevens opinion was "poorly reasoned, has created no significant reliance interests and is ultimately unworkable."[56]

Justice Stevens fired back in his dissenting opinion, accusing the majority of "a misinterpretation of *Jackson*'s rationale and a gross undervaluation of the rule of *stare decisis* [concerning adherence to precedents]."[57] He asserted that "*Jackson* protects a fundamental right that the Court now dishonors" and declared that the majority "flagrantly misrepresented *Jackson*'s underlying rationale"[58] in making an "unwarranted" decision to overrule the precedent.[59] He objected to the majority reaching out to overrule *Jackson* without the issue being raised by the parties or any demonstration that the precedent caused problems.[60]

The depth of Stevens's concern about and disagreement with the majority's decision to overrule *Jackson* was especially evident in his decision to dissent orally from the bench when the *Montejo* decision was announced. Justice Stevens stated in interviews that he believed there should be oral dissents each term as a matter of maintaining the Court's practices and illuminating conscientious debate among the justices. This was the view of Justice Harlan and it was passed along to Stevens by Harlan's colleague, Justice Potter Stewart, when Stevens first arrived at the Court.[61] The *Montejo* case was only the twenty-first time in his then-thirty-four-year career on the Supreme Court that Stevens had announced an oral dissent and none of his prior oral dissents had been in *Miranda*-related or right to counsel cases.[62] Presumably, the oral dissent was based on Stevens's strong objections to the proactive overruling of a precedent that he had personally articulated and strongly defended over a period of more than two decades. As Stevens said in response to an interview question about oral dissents, "You may not persuade anyone but you get it off your chest when you feel so strongly about it."[63]

In his written opinion, Stevens raised concerns about how the majority's "decision can only diminish the public's confidence in the reliability and fairness of our system of justice."[64] In his oral dissent, however, he spoke specifically about other undesirable consequences by saying that the Court's "unwise" decision to overrule *Jackson* "can only have an adverse impact on the law enforcement profession and the rule of law itself."[65]

In addition, while the written dissent used only a brief footnote to argue that prosecutors and, by extension, their agents, the police, are ethically obligated through lawyers' rules of professional conduct to refrain from direct contact with defendants who are represented by counsel, the oral dissent emphasized this issue. Justice Stevens's oral dissent, lasting only two minutes and twenty seconds, devoted attention to his view that ethical prosecutors, who constitute the vast majority of prosecutorial officials in the United States according to Stevens, will respect the ethical rules that effectively require them to act in accordance with the now-overruled *Jackson* precedent. Thus, he claimed that it was "only the rare unethical prosecutor whose conduct is endorsed by the Court today" in overruling *Jackson*.[66] Justice Stevens's life experiences, especially his representation of the police-torture victim Arthur LaFrana in Chicago, made him keenly aware of the risks that police and prosecutors will violate rules in their efforts to obtain convictions. Thus, it seemed possible that Stevens was looking for a way to preserve the *Michigan v. Jackson* rule in practice even as it lost its stature as constitutional law. Stevens's oral dissent did not emphasize in an elaborate fashion the risks of deceptive conduct by justice system officials, as he had done in written opinions over the years. Instead, Stevens apparently sought to have his oral pronouncement, with national news media reporters in attendance at the Court, instruct prosecutors about their ethical obligation to, in effect, follow the now-overruled *Jackson* principle unless they wanted to place themselves into the undesirable category he had labeled as "the rare unethical prosecutor."[67] If this was his intended strategy, it was consistent with his response to an interview question about oral dissents: "There is a different audience [than your colleagues]. You do make the point that you think it is a matter of some importance."[68]

For Stevens, the strong advocate of an idealistic conception of the adversarial system of justice, an ethical attorney will not engage in, encourage, or seek benefits from direct communications with an opposing party who is represented by counsel. Thus he hoped to steer prosecutors and their agents, the police, from seeking to talk to and gain a waiver of counsel from defendants in custody who have had attorneys appointed to represent them. When his brief statement concluded by highlighting his assertion that the majority decision "can only have an adverse impact on the law enforcement profession and the rule of law itself,"[69] Stevens was effectively seeking to tell prosecutors that not only will they violate ethics rules if they stop following the *Jackson* principle, they will also fundamentally harm their profession and society itself if they seek to exploit the new opportunity to question defendants outside of the presence of defense counsel. Justice Stevens sought to use the means available to him to reframe the issue as one advancing the professional self-interest of law enforcement officials. He also sought to disseminate his message in a way that might maximize the interest and attention of the news media. However, it seems unlikely that this message or the underlying ethical obligation of prosecutors will guide the actual behavior of police officers who are seeking to solve crimes and gain incriminating statements from criminal suspects. Indeed, it is possible that prosecutors will be quite tempted to turn a blind eye to the ethical concerns highlighted by Stevens and willingly benefit from police officers' *Montejo*-established opportunity to question already charged and represented defendants.

The oral dissent by Stevens appeared to be similar to oral dissents in other cases by Justice Ruth Bader Ginsburg that were characterized as "signifying an increasing frustration"[70] as the conservative majority on the Roberts Court moved the law in new directions. The oral dissent may have reflected Stevens's recognition, as the inevitability of retirement approached, that the *Montejo* decision could be one of his last opportunities to raise his voice against the diminution of *Miranda* rights and the right to counsel.[71] In speaking out on these issues, Stevens fulfilled John Barrett's view that "[a] Supreme Court Justice who chooses to give personal voice [through oral dissents] . . . is engaging in a public-addressing, publicly accountable and thus commendable part of his or her judicial service."[72] Whether or not the content and emphases in his oral dissent are remembered, the fact of his oral dissent was recorded for history as an exclamation point on years of carefully crafted and consistently forceful judicial opinions embodying his exceptional advocacy for *Miranda* and the right to counsel in contexts when police seek to question suspects and defendants.

The following year, his final one on the Court, Stevens had more opportunities to finish his career by defending *Miranda* and the right to counsel. In *Maryland v. Shatzer* (2010), the Court considered when police are permitted to initiate questioning after a suspect has invoked the right to counsel. In *Shatzer*, the majority opinion by Justice Scalia declared that if there is a break of two weeks or longer in a suspect's custody status under *Miranda*, then police are permitted to initiate questioning and seek a waiver of *Miranda* rights because the *Edwards* invocation of counsel should not be regarded as continuing indefinitely. In the actual situation in *Shatzer*, there had been a two-year break between the invocation of *Miranda* rights and the subsequent reinitiation of questioning. Scalia established the two-week rule arbitrarily in order to create a clear rule for police about when they could again ask questions.

Justice Stevens wrote an opinion concurring in judgment because he did not believe that an *Edwards* rights invocation mandated suppression of a subsequent statement when there was a two-year break in custody between the invocation of *Miranda* and the newly initiated questioning, as occurred in *Shatzer*. However, Stevens strongly disagreed with Scalia's relatively brief fourteen-day break-in-custody rule. He saw it as "insufficiently sensitive to the concerns that motivated the *Edwards* line of cases."[73] In Stevens's view, Scalia's rule not only undervalued the coercive pressures of custodial questioning outside of the presence of counsel, it could actually increase coercive pressure:

> A fourteen-day break in custody does not change the fact that custodial interrogation is inherently compelling. It is unlikely to change the fact that a detainee "considers himself unable to deal with the pressures of custodial interrogation without legal assistance." . . . And in some instances, a fourteen-day break in custody may make matters worse "[w]hen a suspect understands his (expressed) wishes to have been ignored" and thus "may well see further objection as futile and confession (true or not) as the only way to end his interrogation."[74]

In a footnote, Stevens also seized the opportunity to reinforce his strong views about the essential role that defense counsel must play in protecting the rights of criminal suspects. He noted that a defense attorney "can curb an officer's overbearing conduct, advise a suspect of his rights, and ensure there is an accurate record of the interrogation."[75] He reiterated his consistent position that "the right to have counsel present at interrogation is indispensable to the protection of the Fifth Amendment privilege [against compelled self-incrimination]."[76]

In 2010, the Court also issued its decision in *Florida v. Powell*, a case that directly addressed the required content of *Miranda* warnings. Justice Ginsburg's majority opinion rejected a defendant's claim that the police officer's statements that "you have a right to talk to a lawyer *before* answering any of our questions" [emphasis supplied] and "you have a right to use any of these rights at any time you want during this interview" did not clearly inform him that he had a right to have counsel *present during* questioning.[77] Ginsburg and the majority found that these statements satisfied the requirements of *Miranda*.

In a dissenting opinion joined, in part, by Justice Breyer, Stevens complained that the "natural reading of the warning . . . is that [the suspect] only had the right to consult with an attorney before the interrogation began."[78] To Stevens, "the warning entirely failed to inform [the suspect] of the separate and distinct right 'to have counsel present during any questioning,'" as required by the original *Miranda* precedent.[79] Therefore, as summarized in the words of Stevens, "this is, I believe, the first time the Court has approved a warning which, if given its natural reading, entirely omitted an essential element of a suspect's rights."[80]

DEFENDER OF RIGHTS

Justice Stevens distinguished himself as one of the Supreme Court's foremost defenders of both *Miranda* rights and certain aspects of the right to counsel. Because of the Court's increasingly conservative composition during the time period in which he served, he necessarily used dissenting opinions to defend the importance of *Miranda* and the right to counsel. Justice Stevens left a legacy of *Miranda*-related opinions containing strongly argued justifications for the protection of criminal suspects and proper respect for the important role of defense attorneys. In light of his special role as the defender of *Miranda* and the right to counsel, the retirement of Stevens cost the nation's highest court its strongest, most articulate voice of the later Rehnquist Court and early Roberts Court eras that defended the adversary system of justice, opposed deceptive practices by police, and demonstrated sensitivity to the vulnerability of suspects in police custody. With respect to this last issue, as Stevens noted in his *Montejo* dissent, the expansion of police officers' opportunities to question suspects and defendants without providing complete and clear *Miranda* warnings was likely to "be confusing to anyone, but would be especially baffling to defendants with mental disabilities and other impairments."[81] This important point clearly reflected the central element of his judicial philosophy that emphasized fairness and the consideration of the human consequences of judicial decisions.

NOTES

1. *Haley v. Ohio*, 332 U.S. 596 (1948); *Lee v. Mississippi*, 332 U.S. 742 (1948); *Taylor v. Alabama*, 335 U.S. 252 (1948).

2. John Paul Stevens, "Random Recollections," Speech at the Nathaniel L. Nathanson Memorial Lecture at the University of San Diego (April 7, 2004), *San Diego Law Review* 42 (2005): 269; Justice John Paul Stevens, interview with author, U.S. Supreme Court, Washington, D.C., July 12, 2006; John Paul Stevens, *Five Chiefs: A Supreme Court Memoir* (Boston: Little, Brown, 2011), 78–80.

3. *United States v. Springer*, 460 F.2d 1344 (7th Cir. 1972); *United States v. Fowler*, 476 F.2d 1091 (7th Cir. 1973); *United States v. Oliver*, 505 F.2d 301 (7th Cir. 1974).

4. Stevens, *Five Chiefs*, 98.

5. Ibid.

6. Christopher E. Smith, "Justice John Paul Stevens: Staunch Defender of *Miranda* Rights," *DePaul Law Review* 60 (2010): 102–5.

7. *Kansas v. Ventris*, 129 S.Ct. 1841, 1848 (2009) (Stevens, J., dissenting).

8. *The Nomination of John Paul Stevens to be Associate Justice of the Supreme Court of the United States: Hearings Before the Senate Committee on the Judiciary, United States Senate*, 94th Congress (1975), 78.

9. *Penson v. Ohio*, 488 U.S. 75, 84 (1988).

10. Ibid. (quoting Irving R. Kaufman, "Does the Judge Have a Right to Qualified Counsel?" *American Bar Association Journal* 61 (1975): 569).

11. *United States v. Cronic*, 466 U.S. 648, 653–54 (1984).

12. *Lassiter v. Department of Social Services*, 452 U.S. 18, 60 (1981) (Stevens, J., dissenting).

13. Ibid.

14. Ibid., 59, 60 (Stevens, J., dissenting).

15. *Walters v. Radiation Survivors*, 473 U.S. 305, 371 (1985) (Stevens, J., dissenting).

16. Ibid.

17. Ibid., 371 fn. 24 (Stevens, J., dissenting).

18. Ward Farnsworth, "Realism, Pragmatism, and John Paul Stevens," in *Rehnquist Justice: Understanding the Court Dynamic*, ed. Earl M. Maltz (Lawrence, Kan.: University Press of Kansas, 2003), 170–71.

19. Charles J. Ogletree, Jr., "The Rehnquist Revolution in Criminal Procedure," in *The Rehnquist Court: Judicial Activism on the Right*, ed. Herman Schwartz (New York: Hill and Wang, 2002), 63.

20. Charles M. Lamb, "Chief Justice Warren E. Burger: A Conservative Chief for Conservative Times," in *The Burger Court: Political and Judicial Profiles*, eds. Charles M. Lamb and Stephen C. Halpern (Urbana, Ill.: University of Illinois Press, 1991), 154.

21. *Rhode Island v. Innis*, 446 U.S. 291, 312 (Stevens, J., dissenting).

22. Ibid., 313–14 (Stevens, J., dissenting).

23. *Moran v. Burbine*, 475 U.S. 412, 438–39 (Stevens, J., dissenting).

24. Ibid., 465 (Stevens, J., dissenting).

25. *Oregon v. Elstad*, 470 U.S. 298, 364-65 (Stevens, J., dissenting).

26. *Moran v. Burbine*, 475 U.S. at 463 (Stevens, J., dissenting).

27. Ibid., 467.

28. Ibid.

29. Ibid., 468.

30. Rosemary Simota Thompson, "Justice John Paul Stevens: Chicago's Native Son," *Chicago Bar Association Record* 24 (September 2010): 34.

31. Stephen B. Bright, "Counsel for the Poor: The Death Sentence Not for the Worst Crime but for Worst Lawyer," *Yale Law Journal* 103 (1994): 1835–83.

32. *Taylor v. Illinois*, 484 U.S. 410, 418 (1988).

33. Ibid., 419 (Brennan, J., dissenting).

34. Ibid., 433.

35. Thomas R. Hensley, Christopher E. Smith, and Joyce A. Baugh, *The Changing Supreme Court: Constitutional Rights and Liberties* (Belmont, Calif.: West/Wadsworth, 1997), 538.
36. *Scott v. Illinois*, 449 U.S. 367, 376 (1979) (Brennan, J., dissenting).
37. *Michigan v. Jackson*, 475 U.S. 625, 631 (1986).
38. Ibid., 636.
39. *Patterson v. Illinois*, 487 U.S. 285, 301 (1988) (Stevens, J., dissenting).
40. *Michigan v. Harvey*, 494 U.S. 344, 369 (1990) (Stevens, J., dissenting).
41. Ibid.
42. *McNeil v. Wisconsin*, 501 U.S. 171, 183 (1991) (Stevens, J., dissenting).
43. Ibid., 187–88.
44. Ibid., 189.
45. Ibid., 188–89.
46. Ibid., 189.
47. Ibid.
48. Ibid., 188.
49. Ibid., 189.
50. Brian Sagona, "Argument Recap: *Montejo v. Louisiana*," SCOTUS blog website, January 14, 2009, accessed July 2, 2015, http://www.scotusblog.com/2009/01/argument-recap-montejo-v-louisiana/.
51. Mark Sherman, "Obama Legal Team Wants to Limit Defendants' Rights," *Chico* (Calif.) *Enterprise-Record*, April 23, 2009, accessed July 2, 2015, http://www.chicoer.com/general-news/20090423/obama-legal-team-wants-to-limit-defendants-rights.
52. Ibid.
53. Smith, "Justice John Paul Stevens: Staunch Defender of *Miranda* Rights," 103.
54. *Dickerson v. United States*, 530 U.S. 428, 444 (2000) (Scalia, J., dissenting).
55. *Montejo v. Louisiana*, 129 S.Ct. at 2100-101 (Stevens, J., dissenting).
56. Audio recording of opinion announcement for *Montejo v. Louisiana*, 129 S.Ct. 2079 (2009), accessed July 2, 2015, http://www.oyez.org/cases/2000-2009/2008/2008_07_1529.
57. *Montejo v. Louisiana*, 129 S.Ct. at 2094 (Stevens, J., dissenting).
58. Ibid., 2096.
59. Ibid., 2101.
60. Ibid., 2094.
61. Justice John Paul Stevens, interview with author, U.S. Supreme Court, Washington, D.C., July 29, 2010; see also Stevens, *Five Chiefs*, 182.
62. Jill Duffy and Elizabeth Lambert, "Dissents from the Bench: A Compilation of Oral Dissents by U.S. Supreme Court Justices," *Law Library Journal* 102 (2010): 26–31.
63. Justice John Paul Stevens, interview with author, U.S. Supreme Court, Washington, D.C., July 29, 2010.
64. *Montejo v. Louisiana*, 129 S.Ct. at 2099 (Stevens, J., dissenting).
65. Audio recording of opinion announcement for *Montejo v. Louisiana*, 129 S.Ct. 2079 (2009), accessed July 2, 2015, http://www.oyez.org/cases/2000-2009/2008/2008_07_1529.
66. Ibid.
67. Ibid.
68. Justice John Paul Stevens, interview with author, U.S. Supreme Court, Washington, D.C., July 29, 2010.
69. Audio recording of opinion announcement for *Montejo v. Louisiana*, 129 S.Ct. 2079 (2009), accessed July 2, 2015, http://www.oyez.org/cases/2000-2009/2008/2008_07_1529.
70. Robert Barnes, "Over Ginsburg's Dissent, Court Limits Bias Suits," *Washington Post*, May 30, 2007, accessed July 2, 2015, http://www.washingtonpost.com/wp-dyn/content/article/2007/05/29/AR2007052900740.html.
71. Adam Liptak, "At 89, Stevens Contemplates the Law, and How to Leave It," *New York Times*, April 4, 2010, accessed May 21, 2015, http://www.nytimes.com/2010/04/04/us/04stevens.html?_r=0.
72. John Q. Barrett, "Opinion-Editorial: Commending Opinion Announcements by Supreme Court Justices," National Public Radio *Talking Justice* blog, June 4, 2007, accessed July 2, 2015, http://www.stjohns.edu/sites/default/files/documents/law/john-q-barrett/070604-comm

ending-opinion-announcements.pdf.

73. *Maryland v. Shatzer*, 130 S.Ct. 1213, 1229 (2010) (Stevens, J., concurring in the judgment).

74. Ibid., 1231.

75. Ibid., 1230.

76. Ibid.

77. *Florida v. Powell*, 130 S.Ct. 1195, 1200 (2010).

78. Ibid., 1211 (Stevens, J., dissenting).

79. Ibid., 1212–13.

80. Ibid., 1210–11.

81. *Montejo v. Louisiana*, 129 S.Ct. at 2100, fn. 8 (Stevens, J., dissenting).

Chapter Six

Trial by Jury

As a staunch defender of the adversarial system, Justice Stevens sought to protect and strengthen the elements of the trial process. In addition to emphasizing the role of lawyers, Stevens expressed strong views on the importance of the jury in fulfilling the ideals of the American criminal justice process. The Sixth Amendment guarantees a right to trial by jury in "all criminal prosecutions." However, Stevens believed that his colleagues improperly diminished this right and undervalued the role of a fairly selected jury in a number of decisions defining both Sixth Amendment rights and the Fourteenth Amendment right to equal protection in jury selection. As described in chapters 2 and 3, Stevens pointed to his years as a trial attorney and, while serving on the Seventh Circuit U.S. Court of Appeals, his brief service as a substitute trial judge in the U.S. district court in Hammond, Indiana, as important experiences that reinforced his faith in the jury process. He brought the memories and values derived from these experiences when he began his service on the Supreme Court.

One element underlying Stevens's support for jury decision making was his skepticism about elected state judges and their susceptibility to political pressure. As Stevens wrote in a tax fraud case, "[H]istory . . . provides powerful support for my view that this Court has not been properly sensitive to the importance of protecting the right to have a jury resolve critical issues of fact when there is a special danger that elected judges may listen to the voice of the voters rather than witnesses."[1] As chapter 8 will discuss with respect to capital punishment, Stevens expressed concern about "the Court's distance from the realities of an elected state trial bench"[2] in considering the jury's proper role in death penalty cases.

In an instructive example that illuminated the strength of his views, Justice Stevens highlighted the importance of the jury's role in *Scott v. Harris*

(2007), a case concerning a civil lawsuit against police officers. In that case, as discussed in chapter 2, Stevens was the lone dissenter who objected to a summary judgment that dismissed a driver's lawsuit against police officers for causing his permanent paralysis by ramming his car when trying to stop him on a roadway. After watching the video from the police cruiser's dash-mounted camera that recorded the driver's failure to stop when the pursuing police car used its lights and siren, the majority of justices concluded that the driver was responsible for his own injuries. Justice Stevens, alone among the justices, was very dismayed that the permanently injured man was denied the opportunity to have a jury decide his lawsuit. The *New York Times* report about the case said, "With understated sarcasm, [Stevens] highlighted the new role his colleagues had taken on. 'Eight jurors of this court,' Justice Stevens said, 'reach a verdict that differs from the views of the judges [in Georgia] . . . who are surely more familiar with the hazards of driving on Georgia roads than we are.'"[3] As Stevens later said in an interview, "To me [*Scott v. Harris* was] one of the worst decisions the Court made—it was 8-to-1—where the police rammed the guy from behind. . . . [The other justices] totally overlooked the fact—what would [a jury] have done if they had expert witnesses and a lawyer explaining what went on there [in the police video of the chase]. You don't know what the jury would have done."[4] Stevens objected so strongly to his colleagues' decision that he announced his dissent orally in Court. As indicated by Stevens's words and his decision to announce an oral dissent, he strongly objected to permitting judges to substitute their judgments for those of citizen-jurors drawn from the community.

THE RIGHT TO TRIAL BY JURY

In his service on the Supreme Court, Justice Stevens established himself as an advocate of an expansive vision of the Sixth Amendment right to trial by jury. Much like *Miranda* and right-to-counsel issues discussed in chapter 5, Stevens emerged as a justice whose protective approach to criminal defendants' jury rights was comparable to that of the Court's most rights-conscious liberal justices, such as Thurgood Marshall.

At the outset of his Supreme Court service, Stevens immediately demonstrated that he had arrived at the high court with an expansive view of the right to trial by jury. In a case that was argued less than five months after Stevens was sworn in as an Associate Justice, Stevens wrote a dissenting opinion, joined by Marshall, Brennan, and Stewart, that strongly asserted the Sixth Amendment right. The case of *Ludwig v. Massachusetts* (1976) represented a challenge to the two-tier court system used in Massachusetts. For certain crimes, the accused was first tried in a lower-level court where no jury trial was available. If convicted, the accused could file a timely appeal and gain a re-trial in front of a jury in a higher trial court. Ludwig claimed that the two-tier system for trials improperly burdened the exercise of the right to trial by jury by imposing extra financial and psychological burdens on defendants who must endure an initial bench trial before gaining a second trial in front of a jury. The Supreme Court majority concluded that the Massachusetts system was permissible because defendants do, indeed, have the opportunity for a jury trial in the second proceeding. Moreover, the majority did not believe that the two-tier system improperly burdened the exercise of the Sixth Amendment right.

In his dissenting opinion, Stevens objected to the burdens imposed on the defendants who were required to go through the initial bench trial. He recognized the practical likelihood that some defendants would not be able to endure the financial and psychological strain of going through a second trial. Therefore, some defendants' convictions would become final before they had any opportunity to have a jury trial. As a result, while the majority regarded the initial bench trial as a meaningless procedural step for defendants who want a jury trial, Stevens characterized the issue in the case much more starkly in light of the human consequences produced by the Massachusetts system. According to Stevens, "[t]he question in this case is whether Massachusetts may convict a defendant of a crime and sentence him to prison for a period of five years without a jury trial."[5]

Justice Stevens criticized the majority for not requiring Massachusetts to demonstrate a legitimate purpose for the two-tier system. In Stevens's analysis, the only plausible reason for the two-tier approach was to discourage jury trials in some cases in which they might otherwise have occurred. Moreover, he saw adverse practical impacts from the system as the judge in the second trial, as well as any jurors with knowledge of the court system, would know that the defendant must have been convicted in the first bench trial in order for the second jury trial to even take place. Thus the two-tier system created a risk of bias that would adversely affect the defendant's entitlement to a presumption of innocence. Justice Stevens concluded his dissenting opinion with a strong statement about the right to trial by jury:

> Unquestionably, in a great majority of proceedings the two-tier system may expedite the disposition of cases and, indeed, may give a defendant two opportunities to establish his innocence. But that fact is of no significance to the individual who wants only one trial and who wants that trial to be conducted before a jury. The Constitution guarantees him that protection; that guarantee is not fulfilled by a State which eventually offers the defendant the kind of trial he is entitled to receive in the first instance. . . . The burden on the right to a jury trial imposed by Massachusetts is especially unacceptable because the Commonwealth has offered no legitimate justification for its *requirement* of a first-tier-nonjury trial.[6] (emphasis in original)

The expansive nature of Stevens's view of the Sixth Amendment right was most evident in *Lewis v. United States* (1996), a case that examined when criminal defendants have a constitutional right to demand a jury trial and when they can be required to have a bench trial. By that time, Stevens's allies in the *Ludwig* case, Justices Marshall, Brennan, and Stewart, had all retired. Thus Stevens stood out, along with Justice Ginsburg, as the foremost defenders of the right to trial by jury.

Lewis was an employee of the U.S. Postal Service who was arrested for opening and stealing the contents of mail. He was charged with two counts of obstructing the mail. Upon conviction, each count carried a maximum sentence of six months of incarceration. Thus, a conviction on both counts and the imposition of the maximum sentence could possibly lead to one year of imprisonment if the sentences were ordered to be served consecutively rather than concurrently. Lewis requested a jury trial but his request was denied by the U.S. magistrate judge presiding over the case. The U.S. magistrate judge told Lewis that because she would not, under any circumstances, sentence him upon conviction to more than six months' imprisonment, he was not entitled to a jury trial. Lewis appealed the denial of a jury trial and lost in the Second Circuit U.S. Court of Appeals before bringing his case to the Supreme Court.

The literal words of the Sixth Amendment say, "In all criminal prosecutions, the accused shall enjoy the right to a speedy and public trial, by an impartial jury."[7] The administrative consequences of following a literal interpretation of the Sixth Amendment loom large, especially in the numerous cases concerning relatively minor criminal charges, and presumably deter judges from following the precise words of the amendment with respect to the jury trial right. Because the Supreme Court incorporated the right to trial by jury and applied the right to the states in *Duncan v. Louisiana* (1968), the costs and consequences for local governments would be significant if every defendant could demand an expensive jury trial. In effect, the justice system faces a difficult question with respect to the Sixth Amendment's actual words: Can local court systems afford the time and expense of jury trials for people accused of minor crimes such as shoplifting or disorderly conduct? As a parallel matter, the Seventh Amendment right to jury trials in civil cases, literally stated as "[i]n suits at common law, where the value in controversy shall exceed twenty dollars,"[8] is one of only a small number of provisions in the Bill of Rights that have never been incorporated and applied to state court systems. Like the Sixth Amendment criminal jury trial right, the Seventh Amendment, by its literal terms, would impose potentially tremendous costs on state and local court systems if it granted a right to jury trials for small claims court cases and other civil disputes over small amounts of money in state courts.

In interpreting the Sixth Amendment, courts did not follow the amendment's literal declaration about an entitlement to jury trials in "all criminal prosecutions." Instead, the right was typically treated as applying only to offenses that were classified as "serious" rather "petty" or to offenses that presented the prospect of imprisonment for more than six months. The traditional definition of a petty offense is one that leads to punishments that do not exceed a sentence of six months of incarceration. Thus the U.S. magistrate judge's promise to Lewis placed his case into both categories that courts had used to deny a right to trial by jury: he was charged with petty offenses and was promised that any term of imprisonment would not exceed six months. Because federal appellate courts had issued conflicting decisions about which criminal charges make a defendant entitled to demand a jury trial, the Supreme Court accepted Lewis's case to clarify the Sixth Amendment right.

Justice O'Connor wrote the opinion for the Court. On behalf of the majority, she declared:

> We conclude that no jury trial right exists where a defendant is prosecuted for multiple petty offenses. The Sixth Amendment guarantee of the right to a jury trial does not extend to petty offenses, and its scope does not change where a defendant faces a potential aggregate prison term in excess of six months for petty offenses charged.[9]

In sum, O'Connor and the majority decided that the right to a jury trial is triggered by the classification of the offense charged and not by the potential aggregate sentence. If, hypothetically, Lewis had stolen twenty pieces of mail and had been convicted of a separate charge for each letter stolen, he could have received a ten-year prison sentence—six months for each offense and an order to serve the sentences consecutively—without having a right to a jury trial under O'Connor's reasoning.

Justice Kennedy, joined by Justice Breyer, wrote an opinion concurring in judgment. Their opinion argued that the right to trial by jury is triggered whenever a defendant faces the possibility of more than six months of incarceration, whether or not the offenses are classified as petty. However, Kennedy and Breyer accepted the U.S. magistrate judge's promise of imposing a sentence of no more than six months as avoiding the right to a jury trial in Lewis's case. Thus they agreed with the outcome of Lewis's case but not the rule produced by the majority opinion. Strong language in Kennedy's concurrence indicated stark disagreement with O'Connor's reasoning on behalf of the majority. Justice Kennedy wrote about what he characterized as "today's unfortunate decision":[10] "The holding in both its doctrinal formulation and in its practical effect is one of the most serious incursions on the right to jury trial in the Court's history, and it cannot be squared with our precedents."[11]

By contrast, Stevens established himself in *Lewis v. United States* as the Rehnquist Court era's foremost advocate of an expansive right to trial by jury. Justice Stevens wrote a dissenting opinion, joined by Justice Ginsburg, which shared Kennedy's perspective on defining the jury trial right by the potential sentence rather than the classification of the offense. Justice Stevens did not argue for a literal application of the Sixth Amendment's words of applying the right to jury trial in "all criminal prosecutions." He said "I do not quarrel with the established view that only defendants whose alleged misconduct is deemed serious by the legislature are entitled to be judged by a jury."[12] However, Stevens argued for a different definition of what constitutes a "serious" offense than that employed by O'Connor, who focused on the possible sentence for a specific crime. Instead, Stevens asserted that "the legislature's determination of the severity of the charges against a defendant is properly measured by the maximum sentence for the prosecution as a whole."[13] Thus Stevens focused on the actual possible sentence for a defendant, such as Lewis, who was prosecuted for multiple petty offenses.

In addition, Stevens distinguished himself from Kennedy, with whom he shared a similar view about looking at the actual possible sentence, by insisting that "the right to jury trial attaches when the prosecution begins,"[14] namely when the prosecutor decides which charges to pursue. Thus, under Stevens's formulation, the right to trial by jury is more expansive because a judge cannot preclude entitlement to a jury as the trial phase of the case approaches by merely promising that any sentence will not exceed six months. Justice Stevens observed that all justices on the Court agreed that, if a defendant is facing serious armed robbery, rape, or other felony charges, "a judge may not strip a defendant of the right to a jury trial for a serious crime by promising a sentence of six months or less."[15] In Stevens's view, the same principle must apply to prevent a judge from denying a defendant the right to trial by jury when there is a prosecution for multiple lesser charges that can lead to an aggregate sentence in excess of six months' imprisonment. As stated by Stevens, "[b]ecause the right attaches at the moment of prosecution, a judge may not deprive a defendant of a jury trial by making a pretrial determination that the crimes charged will not warrant a sentence exceeding six months."[16] As a result, the dissenting opinion by Stevens in the *Lewis* case represented the Court's most expansive viewpoint on when criminal defendants were entitled to a jury trial.

JURY SELECTION

Justice Stevens stood out from other justices in his efforts to combat an aspect of bias in jury selection: the exclusion of jurors due to their race or gender. On the Supreme Court, he continued to object to racial bias in jury selection just as he did in his Seventh Circuit opinion in *United States v. Booker* (1974). Early in Justice Stevens's tenure on the Supreme Court he asserted his concerns about the potential for juries to be infected with bias if jury selection was not conducted properly. In *Rosales-Lopez v. United States* (1981), he wrote a dissent, joined by his most liberal colleagues, Brennan and Marshall, that urged the majority to require trial judges to ask potential jurors about their racial and ethnic biases when a defense attorney requested such an inquiry. In the case, Stevens concluded that:

> [T]he *voir dire* [questioning of prospective jurors] was inadequate as a matter of law because it wholly ignored the risk that the potential jurors in the Southern District of California might be prejudiced against the defendant simply because he is a person of Mexican descent. Because the defendant's lawyer perceived a risk of such irrational prejudice in that District, his request for a specific question concerning it should have been granted.[17]

Such efforts over the years to define law and policy in ways that would combat discrimination led one commentator to summarize Stevens's career by saying that he "emerged as the Court's foremost critic of unequal treatment under the law" after the retirements of Brennan and Marshall in 1990 and 1991 respectively.[18]

The Supreme Court during Stevens's tenure addressed a series of cases that dealt with the issue of discrimination in jury selection beginning with *Batson v. Kentucky* (1986). In *Batson*, Stevens joined the majority opinion that permitted criminal defense attorneys to question prosecutors' actions in using peremptory challenges to exclude potential jurors of a particular race during jury selection. In such cases, defense attorneys are attempting to establish that the prosecutor has engaged in impermissible racial discrimination in jury selection. Peremptory challenges are a limited number of discretionary juror exclusions that attorneys for each side are traditionally able to apply without providing any reason. Peremptory challenges are different from challenges for cause in which an attorney asks a judge to excuse a juror because of a specific indication that the juror possesses a bias.

After *Batson*, defendants no longer needed to establish a pattern of discriminatory exclusions by prosecutors in a series of cases, as required by the prior precedent, *Swain v. Alabama* (1965). Instead, defense attorneys could ask the trial judge to question the prosecutor during a specific trial's jury selection process about whether peremptory challenges were being applied based on the race of potential jurors. The Court had ruled that race-based exclusions of jurors by prosecutors violated the Fourteenth Amendment right to equal protection of the laws. Justice Stevens wrote only a brief concurring opinion to respond to criticism directed at him in Chief Justice Burger's dissenting opinion. Although Stevens did not play a key role in writing opinions in *Batson*, he was a key figure in subsequent cases seeking to strengthen the effort to block discrimination. According to an observation made by Nancy Mardar during the final terms of his career, "As long as *Batson* remains on the books it must retain its integrity, and Justice Stevens has assumed the role of watchdog."[19]

In *Holland v. Illinois* (1990), the Court considered whether the fair cross-section requirement of the Sixth Amendment jury trial right was violated when prosecutors excluded African American prospective jurors in the criminal trial of a white defendant. The majority opinion written by Justice Scalia concluded that there was no Sixth Amendment violation. According to Scalia, the Sixth Amendment requires that the jury pool be drawn from a fair cross-section of the community, but the amendment does not require that the actual trial jury selected from that pool meet any standards of representativeness. Justice Marshall, joined by Justices Brennan and Blackmun, wrote a strident dissent that criticized Scalia's characterization of the limited nature of the fair cross-section requirement under the Sixth Amendment. By contrast, Justice Stevens wrote his own solo dissent in the case.

Justice Stevens argued that a clear Equal Protection Clause violation had been established in the case even though the petitioner had failed to raise an equal protection claim in the U.S. Supreme Court after losing on that issue in the Illinois Supreme Court. Stevens also emphatically rejected the idea that a white defendant did not have standing to challenge the systematic exclusion of African American jurors. According to Stevens, "the suggestion that only defendants of the same race or ethnicity as the excluded jurors can enforce the jurors' right to equal treatment and equal respect recognized in *Batson* is itself inconsistent with the central message of the Equal Protection Clause."[20] Much of the Stevens dissent provided a careful recitation of the history and precedents regarding the fair-cross-section requirement in order to argue that the Sixth Amendment protects against the exclusion of jurors based on their race. In Stevens's view, the Court's ruling in *Taylor v. Louisiana* (1975) that clearly applied the fair-cross-section requirement with respect to the exclusion of women jurors "was novel [but] the constitutional principle vindicated was ancient."[21] As part of his thorough recitation of precedents, Stevens explained:

> Long before *Duncan v. Louisiana* . . . (1968), held that the Sixth Amendment is applicable to the States, it was "part of the established tradition in the use of juries as instruments of public justice that the jury be a body truly representative of the community," *Smith v. Texas* . . . (1940), and exclusion of a cogniz-

> able group from jury service was considered to "contravene[e] the very idea of a jury," *Carter v. Jury Commission of Greene County* . . . (1970).[22]

In sum, Stevens declared that "[t]he fair-cross-section principle is central to our understanding of the Sixth Amendment."[23]

Why did Stevens decline to join Marshall's dissent and instead choose to write his own dissent? Justice Stevens was clearly in agreement with Marshall and, indeed, Marshall's dissent regularly cited the Stevens dissent to reinforce the points that he was making. It is possible that the combative tone of the Marshall opinion, which elicited pointedly sarcastic responses in the Scalia majority opinion, did not appeal to Stevens. For example, Marshall used strong language to express his views, including the following: "To reach this startling result, the majority misrepresents the values underlying the fair-cross-section requirement, overstates the difficulties associated with the elimination of racial discrimination in jury selection, and ignores the clear import of well-grounded precedents."[24] The sarcasm in Justice Scalia's response included a harsh characterization that seemed to point criticism at other opinions by Marshall in addition to the *Holland* dissent. In Scalia's words, "Justice Marshall rolls out the ultimate weapon, the accusation of insensitivity to racial discrimination—which will lose its intimidating effect if it continues to be fired so randomly. It is not remotely true."[25] Perhaps Stevens sought to steer clear of a conflict within these opinions that seemed to express the personal annoyance that Marshall and Scalia felt for each other at times during Marshall's final years on the Court.[26] With a more dispassionate discussion of the precedents and presentation of analysis, the Stevens dissent may have avoided the dismissive treatment that Marshall's dissent attracted in the majority opinion. Whatever the reason, Stevens's decision to write a thorough, separate dissent apparently reflected the importance of the jury selection issue to him and it made Stevens stand out as a strong advocate of eliminating mechanisms for discrimination in jury selection.

As it turned out, the following year in *Powers v. Ohio* (1991), the Supreme Court declared that a defendant can raise an equal protection violation claim when prosecutors exclude jurors of a race different than the defendant's. Justice Stevens joined the seven-justice majority without issuing any separate opinion. In effect, when faced with the precise issue of equal protection rights for jurors who are improperly excluded because of their race, the Court agreed with the conclusion that Stevens had presented the previous year in the *Holland* dissent.

The Supreme Court's next decisions in this series of cases expanded the protections against attorneys' discriminatory uses of peremptory challenges in jury selection. These cases all focused on discriminatory exclusions as violations of potential jurors' equal protection rights and not as violations of a defendant's or litigant's right to trial by jury, as had been debated in the

Holland case. The Court ruled in *Edmonson v. Leesville Concrete Co.* (1991) that race-based exclusions of potential jurors by private attorneys in civil lawsuits violated the Fourteenth Amendment equal protection rights of the excluded individuals. The majority made a similar ruling in *Georgia v. McCollum* (1992) by barring defense attorneys in criminal cases from using race as the basis for excluding potential jurors. In *J. E. B. v. Alabama ex rel. T. B.* (1994), a majority of justices barred the use of gender-based exclusions during jury selection. Because each of these decisions enhanced the protections against discrimination in jury selection, Stevens joined the majority opinions without writing any separate opinions of his own. He obviously agreed that the protection against category-based applications of peremptory challenges should be expanded to additional trial contexts beyond the original *Batson* case that focused solely on prosecutors' use of race in jury selection. However, in cases concerning *how* the courts were to handle instances when discrimination appeared to exist, Stevens spoke up strongly against the majority's weak enforcement of the prohibitions on discriminatory race- and gender-based peremptory challenges.

In *Hernandez v. New York* (1991), a Latino defendant on trial for attempted murder objected to the prosecutors' exclusion of Latino jurors. Under the *Batson* framework, when asked by the judge why the jurors were excluded, the prosecutor said he lacked confidence that these bilingual jurors would be willing to accept the court interpreter's presentation of testimony that had been delivered by witnesses in Spanish rather than use their own Spanish skills to understand that testimony. The potential jurors had hesitated when asked if they could accept and abide by the court interpreter's presentation of the testimony. Thus there would be a purported risk of multiple interpretations of what was said during the trial if all jurors did not uniformly follow the court interpreter's translation. The Supreme Court analyzed whether the prosecutor had presented a race-neutral explanation for excluding these jurors. A majority of justices—four on the plurality opinion and two on a separate concurring opinion—concluded that it was, indeed, race-neutral. According to Justice Kennedy's plurality opinion, the prosecutors' criterion for excluding Spanish-speaking jurors "would include both Latinos and non-Latinos. While the prosecutor's criterion might well result in the disproportionate removal of prospective Latino jurors, that disproportionate impact does not turn the prosecutor's actions into a *per se* violation of the Equal Protection Clause."[27] Justice Kennedy further explained that the determination of a rights violation rests on the intention expressed in the justification for excluding a category of jurors. In Kennedy's words:

> Equal protection analysis turns on the intended consequences of the government classifications. Unless the government actor adopted a criterion with the intent of causing the impact asserted, that impact itself does not violate the

> principle of race neutrality. Nothing in the prosecutor's explanation shows that he chose to exclude jurors who hesitated in answering questions about following the interpreter *because* he wanted to prevent bilingual Latinos from serving on the jury.[28] (emphasis in original)

In a dissenting opinion joined by Marshall and Blackmun, Justice Stevens asserted his disagreement with the Court's weak enforcement of the prohibition on improper discrimination in jury selection. Stevens argued that a challenge to categorical exclusions of jurors should not fail "whenever the prosecutor advances a nonpretextual justification that is not facially discriminatory."[29] Unlike the majority, Stevens was highly conscious of the discriminatory *impact* of categorical exclusions, even in cases without admissions from the prosecutor about a discriminatory purpose. As Stevens observed, "The line between discriminatory purpose and discriminatory impact is neither as bright nor as critical as the Court appears to believe."[30] Thus Stevens criticized the majority for placing its emphasis solely on the prosecutor's subjective intentions as indicated by the prosecutor's explanation for categorical exclusions of jurors through the use of peremptory challenges. His arguments against relying on an official's subjective intentions as the basis for identifying rights violations paralleled the identical argument he made in *Estelle v. Gamble* (1976) and subsequent Eighth Amendment prison cases discussed in Chapter 4. As Stevens explained with respect to jury selection:

> The Court therefore errs in focusing the entire inquiry on the subjective state of mind of the prosecutor. In jury selection challenges, the requisite invidious intent is established once the defendant makes out a prima facie case. . . . By requiring that the prosecutor's explanation itself provide additional, direct evidence of discriminatory motive, the Court has imposed on the defendant the added requirement that he generate evidence of the prosecutor's actual subjective intent to discriminate. Neither *Batson* nor our other equal protection holdings demand such a heightened quantum of proof.[31]

Justice Stevens noted that the "Court overlooks, however, the fact that the 'discriminatory purpose' which characterizes violations of the Equal Protection Clause can sometimes be established by objective evidence that is consistent with a decisionmaker's honest belief that his motive was entirely benign."[32] Thus Stevens's approach took account of the likelihood that prosecutors may not recognize the discriminatory consequences of categorical exclusions that they erroneously believed were race neutral. Although he did not address the issue directly, Stevens's approach also provided better protection against the possibility that a prosecutor may, in fact, manufacture a pretextual excuse for race-based exclusions and fail to honestly reveal the intentions behind the exclusions when asked about them by the judge. After all, would any prosecutors really admit to discriminatory intentions, even when they existed? Yet under the majority's approach, it appeared as if such an unlikely admission might be necessary in order to block discriminatory exclusions.

In looking at the facts in *Hernandez*, Stevens concluded that an "explanation that is 'race neutral' on its face is nonetheless unacceptable if it is merely a proxy for a discriminatory practice."[33] Moreover, Stevens noted that the prosecutor's concerns could have been handled through means other than categorical exclusion of these bilingual jurors. As Stevens said, "the jury could have been instructed that the official translation alone is evidence; bilingual jurors could have been instructed to bring to the attention of the judge any disagreements they might have had with the translation so that any disputes could be resolved by the court."[34] Stevens also argued that if the prosecutor's concerns about possible interpretation problems had been valid and persuasive, then there could have been a request for an exclusion based on a challenge for cause if the judge agreed about the seriousness of the issue. The prosecutor could have attempted to persuade the judge about the indications of bias for each individual bilingual juror rather than simply use a discretionary peremptory challenge to sweep them aside.

The issue of enforcing the prohibition on discriminatory applications of peremptory challenges in jury selection arose more starkly in the case of *Purkett v. Elem* (1995). The Supreme Court decided *Purkett* based on the petition for a writ of certiorari filed by the convicted offender seeking review of his case. Normally, the Court simply denies such petitions when there are not at least four justices who vote to accept the case for hearing. In a very small number of cases, the Court may issue a decision based on the petition and this was one of those atypical cases.

Elem was on trial for second-degree robbery in a Missouri state court. During jury selection, the prosecutor used peremptory challenges to exclude two African American men from the jury. Elem's attorney objected to the apparent effort to exclude jurors of a particular race. In accordance with the Supreme Court's ruling in *Batson v. Kentucky* (1986), the judge asked the prosecutor to explain the basis for the exclusions. The prosecutor explained by saying:

> I struck [juror] number twenty-two because of his long hair. He had long curly hair. He had the longest hair of anybody on the panel by far. He appeared to me to not be a good juror for that fact, the fact that he had long hair hanging down shoulder length, curly, unkempt hair. Also, he had a mustache and a goatee type beard. And juror number twenty-four also had a mustache and goatee type beard. Those are the only two people on the jury . . . with the facial hair. . . . And I don't like the way they looked, with the way the hair is cut, both of them. And the mustaches and the beards look suspicious to me.[35]

Upon hearing the explanation, the trial judge overruled Elem's objection and proceeded with the trial. Elem later appealed the jury selection issue to the Missouri Court of Appeals. The state appellate court determined that the prosecutor's actions were acceptable as a "legitimate 'hunch'" and concluded that these circumstances did not raise an inference of discrimination.[36]

After his unsuccessful appeals in the Missouri court system, Elem filed a habeas corpus petition in the federal courts to pursue his claim of a Sixth Amendment violation in the jury selection process. The U.S. district court denied his claim after concluding that it was obligated to presume that the state courts' finding of no discrimination was correct. On appeal to the Eighth Circuit U.S. Court of Appeals, however, Elem found support when the federal appellate judges concluded that the prosecutor had failed to provide a "plausible race-neutral reason for believing that those factors will somehow affect the person's ability to perform his or her duties as a juror."[37] In other words, the Eighth Circuit panel concluded that because goatee beards and curly, long hair have no bearing on an individual's ability to serve as a juror, the prosecutor's exclusion of these jurors in reliance on that excuse was merely a pretext to avoid revealing that these were race-related exclusions. As indicated by the appellate judges' conclusion, the prosecutor's explanation in Elem's case was strikingly different than the explanation at issue in *Hernandez*. In *Hernandez*, the explanation was plausibly related to the jurors' ability to perform their duties since there was a concern about multiple interpretations of Spanish-language testimony affecting the jurors' understanding of the facts. By contrast, in Elem's case the prosecutor's explanation was based on nothing other than speculative hunches that an individual's facial hair and physical appearance indicated that specific, undesirable aspects existed in that individual's thinking.

The Supreme Court issued a per curiam opinion, supported by seven justices, that reversed the Eighth Circuit decision. In reliance on a concurring opinion by Justice O'Connor in *Hernandez v. New York* (1991), the per curiam opinion declared that when judges inquire about the reasons for peremptory challenges that raise suspicions about racially discriminatory motivations, the inquiry "does not demand an explanation that is persuasive, or even plausible."[38] According to the guidance from O'Connor's *Hernandez* opinion, "[u]nless a discriminatory intent is inherent in the prosecutor's explanation, the reason offered will be deemed race neutral."[39] At that point, the trial judge has the opportunity to decide whether the party challenging the exclusion has proven the existence of purposeful discrimination. However, the judge is not obligated to disbelieve explanations that are unrelated to actual juror qualifications, even if those explanations are silly or superstitious.

Consistent with the previous concerns he expressed about the Court's weak enforcement of the prohibition on race-based discrimination in jury selection, Stevens wrote a dissenting opinion, joined by Justice Breyer, which articulated even graver concerns about the direction in which the Court was moving. Stevens agreed with the court of appeals decision that found a violation of the Equal Protection Clause when the prosecutor failed to provide an explanation for the exclusions that was related to the jurors' actual qualifications and capabilities. In Stevens's view, the Court had changed the *Batson* standard and thereby weakened the protection against discrimination in jury selection. Even worse, the Court had made this change without the benefit of full written and oral arguments from each side in the case, relying instead on the less-extensive petition for a writ of certiorari alone. Justice Stevens was quite blunt in describing his disagreement with the majority:

> Today, without argument, the Court replaces the *Batson* standard with the surprising announcement that any neutral explanation, no matter how "implausible or fantastic," . . . even if it is "silly or superstitious," . . . is sufficient to rebut a prima facie case of discrimination. A trial court must accept that neutral explanation unless a separate "step three" inquiry leads to the conclusion that the preemptory challenge was racially motivated. . . . It is not too much to ask that a prosecutor's explanation for his [peremptory challenges] be race neutral, reasonably specific, *and* trial related. Nothing less will serve to rebut the inference of race-based discrimination that arises when the defendant has made out a prima facie case.[40] (emphasis in original)

Justice Stevens stood out among his colleagues for strongly arguing against an approach that would permit rather than prohibit discrimination. As one commentator observed with respect to the Court's weak approach to enforcing the prohibition on discrimination in jury selection: "*Batson* and its progeny have proven less an obstacle to discrimination than a roadmap to it. Parties now have a good idea of what they can and cannot get away with in eliminating jurors and adjust their means to suit their desired end."[41] For those attorneys who wish to engage in race- or gender-based discrimination in jury selection, the Court's decisions in *Henandez v. New York* and *Purkett v. Elem* sent out a message: when asked about categorical exclusions, make up any excuse and you may very well succeed as long as you do not admit to discrimination. As a result, the expanded protections against discriminatory peremptory challenges announced in the series of cases from *Batson* to *Edmonson* to *Georgia v. McCollum* to *J. E. B. v. Alabama ex rel. T. B.* actually provide only the illusion of protection when trial judges blindly accept pretextual excuses put forth by attorneys engaged in suspicious categorical exclusions.[42] Justice Stevens was nearly alone in speaking out against the Court's apparent tolerance for the risks of both pretext-obscured discriminatory intentions and obvious discriminatory consequences in jury selection.

In 2005, Stevens had the opportunity to curb one of the discriminatory risks unleashed by *Purkett v. Elem*'s grant of discretion to trial judges. In *Johnson v. California* (2005), the defense attorney objected at trial to the prosecutor's exclusion of African Americans from the jury pool through the use of peremptory challenges. However, the judge declined to ask the prosecutor to explain the basis for the exclusions. Instead, the judge "explained that her own examination of the record had convinced her that the prosecutor's strikes could be justified by race-neutral reasons. Specifically, the judge opined that the black venire members had offered equivocal or confused answers in their written questionnaires."[43] The California Supreme Court ultimately upheld the trial judge's actions because it concluded that the defense had not carried its burden to show that the exclusions were based on race. The state high court said that *Batson* "permits a court to require the objector to present, not merely 'some evidence' permitting the inference, but 'strong evidence' that makes discriminatory intent *more likely than not* if the challenges are not explained."[44]

On behalf of an eight-member majority, Justice Stevens's opinion reversed the California Supreme Court's decision. According to Stevens, "Although we recognize that States do have flexibility in formulating appropriate procedures to comply with *Batson*, we conclude that California's 'more likely than not' standard is an inappropriate yardstick by which to measure the sufficiency of a prima facie case."[45] Justice Stevens noted that the *Batson* decision did not intend to place an onerous burden on the party questioning the exclusions to prove that they occurred due to discrimination. Instead, *Batson* intended to require trial judges to ask prosecutors to explain their categorical use of peremptory challenges when the defense "produc[es] evidence sufficient to permit the trial judge to draw an inference that discrimination had occurred,"[46] such as when all of the members of one racial group are excluded. Thus the systematic exclusion of African American jurors in Johnson's case should have been enough evidence to raise the inference of discrimination and trigger an inquiry about the prosecutor's reasons.

At one point in the opinion, Stevens addressed the reasons that it is essential to prevent racial discrimination in jury selection. In characterizing the importance of the antidiscrimination effort, he said one must look beyond the interests of the individual defendants and jurors affected in the specific trial. According to Stevens:

> The constitutional interests *Batson* sought to vindicate are not limited to the rights possessed by the defendant on trial, [and] . . . those citizens who desire to participate "in the administration of the law, as jurors," *Strauder v. West Virginia*, . . . (1880). Undoubtedly, the overriding interest in eradicating discrimination from our civic institutions suffers whenever an individual is excluded from making a significant contribution to governance on account of his race. Yet the "harm from discriminatory jury selection extends beyond that

> inflicted on the defendant and the excluded juror to touch the entire community. Selection procedures that purposefully exclude black persons from juries undermine public confidence in the fairness of our system of justice." *Batson*, 476 U.S. at 87.[47]

Justice Stevens was eighty-five years old when he wrote these words. Obviously, he knew at that time that he was nearing the end of his career on the Supreme Court. Thus his decision to include a justification for the importance of preventing discrimination in jury selection and the breadth of that justification effectively serve as an exhortation to his colleagues—and to future justices, since the Court's decision in *Purkett v. Elem* gave him good reason to worry about other justices' commitment to actually enforcing the nondiscrimination promise of *Batson*.

The *Johnson* opinion by Stevens did not eliminate the risks of discrimination in peremptory challenges; it merely reduced trial judges' discretion to decline to ask for explanations when one party objects to categorical exclusions by race or gender in the jury process. As Professor Mardar noted, however, problems still remained, such as attorneys' ability to present pretextual justifications and trial judges' authority to accept such justifications that mask the existence of actual discriminatory motives and actions.[48] Justice Marshall had argued that the only solution was to eliminate peremptory challenges entirely in order to remove attorneys' ability to make discretionary exclusions, and thereby only permit challenges for cause when there is evidence that a potential juror possesses a bias.[49] Justice Stevens consistently raised his voice against discrimination in the jury selection process, but he never went as far as Marshall by arguing for the abolition of peremptory challenges. Perhaps these differing conclusions reflected the different life experiences of the Supreme Court's two most experienced trial lawyers from recent decades. As the nation's leading civil rights lawyer from the 1930s to the 1960s, Marshall had long experience with and intimate exposure to seeing those inclined to engage in discrimination use every opportunity to do so. Moreover, he undoubtedly saw that individuals positioned to resist discrimination, such as trial judges during the jury selection process, may not use that authority if they are insufficiently sensitive to the risk of discrimination and not able to fully recognize all of its subtle manifestations. By contrast, Professor Mardar, a former law clerk to Justice Stevens, described his commitment to the preservation of more closely supervised peremptory challenges as reflecting his confidence in legal professionals and the traditions of the American trial process. In Mardar's words, "Justice Stevens's commitment to preserving the peremptory challenge reflects both a lawyer's respect for maintaining a useful litigation tool and a judge's regard for preserving legal traditions."[50]

Justice Stevens expressed another important concern about jury selection. He was critical of the impact of Supreme Court precedents, dating back to *Witherspoon v. Illinois* (1968), which permitted the exclusion from capital juries of jurors who are opposed to the death penalty and whose views would prevent them from fulfilling their duty to make fair decisions according to governing law. He believed that the Court had gone too far in excluding potential jurors who merely expressed skepticism about the death penalty. In his view, the Court thereby facilitated the selection of juries that were prone to being unfairly biased in favor of conviction and the imposition of death sentences. In Stevens's own words, "because the prosecutor can challenge jurors with qualms about the death penalty, the process creates a risk that a fair cross-section of the community will not be represented on the jury.[51]

When the Court announced a decision on this issue in *Uttecht v. Brown* (2007), Stevens used the occasion to announce his dissent orally from the bench in order to emphasize the intensity of his disagreement. As Stevens said from the bench,

> In the past we have protected against such jurors [who express qualms about the death penalty but not complete opposition] being [excluded] for cause in order to prevent the jury from being unfairly biased in favor of the death penalty. Today the Court has done away with that protection, rendering countless Americans ineligible to serve as capital jurors and more importantly, preventing countless defendants from being tried [by] a fair and impartial jury. Because the Court's decision is wholly unsupported by the record or our prior precedents, I respectfully dissent.[52]

For Stevens, this aspect of discrimination in jury selection created a grave risk of unfairness in capital trials. As chapter 8 will explain, this issue was a key element in Stevens's increasingly critical opinions concerning capital punishment over the course of his Supreme Court career.

THE JURY AND SENTENCING

The punishments for criminal offenses are defined in statutes enacted by elected representatives in legislatures. Legislative bodies also define sentencing processes, including the extent to which judges possess discretionary authority to choose a specific sentence for a particular offender and offense. Legislatures' authority over criminal sentencing is limited by judicial oversight to ensure that punishments and associated processes comply with constitutional requirements. Thus specific sentences defined by legislatures may be invalidated if they collide with the Eighth Amendment prohibition on cruel and unusual punishments, including that prohibition's ban on sentences that are either disproportionate to the crime or torturous in nature. Sentencing processes must meet the requirements of due process and the various trial rights contained in the Sixth Amendment. It is with respect to the latter issues that Justice Stevens influenced the law through his views about the primacy of the jury as the fact finder in criminal trials.

In evaluating capital punishment processes, Justice Stevens argued strongly that a jury, as the representative of the community, must decide whether or not the death penalty will be imposed on a convicted murderer. In *Spaziano v. Florida* (1984), a trial judge overrode a jury's recommendation for a sentence of life imprisonment and imposed the death penalty instead. Florida's sentencing procedures permitted such decisions as the jury's sentence determination was treated as merely a recommendation. A majority of justices stated that neither the Sixth Amendment's right to trial by jury nor the Eighth Amendment's protection against cruel and unusual punishments required that a jury determine capital sentences. Justice Stevens wrote a lengthy dissenting opinion, joined by Brennan and Marshall, objecting to this aspect of the majority's decision. The Stevens dissent argued that the Eighth Amendment requires that jurors, as representatives of the community, make the important decision about life or death in capital sentencing. He pointed to the fact that Florida was one of the only states to grant that decision-making authority to judges rather than juries. He used this point as a means to demonstrate that Florida's procedures violate the contemporary societal standards that define "cruel and unusual punishments" under the Supreme Court's guiding precedent in *Trop v. Dulles* (1958). In highlighting the historical importance of juries in the American justice system, Stevens said:

> The same consideration that supports a constitutional entitlement to a trial by a jury rather than a judge at the guilt or innocence stage—the right to have an authentic representative of the community apply its lay perspective to the determination that must precede a deprivation of liberty—applies with special force to the determination that must precede a deprivation of life. [53]

To Stevens, the jury's voice not only provided legitimacy to the ultimate exercise of the state's power over an individual, but it also helped to ensure that criminal punishments were consistent with the contemporary societal standards that define the Eighth Amendment.

Although Stevens based his dissent on his conclusion that Florida's capital sentencing process violated the Eighth Amendment, he also made reference to the Sixth Amendment: "The constitutional legitimacy of capital punishment depends upon the extent to which the process is able to produce results which reflect the community's moral sensibilities. Judges simply cannot acceptably mirror these sensibilities—the very notion of a right to a jury trial is premised on that realization."[54]

Subsequently, the Court examined the sentencing procedures in Arizona, one of the few other states that gave judges the authority to impose capital punishment. In *Walton v. Arizona* (1990), Justice White's majority opinion rejected a challenge to Arizona's capital punishment process. The defendant asserted unsuccessfully that juries, rather than judges, must make the fact-finding decisions about the existence of aggravating and mitigating factors concerning the offender and the commission of the offense that, respectively, either justify or lead away from imposition of the death penalty.

Justice Stevens joined Justice Blackmun's lengthy dissent concerning the details of how evidence was evaluated under Arizona's procedures, but he also wrote his own separate dissent to emphasize the importance of the jury's role. With respect to the role of the jury, Stevens contrasted his conclusions with those of the majority: "The Court holds in Part II of its opinion that a person is not entitled to a jury determination of facts that must be established before the death penalty may be imposed. I am convinced that the Sixth Amendment requires the opposite conclusion."[55] He also quoted at length from the Court's precedent that applied the right to trial by jury to the states by saying, "Justice White's eloquent opinion for the Court in *Duncan v. Louisiana* . . . (1968) was faithful to the history and meaning of the Sixth Amendment."[56] He concluded this section of his dissent by again explicitly praising White's opinion with the words "it is not too late to change our course and follow the wise and inspiring voice that spoke for the Court in *Duncan v. Louisiana*."[57] It seemed very obvious that Stevens praised and emphasized White's *Duncan* opinion, at least in part, as a means to call attention to the fact that White wrote the opinion for the Court in *Walton* against which Stevens was dissenting and to perhaps highlight the tensions he saw between White's reasoning in the two cases. Overall, Stevens argued that by failing to remain true to the history and meaning of the Sixth Amendment right to trial by jury, the Supreme Court's "decisions have encroached upon the fact-finding function that has so long been entrusted to the jury."[58]

Over the same time period as the Supreme Court's decisions in *Spaziano* and *Walton*, Stevens also asserted his view about the importance of juries for aspects of sentencing in non-capital cases. During most of the twentieth century, legislatures defined criminal sentences in a manner that granted discretionary authority to judges to choose the precise sentence from within a range of punishment options, such as probation, fines, jail, or prison. The application of this discretionary authority led to concerns about inconsistent choices of punishments and sentence lengths for similar offenders convicted of the same charge as well as discriminatory sentences applied to African Americans and the poor.[59] To address the issues of inconsistency and unfairness, legislatures began to reform sentencing through the creation of sentencing guidelines that limited the discretion of judges and mandated similar sentences for similar offenders and offenses. Beginning with the development of Minnesota's sentencing guidelines in the late 1970s, other states, and eventually Congress as well, created sentencing schemes that required judges to use an offender's offense history and current offense as the primary factors that determined the criminal punishment. Only a narrow range of sentence lengths and alternative punishment choices were left to the judge's discretion.[60] Other sentencing reforms of the era included the creation of mandatory minimum sentences that sought to prevent judges from imposing any sentences below a certain length of imprisonment for specific offenses. Many judges were unhappy about their loss of discretionary authority. These judges believed such discretion enabled them to tailor punishments for individual offenders, including appropriate opportunities to reward deserving offenders with leniency as well as to impose extra retributive and incapacitative impacts on other selected offenders whose prior records or evident attitudes made them deserving of severe sanctions. On the other hand, social scientists observed that the standardization effects in legislatively mandated sentencing guidelines reduced many of the disparities evident under the previous discretion-based system.

In *McMillan v. Pennsylvania* (1986), the Supreme Court examined a challenge to a state law that imposed a mandatory minimum sentence of five years' imprisonment for anyone convicted of a crime "if the sentencing judge finds, by a preponderance of the evidence, that the person 'visibly possessed a firearm' during the commission of the offense."[61] Several individuals who had each been convicted of crimes that involved the use of a firearm challenged the statute for failing to fulfill their asserted right to have every element of the offense proven "beyond a reasonable doubt." The Pennsylvania statute permitted the judge to impose the mandatory minimum sentence by employing the lesser standard of proof, "preponderance of the evidence," to find the existence of the triggering factor of visible possession of a firearm. In an opinion written by Justice Rehnquist for a slim five-member majority, the Court upheld the Pennsylvania statute by concluding that the "visibly possessed a firearm" element was merely a "sentencing factor," and therefore not subject to the reasonable-doubt standard that applies for proof of underlying elements of an offense in order to obtain a criminal conviction.

Justice Stevens wrote a solo dissenting opinion that Douglas Berman described as "passionate."[62] Justice Marshall, on behalf of Brennan and Blackmun, wrote a separate brief dissent that expressed agreement "with much in Justice Stevens'[s] dissent."[63] In his opinion, Stevens argued that "Once a State defines a criminal offense, the Due Process Clause requires it to prove any component of the prohibited transaction that gives rise to both a special stigma and a special punishment beyond a reasonable doubt."[64] In essence, Stevens argued that criminal defendants are entitled to accurate fact finding concerning issues that will impact their punishments. In Stevens's words, "a State may not advance the objectives of its criminal laws at the expense of accurate fact finding owed to the criminally accused."[65] The reasonable-doubt standard represents an especially high level of proof and thus is applied in determinations of criminal guilt because the highest American value, individual liberty, is at stake from the factual determinations made in criminal cases. In reviewing the due process-based right to the reasonable-doubt standard as established in the case of *In re Winship* (1970), Stevens emphasized the importance of this right to the American justice system. He referred to "the heritage of the rule that Justice Frankfurter characterized as 'basic in our law and rightly one of the boasts of a free society.'"[66]

Professor Berman credited Justice Stevens with raising important procedural issues early in the sentencing reform era. According to Berman, "*McMillan* could have had a profound impact, both conceptually and practically, on modern sentencing laws if Justice Stevens's view had carried the day or if the Court's opinion had suggested that the Constitution imposed some significant requirements on the sentencing process."[67] In Berman's view, the failure of the Court to follow Stevens's view led legislatures, as well as the sentencing commissions to whom legislatures frequently delegated authority to design sentencing guidelines, to "neglect procedural matters when reforming the substance of sentencing laws."[68]

In subsequent decisions about sentencing processes, Stevens emphasized the importance of the jury's role. In *Jones v. United States* (1999), the Court looked at specific factual conditions that triggered enhanced sentences in a criminal statute concerning carjacking. At issue in the case was the victim's assertion that he suffered serious bodily harm during the commission of the crime. The majority opinion written by Justice Souter concluded that a jury should have made the factual determination about the existence of any sentence-enhancement-triggering facts under this statute. Justice Stevens joined the majority opinion but also wrote a separate concurring opinion to emphasize his view that jury decision making was required for the determination of sentence-defining facts in all cases and not just in the circumstances of this particular case. In the words of Stevens:

> I am convinced that it is unconstitutional for a legislature to remove from the jury the assessment of facts that increase the prescribed range of penalties to which a criminal defendant is exposed. It is equally clear that such facts must be established by proof beyond a reasonable doubt. . . . To permit anything less "with respect to a fact which the State deems so important that it must be either proved or presumed is impermissible under the Due Process Clause." This principle was firmly embedded in our jurisprudence through centuries of common-law decisions.[69]

Two years later, Stevens wrote one of his most influential criminal justice opinions. One commentator called the opinion "trail-blazing,"[70] but Professor Berman went even further by saying that it "shook the world of sentencing with a 'watershed' Supreme Court ruling."[71] In *Apprendi v. New Jersey* (2000), the defendant admitted to firing several bullets into the home of an African American family that had moved into a previously all-white neighborhood. According to the police, he initially admitted—but later retracted—a statement in which he said that he shot at the house because he did not want African Americans to live in the neighborhood. The defendant entered a guilty plea but reserved the right to challenge any sentence enhancement that might be imposed under the state's hate crimes law. The law permitted trial judges to increase prison sentences by periods ranging from ten to twenty years "if the trial judge finds, by a preponderance of the evidence, that '[t]he defendant in committing the crime acted with a purpose to intimidate an individual or group of individuals because of race, color, gender, handicap, religion, sexual orientation, or ethnicity."[72] At the sentencing hearing, the defendant claimed that he had been under the influence of alcohol at the time of the shooting and he brought forward character witnesses to testify that he did not harbor racial animosity toward African Americans. The judge, however, found the police officer's testimony to be credible concerning the defendant's original admission of racial motives and imposed a longer sentence under the hate crimes statute.

The issue presented to the Supreme Court for decision was "whether the Due Process Clause of the Fourteenth Amendment requires that a factual determination authorizing an increase in the maximum prison sentence for an offense from ten to twenty years be made by a jury on the basis of proof beyond a reasonable doubt."[73] When the Supreme Court announced the decision in June 2000 and Chief Justice Rehnquist introduced Justice Stevens as the justice to announce the Court's decision, interested observers undoubtedly knew how the case had been decided, in light of Stevens's prior opinions on this issue. Indeed, there was audible laughter in the courtroom when Stevens began his announcement by saying, "I am happy to be on the majority in this case,"[74] as numerous observers recognized that he had pushed for many years to place the primacy of the jury into the case law defining sentencing procedures.

Justice Stevens attracted an unusual combination of four justices—his two liberal colleagues Ginsburg and Souter and his two conservative colleagues Scalia and Thomas—to join him in forming a majority supporting the principle of jury fact-finding for sentencing that he had long advocated. In his brief oral announcement of the decision, Stevens went out of his way to acknowledge Scalia and Thomas, two of his colleagues with whom he was typically least likely to agree in criminal justice-related cases.[75] He credited Scalia with encapsulating the essence of the decision in a concurring opinion. As described by Stevens:

> Justice Scalia has filed a concurring opinion. He ends with the sentence, "The guarantee that in all criminal prosecutions the accused shall enjoy the right to trial by an impartial jury, has no intelligible content unless it means that all the facts which must exist in order to subject the defendant to a legally prescribed punishment must be found by the jury." That's the essence of the holding of the majority.[76]

With respect to Thomas, Stevens said, "Justice Thomas has filed a concurring opinion which is joined by Justice Scalia, which carefully reviews the history of that provision."[77] Typically, Stevens might merely have said that Thomas filed a concurring opinion without also complimenting the opinion with the words "carefully reviews." Presumably this was Stevens's way of expressing gratitude as well as, perhaps, cultivating positive feelings to foster the potential for subsequent support from these justices in other cases.

In his majority opinion, Stevens summarized the Court's newly announced rule and its underlying reasoning by saying:

> In sum, our reexamination of our cases in this area, and of the history upon which they rely, confirms the opinion that we expressed in *Jones*. Other than the fact of a prior conviction, any fact that increases the penalty for a crime beyond the prescribed statutory maximum must be submitted to a jury, and proved beyond a reasonable doubt. With that exception, we endorse the statement of the rule set forth in the concurring opinions in that case.[78]

The concurring opinions to which Stevens referred were his own as well as Justice Scalia's, and he followed with a quote from his own concurring opinion in *Jones*.

After seeing his views about the jury's role and importance finally define the law concerning sentence enhancements, two years later Stevens saw his *Walton* dissent concerning death penalty sentencing transformed into a new law-defining decision when a majority of justices voted to reverse *Walton* in *Ring v. Arizona* (2002). In *Ring*, Justice Ginsburg wrote the majority opinion that followed Stevens's *Apprendi* principle by requiring jury determinations of aggravating and mitigating factors that define whether the death penalty will be imposed in capital cases. In Ginsburg's words, "*Apprendi*'s reasoning is irreconcilable with *Walton*'s holding in this regard, and today we overrule *Walton* in relevant part. Capital defendants, no less than noncapital defendants, we conclude, are entitled to a jury determination of any fact on which the legislature conditions an increase in their maximum punishment."[79]

Because Chief Justice Rehnquist dissented in both *Apprendi* and *Ring*, Stevens was the senior justice in the majority who decided which justice would write the majority opinions. Interestingly, Stevens assigned to himself in *Apprendi* the opportunity to fully explain his long-held principle about the jury's essential fact-finding role for sentencing. In effect, the announcement of his sought-after victory and the elaboration of foundational reasoning for this new precedent were too attractive or too important—or both—to be left in the hands of another justice. By contrast, Stevens assigned to Ginsburg the task of applying *Apprendi* to the death penalty context in *Ring*, and thereby spread the responsibility for the principle of jury fact-finding. In the next important case concerning this principle, *Blakely v. Washington* (2004), a decision that Professor Berman described as an "earthquake" for sentencing processes,[80] Stevens assigned the majority opinion to Justice Scalia. This assignment further spread visible responsibility for the principle, but perhaps also served to acknowledge Scalia's endorsement of the jury's role in cases such as *Jones* that pre-dated the formation of majority support in *Apprendi*.

In *Blakely*, the same slim majority applied the principle of jury fact-finding to a state's comprehensive sentencing guidelines system in a case for which a judge had enhanced a sentence based on a finding that a kidnapper had acted with "deliberate cruelty." Justice Scalia summarized the majority's decision with reference to his originalist approach to constitutional interpretation by saying:

> Petitioner was sentenced to prison for more than three years beyond what the law allowed for the crime to which he confessed, and on the basis of a disputed finding that he had acted with "deliberate cruelty." The Framers would not have thought it too much to demand that, before depriving a man of three more years of his liberty, the State should suffer the modest inconvenience of submitting its accusation to "the unanimous suffrage of twelve of his equals and neighbours," [quoting Blackstone] . . . rather than a lone employee of the State.[81]

The aspect of *Blakely* that shook court systems throughout the country was, as Berman observed, that it "impacted guideline sentencing outcomes *within* otherwise applicable statutory ranges."[82] In other words, jury decisions were required not merely for fact-finding that would lead to sentence enhancements beyond the punishment prescribed by the legislature for the crime, as when New Jersey added to Apprendi's sentence by finding a fact about his racial motives that triggered a separate hate crimes statute. Jury fact-finding was now also required for facts that would determine where within the defined punishment ranges established in sentencing guidelines a particular offender's sentence would be set. Professor Berman described the impact of *Blakely* as "truly staggering" because it collided directly with the judge-centered administrative process of sentencing that had been designed as a central element in sentencing reform efforts that resulted in the establishment of guidelines.[83] Guidelines schemes recognized that most offenders are convicted through guilty pleas. Thus the systems gave judges the responsibility to engage in fact-finding during sentencing hearings that would enhance and consequently establish the precise punishment from within the permissible range. In *Blakely*, that conception of fact-finding for increasing sentences had been blocked by a slim majority on the Supreme Court led by Justice Stevens.

The Supreme Court followed *Blakely* with the decision that observers expected would come next, application of the same jury fact-finding role to the federal sentencing guidelines in *United States v. Booker* (2005). *Booker* created an unusual situation for Stevens. He assigned to himself the majority opinion, perhaps because this was the case concerning jury fact-finding in sentencing that invalidated an approach designed by Congress, a co-equal branch of the federal government. In addition, the Court was more fractured in this case as Justice Ginsburg supported Stevens's application of the *Apprendi* principle to federal sentencing guidelines but then left to join a different majority opinion by Justice Breyer concerning whether certain provisions of federal sentencing law continued to be mandatory in determining decisions by federal judges. Thus Stevens wrote both a majority opinion and a dissenting opinion in *Booker* with respect to the two separate issues. According to Berman, the Court's split decision watered down the jury fact-finding principle advanced by Stevens because Breyer's majority opinion on the separate issue, making the federal sentencing guidelines advisory rather than mandatory, effectively transferred greater flexibility and discretion back to trial judges in the sentencing process.[84] Instead of engaging in the formal fact-finding envisioned by the sentencing guidelines, judges could base their sentencing decisions on unstated conclusions. In effect, it was arguably a move back toward the old sentencing process based on judicial discretion that, in practice, could undercut the goals of consistency and fairness that motivated the creation of the guidelines in the first place. Professor Berman, although an acknowledged admirer of Justice Stevens's opinion in *Apprendi*,[85] was one of several analysts who criticized the practical results of *Apprendi*'s subsequent broader application to sentencing guidelines in *Blakely* and *Booker*. Other critics argued that the Court's mixed decision in *Booker* "paralyze[d] the generally beneficial structured sentencing movement with the result that promising avenues toward improved substantive and procedural sentencing justice have been blocked."[86]

THE JURY'S ADVOCATE

Justice Stevens was arguably the Supreme Court's foremost advocate of the jury's role in the justice system. He placed his imprint on the law governing sentencing procedures through his advocacy for the jury's authority and role. His view of the jury's important role in any fact-finding that affects sentencing, and especially sentencing enhancements, eventually gained majority support and changed the rules for both capital and non-capital sentencing. In part, his advocacy of jury fact-finding was based on the traditional role of the jury in representing the community and providing legitimacy for important punishment decisions. His efforts were also an understandable component of his advocacy for the adversarial system throughout the criminal justice process. These efforts reflected his resistance to the delegation to the solitary trial judge of powers more like those in an inquisitorial system in which the individual judicial officer makes the important decisions that determine the fate of the defendant.

Justice Stevens's advocacy for the jury's role in fair criminal trial processes reflected his commitment to the adversarial system as well as his concern for both due process and equal protection of the law. These priorities, which were evident in his opinions in cases concerning various criminal justice issues, had links to his life experiences as well as to the elements of his judicial philosophy that were well-established prior to his appointment to the Supreme Court. As noted in this chapter and the preceding chapter, Stevens's experiences as a trial lawyer reinforced his concerns about maintaining the elements of the country's tradition of an adversarial legal system. Moreover, his brief experience as a substitute trial judge enhanced his views about the jury's role and beneficial contributions to a fair system of justice. With respect to discrimination, as discussed in chapter 2, Stevens described childhood experiences seeing rigid racial segregation in southern states as well as the unfair treatment of his Jewish friends in college as enhancing his sensitivity to equal protection violations. Thus he had long-standing sensitivity to unfair discrimination that he brought with him to the Supreme Court and expressed in the jury selection cases.

NOTES

1. *Neder v. United States*, 527 U.S. 1, 28 (1999) (Stevens, J., concurring in part and concurring in the judgment).
2. *Baldwin v. Alabama*, 472 U.S. 372, 397–98 (1985) (Stevens, J., dissenting).
3. Adam Liptak, "Supreme Court Enters the YouTube Era," *New York Times*, March 2, 2009, accessed July 2, 2015, http://www.nytimes.com/2009/03/03/us/03bar.html.
4. Justice John Paul Stevens, interview with author, U.S. Supreme Court, Washington, D.C., July 29, 2010.
5. *Ludwig v. Massachusetts*, 427 U.S. 618, 632 (1976) (Stevens, J., dissenting).
6. Ibid., 637–38 (Stevens, J., dissenting).
7. U.S. Constitution, Amendment VI.
8. U.S. Constitution, Amendment VII.
9. *Lewis v. United States*, 518 U.S. 322, 323–24 (1996).
10. Ibid., 330 (Kennedy, J., concurring).
11. Ibid., 331.
12. Ibid., 340. (Stevens, J. dissenting).
13. Ibid.
14. Ibid., 339.
15. Ibid., 341.
16. Ibid.

17. *Rosales-Lopez v. United States*, 451 U.S. 182, 202–3 (Stevens, J., dissenting).

18. Scott Lemieux, "Stevens' Long Battle for Equality," *The American Prospect* (online edition), December 9, 2010, accessed July 2, 2015, http://prospect.org/article/stevens-long-battle-equality-0.

19. Nancy S. Mardar, "Justice Stevens, the Peremptory Challenge, and the Jury," *Fordham Law Review* 74 (2006): 1684.

20. *Holland v. Illinois*, 493 U.S. 474, 507 (1990) (Stevens, J., dissenting).

21. Ibid., 509.

22. Ibid., 510.

23. Ibid., 511.

24. Ibid., 490 (Marshall, J., dissenting).

25. *Holland v. Illinois*, 493 U.S. at 486.

26. Mark V. Tushnet, *Making Constitutional Law: Thurgood Marshall and the Supreme Court, 1961–1991* (New York: Oxford University Press, 1997), 49–51.

27. *Hernandez v. New York*, 500 U.S. 352, 361 (1991).

28. Ibid., 362.

29. Ibid., 376 (Stevens, J., dissenting).

30. Ibid., 378.

31. Ibid.

32. Ibid., 377.

33. Ibid., 379.

34. Ibid.

35. *Purkett v. Elem*, 514 U.S. 765, 767 (1995).

36. Ibid.

37. Ibid.

38. Ibid., 768.

39. Ibid.

40. Ibid., 775 (Stevens, J., dissenting).

41. Karen Bray, "Reaching the Final Chapter in the Story of Peremptory Challenges," *U.C.L.A. Law Review* 40 (1992): 554–55.

42. Christopher E. Smith, "Law and Symbolism," *Detroit College of Law at Michigan State University Law Review* (1997): 946.

43. *Johnson v. California*, 545 U.S. 162, 165 (2005).

44. Ibid., 167.

45. Ibid., 168.

46. Ibid., 170.

47. Ibid., 171–72.

48. Mardar, 1706–7.

49. *Batson v. Kentucky*, 476 U.S. at 102-3 (Marshall, J., concurring).

50. Mardar, 1684.

51. John Paul Stevens, "Address to the American Bar Association Thurgood Marshall Awards Dinner," Chicago, Ill., August 6, 2005, accessed May 21, 2015, http://www.supremecourt.gov/publicinfo/speeches/viewspeech/sp_08-06-05.

52. Audio and transcript of opinion announcement in *Uttecht v. Brown*, June 4, 2007, available at website of the Oyez Project at IIT Chicago-Kent College of Law, accessed July 2, 2015, www.ozez.org/cases/2000-2009/2006/2006_06_413.

53. *Spaziano v. Florida*, 468 U.S. 447, 482–83 (1984) (Stevens, J., concurring in part and dissenting in part).

54. Ibid., 490.

55. *Walton v. Arizona*, 497 U.S. 639, 709 (1990) (Stevens, J., dissenting).

56. Ibid., 711.

57. Ibid., 714.

58. Ibid., 713.

59. Douglas A. Berman, "Foreward: Beyond *Blakely* and *Booker*: Pondering Modern Sentencing," *Journal of Criminal Law and Criminology* 95 (2005): 655–57.

60. Ibid., 657–58.

61. *McMillan v. Pennsylvania*, 477 U.S. 79, 81 (1986).
62. Berman, 666.
63. *McMillan v. Pennsylvania*, 477 U.S. at 93 (Marshall, J., dissenting).
64. *McMillan v. Pennsylvania*, 477 U.S. at 96 (Stevens, J., dissenting).
65. Ibid., 102.
66. Ibid., 96–97.
67. Berman, 666–67.
68. Ibid., 667.
69. *Jones v. United States*, 526 U.S. 227, 252–53 (Stevens, J., concurring).
70. Adam Sheppard, "Justice Stevens' Role in Making Federal Sentencing Matters More Flexible: A Trail-Blazing Opinion," *Chicago Bar Record* 24 (September 2010): 56.
71. Berman, 670.
72. *Apprendi v. New Jersey*, 530 U.S. 466, 468–69 (2000).
73. Ibid., 469.
74. Audio and transcript of opinion announcement in *Apprendi v. New Jersey*, June 26, 2000, accessed July 2, 2015, website of the Oyez Project at IIT Chicago-Kent College of Law, www.ozez.org/cases/1990-1999/1999/1999_99_478.
75. Christopher E. Smith, Michael McCall, and Madhavi McCall, "Criminal Justice and the 2004–2005 United States Supreme Court Term," *University of Memphis Law Review* 36 (2006): 94–95.
76. Audio and transcript of opinion announcement in *Apprendi v. New Jersey*, accessed July 2, 2015, www.ozez.org/cases/1990-1999/1999/1999_99_478.
77. Ibid.
78. *Apprendi v. New Jersey*, 530 U.S. at 490 (2000).
79. *Ring v. Arizona*, 536 U.S. 584, 589 (2002).
80. Berman, 674.
81. *Blakely v. Washington*, 542 U.S. 296, 313–14 (2004).
82. Berman, 674.
83. Ibid., 675.
84. Ibid., 676.
85. Douglas A. Berman, "Should Juries Be the Guide for Adventures Through *Apprendi*-Land?" *Columbia Law Review Sidebar* 109 (2009): 69.
86. Frank O. Bowman, "Debacle: How the Supreme Court Has Mangled American Sentencing Law and How It Might Yet Be Mended," *University of Chicago Law Review* 77 (2010): 369.

Chapter Seven

Search and Seizure

Justice Stevens arrived at the Supreme Court with established views about the importance of limits on government authority in search and seizure contexts. As we will see in this chapter, he wrote opinions supportive of protections for individuals early in his career. However, he also wrote several opinions supporting police authority during these early years, so he was not yet perceived as among the Court's foremost advocates of broad Fourth Amendment rights. Later, during his final twenty-five years as a justice, his opinions usually dissented against the efforts of his conservative colleagues to expand police officers' authority. Although Stevens's views on certain aspects of searches may have changed over time to become more protective of rights, most of the viewpoints that he expressed about Fourth Amendment issues remained consistent throughout his judicial career. In the final decades of his career, he cast liberal votes in Fourth Amendment cases more frequently than he had done in the first eight years. Alterations in voting patterns are often perceived to reflect changes in a justice's approach to decision making for a specific issue. In the case of Stevens, by contrast, the different voting pattern may be largely attributable to changes in the number and nature of search and seizure cases accepted by the Court for hearing and not necessarily to changes in Stevens's approach or viewpoint.

Because he had five years of experience on the court of appeals, Stevens had exposure to search and seizure issues that developed his judicial values and approach to decision making on the Fourth Amendment. The viewpoints that Stevens brought with him to the Supreme Court concerning search and seizures issues can be illustrated through decisions early in his career on the high court. During his earliest years as a justice, Stevens wrote opinions demonstrating that he had arrived at the Supreme Court with a protective viewpoint toward people's rights in certain search contexts. For example, in

Dalia v. United States (1979) Stevens objected to FBI agents' nighttime, forced entry into a building through a window in order to plant electronic listening devices without any specific authorization for such an entry. Although completing just his fourth term on the Court at that time, Stevens's dissenting opinion took note of two earlier cases in which he had also objected to invasive investigative actions:

> For this is the third time in as many years that [the Court] has condoned a serious intrusion on privacy that was not explicitly authorized by statute and that admittedly raised a substantial constitutional question. In *United States v. Ramsey*, . . . [(1977)], the Court upheld an Executive regulation authorizing postal inspectors to open private letters without probable cause to believe they contained contraband. In *United States v. New York Telephone Co.*, . . . [(1977)], the Court upheld orders authorizing the surreptitious pen register surveillance of an individual and directing a private company to lend its assistance in that endeavor.[1]

In all three cases, the Court's most liberal Warren Court holdovers, Brennan and Marshall, joined Stevens's dissenting opinions. Similarly, Stevens dissented in the well-known case of *Zurcher v. Stanford Daily* (1978) in which a warrant was issued to search for evidence of wrongdoing that was believed to be in the possession of a university's student newspaper. Justice Brennan did not participate in the decision, but the other dissenters in *Zurcher* were Marshall and Stewart. These cases provided an initial indication that he came to the Court with skepticism about endorsing law enforcement authority at the expense of protecting individuals and their homes from invasive investigatory actions. Indeed, as early as 1979, Stevens wrote with respect to federal wiretapping statutes, "until Congress has stated otherwise, our duty to protect the rights of the individual should hold sway over the interest in more effective law enforcement."[2] The presumption underlying this declaration served as an early indicator of Stevens's consistent, career-long resistance to his colleagues' efforts to expand law enforcement authority at the expense of Fourth Amendment interests.

THE SUPREME COURT AND THE FOURTH AMENDMENT

A steady stream of Fourth Amendment cases constitutes a significant segment of the Supreme Court's criminal justice docket. The number of search and seizure cases decided by the Court during Justice Stevens's long career reflected several important underlying factors. First, it is extremely difficult for judges to establish clear guidelines for police officers' investigatory actions that will cover all circumstances that may arise. The Fourth Amendment provides protection against "unreasonable searches and seizures" and also requires that judicial officers ensure that warrants for searches and arrests are supported by "probable cause." None of these terms—unreasonable, searches, seizures, and probable cause—has a self-evident meaning for all of the situations in which police officers' assertions of investigative authority collide with individuals' desire to retain their liberty, privacy, or control over property. New factual circumstances arise continuously and challenge the justices to determine whether these contexts of police-citizen encounters should fall under the rules established for other, slightly different circumstances, or whether a newly examined situation requires a different limitation on police actions in order to fulfill the Fourth Amendment's protections. Thus each term brings new requests for the Supreme Court to evaluate whether police officers acted properly in conducting searches and making seizures of persons and property in contexts that differ from those that were examined in the Court's prior decisions.

Second, societal changes, including the development of new technologies, new laws defining crimes, and new forms of criminal behavior, produce new contexts for police investigations that were not anticipated in the Supreme Court's prior decisions. For example, the creation of new technologies for eavesdropping and surveillance inevitably leads to legal challenges that test the applications of those technologies by government. Similarly, the use of cellphones and computers for criminal activities triggers law enforcement officers' efforts to access information on those devices.

Third, throughout the time period of Justice Stevens's career, the justices were deeply divided when called upon to articulate the proper balance between the scope of permissible law enforcement authority and the nature of individuals' protected interests in liberty, privacy, and property. The Warren Court's decisions had sought to strengthen individuals' rights and limit police officers' search and arrest authority, especially through the application of the exclusionary rule in *Mapp v. Ohio* (1961) as a deterrent sanction for police officers' violations of the Fourth Amendment. In the years immediately preceding Stevens's appointment to the Supreme Court, President Nixon sought to advance his law-and-order objectives by placing on the high court four new justices (Warren Burger, William Rehnquist, Lewis Powell, and Harry Blackmun) who were less supportive than were their immediate predecessors of strong Fourth Amendment protections for individuals. Disagreements about the Fourth Amendment divided the Court as Presidents Reagan and George H. W. Bush later appointed additional justices who supported expanded authority for police and President Clinton appointed two justices who favored the retention of the exclusionary rule and other limits on police. Thus, amid a changing mix of colleagues, Stevens participated in decisions concerning new search and arrest situations as well as cases that tested whether earlier rights-protecting decisions would remain as law-defining precedents.

As in other topical areas of criminal justice, Stevens's voting patterns and opinion authorship created an overall record of liberal support for individuals' rights and limitations on police authority. Justices Brennan and Marshall, who were Stevens's colleagues during the first fifteen years of his career and holdovers from among the liberal justices of the Warren Court era, nearly always supported individuals' Fourth Amendment claims. By contrast, Stevens's evaluation of the proper balance between law enforcement authority and Fourth Amendment protections led him to support governmental authority in many but not all cases, especially in the first half of his Supreme Court career. Indeed, Stevens wrote seventeen opinions supporting governmental authority in Fourth Amendment cases while serving with both Brennan and Marshall, including four majority opinions,[3] eleven concurring opinions,[4] and two dissenting opinions.[5] In thirteen of those cases, Brennan and Marshall disagreed with Stevens and supported the protection of individuals' rights.[6] Thus Stevens was not the Supreme Court's leading protector of Fourth Amendment rights during the first fifteen years of his career. Yet Stevens was assertive in his advocacy of limitations on police authority concerning searches and seizures during that initial period on the Court. He wrote a larger number of opinions—twenty-eight—supporting individuals' rights during this time period,[7] only one of which was a majority opinion assigned to him by the senior justice in the majority, William Brennan.[8] The others were self-initiated concurring and dissenting opinions.

After the retirements of Brennan (1990) and Marshall (1991), Stevens wrote only three pro-government opinions in Fourth Amendment cases in the final two decades of his career (1991–2010) while producing twenty-two pro-rights opinions (two of which were written during Marshall's final term on the Court). Stevens became a more prominent advocate for Fourth Amendment rights in the absence of the two liberal Warren Court holdovers as he less frequently voiced support for government authority concerning searches and arrests. This development apparently reflected both his assumption, either by choice or default, of the role as the leader of the liberal wing, as well as his desire to resist aggressive efforts by his conservative colleagues to accept and decide cases that would reshape Fourth Amendment doctrines. In both the first fifteen years of his career and the subsequent two decades after his most liberal colleagues, Brennan and Marshall, retired from the Court, Stevens wrote a number of notable dissents arguing against a reduction in Fourth Amendment protections.

INFLUENCES ON FOURTH AMENDMENT DECISIONS

Justice Stevens's opinions in these cases were linked to aspects of his judicial philosophy and approach to decision making as well as to his formative experiences as a lawyer and court of appeals judge. Opinions by Justice Stevens regularly highlighted the importance of the Fourth Amendment's protection of individuals' liberty. For example, in *Michigan Dept. of State Police v. Sitz* (1990), a five-member majority approved the use of temporary sobriety checkpoints in which law enforcement officials blocked a highway and stopped all drivers briefly to attempt to detect whether they were driving under the influence of alcohol. In dissent, Stevens strongly objected to this suspicionless intrusion on people's protected liberty:

> In my opinion, unannounced investigatory seizures are, particularly when they take place at night, the hallmark of regimes far different from ours; the surprise intrusion upon individual liberty is not minimal. On that issue, my difference with the Court may amount to nothing less than a difference in our respective evaluations of the importance of individual liberty, a serious albeit inevitable source of constitutional disagreement. On the degree to which the sobriety checkpoint seizures advance the public interest, however, the Court's position is wholly indefensible.[9]

In another example, *Maryland v. Wilson* (1997), a seven-member majority approved the authority of police officers during traffic stops to order passengers out of vehicles without any articulated suspicion of wrongdoing by those passengers. Justice Stevens's dissent complained that the majority's decision struck the wrong balance between necessary law enforcement authority and individuals' liberty:

> The majority suggests that the personal liberty interest at stake here . . . is outweighed by the need to ensure officer safety. . . . But countless citizens who cherish individual liberty and are offended, embarrassed, and sometimes provoked by arbitrary official commands may well consider the burden to be significant. In all events, the aggregation of thousands upon thousands of petty indignities has an impact on freedom that I would characterize as substantial, and which in my view clearly outweighs the evanescent safety concerns pressed by the majority.[10]

A second element of Stevens's approach to judicial opinions that affected his Fourth Amendment analysis stemmed from his emphasis on fact-specific, case-by-case decision making rather than any aspiration to create broad rules. As described in chapter 2, Stevens attributed his focus on cases and facts to the teaching methods that shaped his legal education at Northwestern University School of Law.[11] He contrasted his learning and approach from those of justices, such as Antonin Scalia, who were taught through "the rule-oriented approach that the Michigan and Harvard law schools followed."[12] In *Maryland v. Wilson* (1997), for example, concerning police officers' authority to order passengers out of a vehicle during a traffic stop, Stevens noted that the facts of the particular case justified the police officers' action:

> I am satisfied that under the rationale of *Terry* v. *Ohio*, . . . (1968) [for stop-and-frisk searches] if a police officer conducting a traffic stop has an articulable suspicion of possible danger, the officer may order passengers to exit the vehicle as a defensive tactic without running afoul of the Fourth Amendment. Accordingly, I assume that the facts recited in the majority's opinion provided a valid justification for this officer's order commanding the passengers to get out of this vehicle.[13]

However, as previously described, Stevens objected vigorously to the Court's creation of a broad rule authorizing police intrusions on passengers in *all* traffic stop situations. As Stevens declared, "But the Court's ruling goes much further. It applies equally to traffic stops in which there is not even a scintilla of evidence of any potential risk to the police officer. In those cases, I firmly believe that the Fourth Amendment prohibits routine and arbitrary seizures of obviously innocent citizens."[14] Because Fourth Amendment cases present varied and novel factual situations, Stevens looked closely at the circumstances of each case and expressed disagreement when he concluded that his colleagues had articulated overly broad expansions of police authority, even when he might endorse a police officer's action in the specific case at hand. Justice Stevens's fact-specific approach and resistance to the creation of broad rules provided the basis for one of his most well-known dissenting opinions that favored police authority. In *Kyllo v. United States* (2001), Justice Scalia wrote a majority opinion that found a rights violation when police officers acted without a warrant to point a thermal-imaging device at a home to detect the indoor cultivation of marijuana through the use of heat-producing lights. Scalia concluded that the use of the heat-detection device constituted an improper warrantless search. Writing for the dissenters, who included Chief Justice Rehnquist and Justices O'Connor and Kennedy, Stevens argued that the homeowner's reasonable expectation of privacy was not violated by having a heat-detection device pointed at the home's outside walls. Thus, in Stevens's view, the police actions did not constitute a "search" that fell under the protections of the Fourth Amendment. Under his assessment of the facts, the device only detected heat, something that he said neighbors or passersby might detect through the ordinary use of their senses, and thereby did not provide any information about the interior of the house that would be protected by a reasonable expectation of privacy.

In addition, Stevens voiced his concern about the creation of overly broad rules by saying, "Moreover, I believe that the supposedly 'bright-line' rule the Court has created in response to its concerns about future technological developments is unnecessary, unwise, and inconsistent with the Fourth Amendment."[15] Stevens argued that the Court's effort to create a general rule about the use of sense-enhancing technology would hamper legitimate government needs for the use of technology to protect public safety. In

Stevens's words, "public officials should not have to avert their senses or their equipment from detecting emissions in the public domain such as excessive heat, traces of smoke, suspicious odors, odorless gases, airborne particulates, or radioactive emissions, any of which could identify hazards to the community."[16]

Justice Stevens's focus on the specific facts of each case also emphasized the realities of human behavior. In *Illinois v. Wardlow* (2000), Stevens's understanding of the specific factual context of the search led to him to argue in dissent that it was not necessarily reasonable for police officers to suspect that criminal activity was afoot because they saw an individual running away as they arrived in a high crime area. Stevens argued that an innocent person could reasonably conclude that the arrival of police meant that trouble had been reported in the vicinity and thus decide to leave quickly as a matter of rational self-protection. Moreover, Stevens evinced his sensitivity to issues of race and police-community relations by noting that:

> Among some citizens, particularly minorities and those residing in high crime areas, there is also the possibility that the fleeing person is entirely innocent, but, with or without justification, believes that contact with the police can itself be dangerous, apart from any criminal activity associated with the officer's sudden presence. For such a person, unprovoked flight is neither "aberrant" nor "abnormal." Moreover, these concerns and fears are known to the police officers themselves, and are validated by law enforcement investigations into their own practices.[17]

Stevens's attentiveness to the particular facts of the situation and his realistic assessment of human behavior made him skeptical of the majority's expansion of "stop-and-frisk" search authority based on officers' claims about observing an individual running down the sidewalk.

Justice Stevens criticized the Court's lack of appropriate deference to other decision makers in *Michigan v. Long* (1983).[18] In that case, a six-member majority of the Court endorsed the warrantless search of the passenger compartment of an unoccupied car when the driver was found standing outside of the vehicle. Justice Stevens argued that the majority was too actively seeking to create a rule to expand law enforcement authority. In Stevens's view, the nation's highest court should concern itself with circumstances in which individuals' rights receive too little protection, not those in which state courts have protected one of their own citizens:

> In this case, the State of Michigan has arrested one of its citizens and the Michigan Supreme Court has decided to turn him loose. The respondent is a United States citizen as well as a Michigan citizen, but since there is no claim that he has been mistreated by the State of Michigan, the final outcome of the state processes offended no federal interest whatever. Michigan simply pro-

> vided greater protection to one of its citizens than some other State might provide or, indeed, than this Court might require throughout the country.
>
> I believe that, in reviewing the decisions of state courts, the primary role of this Court is to make sure that persons who seek to *vindicate* federal rights have been fairly heard. That belief resonates with statements in many of our prior cases.[19]

Expressions of concern about the identification of and deference to appropriate decision makers can been seen all the way back to early decisions during Stevens's career on the Seventh Circuit U.S. Court of Appeals. In *United States v. Dichiarinte* (1971), for example, a majority on the Seventh Circuit panel concluded evidence of criminal tax evasion must be excluded from use in a prosecution because it was unreasonable for federal officers to seize the defendant's papers when he had only consented to a search of his home for narcotics. Here, Stevens's expressed concern for deference to appropriate decision makers placed him on the side of the government rather than in support of the individual's rights claims. In his dissenting opinion, Stevens argued that the appellate judges should have deferred to the fact-finding by the trial judge who actually heard the witness testimony about the consent and was the appropriate decision maker for determining the credibility of the testimony by the defendant and the federal officers.

THE EXCLUSIONARY RULE

Justice Stevens endorsed the exclusion of evidence as a necessary remedy for Fourth Amendment violations. As described in chapter 3, Stevens supported the exclusionary rule in his opinions as a judge on the court of appeals. He saw the exclusionary rule as mandated by the Constitution and he emphasized this point explicitly by saying in one opinion, "I add this comment merely to endorse Justice Stewart's conclusion that the 'rule *is* constitutionally required, not as a 'right' explicitly incorporated in the [F]ourth [A]mendment's prohibitions, but as a remedy necessary to ensure that those prohibitions are observed in fact.'"[20] However, his conception of the exclusionary rule's applicability was a bit narrower than that of his liberal colleagues, Brennan and Marshall. His disagreements with Brennan and Marshall did not concern whether the exclusionary rule should apply to remedy a particular rights violation, because Stevens strongly and consistently advocated the application of the exclusionary rule to remedy rights violations. Instead, his more limited view of the exclusionary rule's applicability stemmed from occasional disagreements with Brennan and Marshall about when a rights violation had actually occurred. In some cases, his liberal, holdover colleagues from the Warren Court identified a rights violation, but Stevens concluded that police acted within their authority in that specific situation. In *Maryland v. Garrison* (1987), for example, Stevens wrote a majority opinion, from which Brennan, Marshall, and Blackmun dissented, finding no Fourth Amendment violation when police officers searched the wrong apartment because in obtaining a warrant to search the third floor of a building, the officers did not realize that there was more than one apartment on that floor.

In several cases concerning warrantless searches of containers within automobiles, Brennan and Marshall argued that Fourth Amendment violations had occurred that required the exclusion of evidence. By contrast, Stevens concluded that the existence of probable cause made certain warrantless searches of the automobiles and their contents "reasonable" and permissible under the Fourth Amendment, thereby avoiding any rights violations that would require the remedy of excluding evidence from use by the prosecution.[21] Similarly, Brennan and Marshall disagreed with Stevens's view that the Fourth Amendment does not cover searches conducted in foreign countries by American law enforcement officials (*United States v. Verdugo-Urquidez*, 1990).

Justice Stevens's more limited view of Fourth Amendment protections and, by extension, the applicability of the exclusionary rule, was reflected in several of his majority opinions that endorsed governmental search authority. In *Horton v. California* (1990), for example, a case for which Stevens wrote the majority opinion on behalf of seven justices, he simply disagreed with Brennan's and Marshall's perspective on the "plain view doctrine" when he concluded that officers using a warrant that authorized a search for the proceeds of a robbery could also seize weapons found in the residence, even though this discovery was not inadvertent. The officers had admitted that they were looking for other evidence from the robbery beyond the financial proceeds described in the warrant. An earlier Stevens majority opinion, in *United States v. Caceres* (1979), had also parted company with Brennan's and Marshall's views, by concluding that the exclusion of evidence was not required for a violation of Internal Revenue Service regulations related to taping conversations of individuals under investigation.

In contrast to the foregoing examples, when Stevens identified an actual violation of the Fourth Amendment, he argued strongly for the remedy of exclusion and he objected to his conservative colleagues' efforts to reduce the applicability of the rule. In dissenting against the Burger Court majority's diminution of the exclusionary rule, Stevens emphasized the importance of the rule's deterrent purposes. In *Segura v. United States* (1984), for example, Stevens's dissenting opinion, joined by Brennan, Marshall, and Blackmun, objected to officers' warrantless entry and occupation of an apartment for eighteen hours before a search warrant was obtained. Moreover, he disagreed with the majority's decision to permit the officers to use evidence that they had obtained through these actions. In emphasizing the importance of the exclusionary rule's deterrence rationale, Stevens said,

> [T]he policies underlying the exclusionary rule demand that some deterrent be created to this kind of unconstitutional conduct. Yet the majority's disposition of this case creates none. Under the majority's approach, the agents could have remained indefinitely—impounding the apartment for a week or a month—without being deprived of the advantage derived from the unlawful impoundment. We cannot expect such an approach to prevent similar violations of the Fourth Amendment in the future.[22]

As Stevens said early in his Supreme Court career in *Dunaway v. New York* (1979), he saw the deterrent purpose of the exclusionary rule as intended to encourage the creation of appropriate policies and practices by police departments that will protect Fourth and Fifth Amendment rights: "The justification for the exclusion of evidence obtained by improper methods is to motivate the law enforcement profession as a whole—not the aberrant individual officer—to adopt and enforce regular procedures that will avoid the future invasion of the citizen's constitutional rights."[23]

Deterrence was not the only important purpose, however. Justice Stevens argued that both the Fourth Amendment and the exclusionary rule advance a "majestic conception" of safeguarding people, their privacy, and their property from unreasonable intrusions by government.[24] As a result, he saw purposes that went beyond merely deterring police officers from improper actions. In his view, "the Fourth Amendment and particularly the exclusionary rule, which effectuates the Amendment's commands . . . [are] constraint[s] on the power of the sovereign, not merely on some of its agents. The remedy for [Fourth Amendment] violation[s] imposes costs on that sovereign, motivating it to train all of its personnel to avoid future violations."[25] Thus the exclusionary rule also served to push government agencies to ensure that laws and proper procedures were followed by their agents.

Justice Stevens's defense of the exclusionary rule was also based on his concern that the judicial branch should be committed to preventing and remedying rights violations and therefore not participate in the utilization of improperly obtained evidence. In *United States v. Leon* (1984), the decision that created a "good faith" exception to the exclusionary rule when police rely on an improperly issued search warrant, Stevens complained about the majority's failure to insist on fulfillment of the judiciary's proper role:

> Today, for the first time, this Court holds that, although the Constitution has been violated, no court should do anything about it at any time and in any proceeding. In my judgment, the Constitution requires more. Courts simply cannot escape their responsibility for redressing constitutional violations if they admit evidence obtained through unreasonable searches and seizures,

> since the entire point of police conduct that violates the Fourth Amendment is to obtain evidence for use at trial. If such evidence is admitted, then the courts become not merely the final and necessary link in an unconstitutional chain of events, but its actual motivating force.[26]

Because he was concerned about the judiciary's duty to remedy rights violations, Stevens was especially concerned about his colleagues' efforts to identify an increasing number of contexts in which evidence could be used despite improper conduct and rights violations by police. For Stevens, such actions undercut the judiciary's fundamental responsibility to uphold the Bill of Rights. He expressed this view in strong terms in his *Leon* opinion:

> Nor should we so easily concede the existence of a constitutional violation for which there is no remedy. To do so is to convert a Bill of *Rights* into an unenforced honor code that the police may follow in their discretion. The Constitution requires more; it requires a *remedy*. If the Court's new rule [permitting the use of improperly obtained evidence] is to be followed, the Bill of Rights should be renamed.[27] (emphasis in original)

Supreme Court justices who seek to reduce the scope of the exclusionary rule often claim that the costs imposed on society from permitting criminals to escape proper punishment outweigh the benefits of protecting rights through exclusion. In the *Leon* majority opinion, for example, Justice White wrote that "We conclude that the marginal or nonexistent benefits produced by suppressing evidence obtained in objectively reasonable reliance on a subsequently invalidated search warrant cannot justify the substantial costs of exclusion."[28] As a dissenter in *Leon* and other cases that diminished the exclusionary rule, Stevens obviously did not agree with such assessments of the costs and benefits involved. Indeed, in a case concerning improper police questioning, Stevens made clear that he viewed the nature of the exclusionary rule's costs differently than did his conservative colleagues, who defined costs solely in terms of crime control objectives. He acknowledged that the rule imposed risks and costs for the goal of convicting and punishing criminal offenders. However, he saw costs to society, even beyond the harm to individuals' rights, if police officers were permitted to violate procedures. Justice Stevens wrote:

> The majority refers to the "societal cost" of excluding probative evidence. In my view, the more relevant cost is that imposed on society by police officers who decide to take procedural shortcuts instead of complying with the law . . . [thus leading to] years and years of unnecessary but costly litigation [when there are appeals and new trials resulting from rights violations].[29]

In light of his strongly held views about the deterrent value of the exclusionary rule and the judiciary's duty to remedy rights violations, Stevens disagreed consistently with decisions that created exceptions to the exclusionary rule. He saw the "good faith" exception in *Leon* as directly violating the animating purposes of the Fourth Amendment. Because the framers were deeply concerned about warrants based on insufficient justification as well as those that authorized general searches, they wrote specific requirements into the amendment. As Stevens noted:

> The notion that a police officer's reliance on a magistrate's warrant is automatically appropriate is one the Framers of the Fourth Amendment would have vehemently rejected. . . . Those who sought to amend the Constitution to include a Bill of Rights repeatedly voiced the view that the evil which had to be addressed was the issuance of warrants on insufficient evidence.[30]

Thus he used unusually sharp language in criticizing the majority's decision in *Leon*: "The Court's view that it is consistent with our Constitution to adopt a rule that it is presumptively reasonable to rely on a defective warrant is the product of constitutional amnesia."[31]

In short dissents, Stevens noted his objections to permitting the use of improperly obtained evidence in immigration deportation proceedings[32] and parole revocation hearings.[33] In *Arizona v. Evans* (1995), concerning a search incident to an arrest based on a nonexistent warrant erroneously listed in a computer database, Stevens forcefully, but unsuccessfully, advocated for the exclusion of evidence based on the Fourth Amendment violation. In Stevens's words, "The use of general warrants to search for evidence of violations of the Crown's revenue laws understandably outraged the authors of the Bill of Rights. . . . The offense to the dignity of the citizen who is arrested, handcuffed, and searched on a public street simply because some bureaucrat has failed to maintain an accurate computer data base strikes me as equally outrageous."[34]

As in several other cases that expanded police authority at the expense of the exclusionary rule's protections, the Court's majority preferred to ask "did the police officer do anything wrong?" rather than give priority to the question "were any Fourth Amendment rights violated?" Because the error was made by clerks responsible for the database and not by the police officers who made the traffic stop, arrest, and search in reliance on the database, the majority concluded that there was no reason to exclude the evidence found during the search. Justice Stevens expressed grave concern about the "serious impact . . . on the otherwise innocent citizen who is stopped for a minor traffic infraction and is wrongfully arrested based on erroneous information in a computer database."[35] This concern was especially important because the Court's approach seemed to preclude the possibility of winning a civil lawsuit against the officer or the law enforcement agency for violating Fourth Amendment constitutional rights with an unjustified arrest in this context.

The lack of an alternative mechanism to protect people's rights led Stevens to argue that "if courts are to have any power to discourage official error of this kind, it must be through application of the exclusionary rule."[36] The dissenting opinion written by Stevens in *Arizona v. Evans* later became a central source of quoted language for a similar dissenting opinion written by Justice Ginsburg, and joined by Justices Stevens, Souter, and Breyer, in another case in which computer database errors led to an improper arrest and attendant search that revealed criminal evidence (*Herring v. United States*, 2009).

As illustrated by the *Herring* case, Stevens joined dissenting opinions written by other justices advocating preservation of the exclusionary rule in a variety of contexts. For example, he joined dissents asserting that evidence should be excluded from administrative searches that relied on statutes later declared to be unconstitutional[37] and searches in which officers erroneously rely on consent from a person who lacks authority over the premises to be searched.[38]

STOP AND FRISK

As described in chapter 3, Stevens's court of appeals opinion on the stop-and-frisk issue in *United States v. Jeffers* (1975) endorsed police officers' removal of a woman's calf-length boot to discover an illegal narcotic capsule hidden inside. By approving removal of the boot rather than relying on a patdown for weapons at the lower leg and ankle, Stevens's opinion seemed to stretch the rationale of *Terry v. Ohio* (1968) beyond the Supreme Court's stated intention of permitting a frisk search to protect public safety when an officer could reasonably conclude that specific facts indicated the potential for danger. Judge Stevens's opinion demonstrated both deference to law enforcement authority and a relaxed application of the *Terry* holding regarding the factual circumstances justifying a stop-and-frisk search. Neither of these elements was consistently evident across Stevens's later votes and opinions on Fourth Amendment issues as a Supreme Court justice. Indeed, stop-and-frisk searches appear to be a specific category for which Stevens's approach as a Supreme Court justice was more protective of individuals than the analysis he applied in his *Jeffers* opinion as a court of appeals judge.

For example, *Maryland v. Buie* (1990) was a case in which dissenters Brennan and Marshall complained that "[t]oday the Court for the first time extends *Terry v. Ohio* . . . into the home."[39] Contrary to his earlier *Jeffers* opinion, Stevens's concurring opinion seemed to show concern about the facts used by officers to justify acting upon a reasonable suspicion of danger, even as he supported the idea of a *Terry*-like protective sweep inside a home. Moreover, the specific questions Stevens raised about whether the facts supported reasonable suspicion to justify the protective sweep in this case so alarmed Justice Kennedy about their potential to limit police authority that he wrote a very short "please-do-not-listen-to-Stevens" concurring opinion that criticized Stevens's "gratuitous observation."[40] Justice Kennedy claimed that his own one-paragraph opinion was "necessary, lest by acquiescence the impression be left that Justice Stevens'[s] views can be interpreted as authoritative guidance for application of our ruling to the facts of the case."[41] Similarly, in both *Illinois v. Wardlow* (2000), concerning the stop-and-frisk of the man seen running in a "high-crime area," and *Alabama v. White* (1990), concerning a stop and search based on an anonymous tip that was consistent with police officers' observations, Stevens wrote dissenting opinions demanding more specific information and police observations as the basis for such searches.

In a related case, *New Jersey v. T.L.O.* (1985), Stevens objected to the majority endorsing school officials' authority to search students' purses based on a suspicion of violations of trivial school rules rather than insisting that such invasions of privacy should be based on *Terry*-type concerns about safety. The *Jeffers* case may have helped to initially familiarize Stevens with stop-and-frisk issues, but it did not necessarily reflect a settled viewpoint, especially because he would have later opportunities to learn and consider more aspects of the situations in which these searches can arise. In the later cases, he appeared to be more insistent that search authority be justified by guidance from *Terry*'s fact-specific holding.

VEHICLE SEARCHES

Justice Stevens's reasoning appeared to be especially consistent over his career in cases concerning searches of vehicles and their contents. A superficial examination of his voting record on this issue might lead one to conclude that he supported police authority early in his career and then shifted to support individuals' rights in later years. In fact, however, Stevens's later opinions articulated his objections to the Court's aggressive efforts to expand police authority to search vehicles beyond the scope of the authority that he helped to define in his early opinions on the issue.

In the first decade of his career, Stevens wrote several opinions endorsing police authority in vehicle search cases. In his dissenting opinion in *Robbins v. California* (1981), Stevens expressed the view that when a vehicle is lawfully stopped and its driver is lawfully arrested, officers can search the vehicle and containers within the vehicle when they have probable cause to believe that evidence of a crime may be found there. In *Robbins*, probable cause was based on the officer smelling the aroma of marijuana so Stevens argued that it was proper for the officer to open the trunk and examine a package within the trunk that was found to contain marijuana. However, he expressed grave concern about the potential expansion of police authority from the Court's decision in a parallel case, *New York v. Belton* (1981). In *Belton*, the majority relied on the rationale of a search incident to a lawful arrest as the justification for searching a jacket found within a vehicle. Stevens feared that officers may manufacture reasons to make arrests in order to use that justification for searches. Instead, he argued that both cases should fall under the "automobile exception" to the warrant requirement that, in his view, permitted searches of vehicles and containers when officers have probable cause to search for contraband without any specific knowledge about where the contraband might be. He sought to impose a strict requirement on officers through his expectation that probable cause exist to justify such searches. Moreover, his expectation about the existence of probable cause defined permissible searches as arising within a more limited set of factual circumstances than searches based on officers' authority to explore an area and objects within the immediate area to make sure that an arrestee did not have weapons or evidence.

The following year, in *United States v. Ross* (1982), Stevens wrote for a six-member majority in seeking to clarify the law of vehicle searches by holding that:

> [T]he scope of the warrantless search authorized by that [automobile] exception [to the Fourth Amendment's warrant requirement] is no broader and no narrower than a magistrate could legitimately authorize by warrant. If probable cause justifies the search of a lawfully stopped vehicle, it justifies the search of every part of the vehicle and its contents that may conceal the object of the search.[42]

Justices Brennan, Marshall, and White disagreed with Stevens and dissented, thereby advocating a narrower scope of police authority to search vehicles and their contents.

The *Ross* decision rejected the holding of the prior year's *Robbins* (1981) case for which Stevens had written a dissent. In *Ross*, Stevens emphasized the importance of the existence of probable cause to justify the warrantless search and its scope. He also emphasized the need to permit deviation from the Fourth Amendment's warrant requirement only in cases of carefully delineated exceptions and he sought to define the automobile exception in a careful, specific manner. His explicit intent was to provide clarity for the rule that officers would apply to vehicle searches because the justices' decisions in several earlier cases appeared to make potentially confusing distinctions between the types of containers found within vehicles. He emphasized the Fourth Amendment's protection of individuals and, unlike some of his colleagues in other search cases, he did not identify any need to reduce impediments to officers' authority to search. Thus one does not see within Stevens's opinion any explicit effort to enhance the crime control mission of police officers. Yet, the rule he articulated in *Ross* effectively granted police officers significant authority because they would make their own determinations about the existence of probable cause without the intervening judgment of a neutral magistrate, as in the cases for which they must seek warrants. Such determinations could be retrospectively challenged and examined by judicial officers in suppression hearings during the prosecution process. However, officers would have the time and opportunity in such circumstances to strengthen—and potentially exaggerate—their description of the facts that purportedly justified the existence of probable cause in vehicle search contexts. Despite this risk, in Stevens's view, practical necessity justified permitting police to open containers within vehicles when probable cause exists, in part, because requiring officers to seek warrants merely served to increase the inconvenience and intrusion on privacy interests suffered by individuals at the scene of traffic stops. As Stevens explained:

> But prohibiting police from opening immediately a container in which the object of the search is most likely to be found, and instead forcing them first to comb the entire vehicle, would actually exacerbate the intrusion on privacy interests. Moreover, until the container itself was opened, the police could never be certain that the contraband was not secreted in a yet undiscovered portion of the vehicle; thus, in every case in which a container was found, the vehicle would need to be secured while a warrant was obtained.[43]

In these three conservative decisions—*Robbins*, *Belton*, and *Ross*—Stevens did not advocate overturning prior precedents that required officers to obtain warrants when they lacked probable cause to search a vehicle and only had probable cause to believe that a specific container placed within a vehicle contained contraband. In such cases, they were expected to seek a search warrant from a judicial officer after seizing the container for which they claimed to have probable cause to search. In *United States v. Chadwick* (1977), a warrant was required when narcotics officers seized from a vehicle the luggage that they had probable cause to believe contained illegal drugs. Similarly, in *Arkansas v. Sanders* (1979), the Court required a warrant before searching luggage that was seized from a drug suspect riding in a taxi cab. These precedents distinguished searches permitted when there was probable cause to search a vehicle from those based solely on probable cause for a specific container that had been placed within the vehicle. Justice Stevens reiterated this view in his concurrence in *Texas v. Brown* (1983), a case concerning the plain view doctrine-based seizure of a balloon that was visible in the car and appeared to be of the type used to carry small quantities of illegal drugs. Joined by Justices Brennan and Marshall, Stevens agreed that the balloon could be seized under the plain view doctrine but argued that the evidence revealed by opening the balloon on the spot without a warrant must be excluded unless on remand to the lower courts the state provided additional facts to establish probable cause or exigent circumstances.

In *Robbins*, *Belton*, and *Ross*, Stevens supported the exercise of police authority in opposition to the views of his colleagues Brennan, Marshall, and White, who wanted greater protection for individuals under the Fourth Amendment in the context of vehicle searches. However, throughout the remainder of his career, with the exception of one opinion, Stevens's opinions concerning vehicle searches consistently supported the protection of individuals' rights and opposed the expansion of police authority to conduct such searches. The one exception was *Illinois v. Cabelles* (2005) in which his majority opinion ruled that a trained police dog sniffing around the exterior of a vehicle during a lawful traffic stop did not constitute a search and therefore was not covered by the Fourth Amendment's protections.

The Supreme Court's decision in *Michigan v. Long* (1983) and Stevens's reaction to that decision in his dissenting opinion provided a glimpse of what was to come in defining his role in vehicle search cases for the final quarter-century of his career on the Supreme Court. In *Michigan v. Long*, Stevens objected to the Court's reaching out to overrule a Michigan Supreme Court decision that declared officers lacked a proper basis to search a vehicle after conducting a *Terry*-based frisk of a driver found standing outside of the car. Justice Stevens complained that throughout the Court's history the justices had not accepted and overruled decisions in which a state supreme court had protected its own citizens' rights. He warned against the then-recent development of the Supreme Court taking such cases in order to expand police authority under the claim of seeking to enhance uniformity:

> Sometime during the past decade, perhaps about the time of the 5-to-4 decision in *Zacchini v. Scripps-Howard Broadcasting Co.*, . . . (1977), our priorities shifted. The result is a docket swollen with requests by States to reverse judgments that their courts have rendered in favor of their citizens. I am confident that a future Court will recognize the error of this allocation of resources. When that day comes, I think it likely that the Court will also reconsider the propriety of today's expansion of our jurisdiction.[44]

He wrote these words as the composition of the Supreme Court was soon to change with the addition of newcomers appointed by Presidents Ronald Reagan and George H. W. Bush. Several of these new justices contributed to more assertive efforts to expand police authority. Thus in vehicle search cases, as in other cases concerning the exclusionary rule and other search contexts, Stevens appeared to devote most of his attention and energy to resisting efforts to diminish Fourth Amendment protections for individuals.

Although the Stevens dissent in *Michigan v. Long* (1983) focused on his criticism of the Court's overreaching and did not engage the majority opinion's substantive analysis of the actual search, two years later he wrote another dissent that similarly complained about overreaching and also criticized the majority's substantive analysis. In *California v. Carney* (1985), the California Supreme Court had ruled that police officers must obtain a warrant in order to conduct a non-exigent search of a mobile home. The majority of U.S. Supreme Court justices reversed that decision and treated the mobile home like an automobile, a search location with a diminished expectation of privacy and a risk of flight that more easily justified warrantless searches. In his dissenting opinion, joined by Brennan and Marshall, Stevens argued that mobile homes should be treated like houses. He said they should be recognized as places with reasonable expectations about significant privacy interests for individuals that deserved a high level of Fourth Amendment protection. He also strongly reiterated his complaints about the Court's "aggressiveness" in expanding police search authority by improperly accepting too many cases inappropriately for hearing.[45] In Stevens's words:

> In recent Terms, the Court has displayed little confidence in state and lower federal court decisions that purport to enforce the Fourth Amendment. Unless an order suppressing evidence is clearly correct, a petition for certiorari is likely to garner the four votes required for a grant of plenary review—as the one in this case did. Much of the Court's "burdensome" workload is a product of its own aggressiveness in this area. By promoting the Supreme Court of the United States as the High Magistrate for every warrantless search and seizure, this practice has burdened the argument docket with cases presenting fact-bound errors of minimal significance. It has also encouraged state legal officers to file petitions for certiorari in even the most frivolous search and seizure cases.[46]

Justice Stevens repeated his criticism of the Court's "activism" in a concurring opinion in *Florida v. Wells* (1990). He expressed grave concern about the Court's encouragement of standardless, discretionary decisions by officers to search containers in impounded vehicles. Justice Stevens effectively accused his colleagues of being too preoccupied with expanding police authority when he said, "Apparently the mere possibility of a minor burden on law enforcement interests is enough to generate corrective action by this Court."[47] He complained that, "Thus, luggage, briefcases, handbags, brown paper bags, violin cases—indeed, virtually all containers except goldfish bowls—could be opened at the whim of the officer, whether locked or unlocked."[48]

The following year, in *California v. Acevedo* (1991), Stevens wrote an extensive dissenting opinion objecting to the majority running roughshod over the careful distinctions between vehicles and containers that he had sought to articulate in his majority opinion in *United States v. Ross* (1982). The Court permitted officers to undertake a warrantless search of a package for which they had probable cause to search. After they saw it placed in an automobile, they then stopped the vehicle and seized the package. The majority specifically reversed the *Arkansas v. Sanders* (1979) precedent that previously required officers to seek a search warrant after such a seizure when there was no probable cause to search the vehicle in which the container was located.

In presenting his review of the purposes of the Fourth Amendment and the Court's precedents concerning containers within vehicles, he drew from his prior experience by emphasizing a quote from Justice Jackson's opinion in *Johnson v. United States* (1948), an opinion that his mentor Justice Rutledge had joined during Stevens's clerkship year at the Court. Justice Stevens systematically refuted the majority's justifications for expanding police authority by rejecting assertions that the prior rule was too confusing and unnecessary for protecting privacy interests. He was highly critical of the majority for removing Fourth Amendment protections from containers merely because they have been placed inside motor vehicles. As Stevens noted:

> For surely it is anomalous to prohibit a search of a briefcase while the owner is carrying it exposed on a public street, yet to permit a search once the owner has placed the briefcase in the locked trunk of his car. One's privacy interest in one's luggage can certainly not be diminished by one's removing it from a public thoroughfare and placing it—out of sight—in a privately owned vehicle.[49]

In addressing the majority's claim that the prior rule was an impediment to law enforcement efforts to control crime, Stevens issued a sharp retort:

> No impartial observer could criticize this Court for hindering the progress of the war on drugs. On the contrary, decisions like the one the Court makes today will support the conclusion that this Court has become a loyal foot soldier in the Executive's fight against crime.
>
> Even if the warrant requirement does inconvenience the police to some extent, that fact does not distinguish this constitutional requirement from any other procedural protection secured by the Bill of Rights. It is merely a part of the price that our society must pay in order to preserve its freedom.[50]

Justice Stevens had been very consistent in his approach to defining police authority to conduct warrantless searches of containers within automobiles, yet this dissenting opinion made clear that the Court majority's efforts to expand that authority had pushed him to strongly defend the Fourth Amendment protections that he saw shrinking. He concluded his *Acevedo* dissent with stark criticisms of the majority's action: "It is too early to know how much freedom America has lost today. The magnitude of the loss is, however, not nearly as significant as the Court's willingness to inflict it without even a colorable basis for its rejection of prior law."[51] In this case and other vehicle search cases, his voting record became more liberal under the counting and classifying methods of social scientists, yet this reflected only his resistance to the change in the direction of the Court's decisions and not a change in his own reasoning.

Justice Stevens continued to argue in favor of requiring warrants in circumstances that did not fit his assessment of the exigencies that must exist in order to trigger his conception of the automobile exception. In *Florida v. White* (1999), joined only by Justice Ginsburg, he objected to the warrantless search of an automobile when the police had information months earlier about the vehicle's apparent use in drug transactions yet they never bothered to get a warrant. He complained that, "[O]ne must assume that the officers who seized White's car simply preferred to avoid the hassle of seeking approval from a judicial officer. I would not permit bare convenience to overcome our established preference for the warrant process as a check against arbitrary intrusions by law enforcement agencies.[52]

In *Wyoming v. Houghton* (1999), as in *Florida v. White,* the Supreme Court majority expanded law enforcement authority by reversing a state supreme court decision that protected individuals' rights. In *Houghton,* the majority concluded that the search of a vehicle passenger's purse was justified by the discovery in the shirt pocket of the driver of a hypodermic needle used for injecting drugs. In an opinion written by Justice Scalia, the majority declared that the formation of probable cause to search for drugs in the vehicle based on the discovery of the hypodermic needle justified searching in every location within the vehicle where drugs might be, even if that location affected the possessions of passengers who were unconnected to the basis for the probable cause determination.

With the support of Justices Ginsburg and Souter, Stevens dissented against this expansion of police authority. As in other cases, he cited a precedent that was familiar to him from his clerkship year on the Court when he said, "In the only automobile case confronting the search of a passenger defendant, *United States v. Di Re,* . . . (1948)—the Court held that the exception to the warrant requirement did not apply. . . . In *Di Re,* as here, the information prompting the search directly implicated the driver, not the passenger."[53] He referred to the *Di Re* case several more times in his dissenting opinion, including a long quote from Justice Jackson's *Di Re* majority opinion that concluded with the words "'We are not convinced that a person, by mere presence in a suspected car, loses immunities from search of his person to which he would otherwise be entitled.' *Di Re,* 332 U. S., at 587."[54]

Justice Stevens also relied on his own majority opinion in *United States v. Ross* (1982) to illustrate the expansion of police authority reflected in the majority's *Houghton* opinion and to argue against the intrusion on passengers' privacy interests:

> Ironically, while we concluded in *Ross* that "[p]robable cause to believe that a container placed in the trunk of a taxi contains contraband or evidence does not justify a search of the entire cab," . . . the rule the Court fashions would apparently permit a warrantless search of a passenger's briefcase if there is probable cause to believe the taxidriver had a syringe somewhere in his vehicle.
>
> Nor am I persuaded that the mere spatial association between a passenger and a driver provides an acceptable basis for presuming that they are partners in crime or for ignoring privacy interests in a purse. Whether or not the Fourth Amendment required a warrant to search Houghton's purse, . . . at the very least the trooper in this case had to have probable cause to believe that her purse contained contraband. The Wyoming Supreme Court concluded that he did not [have probable cause]. . . . Finally, in my view, the State's legitimate interest in effective law enforcement does not outweigh the privacy concerns at issue.[55]

Justice Stevens laid the groundwork in *Thornton v. United States* (2004) for a subsequent rare opportunity to successfully limit the expansion of law enforcement officers' authority to search vehicles and containers within vehicles. In *Thornton*, Justice Stevens used a dissenting opinion, joined only by Justice Souter, to renew the objections he raised in *New York v. Belton* (1981) concerning the Court's use of the incident-to-lawful-arrest rationale for searches when an individual is arrested outside of the vehicle. To Stevens, the "rule should provide the same protection to a 'recent occupant' of a vehicle as to a recent occupant of a house,"[56] namely limiting police to searching the individual and the area around the individual for weapons and evidence but not entering and searching new areas. He also complained that the majority gave no guidance on the meaning of "recent" in declaring that officers can search vehicles of arrestees who were recent occupants of vehicles. In Stevens's view, "the Court extends *Belton*'s reach without supplying any guidance for the future application of its swollen rule."[57] Justice Stevens complained that "[w]ithout some limiting principle, I fear that today's decision will contribute to 'a massive broadening of the automobile exception,' . . . when officers have probable cause to arrest an individual but not to search his car."[58]

Subsequently, Stevens gained the opportunity to write a majority opinion that defined a limitation on the expansion of police authority incident to arrests that had occurred in *Belton* and *Thornton*. In *Arizona v. Gant* (2009), as the senior justice in the majority, Stevens assigned to himself an opinion on behalf of a narrow five-member majority, including Justices Ginsburg, Souter, Scalia, and Thomas. In *Gant*, police officers searched the vehicle after arresting Gant, handcuffing him, and placing him in the back of the patrol car. The original justification for a warrantless search incident to a lawful arrest inside a home in *Chimel v. California* (1969) was based on officers' need to protect themselves from weapons within reach of the arrestee and to prevent the arrestee from destroying nearby evidence. Justice Stevens concluded that these justifications could not exist when the arrestee was handcuffed and placed in a patrol car. Therefore officers could not automatically conduct a vehicle search simply because they had arrested the recent occupant of a vehicle. Although this case provided a legal limit on officers' authority, it was not immune from subversion by the adaptive behavior of officers who were determined to conduct a vehicle search. If officers, for example, held the arrestee by the arm outside of the vehicle without handcuffing him and placing him into the patrol car, then they could likely rely on the *Belton* and *Thornton* precedents to conduct their desired vehicle search. Notwithstanding Stevens's inability to control exactly how police would respond and implement the rule he articulated in *Gant*, he did succeed—barely, by one vote—in halting, at least momentarily, the continued expansion of police search authority in this arrest context.

VEHICLE STOPS

With respect to the related issue of vehicle stops, Stevens experienced mixed results in seeking to have his preferred interpretations of the Fourth Amendment placed into law. During his first term on the Supreme Court, Stevens joined Justice Powell's majority opinion in *United States v. Martinez-Fuerte* (1976) that approved brief, suspicionless stops of all drivers at a police checkpoint to detect the smuggling of undocumented workers into the country. In 1979, Stevens was among an eight-justice majority endorsing an opinion by Justice White in *Delaware v. Prouse* (1979) that forbade police officers from making random, discretionary stops of vehicles in order to check drivers' licenses and registration papers. Unlike Justice Blackmun, Stevens did not write a concurring opinion to explain or disavow a statement in White's reasoning that appeared to endorse the possibility of vehicle checkpoints for purposes other than detecting smuggling. Justice White wrote that "This holding does not preclude the State of Delaware or other States from developing methods for spot checks that involve less intrusion or that do not involve the unconstrained exercise of discretion. Questioning of all oncoming traffic at roadblock-type stops is one possible alternative."[59] Because this language was not part of the holding of the case, one must hesitate to assume that it was supported by all of the justices who joined the opinion. On the other hand, Justice Stevens was such a prolific writer of concurring and dissenting opinions that he often carefully distinguished his precise views from those of other justices. The fact that he did not comment on this language, as Blackmun did in a short concurring opinion, leaves open the inference that Stevens was open to the possibility of permitting vehicle checkpoints for various purposes at that time.

In the later case of *Michigan Dept. of State Police v. Sitz* (1990), by contrast, Stevens dissented on behalf of Brennan and Marshall when the Court approved sobriety checkpoints at which all drivers were stopped briefly to detect whether they were driving under the influence of alcohol. He had not changed his mind about the propriety of certain vehicle checkpoints. Instead, he saw critical distinctions between the sobriety checkpoint and the checkpoint that he had approved in *Martinez-Fuerte*. In particular, he saw the surprise checkpoint in *Sitz* as more intrusive than the checkpoint in *Martinez-Fuerte* that was announced by road signs in advance of the stop. He also saw the justification for the checkpoint to stop smuggling as more compelling than the sobriety checkpoint that he viewed as symbolic and ineffective. According to Stevens:

> [T]he sobriety checkpoint is driven by nothing more than symbolic state action—an insufficient justification for an otherwise unreasonable program of random seizures. Unfortunately, the Court is transfixed by the wrong symbol—the illusory prospect of punishing countless intoxicated motorists—when it should keep its eyes on the road plainly marked by the Constitution.[60]

Justice Stevens appeared to play a key role in a subsequent vehicle checkpoint case, *City of Indianapolis v. Edmond* (2000). A six-member majority of the Court, including Stevens, disallowed the use of checkpoints for the general law enforcement purpose of seeking to discover illegal drugs. With Chief Justice Rehnquist among the dissenters, Stevens was the senior justice in the majority. In that role, Stevens assigned the majority opinion to Justice O'Connor, who had supported sobriety checkpoints in *Michigan Dept. of State Police v. Stiz* (1990). In interviews, Stevens acknowledged that, in his role as senior majority justice, when he assigned opinion-writing duties, "[s]ometimes . . . in all candor, if you think somebody might not be solid . . . it might be wiser to let that person write the opinion . . . [as he or she] may tend to become more convinced" in the process of articulating the reasoning for the decision.[61] Thus Stevens may have strategically selected O'Connor to write the opinion in order to retain her vote, as well as that of Justice Kennedy, against drug enforcement checkpoints, as both had supported sobriety roadblocks in *Sitz*.

Subsequently, in *Illinois v. Lidster* (2004), Stevens wrote an opinion concurring in part and dissenting in part, joined by Ginsburg and Souter, in a case concerning a temporary checkpoint to ask drivers if they had witnessed a fatal hit-and-run collision at that location on a previous day. The case arose because the checkpoint led to the inadvertent discovery that Lidster was driving under the influence of alcohol when he was stopped to ask if he had witnessed the hit-and-run incident. In the concurring portion of the opinion, Stevens agreed with the majority that the checkpoint was not precluded by the Court's decision in *Edmond* because "There is a valid and important distinction between seizing a person to determine whether she has committed a crime and seizing a person to ask whether she has any information about an unknown person who committed a crime a week earlier."[62] In the dissenting portions, however, he disagreed with the majority's decision to analyze the factual circumstances of the event and reach the conclusion that the checkpoint was constitutional. Consistent with his oft-stated concerns about looking carefully at each case's underlying factual circumstances and his concern about the Supreme Court's appropriate role, he argued that the case should be remanded to the Illinois courts, which had not analyzed the facts but merely applied the *Edmond* precedent when the case moved through state court system. As Stevens observed, "We should be especially reluctant to abandon our role as a court of review in a case in which the constitutional inquiry requires analysis of local conditions and practices more familiar to judges closer to the scene."[63]

Justice Stevens's views on the permissibility of vehicle checkpoints help to illustrate why commentators initially found it difficult to pigeonhole his judicial decision making into the familiar categories of "liberal" and "conservative." Because of his concern with the factual circumstances of each case and the need to balance the interests of individuals and the state in assessing the definition of Fourth Amendment rights, he did not reflexively either endorse or oppose vehicle checkpoints. Justices Brennan and Marshall consistently rejected the constitutionality of suspicionless, checkpoint stops of drivers inside the country's borders while Scalia, Thomas, and Rehnquist consistently supported such police authority. By contrast, Stevens was among the justices who saw distinctions between the circumstances and justifications for checkpoints. When Stevens was ultimately labeled as "liberal" for such cases, it was based on a relative assessment of the limited circumstances in which he would endorse the permissibility of checkpoints. Most of his colleagues had a broader view of police authority under the Fourth Amendment as evidenced by the majority decisions that Stevens criticized in *Sitz* and *Lidster*.

In a parallel fashion, Stevens reached specific conclusions about the circumstances that justified warrantless searches of vehicles and containers within vehicles. He articulated a view of the "automobile exception" to the warrant requirement that permitted warrantless searches when officers possessed probable cause. However, he consistently opposed using the incident-to-a-lawful-arrest rationale to justify broad searches of vehicles and containers, just as he opposed permitting warrantless searches when officers had probable cause to search only containers that were placed into vehicles. Because he believed strongly in the presumption that the Fourth Amendment required police to obtain search warrants from judicial officers when possible, he did not endorse warrantless searches of containers in police custody, even when police officers concluded that they had probable cause to search.

The votes cast by Stevens in vehicle stop and search issues became more frequently liberal over the course of his career, but this change in his voting record reflected his reaction to changes in the Court's composition, the new majority's aggressiveness in reshaping Fourth Amendment law, and the nature of issues accepted for hearing. A close examination of his opinions indicated great consistency in his analysis of Fourth Amendment rights and the appropriate limits of police authority to conduct warrantless searches of vehicles.

SEIZURES

The cases concerning vehicle stops reflected Stevens's consistent concern about limiting police authority to undertake seizures and ensuring that any seizures were appropriately justified in light of the Fourth Amendment's purposes and protections. In other kinds of cases, Stevens stood out as a particularly strong advocate of protecting individuals' rights against inappropriate warrantless seizures. Early in his career, Stevens, along with Brennan and Marshall, joined a dissenting opinion by Justice White in *United States v. Mendenhall* (1980). In that case, a woman at the Detroit airport was approached by agents of the federal Drug Enforcement Agency and was asked to accompany the agents to an office at the airport to answer questions. The agents thought that she was suspicious because she had arrived on a flight from Los Angeles without any luggage. At the office, she agreed to a search and the search revealed that she was carrying illegal drugs under her clothing. Justice Stevens joined the dissenting opinion that concluded the woman was "seized" in Fourth Amendment terms because she was not free to leave and that the agents lacked a sufficient basis for the seizure, therefore constituting a rights violation as an unreasonable seizure. Justice Stevens's agreement with the Warren Court holdovers' protective view of the Fourth Amendment right against unreasonable seizures provided an early indication that he would look closely at the facts of each case and be concerned about whether individuals were genuinely free to leave certain police-initiated interactions.

In later cases, Stevens asserted his views in concurring and dissenting opinions, and thereby established himself as more protective of individuals' rights related to warrantless seizures than any other justices except Brennan and Marshall. In *Brower v. County of Inyo* (1989), Stevens wrote a concurring opinion, joined by Brennan, Marshall, and Blackmun, that viewed the other five justices' definition of seizures as too narrow. According to Stevens, "The intentional acquisition of physical control of something is no doubt a characteristic of the typical seizure, but I am not entirely sure that it is an essential element of every seizure, or that this formulation is particularly helpful in deciding close cases."[64]

The concern expressed by Stevens in *Brower* came to fruition two years later in *California v. Hodari D.* (1991) and clearly established Stevens as more protective of Fourth Amendment rights on this issue than were his colleagues. In *Hodari D.*, a young man discarded rocks of crack cocaine just prior to being tackled by an officer who was chasing him. The chase began when several young people ran at the sight of a police car; the police did not otherwise have information that these individuals were involved with illegal drugs. The majority opinion by Justice Scalia concluded that the subject had not been seized at the time that he discarded the drugs while running because a seizure in this case would require either the application of physical force by the officer or the subject's submission to the officer's assertion of authority. In this case, Hodari D. had not yet been physically touched by the officer and, by running, he clearly did not submit to the officer's authority on his own.

In a strong dissenting opinion, joined only by Marshall in the aftermath of Brennan's retirement during the prior year, Stevens argued that the majority had deviated from prior precedents and defined too narrowly the concept of seizure under the Fourth Amendment. For Stevens, an individual can be "not free to leave" and therefore seized as a result of an officer's show of force, without regard to whether physical contact has occurred. Moreover, he did not believe that seizures should be defined by a citizens' reaction—submission or not—in part, because time intervals between a show of force and a decision to submit still place an individual in the position of being "not free to leave." In the words of Stevens's opinion,

> [T]he same issue would arise if the show of force took the form of a command to "freeze," a warning shot, or the sound of sirens accompanied by a patrol car's flashing lights. In any of these situations, there may be a significant time interval between the initiation of the officer's show of force and the complete submission by the citizen. At least on the facts of this case, the Court concludes that the timing of the seizure is governed by the citizen's reaction, rather than by the officer's conduct. . . . One consequence of this conclusion is that the point at which the interaction between citizen and police officer becomes a seizure occurs, not when a reasonable citizen believes he or she is no longer free to go, but rather only after the officer exercises control over the citizen.[65]

As in some other cases, Stevens's assessment of individuals' thoughts and actions, in particular the reality of feeling not free to leave, seemed to reflect a more precise analysis of the facts and realistic assessment of human behavior than that employed by his colleagues. One of his examples in the *Hodari*

D. opinion provided an especially stark illustration of the real-world possibilities that his colleagues failed to recognize and consider:

> In an airport setting, may a drug enforcement agent now approach a group of passengers with his gun drawn, announce a "baggage search," and rely on the passengers' reactions to justify his investigative stops? The holding of today's majority fails to recognize the coercive and intimidating nature of such behavior, and creates a rule that may allow such behavior to go unchecked.[66]

Justice Stevens stood out from his colleagues as the lone dissenter in *Ohio v. Robinette* (1996). A motorist had been stopped for speeding. At the conclusion of his encounter with the police officer, the officer expressed a desire to ask "one more question before you get gone."[67] The officer asked if there was any contraband in the vehicle and then asked for consent to conduct a search. Consent was granted and illegal drugs were discovered. Justice Stevens agreed with his colleagues' conclusion that there is no constitutional requirement that a police officer inform a driver that he is free to leave or to decline to consent to a search. However, Stevens was alone among the justices in concluding that the driver was not free to leave at the time that the officer asked the crucial questions. Therefore, in his view, the consent to search was invalid because it was the product of an illegal seizure, namely the unjustified continued detention of the driver after the speeding infraction had been handled. As in other opinions, Stevens focused on a realistic understanding of human motives and behaviors in questioning government assertions that such consents are voluntary because people are free to leave at that point in the encounter. With respect to people's reasonable assessment of whether or not they have been released from the traffic stop, Stevens observed:

> The fact that this particular officer successfully used a similar method of obtaining consent to search roughly 786 times in one year, . . . indicates that motorists generally respond in a manner that is contrary to their self-interest. Repeated decisions by ordinary citizens to surrender that interest cannot satisfactorily be explained on any hypothesis other than an assumption that they believed they had a legal duty to do so.[68]

Justice Stevens was also highly critical of police officers' reliance on anonymous tips as a basis for seizures. In *Alabama v. White* (1990), the Court endorsed a stop based on an anonymous tip concerning when a subject would leave a house and where the subject would go. In his dissenting opinion, joined by Brennan and Marshall, Stevens complained that the Court had opened the door to vindictive actions and pranks since officers' corroborating observations that trigger the seizure may be merely of routine, benign daily activities. According to Stevens:

> Millions of people leave their apartments at about the same time every day, carrying an attache case and heading for a destination known to their neighbors. . . . Anybody with enough knowledge about a given person to make her the target of a prank, or to harbor a grudge against her, will certainly be able to formulate a tip. . . . [U]nder the Court's holding, every citizen is subject to being seized and questioned by any officer who is prepared to testify that the warrantless stop was based on an anonymous tip predicting whatever conduct the officer just observed. . . . But the Fourth Amendment was intended to protect the citizen from the overzealous and unscrupulous officer, as well as from those who are conscientious and truthful. This decision makes a mockery of that protection.[69]

JUSTICE STEVENS AND THE FOURTH AMENDMENT

In his earliest years on the Supreme Court, Stevens demonstrated a strong concern for the protection of individuals' privacy rights against excessive exertions of search and seizure authority by law enforcement officials. For example, he objected to government officials' actions in opening private letters (*United States v. Ramsey*, 1977), monitoring telephones (*United States v. New York Telephone Co.*, 1977), and making a warrantless entry in order to plant an electronic listening device (*Dalia v. United States*, 1979). He did not, however, reflexively support Fourth Amendment claims and he was less likely than his colleagues Brennan and Marshall to consistently oppose intrusive investigatory actions by the police. Thus Stevens also wrote a number of opinions supporting law enforcement authority to conduct searches. These opinions were based on his careful examination of the facts of each case and attention to the words, history, and purposes of the Fourth Amendment.

As described in the foregoing discussion of *Robbins v. California* (1981), *United States v. Ross* (1982), and other cases, Stevens remained very consistent in his assessment of appropriate law enforcement authority. The issues faced by the Court in many of his early cases led him to endorse the propriety of searches based on the facts of the cases. As the Court's composition changed and the majority acted to expand law enforcement authority in later cases, Stevens increasingly dissented against the Court's endorsement of police actions. In *Illinois v. McArthur* (2001), for example, Stevens was the lone dissenter who objected to the majority's endorsement of officers who blocked a resident's entry into his home for several hours while seeking a warrant related to a relatively minor drug possession offense. The greater frequency of liberal votes and attendant dissenting opinions later in his career reflected a shift in the Court's orientation and decisions rather than a change in Stevens's approach to Fourth Amendment issues. Throughout his career, Stevens consistently defended the exclusionary rule and urged that it be applied more broadly as an effective deterrent and remedy for Fourth Amendment violations. He also consistently voiced skepticism about broad police authority to conduct warrantless searches. Thus Stevens stood out as an outspoken advocate for halting the Court's trend toward expanding law enforcement authority.

With respect to two specific issues, there is evidence from which one may infer that Stevens changed his position over the course of his judicial career. As previously discussed, Stevens's Seventh Circuit opinion in *United States v. Jeffers* (1975) endorsed a *Terry*-type frisk search under circumstances that may not have received his approval later in his career. The analysis of the justification and scope of the search in *Jeffers* appeared to be more deferential to police discretion than the approach that he applied or endorsed in later cases at the Supreme Court concerning stop-and-frisk searches.

By contrast, the evidence supporting the second possible example of change is more tenuous. Justice Stevens endorsed, without any explanatory opinion of his own, Justice White's majority opinion in *Delaware v. Prouse* (1979) containing language that invited police to develop roadblocks to stop drivers systematically in order to avoid the excessive use of discretion in making investigatory stops not based on reasonable suspicion. When Stevens actually addressed vehicle checkpoints in subsequent cases, he expressed skepticism about specific justifications and circumstances as he opposed the sobriety checkpoints in *Michigan Dept. of State Police v. Sitz* (1990) and drug investigation checkpoints in *City of Indianapolis v. Edmond* (2000). He also questioned the accident investigation checkpoint in *Illinois v. Lidster,* (2004). At the start of his career, he endorsed a checkpoint aimed at discovering undocumented workers who violated immigration laws (*United States v. Martinez-Fuerte*, 1976). He subsequently reaffirmed that endorsement in his *Sitz* dissent by distinguishing its purpose from those of other vehicle checkpoints. Because he did not have a simple, uniform position on all checkpoints, it is difficult to know with certainty whether his criticisms of specific checkpoints later in his career reflected a change in viewpoint.

Justice Stevens's impact on the law of search and seizure was limited. He wrote only a half dozen majority opinions that established protections for individuals. Among these cases, *Payton v. New York* (1980) articulated the important principle that, absent exigent circumstances, police cannot make a warrantless, nonconsensual entry into a home in order to make a routine felony arrest. Other majority opinions served to halt, at least temporarily, further expansions of law enforcement authority after trends in decisions seemed to be moving toward additional diminutions of Fourth Amendment rights concerning warrantless drug testing and vehicle searches. In *Ferguson v. City of Charleston* (2001), Stevens's majority opinion prohibited hospital officials from voluntarily giving pregnant women's medical test results to law enforcement officials despite claims that such warrantless actions were needed to prosecute narcotics-abusing expectant mothers who exposed their unborn children to addictive drugs. Similarly, *Arizona v. Gant* (2009) served to limit police authority to conduct vehicle searches incident to an arrest when the arrestee was handcuffed and sitting in the patrol car. The survival of such contested line-drawing decisions will depend entirely on changes in the Court's composition and the justices' decisions about which issues to examine in future cases. Justice Stevens's most significant contribution may ultimately be through his role as a dissenter against expansions of law enforcement authority to carry out searches and seizures. He articulated reasoning in many opinions that will be available for justices to consider in future cases. For example, his warning in *Arizona v. Evans* (1995) about the threat to individual rights from reliance by law enforcement officials on inaccurate computer databases may ultimately reflect his insightful anticipation of an issue which, as it expands in frequency and effect, may arouse broader concern among citizens and judges.

NOTES

1. *Dalia v. United States*, 441 U.S. 238, 265 (Stevens, J., dissenting).
2. Ibid., 262 (Stevens, J., dissenting).
3. *United States v. Caceres*, 440 U.S. 741 (1979); *United States v. Ross*, 456 U.S. 798 (1982); *Maryland v. Garrison*, 480 U.S. 79 (1987); *Horton v. California*, 496 U.S. 128 (1990).
4. *United States v. Santana*, 427 U.S. 38 (1976); *Donovan v. Dewey*, 452 U.S. 594 (1981); *New York v. Belton*, 453 U.S. 454 (1981); *Texas v. Brown*, 460 U.S. 730 (1983); *United States v. Knotts*, 460 U.S. 276 (1983); *Immigration and Naturalization Service v. Delgado*, 466 U.S. 210 (1984); *Massachusetts v. Shepherd*, 468 U.S. 981 (1984); *United States v. Montoya de Hernandez*, 473 U.S. 531 (1985); *Skinner v. Railway Labor Executives' Association*, 489 U.S. 602 (1989); *United States v. Verdugo-Urquidez*, 494 U.S. 259 (1990); *Maryland v. Buie*, 494 U.S. 325 (1990).
5. *Marshall v. Barlow's Inc.*, 436 U.S. 307 (1978); *Robbins v. California*, 453 U.S. 420 (1981).
6. *United States v. Santana*, 427 U.S. 38 (1976); *United States v. Caceres*, 440 U.S. 741 (1979); *Robbins v. California*, 453 U.S. 420 (1981); *New York v. Belton*, 453 U.S. 454 (1981); *United States v. Ross*, 456 U.S. 798 (1982); *Immigration and Naturalization Service v. Delgado*, 466 U.S. 210 (1984); *Massachusetts v. Shepherd*, 468 U.S. 981 (1984); *United States v. Montoya de Hernandez*, 473 U.S. 531(1985); *Maryland v. Garrison*, 480 U.S. 79 (1987); *Skinner v. Railway Labor Executives' Association*, 489 U.S. 602 (1989); *Horton v. California*, 496 U.S. 128 (1990); *United States v. Verdugo-Urquidez*, 494 U.S. 259 (1990); *Maryland v. Buie*, 494 U.S. 325 (1990).
7. *United States v. Donovan*, 429 U.S. 413 (1977); *United States v. Ramsey*, 431 U.S. 606 (1977); *United States v. New York Telephone Co.*, 434 U.S. 159 (1977); *Michigan v. Tyler*, 436 U.S. 499 (1978); *Zurcher v. Stanford Daily*, 436 U.S. 547 (1978); *Dunaway v. New York*, 442 U.S. 200 (1979); *Dalia v. United States*, 441 U.S. 238 (1979); *Payton v. New York*, 445 U.S. 573 (1980); *Walter v. United States*, 447 U.S. 649 (1980); *Michigan v. Long*, 463 U.S. 1032 (1983); *Illinois v. Gates*, 462 U.S. 213 (1983); *United States v. Leon*, 468 U.S. 897 (1984); *Immigration and Naturalization Service v. Lopez-Mendoza*, 468 U.S. 1032 (1984); *Michigan v. Clifford*, 464 U.S. 287 (1984); *Segura v. United States*, 468 U.S. 796 (1984); *Hudson v. Palmer*, 468 U.S. 517 (1984); *United States v. Karo*, 468 U.S. 705 (1984); *California v. Carney*, 471 U.S. 386 (1985); *New Jersey v. TLO*, 469 U.S. 325 (1985); *Griffin v. Wisconsin*, 483 U.S. 868 (1987); *Murray v. United States*, 487 U.S. 533 (1988); *Brower v. County of Inyo*, 489 U.S. 593 (1989); *Florida v. Wells*, 495 U.S. 1 (1990); *Alabama v. White*, 496 U.S. 325 (1990); *Michigan Dept. of State Police v. Sitz*, 496 U.S. 444 (1990); *United States v. Ojeda-*

Rios, 495 U.S. 257 (1990); *Minnesota v. Olson*, 495 U.S. 91 (1990); *James v. Illinois*, 493 U.S. 307 (1990).

8. *Payton v. New York*, 445 U.S. 573 (1980).

9. *Michigan Dept. of State Police v. Sitz*, 496 U.S. 444, 468-69 (1990) (Stevens, J., dissenting).

10. *Maryland v. Wilson*, 519 U.S. 408, 416, 419 (1997) (Stevens, J., dissenting).

11. Justice John Paul Stevens, interview with author, U.S. Supreme Court, Washington, D.C., July 12, 2006.

12. John Paul Stevens, "Commencement Address," Northwestern University School of Law, Chicago, Ill., May 13, 2011, accessed July 2, 2015, http://www.law.northwestern.edu/about/news/newsdisplay.cfm?ID=535.

13. *Maryland v. Wilson*, 519 U.S. at 415–16 (Stevens, J., dissenting).

14. Ibid., 416.

15. *Kyllo v. United States*, 533 U.S. 27, 41 (2001) (Stevens, J., dissenting).

16. Ibid.

17. *Illinois v. Wardlow*, 528 U.S. 119, 132–33 (2000) (Stevens, J., dissenting).

18. *Michigan v. Long*, 463 U.S. 1032 (1983).

19. *Michigan v. Long*, 463 U.S. 1032, 1068 (Stevens, J., dissenting).

20. *Pennsylvania Board of Probation and Parole v. Scott*, 524 U.S. 357, 369 (1998) (Stevens, J., dissenting).

21. *Robbins v. California*, 453 U.S. 420 (1981); *New York v. Belton*, 453 U.S. 454 (1981); *United States v. Ross*, 456 U.S. 798 (1982).

22. *Segura v. United States*, 468 U.S. 796, 837 (1984) (Stevens, J., dissenting).

23. *Dunaway v. New York*, 442 U.S. 200, 221 (Stevens, J., concurring).

24. *Arizona v. Evans*, 514 U.S. 1, 18 (1995) (Stevens, J., dissenting).

25. Ibid.,18–19.

26. *United States v. Leon*, 468 U.S. 897, 977–78 (1984) (Stevens, J., dissenting).

27. Ibid., 978.

28. *United States v. Leon*, 468 U.S. at 922.

29. *Nix v. Williams*, 467 U.S. 431, 457–58 (1984) (Stevens, J., dissenting).

30. *United States v. Leon*, 468 U.S. at 970–71 (Stevens, J., dissenting).

31. Ibid., 972.

32. *Immigration and Naturalization Service v. Lopez-Mendoza*, 468 U.S. 1032 (1984).

33. *Pennsylvania Board of Probation and Parole v. Scott*, 524 U.S. 357 (1998).

34. *Arizona v. Evans*, 514 U.S. 1, 23 (Stevens, J., dissenting).

35. Ibid., 22.

36. Ibid., 22–23.

37. *Illinois v. Krull*, 480 U.S. 340 (1987).

38. *Illinois v Rodriguez*, 497 U.S. 177 (1990).

39. *Maryland v. Buie*, 494 U.S. 325, 339 (1990) (Brennan, J., dissenting).

40. *Maryland v. Buie*, 494 U.S. at 339 (Kennedy, J., concurring).

41. Ibid.

42. *United States v. Ross*, 456 U.S. 798, 825 (1982).

43. Ibid., 821, fn. 28.

44. *Michigan v. Long*, 463 U.S. 1032, 1069–70 (1983) (Stevens, J., dissenting).

45. *California v. Carney*, 471 U.S. 386, 396 (1985) (Stevens, J., dissenting).

46. Ibid.

47. *Florida v. Wells*, 495 U.S. 1, 12 (1990) (Stevens, J., concurring in judgment).

48. Ibid.

49. *California v. Acevedo*, 500 U.S. 565, 598 (1991) (Stevens, J., dissenting).

50. Ibid., 601.

51. Ibid., at 602.

52. *Florida v. White*, 526 U.S. 559, 573 (1999) (Stevens, J., dissenting).

53. *Wyoming v. Houghton*, 526 U.S. 295, 309 (1999) (Stevens, J., dissenting).

54. Ibid., 312.

55. Ibid., 310–11.

56. *Thornton v. United States*, 541 U.S. 615, 636 (2004) (Stevens, J., dissenting).
57. Ibid.
58. Ibid.
59. *Delaware v. Prouse*, 440 U.S. 648, 663 (1979).
60. *Michigan Department of State Police v. Sitz*, 496 U.S. 444, 477 (1990).
61. Jeffrey Rosen, "The Dissenter," *New York Times*, September 23, 2007, 53–54.
62. *Illinois v. Lidster*, 540 U.S. 419, 428 (Stevens, J., concurring in part and dissenting in part).
63. Ibid., 429 (Stevens, J., concurring in part and dissenting in part).
64. *Brower v. County of Inyo*, 489 U.S. 593, 600 (1989) (Stevens, J., concurring).
65. *California v. Hodari D.*, 499 U.S. 621, 643 (1991) (Stevens, J., dissenting).
66. Ibid., 645.
67. *Ohio v. Robinette*, 519 U.S. 33, 35 (1996).
68. Ibid., 48 (Stevens, J., dissenting).
69. *Alabama v. White*, 496 U.S. 325, 333 (Stevens, J., dissenting).

Chapter Eight

Capital Punishment

Justice Stevens arrived at the Supreme Court in December 1975, a pivotal moment in the history of constitutional litigation over capital punishment. The Court had effectively imposed a national moratorium on capital punishment with its 1972 decision in *Furman v. Georgia* declaring that the death penalty was being applied in an unconstitutional manner. The majority of justices did not see capital punishment as inherently unconstitutional under the Eighth Amendment's Cruel and Unusual Punishments Clause, so the Court's decision left the door open for states to revise their death penalty statutes in an effort to remedy the due process deficiencies identified in *Furman*. In April 1975, the Supreme Court had heard oral arguments in *Fowler v. North Carolina*, a case concerning a new capital punishment statute, but with an ailing and soon-to-retire Justice William O. Douglas hospitalized and missing deliberations, the justices deadlocked 4 to 4 and decided to reschedule the issue for reargument in the following term. Thus Stevens, who replaced Douglas, began his service on the Supreme Court at the moment that it was to consider and decide whether capital punishment could resume. In light of the Court's deadlocked vote in the preceding case, some observers perceived the newcomer Stevens as holding the potential deciding vote on the resumption of the death penalty.[1] As the subsequent sections of this chapter will describe, Stevens began his career on the Court by endorsing the constitutionality of the death penalty but ended his career with a clear renunciation of the ultimate criminal punishment.

Social scientists who count and classify the justices' votes assert that "Justice Stevens moved substantially to the left," meaning that he became more liberal in voting on decisions over the course of his career.[2] By contrast, in evaluating himself, Stevens emphasized how the Court's composition changed around him over the years with the addition of justices who were more conservative than their predecessors. In his view, the changing composition conveyed the impression that he was becoming more liberal, but he disagreed by saying, "I don't really think I've changed. I think there have been a lot of changes in the Court."[3] However, as noted in previous chapters, he also admitted that "learning on the bench has been one of the most important and rewarding aspects of my own experience over the last thirty-five years," thereby effectively acknowledging the possibility that his understanding of and approach to certain legal issues changed over time.[4]

Of particular importance for analyses about changes in Stevens's approach to specific issues is the widespread perception that he changed his viewpoint about capital punishment as he moved from endorsing the constitutionality of the death penalty in *Gregg v. Georgia* and its companion cases in 1976 to renouncing his acceptance of the death penalty in *Baze v. Rees* in 2008. This chapter explores the extent to which Stevens's decisions on the issue of capital punishment were consistent with his claim about his career in general that "I don't think that my votes represent a change in my own thinking[;] I'm disagreeing with a change that *others* are making."[5]

THE IMPACT OF STEVENS'S JUDICIAL PHILOSOPHY

Throughout his thirty-five years on the high court, Justice Stevens emphasized two specific issues in analyzing capital punishment cases. First, he sought to narrow and limit the categories of offenders who could be subjected to the death penalty. Second, he demonstrated continuous concern about procedural fairness. These priorities were evident from the very beginning of his service on the Court. These priorities were also closely connected to the kinds of issues addressed by the Supreme Court in death penalty cases. Stevens's experiences as a Supreme Court law clerk, as an attorney handling pro bono cases for the Chicago Bar Association's prisoner assistance committee, and as a judge on a U.S. court of appeals all contributed to his keen awareness of the need for effective defense counsel in criminal cases, including capital trials and appeals. As described in chapter 2, Stevens pointed to his reaction to the U.S. Navy's specific efforts to target and kill Admiral Yamamoto during World War II as spurring him to think about the parallel process of selecting an individual offender for execution in the capital punishment process. He translated his discomfort about this wartime episode into his assessment of the extremely difficult decision that jurors must make in deciding whether a specific defendant should be executed for committing a murder.

At the time of Stevens's nomination for the Supreme Court in 1975, certain aspects of his analytical approach had developed and he provided clues about how his legal education and judicial experience had led him to assess the issue. At the confirmation hearings, Senator Edward Kennedy (D-Mass.) said to Stevens, "But, I would like to know your feelings on capital punishment. Do you believe it serves as a deterrent?"[6] In response, Stevens sought to avoid commenting directly on the issue of capital punishment because, in his words, "that is a matter that will be before the Supreme Court, and I think it would be inappropriate to comment on that."[7]

Despite following the understandable approach of declining to make any comments that might imply that he had prejudged contemporary legal issues, Stevens made two comments that, in retrospect, revealed elements of his approach to the capital punishment issue. First, when Senator Kennedy's follow-up question about capital punishment was phrased as "I am asking you only for your general views on this issue,"[8] Stevens replied by saying:

> I really don't think I should discuss this subject generally, Senator. I don't mean to be unresponsive but in all candor I must say that there have been many times in my experience in the last five years [as a court of appeals judge] where I found that my first reaction to a problem was not the same as the reaction I had when I had the responsibility of [judicial] decisions and I think that if I were to make comments that were not carefully thought through they might be given significance that they really did not merit. I am not trying to be evasive. I am trying to be honest. . . .
>
> I honestly do not think it is appropriate for me to give you a philosophical discussion of what I might do if I were a legislator. I do not intend to be a legislator and my policy thoughts are really not what would be controlling when I face the adjudication of these matters later on.[9]

Stevens's response seemed to imply that his judicial assessment of capital punishment was not fixed, but could be shaped by and potentially change as a result of what he learned as he heard arguments and studied the issue in his role as a judge. Thus, if Stevens's opinions on capital punishment changed over the course of his judicial career, as asserted by commentators, this development would not be inconsistent with the implications of his statement at the confirmation hearings.

Second, in response to a question from Senator John Tunney (D-Calif.) about how he would approach the interpretation of the Eighth Amendment's Cruel and Unusual Punishments Clause, Stevens replied:

> Senator, as I recall the interpretation of the [E]ighth [A]mendment, there are basically two kinds of arguments that are made in support of a claim that punishment is cruel and unusual. One is that the particular punishment is so disproportionate to the particular offense, such as a death sentence for possession of marihuana, that it might seem to be disproportionate and one might apply such an argument.
>
> On the other hand, another kind of argument is that in absolute terms, certain kinds of punishment, such as, I think whipping is an example that is

> given, are considered so barbaric by present-day standards that they would be considered cruel and unusual within the meaning of the amendment. And I would think there is certainly some truth to the notion that one has to consider both the social conditions at the time the amendment was adopted or the intent of the framers and the background in which a particular punishment is being given out today. That is about as much as I can say.[10]

Although it is difficult to describe his response as an endorsement of giving close attention to proportionality issues in punishment, he acknowledged his awareness of the issue and gave an example regarding possession of drugs that implied he might very well find such a sentence to be disproportionate to the crime. Stevens's response provided a clue for anticipating his serious consideration and support during his second term on the Supreme Court for narrowing capital punishment on proportionality grounds by prohibiting the death penalty in rape cases with adult victims in *Coker v. Georgia* (1977).

Moreover, with even greater clarity, his response to Senator Tunney indicated that Stevens accepted the Supreme Court's established interpretive approach that treated the Cruel and Unusual Punishments Clause's meaning as evolving and not fixed. Stevens's viewpoint was consistent with the precedent in *Trop v. Dulles* (1958) in which Chief Justice Warren described the Clause's meaning as "not static . . . [and] draw[ing] its meaning from the evolving standards of decency that mark the progress of a maturing society."[11] Eventually, Stevens became the Supreme Court's most outspoken advocate for interpreting the Cruel and Unusual Punishments Clause according to the evolving standards of contemporary society.

The use of the "evolving standards" test from *Trop v. Dulles* presents potential problems for those jurists who seek to limit or eliminate the death penalty. Because contemporary public opinion polls consistently show that at least half of Americans support the existence of capital punishment, how can a jurist argue that the death penalty or specific applications of the punishment are out of step with the values of current society? Justice Brennan answered the question by thinking in normative terms about the aspirational ideals of society rather than specific empirical evidence about current social values. According to Brennan, "the Constitution embodies the aspirations to social justice, brotherhood, and human dignity that brought this nation into being."[12] Brennan concluded that capital punishment violated the Cruel and Unusual Punishments Clause in all circumstances because:

> [T]he state, even as it punishes, must treat its citizens in a manner consistent with their intrinsic worth as human beings. A punishment must not be so severe as to be utterly and irreversibly degrading to the very essence of human dignity. Death for whatever crime and under all circumstances is a truly awesome punishment. The calculated killing of a human being by the state in-

> volves, by its very nature, an absolute denial of the executed person's humanity. . . . It is thus inconsistent with the fundamental premise of the Clause that even the most base criminal remains a human being possessed of some potential, at least, for common human dignity.[13]

As indicated by Brennan's words, his analysis of the Eighth Amendment did not depend on evidence from public opinion polls or other indicators of society's current values. He advocated a normative viewpoint that focused instead on his assessment of the Constitution's ideals and aspirations for human dignity.

Justice Marshall, another opponent of capital punishment, shared Brennan's view and also addressed the question of contemporary values by applying an idea that became known as "the Marshall Hypothesis." In his dissent in *Furman v. Georgia* (1972), Marshall argued that the American public's expressed support for capital punishment would shrink markedly if people were more knowledgeable about the death penalty, especially the lack of a demonstrable deterrent effect and the discriminatory application of the punishment. Social science research provides support for Marshall's view.[14] Thus Marshall could reject simple public opinion polls' apparent representation of contemporary values. Instead, he could argue that the provision of more information about the death penalty's flaws or more detailed questions, such as whether people would prefer sentences of life without possibility of parole for murderers, would lead to markedly diminished expressed support by the public for capital punishment.

Although Stevens did not make it the centerpiece of his opinions, his reaction to and thoughts about the killing of Admiral Yamamoto during World War II appeared to contribute to what one might call "the Stevens hypothesis." Stevens believed that public opinion polls gauging support for capital punishment did not accurately reflect contemporary values because they were based on generic, abstract questions. Thus they were entirely different, in his view, from the actual death penalty decisions made by citizen-jurors after hearing evidence in a trial and a sentencing proceeding. As Stevens said, "In my mind, there is a difference between statistics and sitting on a jury and deciding whether to kill a single person."[15] He believed that a juror who had heard a complete, well-presented case would be reluctant to impose the death penalty. Thus a juror would likely apply capital punishment only in the narrowest categories of cases, even if that juror would have previously responded to a generic public opinion question by expressing general support for capital punishment. As he said in an interview, "[J]ust on the death penalty, for example, it is very easy to think that executing a person is not a big deal. It happens all the time. But when juries sit on a particular case and they are confronted with a particular individual and particular incident, it is not a statistic. It is a human situation."[16] This analytical perspective, shaped in part by his reaction to the targeted killing of Admiral Yamamoto, influenced Stevens's assessment of the propriety of the death penalty under the *Trop* test for the Eighth Amendment.

THE "CONSERVATIVE" YEARS: 1976–1984

For the cases classified as concerning the issue of "capital punishment" in the Supreme Court Judicial Database, Stevens supported individuals' claims in only twelve of the twenty cases decided from 1976 through 1984. His percentage of liberal votes in capital punishment cases during this time period was much lower than that evidenced in his voting record for the remainder of his career. In his final quarter century on the Court, he supported individuals in forty-nine of fifty-one cases and his two votes for the government in *Oregon v. Guzek* (2006) and *Baze v. Rees* (2008) were not substantive repudiations of the individuals' claims, but concerned procedural and precedential issues. With respect to his early years on the Court, several considerations made Stevens's approach to capital punishment in this initial period less conservative than it may have appeared from his voting record.

First, three of the eight conservative votes during this initial period came in a set of cases—*Gregg v. Georgia*, *Proffitt v. Florida*, and *Jurek v. Texas*—decided on the same day in 1976 that raised closely related issues. Each case examined a particular state's newly designed bifurcated proceedings that mandated, either explicitly or implicitly, consideration of aggravating and mitigating evidence in capital cases. Had these cases been formally joined together, Stevens would have recorded only one conservative vote instead of three. By comparison, Justices Brennan and Marshall each wrote a single dissenting opinion directed at all three cases simultaneously. Moreover, in each of these three cases in which Stevens joined with Justices Stewart and Powell to issue joint opinions that endorsed the constitutionality of capital punishment, the opinions manifested significant concern about the importance of using fair and careful procedures in death penalty cases. In *Jurek v. Texas*, for example, the joint opinion announced by Stevens, he emphasized that the Texas statute approved by the Court narrowed the categories of offenders eligible for the death penalty and thereby served the same purpose as requiring a finding of specific aggravating factors in order to impose capital punishment. He also saw the statute as enabling the jury to "consider whatever evidence of mitigating circumstances the defense can bring before it."[17]

Second, on the same day in 1976 that the Supreme Court reactivated capital punishment with the decisions in *Gregg*, *Proffitt*, and *Jurek*, the three-judge plurality—Stevens, Stewart, and Powell—also led the Court in striking down statutes that mandated the imposition of capital punishment for first-degree murder convictions (*Woodson v. North Carolina*; *Roberts v. Louisiana*). Over the objections of four dissenters (Chief Justice Burger and Justices White, Blackmun, and Rehnquist), Stevens, according to the analysis of James Liebman and Lawrence Marshall, helped to push forward a "commitment to narrowing [the scope of the death penalty] as a way of dealing with flaws in the administration of capital punishment."[18]

Third, the decision announced by Stevens in *Roberts v. Louisiana* (1976) concerning the impermissibility of mandatory punishment statutes emphasized his commitment to interpreting the Eighth Amendment according to the *Trop v. Dulles* (1958) standard of "the evolving standards of decency that mark the progress of a maturing society."[19] The *Trop* standard opened the possibility for Stevens to conclude eventually that *society's* changing values mandated the elimination of capital punishment even if he did not change his own perspective on the desirability or efficacy of the death penalty.

Justice Stevens's first term on the Court was a monumental moment for the development of constitutional law concerning the death penalty. The punishment had effectively been placed "on hold" pending the Court's examination of states' newly designed procedures that were developed after the *Furman* decision. As a newcomer to the Court, Stevens was a key actor in reactivating capital punishment in the *Gregg-Proffitt-Jurek* trilogy, yet he also played a pivotal role in limiting the application of the death penalty in *Woodson* and *Roberts*. Thus he cannot be labeled simplistically as "pro-death penalty." From the beginning of his career on the Court, he demonstrated his concerns about limiting the application of the death penalty and enforcing fair procedures.

The next three Supreme Court terms during his "conservative" era saw Stevens consistently vote in support of individuals' claims and thereby narrow the scope of capital punishment in the eight cases addressed by the Supreme Court.[20] In addition, Stevens was assigned the responsibility for writing the Court's opinion in two of these cases. These opinions concerned the defendant's opportunity to respond to information considered in the sentencing process (*Gardner v. Florida*, 1977) and the capital jury's opportunity to consider the alternative of convicting the defendant for a non-capital, lesser-included offense (*Beck v. Alabama*, 1979). Each of the eight cases narrowed the application of the death penalty except for one noteworthy case, *Dobbert v. Florida* (1977), in which Stevens wrote a dissenting opinion on behalf of himself and his ardent abolitionist colleagues, Brennan and Marshall. With the exception of *Dobbert*, Stevens had been a member of the majority in these cases and he had joined his joint-opinion partners from the important 1976 *Gregg* trilogy of cases, Justices Stewart and Powell. In the 1977 *Dobbert* dissent, Stevens distinguished himself from these partners. He demonstrated that, more so than all of his colleagues other than the abolitionists Brennan and Marshall, from his very first terms on the Court he took a particularly critical view of fairness issues in capital punishment cases.

In *Dobbert*, Stevens argued that the application of the Florida death penalty statute violated the *Ex Post Facto* Clause because the crime occurred several months before the Supreme Court had endorsed the constitutionality of Florida's statute and reactivated the state's capital case procedures in *Proffitt v. Florida* (1976). Stevens used strong language to express his disagreement with the majority's endorsement of capital punishment in this case:

> The Court's "fair warning" test, if it extends beyond this case, would allow government action that is just the opposite of impartial. If that be so, the "fair warning" rationale will defeat the very purpose of the [*Ex Post Facto*] Clause. . . .
>
> If I am correct that the *Ex Post Facto* Clause was intended as a barrier to capricious government action, today's holding is actually perverse. For when human life is at stake, the need to prevent capricious government action is greatest. . . . Yet the Court's holding may lead to results that are intolerably arbitrary. . . .
>
> I assume that this case will ultimately be regarded as nothing more than an archaic gargoyle. It is nevertheless distressing to witness such a demeaning construction of a majestic bulwark in the framework of our Constitution.[21]

Five pro-death penalty votes were cast by Stevens in cases decided from 1982 through 1984. Stevens was not a member of any narrow majorities that upheld capital sentences in closely contested cases. Instead, he joined all of the justices except for the abolitionists Brennan and Marshall in three cases (*Hopper v. Evans*, 1982; *Zant v. Stephens*, 1983; *Pulley v. Harris*, 1984) and six-member majorities in two additional cases when Justice Blackmun joined Brennan and Marshall in dissent (*Barefoot v. Estelle*, 1983; *Barclay v. Florida*, 1983).

Even during the time period of his most conservative voting record on capital punishment issues in his first decade on the Court, there was evidence that his approach to analyzing issues would place him primarily among the justices who were highly critical of states' death penalty statutes and practices. First, in every 5-to-4 capital case, Stevens sided with the individual rather than the state. Second, after the 1981 retirement of Justice Stewart, a justice with whom Stevens agreed in every capital punishment case except one (*Dobbert v. Florida*, 1977), Stevens wrote an opinion that signaled his developing conclusion about the Court's direction. According to Stevens, the Court's majority was moving away from the specific concerns about fair procedures that he regarded as at the heart of *Gregg v. Georgia* and the other cases that reactivated capital punishment in 1976. In his concurring opinion in *Barclay v. Florida* (1983), Stevens wrote:

> Although I agree with the plurality's conclusion, and with much of what is said in its opinion, I think it important to write separately. The plurality acknowledges, of course, the constitutional guarantees that have been emphasized in our cases since *Gregg*. But in some of its language, the plurality speaks with unnecessary, and somewhat inappropriate, breadth. The Court has never thought it sufficient in a capital case merely to ask whether the state court has been "so unprincipled or arbitrary as to somehow violate the United States Constitution." . . . Nor does a majority of the Court today adopt that standard. A constant theme of our cases . . . has been emphasis on procedural protections that are intended to ensure that the death penalty will be imposed in a consistent, rational manner. As stated in *Zant* [*v. Stephens*, 1983], we have stressed the necessity of "genuinely narrow[ing] the class of persons eligible for the death penalty," and of assuring consistently applied appellate review. . . . Accordingly, my primary purpose is to reemphasize these limiting factors in light of the decisions of the Supreme Court of Florida.[22]

Justice Stevens said in 2007 that "I think every judge—with the exception of Justice [Ruth Bader] Ginsburg— . . . who's been appointed to the [C]ourt since . . . Lewis Powell [in 1971], has been more conservative than his predecessor."[23] In light of this statement, it is not surprising that Stevens may have perceived the Court shifting in a direction that was less sensitive to his intense concern about procedural fairness in capital cases. The appointments of Justice O'Connor to replace Justice Stewart in 1981 and Justices Scalia and Kennedy to fill vacancies created by the retirements of Chief Justice Burger and Justice Powell in 1986 and 1987 served to move the Court in a direction that was more accepting and supportive of states' approaches to capital punishment. Moreover, the retirees, Stewart and Powell, had been the two justices with whom Stevens issued the important joint opinions in *Gregg*, *Proffitt*, and *Jurek* that reactivated a more carefully controlled death penalty in 1976.

In the final capital case of his "conservative" era, *Spaziano v. Florida* (1984), Stevens strongly distinguished himself from the non-abolitionist justices by writing an opinion concurring in part and dissenting in part that insisted on juries rather than judges making the determination about whether an offender should be sentenced to death. His reasoning was consistent with his fidelity to the *Trop* standard for assessing cruel and unusual punishments according to evolving societal values. More importantly, the opinion served to separate Stevens from his more conservative colleagues as well as from Justice Powell, someone with whom he had agreed in all but three capital cases over the course of the preceding decade. Writing on behalf of Justices Marshall and Brennan, Stevens said:

> In the twelve years since *Furman v. Georgia*, . . . every Member of this Court has written or joined at least one opinion endorsing the proposition that, because of its severity and irrevocability, the death penalty is qualitatively differ-

> ent from any other punishment, and hence must be accompanied by unique safeguards to ensure that it is a justified response to a given offense. Because it is the one punishment that cannot be prescribed by a rule of law as judges normally understand such rules, but rather is ultimately understood only as an expression of the community's outrage—its sense that an individual has lost his moral entitlement to live—I am convinced that the danger of an excessive response can only be avoided if the decision to impose the death penalty is made by a jury, rather than by a single governmental official. This conviction is consistent with the judgment of history and the current consensus of opinion that juries are better equipped than judges to make capital sentencing decisions. The basic explanation for that consensus lies in the fact that the question whether a sentence of death is excessive in the particular circumstances of any case is one that must be answered by the decisionmaker that is best able to "express the conscience of the community on the ultimate question of life or death." [24]

When the Supreme Court issued decisions in capital punishment cases in 1985 and thereafter, Stevens's commitment to fair procedures in death penalty cases distinguished him from all of the other justices except his abolitionist colleagues, Brennan and Marshall. Moreover, his opinions effectively predicted the subsequent disagreements with the Court majority that would keep Stevens consistently arguing in favor of defendants' claims concerning the fairness of procedures and the need to narrow the applicability of capital punishment.

STEVENS AS DEATH PENALTY CRITIC: 1985–2010

One of the most striking aspects of Justice Stevens's experience with capital punishment issues in the final twenty-five years of his career on the Court was how few majority opinions concerning capital punishment he was assigned—or assigned to himself when he became the senior justice among the liberals after the retirement of Justice Blackmun in 1994. Based on the classification of cases in the Supreme Court Judicial Database, in his first decade on the Court, Stevens was credited with five majority and plurality opinions in death penalty cases. By contrast, he only wrote four such opinions in the next twenty-five years as he found himself most frequently dissenting against decisions by an increasingly conservative majority. Justice Stevens's viewpoint can be illuminated by examining several illustrative opinions during this later period.

In *Baldwin v. Alabama* (1985), a case that the American Civil Liberties Union later labeled as showing strong evidence that Baldwin was not the murderer,[25] Stevens wrote a dissenting opinion joined by Brennan and Marshall. He objected to the approval of a sentencing process that instructed the jury to impose the death sentence if it found the existence of certain aggravating factors but permitted the judge to make the ultimate decision about the sentence. Justice Stevens reiterated his view that the jury must make capital punishment decisions in non-mandatory schemes and argued that "[i]n my view, it is also unconstitutional to present an elected trial judge, who might otherwise regard the arguments for and against a death sentence as equally balanced, with the burden of rejecting a jury verdict of this kind before he can impose a sentence of life."[26] Anticipating contemporary criticisms of the susceptibility of elected judges to political pressures and the passions of the local community, Stevens focused on the problem of judges who must face reelection after bucking local community sentiment:

> Judges in Alabama, as in many States, are elected. . . . They are not insulated from community pressure; indeed, responsiveness and accountability to the community provide the justification for an elected judiciary. Although a judge may understand that a mandatory jury sentence of death is, in some sense, meaningless . . . , the community probably does not. A jury sentence of death is likely to be reported and understood as a real sentence of death, as it was in this case. Whether it "logically" need be so or not, . . . the plain fact is that a judge who later decides to sentence to life in such circumstances is publicly perceived to have rejected the jury's sentence; indeed, the terms of the statute itself embody that perception. The pressures on a judge that inevitably result should not be ignored. In my view, only the Court's distance from the realities of an elected state trial bench can explain its declaration that, as a matter of fact, a jury's mandatory sentence of death will not enter the judge's mind when he considers whether to "refuse" or "accept" the jury's sentence.[27]

In *McCleskey v. Kemp* (1987), a narrow majority on the Supreme Court rejected a systemic challenge to capital punishment based on strong statistical evidence showing Georgia's justice system to be infused with racial discrimination in imposing death sentences. Although Court precedents permitted the use of statistical evidence to demonstrate racial discrimination in employment discrimination and jury selection cases, five justices said that such evidence cannot be used to demonstrate Equal Protection Clause violations in the administration of capital punishment. For some of the justices, the case appeared to represent a test of their priorities. Justice Scalia—unbeknownst to the public at that time—acknowledged in a memo later discovered in the Thurgood Marshall Papers at the Library of Congress that the evidence in *McCleskey* showed the existence of racial discrimination. However, he demonstrated his preference to preserve capital punishment in spite of the apparent existence of racial discrimination by saying "I do not share the view . . . that an effect of racial factors on sentencing, if it could be shown by sufficiently strong statistical evidence, would require reversal."[28] By contrast, although Stevens still believed at that time that the death penalty could be administered fairly, he was quite clear in demonstrating that the prevention of constitutional violations took precedence over the maintenance of the death penalty as an available punishment:

> The Court's decision appears to be based on a fear that the acceptance of McCleskey's claim would sound the death knell for capital punishment in Georgia. If society were indeed forced to choose between a racially discriminatory death penalty (one that provides heightened protection against murder "for whites only") and no death penalty at all, the choice mandated by the Constitution would be plain.[29]

Justice Stevens wrote a plurality opinion in *Thompson v. Oklahoma* (1988) that applied the *Trop* standard of society's evolving values to declare that states could not impose the death penalty on offenders who committed murders at ages younger than sixteen. The decision advanced Stevens's consistent objective of narrowing the categories of offenders and situations to which the death penalty would be applicable. It also laid the groundwork for his later success in helping to form a five-member majority in *Roper v. Simmons* (2005) to forbid the application of capital punishment to offenders who committed their crimes while younger than age eighteen.

He also set the stage for future influence through his dissenting opinion in *Walton v. Arizona* (1990). Reiterating his consistent emphasis on the importance of the jury for fact-finding and sentencing, Stevens insisted that judges could not rely on their own determinations of facts in making sentencing decisions. In his view, relevant factual determinations must be made by the jury during trial. As discussed in chapter 6, ten years later, Stevens continued this theme as he wrote a majority opinion in *Apprendi v. New Jersey* (2000) that forbade judges in non-capital cases from imposing sentence enhancements based on specific facts unless those facts had been found by the jury. Two years later, a majority opinion by Justice Ruth Bader Ginsburg in *Ring v. Arizona* (2002) relied on Stevens's majority opinion in *Apprendi* to overrule the Court's decision in *Walton* and thereby place into law Stevens's dissenting argument in *Walton* that the jury must bear responsibility for fact-finding that affects sentencing decisions in capital cases.

In 1991, the Court's decision in *Payne v. Tennessee* led Stevens to make an especially vocal complaint about the nature and speed of the majority's move in a new direction. In *Payne*, the Court approved the presentation of victim impact statements as a component of sentencing proceedings. Such statements pose the risk that similarly situated defendants will be treated differently, not based on the act committed, but on the degree of sympathy that the jurors or judge feel for a specific victim. For example, in some communities this could lead to harsher sentences for offenders convicted of harming white victims and, in effect, a lower valuation of the lives of victims who are poor or members of minority groups. Stevens saw the Court majority as insufficiently concerned with procedural fairness and the prevention of the arbitrariness that had led to the Court's moratorium death sentences in *Furman v. Georgia* (1972). The *Payne* majority abruptly overturned precedents established just two and four years earlier in *South Carolina v. Gathers* (1989) and *Booth v. Maryland* (1987) that had prohibited the use of victim impact statements. Justice Marshall forthrightly attributed this development solely to the change in the Court's composition as Justices Kennedy and Souter, who both voted with the majority, had joined the Court since the original *Booth* precedent was established. The decision spurred Stevens to take the unusual step of announcing his dissent orally from the bench. In this case, Stevens's decision to read his dissent in open court demonstrated his especially intense feelings of disappointment and concern about the Court's new direction. The strong language in the dissenting opinion expressed Stevens's dismay about the majority's disregard for precedent and introduction of emotion, rather than reason, as the basis for imposing death sentences:

> The novel rule that the Court announces today represents a dramatic departure from the principles that have governed our capital sentencing jurisprudence for decades. . . . Our cases provide no support whatsoever for the majority's conclusion that the prosecutor may introduce evidence that sheds no light on the defendant's guilt or moral culpability, and thus serves no purpose other than to encourage jurors to decide in favor of death, rather than life, on the basis of their emotions, rather than their reason.[30]

Twenty years later when Stevens wrote his memoir about the Supreme Court, he said, "I vividly remember Justice Marshall's outraged reaction to the majority's decision to overrule those recent cases" in *Payne*.[31] Justice Stevens then added, "My reaction to that abysmal *Payne* decision remains every bit as hostile today as Thurgood's was when it was announced."[32]

Justice Stevens wrote several other opinions during the 1990s and shortly thereafter that advocated such things as the primacy of the jury as the decision maker in capital cases (*Harris v. Alabama*, 1995) and that urged the enforcement of careful jury instructions (*Weeks v. Angelone*, 2000). In two cases, *Harris v. Alabama* (1995) and *Hopkins v. Reeves* (1998), he was the lone dissenter against the approval of procedures that he regarded as inadequate. In 1995, however, he had a rare opportunity to write a majority opinion in a capital case to broaden, albeit modestly, opportunities for convicted offenders to seek examination of erroneous conviction claims through the habeas corpus process.

In *Schlup v. Delo* (1995), as senior justice in the majority, Stevens assigned to himself the majority opinion in a 5 to 4 decision. Lloyd Schlup was convicted and sentenced to death for purportedly being one of three white prisoners who murdered an African American prisoner inside a Missouri correctional institution. Twice Schlup came within hours of execution before being spared by additional legal proceedings to review his claims that he was innocent, that his attorney provided ineffective assistance of counsel, and that the state had failed to fulfill its obligation to reveal exculpatory evidence. The case received significant national attention, including a nationally televised documentary film, because of the number of witnesses, including prisoners and a corrections officer, who later said Schlup was not involved in the killing.[33] Prison security video tapes also showed a calm Schlup present in the dining hall sixty-five seconds before the emergency call went out to corrections officers concerning the fatal stabbing that occurred elsewhere in the prison. Schlup's second habeas corpus petition had been dismissed for his failure to meet the standard established in *Sawyer v. Whitley* (1992) that he demonstrate by "clear and convincing evidence" that, but for a constitutional error, no reasonable juror would have found him guilty. Instead, on behalf of the majority, Stevens held that Schlup must merely show that a constitutional violation "probably resulted" in an erroneous conviction.[34] This is a lower burden of proof than the "clear and convincing evidence" standard. According to Stevens's opinion, however, the lower standard fulfills the post-appeals-process goal of "ensur[ing] that petitioner's case is truly 'extraordinary,' . . . while still providing petitioner a meaningful avenue by which to avoid a manifest injustice."[35] The four dissenters, through opinions written by Chief Justice Rehnquist and Justice Scalia, disagreed with Stevens's modest easing of requirements for asserting claims of innocence in conjunction with alleging constitutional rights violations during the trial process.

In 2002, Stevens had another rare opportunity to shape the death penalty law with his majority opinion in *Atkins v. Virginia* (2002). In *Atkins*, Stevens wrote on behalf of a six-member majority to declare that:

> Our independent evaluation of the issue reveals no reason to disagree with the judgment of "the legislatures that have recently addressed the matter" and concluded that death is not a suitable punishment for a mentally retarded criminal. We are not persuaded that the execution of mentally retarded criminals will measurably advance the deterrent or the retributive purpose of the death penalty. Construing and applying the Eighth Amendment in the light of our "evolving standards of decency," we therefore conclude that such punishment is excessive and that the Constitution "places a substantive restriction on the State's power to take the life" of a mentally retarded offender.[36]

As he did consistently in other cases throughout his career that raised issues under the Eighth Amendment's Cruel and Unusual Punishments Clause, Stevens applied the *Trop* standard in providing evidence, such as examples of contemporary legislative enactments, to support his conclusion that the execution of developmentally disabled defendants violated society's "evolving standards of decency." Thus he advanced his longtime goal of narrowing the application of the capital punishment.[37]

In *Roper v. Simmons* (2005), Stevens, in his opinion-assigning role as senior associate justice, was credited with facilitating the Supreme Court's decision that barred the application of the death penalty to offenders who committed capital offenses while under the age of eighteen. Justice Anthony Kennedy wrote the controversial opinion for the five-member majority after siding with the Court's four most liberal justices. This situation fit Walter Dellinger's observation that "Stevens has controlled the assignment of opinions with great skill. . . . Sometimes he has assigned opinions to himself, but more important are the cases in which he gave up the privilege of writing the opinion in landmark cases in order to secure a shaky majority."[38] Presumably, Stevens might otherwise have wished to assign to himself the opportunity to expand the application of the arguments against executing teenagers that he had articulated in 1988 in *Thompson v. Oklahoma*. Other observers have noted that "it's widely assumed that Stevens had Kennedy's ear on at least some important issues"[39] and that "[t]he absence of Stevens'[s] personal touch" in influencing Kennedy would otherwise have led the Court to move to the right in specific cases.[40]

Stevens contributed to one more notable success in narrowing the application of death penalty. He again assigned to Justice Kennedy the responsibility for writing on behalf of a five-member majority as the Court in *Kennedy v. Louisiana* (2008) forbade the application of the death penalty for the crime of child rape that does not result in the death of the victim. In oral arguments for the case, Stevens was credited with using his questions to effectively steer attention toward the legal issues in the case. Thus he prevented the attorney for Louisiana from attempting to lead the justices to focus on the victim's physical injuries which had actually healed within weeks after the crime.[41]

In capital punishment cases, such successes for Stevens in narrowing the application of the death penalty were rare and possibly fleeting. Instead, he spent most of his energy resisting the decision-making trends of the Court majority that became increasingly conservative in the 1980s and early 1990s. This resistance included statements and dissenting opinions that Stevens wrote in the Court's decisions concerning which cases to accept for hearing. One such example was the petition of John Allen Muhammad, the so-called "D.C. sniper," who terrorized the nation's capital by planning random shootings that killed ten people in 2002.[42] The Court declined to grant a stay of execution for Muhammad as Virginia sought to carry out the execution swiftly while Muhammad's attorneys were still filing challenges to his conviction and sentence. Thus Stevens complained that:

> By denying Muhammad's stay application, we have allowed Virginia to truncate our deliberative process on a matter—involving a death row inmate—that demands the most careful attention. This result is particularly unfortunate in

> light of the limited time Muhammad was given to make his case in the District Court.
>
> I continue to believe that the Court would be wise to adopt a practice of staying all executions scheduled in advance of the completion of our review of a capital defendant's first application for a federal writ of habeas corpus.[43]

As illustrated by this quote, Stevens made normative arguments about what the Court ought to do, both with respect to procedural fairness, as in John Muhammad's case, and also with respect to narrowing the applicability of capital punishment. In particular, Stevens argued unsuccessfully for the Court to declare that the Cruel and Unusual Punishments Clause was violated when there was excessive delay in post-conviction reviews thereby leading death row inmates to spend decades in solitary confinement anticipating their executions (*Lackey v. Texas*, 1995). In his final term on the Court, for example, Stevens argued strongly in *Johnson v. Bredesen* (2009) for the Court to recognize a constitutional violation in such circumstances:

> Petitioner Cecil Johnson, Jr., has been confined to a solitary cell awaiting his execution for nearly twenty-nine years. Johnson bears little, if any, responsibility for this delay. . . . I remain steadfast in my view "that executing defendants after such delays is unacceptably cruel," . . . [as] the delay itself subjects death row inmates to decades of especially severe, dehumanizing conditions of confinement.[44]

Near the end of his career, as noted in chapter 6, Stevens was moved once more to read a dissent from the bench in a capital punishment case, *Uttecht v. Brown* (2007), a strategy that one of his former law clerks saw as a means for "expressing righteous anger."[45] Linda Greenhouse described it as "an opinion dissenting from a decision that in retrospect appears to have been, for him, the final straw . . . [as the] majority gave state courts great leeway in death penalty trials to remove jurors who express even mild doubt about capital punishment."[46] Justice Stevens objected strongly to the majority's further expansion of prosecutors' and trial judges' authority to exclude potential jurors who would not apply capital punishment in every possible case. As Stevens wrote in the published dissent:

> Today, the Court has fundamentally redefined—or maybe just misunderstood—the meaning of "substantially impaired" [with respect to a juror's ability to consider state law with regard to possible sentences in murder cases], and, in doing so, has gotten it horribly backwards. [The Court] appears to be under the impression that trial courts should be encouraging the inclusion of jurors who will impose the death penalty.[47]

The concerns that he expressed in this 2007 opinion flowed directly from similar issues he raised in a 2005 speech to the American Bar Association in which he said that "aspects of the process of selecting juries in capital cases are troublesome."[48] Stevens complained that:

> [M]any days are spent conducting voir dire examinations in which prosecutors engage in prolonged questioning to determine whether the venire person has moral or religious scruples that would impair her ability to impose the death penalty. Preoccupation with that issue creates an atmosphere in which jurors are likely to assume that their primary task is to determine the penalty for the presumptively guilty defendant. More significantly, because the prosecutor can challenge jurors with qualms about the death penalty, the process creates a risk that a fair cross-section of the community will not be represented on the jury.[49]

He reiterated this point in an interview in 2010 by saying, "[I]f you pick juries at random and not by a process that loads the dice for the prosecutor, I'm not sure that an awful lot of the death penalty [sentences] would be returned [by juries]."[50]

The American Bar Association speech in 2005 was not merely a precursor to Stevens's oral dissent, which called attention to the biasing of juries in capital cases through a distortion of the jury selection process. The speech also made clear that as early as 2005 Stevens had come to the conclusion that the processes of the justice system tilted unfairly in favor of sentencing murder defendants to death rather than to incarceration. Stevens cited "[t]wo aspects of the sentencing process [that] tip the scales in favor of death."[51] First, he indicated his belief that using elected state judges to "preside and often make the final life-or-death decision [when they] must stand for re-election creates a subtle bias in favor of death."[52] Second, he complained about "the admissibility of victim impact evidence that sheds absolutely no light on either the issue of guilt or innocence, or the moral culpability of the defendant, [and therefore] serves no purpose other than to encourage jurors to decide in favor of death . . . on the basis of their emotions rather than their reason"—the very issue that led to his first oral dissent in a capital case in *Payne v. Tennessee* (1991).

INDEPENDENT JOURNEY OR CHANGING COURT?

John Paul Stevens arrived at the Supreme Court in 1975 with a number of firmly held viewpoints relevant to capital punishment based on his life experience and his judicial philosophy. He believed that careful procedures were necessary in order to have fair criminal prosecutions, that defendants needed high-quality representation by counsel in order for the adversary system to operate properly, and that judges must carefully review claims from all individuals, including those who lack status, power, and public sympathy. Stevens also had personal experiences that made him think deeply about the death penalty. Moreover, his approach to analyzing Eighth Amendment issues made him open to changing the definitions of acceptable criminal punishments. After starting his Supreme Court career as a key member of the three-justice plurality that guided the reactivation of capital punishment in 1976, Stevens eventually, in the words of his biographers, "brought the long journey of his death penalty logic . . . up to the abolitionist goal line" in 2008.[53] Did this reflect an independent journey, as Stevens changed his mind about capital punishment, or did it merely reflect, as Stevens often said about his career in general, an increasing conservatization of the Court that made him appear to become more liberal?

In a 2010 interview with National Public Radio's Nina Totenberg, Stevens identified his 1976 vote to approve the Texas death penalty procedures in *Jurek v. Texas* as the "one vote that [he] would change."[54] This public statement mirrored the 1991 conclusion of Stevens's colleague, Justice Lewis Powell, who voted with him in those cases. Powell had different reasons for looking back with regret at his votes in capital punishment cases. He said that "[c]apital punishment, though constitutional, was not being enforced. I think it reflects discredit on the law to have a major component of the law that is simply not enforced."[55] Thus Powell told his biographer, John C. Jeffries, that he had "come to think that capital punishment should be abolished."[56] Powell was concerned that last-minute appeals and extended litigation kept capital punishment from being implemented and thereby diminished the image of law and courts. By contrast, Stevens looked back with regret because of his concerns about biased jury selection processes, risks of discrimination and error, and other issues of fairness.

In his comments during the Totenberg interview, Stevens candidly discussed the 1976 *Jurek* case as "an incorrect decision."[57] Viewed in isolation, this statement could imply that Stevens's own viewpoints had changed—that what he considered in 1976 to be a proper decision to reactivate the death penalty he now regarded as "incorrect." However, in elaborating on the reasons for the regret about his 1976 vote, Stevens emphasized that it was not his viewpoint that had changed, but rather the Supreme Court and its decisions had changed over the years. As the Court changed, Stevens explained, he lost confidence in the possibility that capital punishment could be implemented fairly:

> But what happened over the years is the Court constantly expanded the cases eligible for the death penalty, so that the underlying premise for my vote in those cases has disappeared in a sense. . . . Not only is it a larger universe [of cases and defendants eligible for the death penalty], but the procedures have been more prosecution friendly. . . . So, I really think that the death penalty today is vastly different from the death penalty that we thought we were authorizing. If the procedures had been followed that we expected to be in

> place, I think I probably would've still had the same views. . . . I think we did not foresee how it would be interpreted.[58]

This explanation was consistent with Stevens's claim that his views did not change at all. Moreover, his reference to the Court's development of troubling doctrines and unfair procedures echoed his detailed critique of capital punishment in *Baze v. Rees* (2008).

In *Baze v. Rees* (2008), the Court examined whether Kentucky's lethal injection protocol violated the Eighth Amendment prohibition on cruel and unusual punishments. Chief Justice John Roberts's plurality opinion announcing the judgment of the Court found that the petitioners had failed to demonstrate that the lethal injection protocol actually caused the severe pain and suffering that were asserted to be risks from this procedure. Justice Stevens later stated that Roberts's opinion convinced him that over time the Court had rejected the premise that the death penalty served a meaningful retributive purpose. In Stevens's words, by requiring relatively painless executions, "[w]e have thus undermined the premise on which public approval of the retribution rationale is based."[59] According to Stevens, "Reflection after reading the Roberts opinion led to my decision to concur in his result but also to write separately."[60] The separate opinion explained Stevens's new conclusion that capital punishment was irretrievably flawed.

Justice Stevens wrote a concurring opinion in which he reluctantly endorsed the Court's judgment as a matter of respect for precedent. However, Stevens simultaneously presented a thorough critique and renunciation of capital punishment. He wrote, "I have relied on my own experience in reaching the conclusion that the imposition of the death penalty represents 'the pointless and needless extinction of life.'"[61] Stevens used the opinion to describe the changes in the Supreme Court's decisions that had moved death penalty jurisprudence away from, in his words, "[o]ur decisions in 1976 upholding the constitutionality of the death penalty [that] relied heavily on our belief that adequate procedures were in place that would avoid the danger of discriminatory application . . . , of arbitrary application . . . , and of excessiveness."[62] Stevens described the Court's decisions that raised "special concern[s]"[63] for him. These decisions increased the risks of jurors not representing a fair cross-section of the community,[64] the risk of error from the infusion of emotion through victim impact statements,[65] and the risk of racial discrimination that "the Court has allowed . . . to continue to play an unacceptable role."[66] With respect to the risk of erroneous convictions, Stevens stated forthrightly, "The risk of executing innocent defendants can be entirely eliminated by treating any penalty more severe than life imprisonment without the possibility of parole as constitutionally excessive."[67] He presented these arguments in support of a point that he made earlier in the opinion, namely his conclusion that "[i]ronically, . . . more recent [Supreme Court] cases have endorsed procedures that provide less protections to capital defendants than to ordinary offenders."[68]

Justice Stevens's reasoning made plausible the idea that his renunciation of capital punishment was merely a *Furman*-like conclusion. In effect, his opinion may be read to argue that the death penalty, as developed by the increasingly conservative Court majority over the preceding three decades, imposed risks of arbitrariness, discrimination, and error that he found to be unacceptable under the views that he had expressed in 1976 about the need for careful, fair procedures in death penalty cases. Thus, these arguments by Stevens can be seen to reinforce his generally stated view that the Court's changes created the perception that he altered his approach to judicial decision making, yet he actually continued to apply the same viewpoints and principles that he expressed in 1976.

On the other hand, it was clear that Stevens was not entirely immune to changing his views on issues. Linda Greenhouse used Justice Blackmun's papers in the Library of Congress to trace changes in Stevens's approach to abortion rights cases.[69] Social scientists who study patterns in justices' decision making have concluded that Stevens became more liberal after joining the Court as, over the course of his career, he voted more frequently to support claims by individuals.[70] With respect to capital punishment, some observers claimed that Stevens showed an increased sensitivity to Sixth Amendment right-to-counsel issues during his Supreme Court career that coincided with his increasing criticism of the majority's conservative decisions concerning the death penalty.[71] Moreover, Stevens himself said that "I know that I, like most of my colleagues, have continued to participate in a learning process while serving on the bench,"[72] thus acknowledging the possibility of development and change in his own decision making.

Even more intriguing was a different section of Stevens's *Baze v. Rees* opinion. In Part II of the opinion, he discussed his conclusion that the governing institutions of the United States had decided "to retain the death penalty as part of our law . . . [as] the product of habit and inattention rather than an acceptable deliberative process that weighs the costs and risks of administering that penalty against its identifiable benefits, and . . . in part on a faulty assumption about the retributive force of the death penalty."[73] He referred to his 1976 joint opinion with Justices Stewart and Powell in *Gregg v. Georgia*[74] to note that at the beginning of his career a plurality of justices had stated that a punishment will "constitute[e] 'gratuitous infliction of suffering' in violation of the Eighth Amendment," if it does not "serve a legitimate penological function."[75] He proceeded to argue that, based on available evidence, the purported justifications for capital punishment—incapacitation, deterrence, and retribution—did not actually fulfill their purposes.

With respect to incapacitation as a justification, Stevens said "the recent rise in statutes providing for life imprisonment without the possibility of parole demonstrates that incapacitation is neither a necessary nor a sufficient justification for the death penalty."[76] In effect, lifetime incarceration fulfills the incapacitation justification and thereby undercuts the claim that the death penalty is necessary for that purpose. In addressing deterrence as a justification, he said that: "Despite thirty years of empirical research in the area, there remains no reliable statistical evidence that capital punishment in fact deters potential offenders. In the absence of such evidence, deterrence cannot serve as a sufficient penological justification for this uniquely severe and irrevocable punishment.[77] Finally, while acknowledging that retribution "provides the most persuasive arguments for prosecutors seeking the death penalty,"[78] he noted that "our society ha[d] moved away from public and painful retribution towards ever more humane forms of punishment."[79] This comment referred to the use of lethal injection that was at the heart of the *Baze v. Rees* case. For Stevens, this meant that "[s]tate-sanctioned killing [wa]s therefore becoming more and more anachronistic,"[80] and that "[t]his trend, while appropriate and required by the Eighth Amendmen[t]. . . , actually undermine[d] the very premise on which public approval of the retribution rationale [wa]s based."[81]

In light of these unfulfilled justifications, Stevens declared that courts and legislatures should reconsider the use of capital punishment. At the end of Part III in the opinion, he brought back these themes and conclusions. He used them as part of his strongest declaration about his newly announced opposition to capital punishment:

> I have relied on my own experience in reaching the conclusion that the imposition of the death penalty represents "the pointless and needless extinction of life with only marginal contributions to any discernible social or public purposes. A penalty with such negligible returns to the State [is] patently excessive and cruel and unusual punishment violative of the Eighth Amendment."[82]

One important aspect of this statement was the implication that Justice Stevens had, based "on [his] own experience,"[83] changed his views about capital punishment. But did this necessarily constitute an admission that he had changed his viewpoint about or approach to capital punishment cases?

In Part III of the opinion, in which his critique of the death penalty was based on decisions that reduced procedural fairness and enhanced the risks of arbitrariness, discrimination, and error, Stevens could conceivably claim that he was merely adjusting his assessment in light of the Court majority's move in a conservative direction. In other words, he still believed in the same procedural protections that he supported in 1976, but the Court's decisions in the preceding three decades had made it impossible to consistently provide those necessary protections for defendants in capital cases. This discussion reflected Linda Greenhouse's observation about the case that "capital punishment had become for him, in the [C]ourt's hands, a promise of fairness unfulfilled."[84]

In Part II of the opinion, by contrast, he focused on the underlying justifications for capital punishment and the evidence of their ineffectiveness and decreasing relevance. Yet this discussion can be interpreted as reflecting his consistent adherence to the Eighth Amendment standard from *Trop v. Dulles* (1958) since Stevens noted how society's evolving values and policy decisions had undercut justifications for capital punishment as "a criminal sanction [that] serves a legitimate penological function."[85] His opinion pointed to changes in society that reduced the incapacitation justification through wider use of life-without-parole sentences and that undercut the retribution rationale as society sought more humane methods of execution. These were not examples of changes in Supreme Court decisions that led the purportedly unchanging Justice Stevens to appear to become more liberal. Instead, these were changes through state legislatures' actions that reflected diminished societal commitment to capital punishment. These arguments can be interpreted as evidence that Stevens did not change his own views about incapacitation and retribution. Instead, he simply adhered to the interpretive approach of defining the Eighth Amendment according to society's evolving values. He had emphatically reinforced his support for this approach to Eighth Amendment interpretation through his concurring opinion in *Roper v. Simmons* (2005). Thus Justice Stevens arguably reached new conclusions about the contemporary inapplicability of incapacitation and retribution as justifications for capital punishment not because he changed his viewpoint, but because he remained consistent in his approach to interpreting the Eighth Amendment in accordance with changes in society.

Despite this evidence that seems to support Stevens's general assessment of himself as having maintained consistency in his judicial decision making, there was one lingering example that appeared instead to reflect a change in his thinking about capital punishment. Justice Stevens's discussion of the *deterrence* justification for the death penalty pointed to years of social science research that failed to provide evidence to support this rationale for capital punishment. In making this point, he did not refer to actions taken by state legislatures to scale back or eliminate capital punishment or to any other societal changes that occurred due to this lack of evidence about deterrence. Moreover, this point was directly at odds with two aspects of the language of the *Gregg* plurality opinion—an opinion for which he was credited as joint author. First, the *Gregg* opinion explicitly said, "Although some of the studies suggest that the death penalty may not function as a significantly greater deterrent than lesser penalties, there is no convincing empirical evidence either supporting or refuting this view."[86] In *Baze*, by contrast, Stevens concluded that the absence of empirical evidence to support the deterrent effects of capital punishment—an absence that existed and was already noted in his joint plurality opinion in *Gregg* more than thirty years earlier—meant that "deterrence cannot serve as a sufficient penological justification for this uniquely severe and irrevocable punishment."[87] Yet in *Gregg*, the joint opinion had concluded that the lack of empirical evidence to support deterrence meant that "[t]he value of capital punishment as a deterrent of crime is a complex factual issue the resolution of which properly rests with the legislatures, which can evaluate the results of statistical studies in terms of their own local conditions and with a flexibility of approach that is not available to the courts."[88] Thus, there appeared to be a change in Stevens's own thinking about the implications of empirical studies concerning deterrence. In *Baze*, Stevens spoke about his own learning and, in effect, change in thinking through scholarly studies that had led him to conclude that deterrence did not provide an appropriate and sufficient justification for the maintenance of capital punishment.

Moreover, in the *Gregg* plurality opinion in 1976, Stevens had endorsed the assumption that, even without supportive empirical evidence, the death penalty deterred some murders:

> We may nevertheless assume safely that there are murderers, such as those who act in passion, for whom the threat of death has little or no deterrent effect. But for many others, the death penalty undoubtedly is a significant deterrent. There are carefully contemplated murders, such as murder for hire, where the possible penalty of death may well enter into the cold calculus that precedes the decision to act.[89]

In *Baze*, by contrast, Stevens evinced no similar assumption about the deterrent effect of capital punishment for "many" potential murderers and, more importantly, no willingness to use any such assumption as a justification to support the constitutionality of capital punishment. With respect to this point, it seemed clear that Stevens did, in fact, change his mind about whether deterrence could serve as a plausible and acceptable justification for the death penalty.

Justice Stevens said in a 2010 interview that he did not recall ever feeling confident about the deterrent effects of capital punishment. In his words, "I'm not sure that I ever thought deterrence ever had much effect—as opposed to life in prison."[90] It is possible that his endorsement of the language in *Gregg* that assumed the effectiveness of deterrence for "many" potential murderers who make "carefully contemplated" decisions was to some extent the product of compromise and accommodation.[91] Perhaps he endorsed the language in order to achieve the goal of producing a plurality opinion that could guide state legislatures on an important, contentious issue. Nevertheless, even if Stevens did not actually have faith in deterrence in 1976, he, like all Supreme Court justices, must have his presumptive viewpoints evaluated according to the language of both opinions that he wrote and those that he joined. In this instance, the treatment of the deterrence issue in the jointly-authored opinion in *Gregg* was markedly different than the treatment of deterrence in Stevens's opinion in *Baze*—a difference that was not grounded in any purported changes in society's treatment of the deterrence rationale. Thus the deterrence issue can appropriately be regarded as evidence of a change in the position of Justice Stevens as expressed in opinions that he wrote or endorsed, albeit while acknowledging the hypothetical possibility that his actual, personal opinion about deterrence may not have changed.

One other bit of evidence regarding a change in thinking by Stevens emerged in his memoir about the Supreme Court. In recalling *Jurek v. Texas* (1976), part of the trilogy of cases, along with *Gregg v. Georgia* (1976), that reactivated capital punishment, Stevens wrote:

> [M]y law clerk George Rutherglen . . . urged me to treat the Texas statute as effectively mandatory because the jury was required to impose the death penalty if it made a particular finding about the dangerous character of the defendant. George failed to persuade me at the time, but I have since concluded that he was right and that I should have voted differently in the Texas case. Of course, unless I could have persuaded Lewis [Powell] and Potter [Stewart] to do so as well, the outcome would not have changed. Nevertheless I regret that vote because experience has shown that the Texas statute has played an important role in authorizing so many death sentences in that state.[92]

Despite the evidence of change in his thinking, Stevens's new conclusion about the specific failure of the deterrence justification was not necessarily the linchpin for his general renunciation of capital punishment in *Baze v. Rees* (2008). Overall, much of Stevens's decision making on capital punishment issues can arguably be viewed as the product of consistent concern for fair procedures and a narrow application of the death penalty as well as adherence to the *Trop* standard for interpreting the Eighth Amendment through society's evolving values. His rejection of the death penalty in *Baze* may have been primarily motivated by his concerns about the Court's diminution of fair procedures rather than his changed view of the deterrence rationale.

JUSTICE STEVENS AND THE DEATH PENALTY

Much of Stevens's decision making on capital punishment issues can be viewed as the product of consistent concerns throughout his Supreme Court career—namely, concerns about fair procedures, narrow application of the death penalty, and consistent adherence to the *Trop* standard for interpreting the Eighth Amendment according to society's evolving values. His opinion in *Baze v. Rees* (2008) demonstrated that he did, in fact, appear to change his view on at least one aspect of capital punishment: the deterrence rationale for the death penalty. Although this change conflicted with Justice Stevens's professed belief that he remained consistent while the Supreme Court changed, it was perfectly consistent with his explicit recognition of the need for judges to learn while serving on the bench. Indeed, he openly stated in his *Baze* opinion that "I have relied on my own experience in reaching the conclusion that the imposition of the death penalty represents 'the pointless and needless extinction of life.'"[93] In an interview in 2010, he acknowledged a component of this experience and learning by pointing to the lessons he drew from observing other jurisdictions. He said, "I think it is appropriate to see the experience of other countries. The fact that no other civilized country uses the death penalty is a pretty good suggestion that they don't think they need it—and a lot of states get along without it."[94]

His ultimate renunciation of capital punishment was also based, in part, on Stevens's determination that society's views about the death penalty had changed. As he said in an interview, "But the very fact that hundreds and hundreds of guys are just going to be dying of old age on death row shows that there really isn't the public interest in enforcing the death penalty. You can't blame it all on federal judges. There just isn't the will to get it done except in [a few states]."[95]

Justice Stevens had a profound impact on the Supreme Court's debates and decisions concerning capital punishment. His role as a member of the three-justice *Gregg v. Georgia* plurality that shaped the reactivation of capital punishment in 1976 placed him at the center of the issue at the very start of his Supreme Court career. Over the years, he succeeded in his goal of narrowing the applicability of the death penalty through his majority opinion that precluded the application of capital punishment to developmentally disabled defendants (*Atkins v. Virginia,* 2002) and through his assignment to Justice Kennedy of responsibility for the majority opinions that eliminated the death penalty for juveniles under age eighteen (*Roper v. Simmons*, 2005) and defendants in child-rape cases (*Kennedy v Louisiana*, 2008). In many cases, however, his role was to resist the increasingly conservative Court's efforts to facilitate capital punishment at the expense of careful, fair procedures

Justice Stevens's opinion in *Baze v.* Rees—highlighting the flaws in both the justifications for capital punishment and the Court's enhancement of risks for arbitrariness, discrimination, and error—represented a comprehensive final judicial opinion on the subject after nearly thirty-five years of careful attention to the issue. It did not, however, represent his final word on the subject. In 2014, four years after his retirement from the Court, he provided a definitive final statement of his views. Justice Stevens published a book entitled *Six Amendments: How and Why We Should Change the Constitution.*[96] One of the six constitutional amendments proposed by Stevens made quite clear the strength of his conclusion that capital punishment should be abolished. His proposed revision of the Eighth Amendment would change the wording to accomplish that task: "Excessive Bail shall not be required, nor excessive fines imposed, nor cruel and unusual punishments *such as the death penalty* inflicted" (emphasis added to new proposed wording).[97]

NOTES

1. See, for example, "Only Four Justices Question Lawyers About Death Penalty," *Deseret News* (Salt Lake City, Utah), April 1, 1976, 2A. ("The views of Stevens, the newest justice, were not known. . . . Since Stewart and Justice Byron White took a midway position [in *Furman v. Georgia*, 408 U.S. 238 (1972)] their votes are crucial in the current series [of death penalty cases heard by the Supreme Court] as is that of Stevens who succeeded Justice William Douglas.")
2. Lee Epstein, "Who or What Changed?" *Legal Times,* April 11, 2010, accessed July 2, 2105, http://legaltimes.typepad.com/justicestevens.
3. William M. Treanor, "Lesson for Obama in Ford's Selection of Stevens," *USA Today*, April 15, 2015, accessed July 2, 2015, http://usatoday30.usatoday.com/news/opinion/forum/2010-04-15-treanor15_st_N.htm.
4. John Paul Stevens, "Learning on the Job," *Fordham Law Review* 74 (2006): 1567.
5. Jeffrey Rosen (Interviewer), "Interview Transcript: Justice John Paul Stevens," *New York Times*, April 12, 2010 (interview conducted June 22, 2007), accessed July 2, 2015, http://www.nytimes.com/2010/04/12/magazine/12stevens-interview.html.
6. *Nomination of John Paul Stevens to be a Justice of the Supreme Court: Hearings Before the Senate Judiciary Committee,* 94th Congress (1975), 26.
7. Ibid.
8. *Nomination of John Paul Stevens*, 26.
9. Ibid., 26–27.
10. Ibid., 72.
11. *Trop v. Dulles*, 356 U.S. 86, 101 (1958).
12. William J. Brennan, Jr., "The Constitution of the United States: Contemporary Ratification," in *Judges on Judging: Views from the Bench*, ed. David M. O'Brien (Chatham, N.J.: Chatham House, 1997), 200.
13. Ibid., 209.
14. Austin Sarat and Neil Vidmar, "Public Opinion, the Death Penalty, and the Eighth Amendment: Testing the Marshall Hypothesis," *Wisconsin Law Review* (1976): 171–206.
15. Diane Marie Amann, "John Paul Stevens, Human Rights Judge," *Fordham Law Review* 74 (2006): 1583.
16. Justice John Paul Stevens, interview with author, U.S. Supreme Court, Washington, D.C., July 29, 2010.
17. *Jurek v. Texas*, 428 U.S. 262, 273 (1976).
18. James S. Liebman and Lawrence C. Marshall, "Less Is Better: Justice Stevens and the Narrowed Death Penalty," *Fordham Law Review* 74 (2006): 1611.
19. *Trop v. Dulles*, 356 U.S. 86, 101 (1958).
20. *Gardner v. Florida*, 430 U.S. 349 (1977) (death sentence cannot be based on information in a presentence report that defense had no opportunity to refute or explain); *Dobbert v. Florida*, 432 U.S. 282 (1977) (application of changes in state law did not violate Ex Post Facto Clause); *Coker v. Georgia*, 433 U.S. 584 (1977) (imposition of death sentence for rape of an adult woman violates the Eighth Amendment as a disproportionate punishment); *Lockett v. Ohio*, 438 U.S. 586 (1978) (Ohio statute did not permit sufficient consideration of mitigating factors); *Bell v. Ohio*, 438 U.S. 637 (1978) (Ohio death penalty statute did not permit sufficient individualized consideration of the offender and offense); *Godfrey v. Georgia*, 446 U.S. 420 (1980) (language of Georgia statute on aggravating factors was too vague); *Beck v. Alabama*,

447 U.S. 625 (1980) (capital jury must be permitted to consider conviction for a lesser-included offense); *Adams v. Texas*, 448 U.S. 38 (1980) (application of Texas rule applied too broadly to exclude potential jurors in capital cases).

21. *Dobbert v. Florida*, 428 U.S. 282, 308–11 (1977) (Stevens, J., dissenting).

22. *Barclay v. Florida*, 463 U.S. 939, 959–60 (1983) (Stevens, J., concurring in judgment).

23. Rosen, "Interview Transcript."

24. *Spaziano v. Florida*, 468 U.S. 447, 468–70 (1984) (Stevens, J., concurring in part and dissenting in part).

25. American Civil Liberties Union, *Broken Justice: The Death Penalty in Alabama* (New York: American Civil Liberties Union, 2005), 9–10, accessed July 2, 2015, http://www.aclualabama.org/WhatWeDo/BrokenJustice_report.pdf (the forensic evidence linked only Baldwin's co-defendant to the murder; there is evidence that teenage suspect Baldwin's confession was extracted through a physically coercive interrogation; the co-defendant admitted that he alone was responsible for the murder; the co-defendant was executed in 1996 and Baldwin was executed in 1999).

26. *Baldwin v. Alabama*, 472 U.S. 372, 394 (1985) (Stevens, J., dissenting).

27. Ibid., 397–98.

28. Christopher E. Smith and Madhavi McCall, "Justice Scalia's Influence on Criminal Justice," *University of Toledo Law Review* 34 (2003): 550.

29. *McCleskey v. Kemp*, 481 U.S. 279, 367 (1987) (Stevens, J., dissenting).

30. *Payne v. Tennessee*, 501 U.S. 808, 856 (Stevens, J., dissenting).

31. John Paul Stevens, *Five Chiefs: A Supreme Court Memoir* (Boston: Little, Brown, 2011), 186.

32. Ibid.

33. Jean Redding, "Evidence of Innocence: The Lloyd Schlup Death Penalty Case," *Variety*, June 18, 1995, accessed July 2, 2015, http://variety.com/1995/tv/reviews/evidence-of-innocence-the-lloyd-schlup-death-penalty-case-1200441896/.

34. *Schlup v. Delo*, 513 U.S. 298, 327 (1995).

35. Ibid.

36. *Atkins v. Virginia*, 536 U.S. 304, 321 (2002).

37. Liebman and Marshall, 1632–75.

38. Jeffrey Toobin, "After Stevens: What Will the Supreme Court Be Like Without Its Liberal Leader?" *The New Yorker*, March 22, 2010, 43.

39. Ross Douthat, "The Further Empowerment of Anthony Kennedy," *New York Times*, April 12, 2010, accessed July 2, 2015, http://douthat.blogs.nytimes.com/2010/04/12/the-further-empowerment-of-anthony-kennedy/.

40. Ibid.

41. Linda Greenhouse, "After a 32-Year Journey, Stevens Renounces Capital Punishment," *New York Times*, April 18, 2008, accessed July 2, 2015, http://www.nytimes.com/2008/04/18/world/americas/18iht-18memo.12124092.html.

42. Tracey D. Samuelson, "DC Sniper Execution: Why His Case Moved So Quickly," *Christian Science Monitor*, November 11, 2009, accessed July 2, 2015, http://www.csmonitor.com/USA/Justice/2009/1111/p02s01-usju.html.

43. *Muhammad v. Kelly*, 130 S.Ct. 541 (2009) (Statement of Stevens, J.).

44. *Johnson v. Bredesen*, 130 S.Ct. 541 (2009) (Statement of Stevens, J.).

45. Andrew Siegel, "Justice Stevens and the Seattle Schools Case: A Case Study on the Role of Righteous Anger in Constitutional Discourse," *UC Davis Law Review* 43 (2010): 934.

46. Greenhouse, "After a 32-Year Journey."

47. *Uttecht v. Brown*, 551 U.S. 1, 35 (2007) (Stevens, J., dissenting).

48. John Paul Stevens, "Address at the American Bar Association Thurgood Marshall Awards Dinner," Chicago, Ill., August 6, 2005, accessed May 21, 2015, http://www.supremecourt.gov/publicinfo/speeches/viewspeech/sp_08-06-05.

49. Ibid.

50. Justice John Paul Stevens, interview with author, U.S. Supreme Court, Washington, D.C., July 29, 2010.

51. Stevens, "Address at the American Bar Association Thurgood Marshall Awards Dinner," 2005.
52. Ibid.
53. Bill Barnhart and Gene Schlickman, *John Paul Stevens: An Independent Life* (DeKalb, Ill.: Northern Illinois University Press, 2010), 218.
54. Nina Totenberg, "Justice Stevens: An Open Mind On a Changed Court," National Public Radio, October 4, 2010, accessed May 21, 2015, http://www.npr.org/templates/story/story.php?storyId=130198344.
55. John C. Jeffries, *Justice Lewis F. Powell, Jr.* (New York: Scribner, 1994), 451.
56. Ibid.
57. Totenberg, "Justice Stevens: An Open Mind On a Changed Court."
58. Ibid.
59. Stevens, *Five Chiefs*, 218.
60. Ibid.
61. *Baze v. Rees*, 553 U.S. 35, 71 (2008) (Stevens, J., concurring in judgment).
62. Ibid.
63. Ibid., 84.
64. Ibid.
65. Ibid., 85.
66. Ibid.
67. Ibid., 86.
68. Ibid., 84.
69. Linda Greenhouse, "Justice John Paul Stevens as Abortion-Rights Strategist," *UC Davis Law Review* 43 (2010): 749–82.
70. Lee Epstein, Andrew D. Martin, Kevin M. Quinn, and Jeffrey A. Segal, "Ideological Drift Among Supreme Court Justices: Who, When, and How Important?" *Northwestern University Law Review* 101 (2007): 1492, 1505.
71. Barnhart and Schlickman, 217.
72. Stevens, "Learning on the Job," 1562.
73. *Baze v. Rees*, 553 U.S. at 71 (Stevens, J., concurring in judgment).
74. *Gregg v. Georgia*, 428 U.S. 153 (1976).
75. *Baze v. Rees*, 553 U.S. at 78 (Stevens, J., concurring in judgment) (quoting *Gregg v. Georgia*, 428 U.S. at 183 and n. 28 (joint opinion of Stewart, Powell, and Stevens, JJ)).
76. Ibid.
77. Ibid., 79.
78. Ibid., 80.
79. Ibid.
80. Ibid.
81. Ibid., 81.
82. Ibid., 86 (Stevens, J., concurring in judgment) (quoting *Furman v. Georgia*, 408 U.S. at 312 (1972) (White, J., concurring)).
83. Ibid., 86 (Stevens, J., concurring in judgment).
84. Greenhouse, "After a 32-Year Journey."
85. *Baze v. Rees*, 553 U.S at 78 (Stevens, J., concurring in judgment).
86. *Gregg v. Georgia*, 428 U.S. 153, 185 (1976).
87. *Baze v. Rees*, 553 U.S. at 78 (Stevens, J., concurring in judgment).
88. *Gregg v. Georgia*, 428 U.S. at 186.
89. Ibid.
90. Justice John Paul Stevens, interview with author, U.S. Supreme Court, Washington, D.C., July 29, 2010.
91. *Gregg v. Georgia*, 428 U.S. at 185–86.
92. Stevens, *Five Chiefs*, 215–16.
93. *Baze v. Rees*, 553 U.S. at 86 (Stevens, J. concurring in judgment).
94. Justice John Paul Stevens, interview with author, U.S. Supreme Court, Washington, D.C., July 29, 2010.
95. Ibid.

96. John Paul Stevens, *Six Amendments: How and Why We Should Change the Constitution*. (New York: Little, Brown, 2014), 107–23.
97. Ibid., 123.

Chapter Nine

Conclusion

Justice Stevens stood out as an outspoken defender of constitutional rights in the criminal justice system. Yet scholars' analyses of his votes make clear that he did not automatically support individuals' claims in these cases. It is easy to identify many cases in which Stevens's fact-based, case-by-case approach led him to reject rights claims and endorse the arguments of prosecutors or the actions of police officers. With respect to certain issues, particularly prisoners' rights, *Miranda* warnings, and, eventually, specific aspects of capital punishment, Stevens's voting record was comparable to those of Warren Court liberals Thurgood Marshall and William Brennan. Compared to the other post-Warren Court appointees to the Court, Stevens stood out as the most rights-supported justice on criminal justice issues. In light of this book's topical discussions based on Stevens's judicial philosophy and opinions, what conclusions can be drawn about his decision making, role, and impact for criminal justice?

CONTINUITY OR CHANGE?

Judicial scholars who focus on attitudes and values as the primary drivers of Supreme Court justices' decisions have struggled to identify and define baseline attitudes for new justices. A pre-appointment baseline assessment is needed in order to avoid the circularity of demonstrating that attitudes motivate judicial votes by relying solely on attitudes reflected in those very judicial votes and opinions. Jeffrey Segal and Albert Cover developed a widely-used method for baseline assessments of new appointees. They utilized characterizations and predictions about those appointees that appeared in editorials published in a specific set of major newspapers reflecting a mix of liberal and conservative political perspectives.[1] Although this measure clearly relies on *perceptions* of new appointees' attitudes and values, their analysis shows a high degree of congruence between the initial reputations of new appointees and their eventual patterns of decision making as Supreme Court justices. Justice Stevens, however, stands out in this analysis as one of the justices whose actual performance in Supreme Court decision making on constitutional rights issues differed significantly from initial perceptions and expectations at the time of his appointment.[2] The major newspapers' editorial assessments of Stevens in 1975 cast him as a conservative, yet his actual voting record established him as a liberal who supported individuals in nearly two-thirds of constitutional rights cases, including those outside the realm of criminal justice.[3] Indeed, by the end of his career in 2010, it was clear that Stevens's voting record defined him as the most liberal justice appointed to the Supreme Court since Thurgood Marshall's appointment in 1967.[4]

Justice Stevens always maintained, in his words, "I don't think of myself as a liberal *at all*. . . . I think as part of my general politics, I am pretty darn conservative."[5] He expressed the view that he merely appeared to be more liberal in observers' eyes over the course of his career because the Court's composition steadily became more conservative. To Stevens, the replacements of Stewart by O'Connor in 1981, Burger by Scalia in 1986, Powell by Kennedy in 1988, Brennan by Souter in 1990, and Marshall by Thomas in 1991 brought to the Court justices who were each more conservative than the specific justices that they replaced. So, too, did the Court's conservatism increase with the later replacement of O'Connor by Alito in 2006. Thus he found himself dissenting against the efforts of his junior Republican colleagues, as well as his senior colleague Rehnquist, to diminish or reverse rights-protecting precedents.[6]

Was Stevens's liberal voting record a result of changes that occurred on the Court, as Stevens asserted, or was it the product of his changing views during his career on the Court? As with other complex questions, there is good reason to resist adopting a simple answer. There is evidence that Stevens, the justice who espoused learning on the bench, changed his views on some issues. Social science studies that account for justices' voting patterns as well as changes in the issues on the Court's docket indicate that Stevens became more liberal over the course of his Supreme Court career.[7] Linda Greenhouse observed with respect to the evolution of his opinions on abortion, "As Justice Stevens would show throughout his career on the Court, he was never willing to take for granted that he had been right in the past without thinking the problem through in each subsequent iteration."[8] Stefanie Lindquist's empirical study led her to speculate that Stevens's five-year experience working with liberal judges on the Seventh Circuit may have contributed to his openness to considering different ideas and approaches. In her words, "Although we have no direct evidence that his interaction with Democratic appointees on the Seventh Circuit influenced Justice Stevens ideologically, it is certainly possible that his respect for his more liberal colleagues on the circuit caused him to be open to alternative viewpoints and ideas."[9] In the realm of criminal justice, as discussed in chapter 8, capital punishment stands out as an issue for which there was evidence of change, especially his eventual rejection of the deterrence rationale as part of his conclusion in *Baze v. Rees* (2008) that the death penalty system became increasingly unfair and not worthy of continuation. As indicated in chapter 7, there was also evidence of possible change with respect to stop-and-frisk criteria for searches as well as vehicle checkpoints under the Fourth Amendment.

Notwithstanding such evidence, Stevens's perception of himself deserves consideration for its potential explanatory power. Justice Stevens's experiences and judicial philosophy unquestionably led him to bring to the Supreme Court values and an approach to decision making that were protective of constitutional rights. The divergence between his ultimately liberal voting record on rights in criminal justice and the original expectations about the anticipated conservatism of a Republican antitrust attorney was clearly not primarily the product of changes in his views. There is consistency in Stevens's endorsement of rights for several issues that extended from his Seventh Circuit opinions to his early opinions on the Supreme Court and then continued for his entire career on the high court. His support for prisoners' rights, *Miranda* rights, right to counsel, and the importance of the jury was evident throughout his judicial career.

Why were initial expectations about Stevens so far off the mark as to enhance the perception that he changed his views as a Supreme Court justice? The original expectations that characterized Stevens as a conservative were shaped by a historical context in which he was replacing the ultraliberal Justice Douglas while other liberal Warren Court justices were either still serving on the Court (i.e., Brennan and Marshall), or, as in the examples of Warren, Black, and Fortas, remained fresh in the recent memories of Court observers. In addition, Stevens's Seventh Circuit opinions that might have signaled the rights-protective nature of his judicial philosophy did not necessarily clash with the perspectives of recognized judicial conservatives of the day, such as Chief Justice Burger. Moreover, in 1975 observers were both unaware of specific life events that shaped Stevens's judicial philosophy, such as his pro bono representation of wrongly convicted Arthur LaFrana and other imprisoned offenders, and unable to anticipate the influence of known life events, such as his service in World War II and his role in the Illinois investigatory commission.

The emergence of Stevens's identification and reputation as a liberal justice also owes much to the historical era in which he served on the Supreme Court. Stevens arrived at the Supreme Court just as legislative restrictions on abortion were about to challenge *Roe v. Wade* repeatedly and thereby lead Stevens to cast a series of liberal votes to preserve the right of choice. Debates about the exclusionary rule and *Miranda* rights heated up as conservative appointees sought to curtail the scope of these rights and Stevens found himself casting votes and writing opinions against the diminution of individuals' legal protections. Similar developments occurred with regard to other constitutional rights issues regularly reexamined by the increasingly conservative Supreme Court. These cases generated liberal votes and opinions as part of Stevens's effort to preserve and maintain existing rights. Thus the nature of the issues accepted for hearing by the Court and conservatizing trends in its decisions concerning many rights issues contributed to the liberal decision-making record produced by Stevens, especially with respect to criminal justice issues. Analysts can point to evidence that Stevens changed his views over the course of his Supreme Court career and became more liberal with respect to specific issues, such as affirmative action and capital punishment. Yet Stevens's liberal record on rights issues and the divergence of that record from the original assumptions about him as a Republican judge seem largely attributable to the experience-based judicial philosophy that he brought to the Court and the historical context in which his record was produced and evaluated.

ROLE AND IMPACT IN CRIMINAL JUSTICE CASES

There are no clear, agreed-upon criteria for determining whether a Supreme Court justice should be considered important and influential and, moreover, how to measure that influence. Edward Rubin put forward the following definition for guiding assessments of justices:

> Influential jurists and courts are characterized by their unity of purpose, the subtle yet dramatic alchemy which can combine particular decisions that must be plausible on their own terms into a coherent pattern that contributes to the governance of the regime. . . . Truly great jurists and great courts are those whose patterns of decisions not only influence the present but survive into the future. They are those whose unity of purpose projects a vision that at least foreshadows and perhaps transfigures the direction their society is headed.[10]

Although Professor Rubin's formulation does not represent either the definitive or final word on assessing justices' influence, it is interesting to bear in mind when evaluating the career of Justice Stevens or any other justice. Justice Stevens is certainly deserving of consideration in light of the consistent aspects of his judicial philosophy and decision making as well as his key role in decisions shaping major issues of his historical era, including prisoners' rights, sentencing, affirmative action, abortion, post-9/11 terrorism suspects' rights, and capital punishment. Transfiguring society? That's a tall order for any individual justice and Rubin presumably had specific court eras in mind, such as the Warren Court and its role in the constitutional rights revolution that reshaped American society. Yet Stevens clearly had important influence over key cases that significantly affected society as well as leaving—through his numerically staggering body of opinions—ideas and reasoning that may very well have profound impacts in the future.

In asserting that a justice was influential, commentators often look first to majority opinions written by that individual. The attribution of influence to the majority opinion author is based on a recognition that the opinion writer shapes the reasoning and articulation of standards and rules presented in the opinion. However, any discussion of personal responsibility and credit for influence flowing from a specific Supreme Court opinion must be approached with caution. After the responsibility for writing the majority opinion is assigned by the chief justice or the senior justice in the majority, a particular justice initiates the opinion-drafting process in each case. In effect, the draft produced by this justice defines the initial terms for the discussions of the opinion's structure and content before the other justices provide input, request changes, and express disagreement. The greater the extent to which the author incorporates suggested changes from others, the less deserving the author becomes of special or sole credit for the opinion's content. Yet outside observers have little ability to know how suggestions shaped any particular opinion unless and until such give-and-take communications and changes are revealed years later in a retired justice's papers. The significant impact of this drafting process on the content of opinions is easily discernible in many case files among Justice Blackmun's papers in the Library of Congress. As chapter 4 described, for example, with respect to the development of majority opinions in the prisoners' rights cases of *Estelle v. Gamble* (1976) and *Houchins v. KQED, Inc.* (1978), the process of circulating draft opinions and incorporating comments can affect both the content of an opinion and the ultimate outcome of a case.

A number of Justice Stevens's significant majority opinions addressed issues other than criminal justice. For example, *Federal Communications Commission v. Pacifica Foundation* (1978) endorsed and clarified governmental authority to regulate indecent material broadcast over the airwaves. Justice Steven's majority opinion in *Chevron U.S.A., Inc. v. Natural Resources Defense Council* (1984) remains one of the most important and frequently cited cases in administrative law. The decision clarified how courts are supposed to evaluate government agencies' interpretations of the statutes that they administer and the circumstances that call for judicial deference to an agency's determinations. In a highly controversial opinion in *Kelo v. New London* (2005), Justice Stevens clarified the meaning of "public use" under the Fifth Amendment's Takings Clause with respect to a city's effort to acquire residential properties in an area that would be redeveloped by a private developer under the city's master plan. These and other important majority opinions serve as a reminder that the focus on policy-shaping criminal justice cases in this book should not obscure Stevens's significant impact on numerous areas of law during his thirty-five years on the Court.

The Supreme Court Judicial Database lists Stevens as the author of majority opinions in sixty-three cases classified as constitutional criminal procedure and prisoners' rights. These majority opinions were not all equally impactful. More importance is usually attributed to those opinions that redefine or clarify the law, expand or curtail rights, and otherwise either break new ground or have broad impacts on society. Justice Stevens certainly wrote opinions deserving of credit as important among those listed for these categories in the database. However, in the area of criminal justice his dissenting opinions objecting to the diminution of established constitutional rights deserve recognition as they were especially numerous as well as notable for their memorable language and reasoning.

Some majority opinions, including those written by Stevens, had a finite lifespan as changes in the Court's composition and other factors led to the alteration of precedents, including complete reversals, in subsequent Supreme Court decisions. For example, Justice Stevens made an effort in *United States v. Ross* (1982) to construct a careful delineation of the limited circumstances in which the existence of probable cause could justify the warrantless search of a container within a vehicle. This precedent was undone a decade later by the Court's decision to relax Fourth Amendment standards and expand police authority in *California v. Acevedo* (1991). Similarly, Justice Stevens's important *Michigan v. Jackson* (1986) precedent concerning the protection of represented criminal defendants from police questioning outside of the presence of counsel was overturned in *Montejo v. Louisiana* (2009) through the proactive efforts of the conservative Roberts Court majority. Other majority opinions by Stevens, however, have had continuing impact.

Majority opinions by Stevens provided important guidance to lower court judges. For example, his opinion in *United States v. Cronic* (1984) concerning standards for identifying Sixth Amendment ineffective-assistance-of-counsel violations provided guidance for innumerable cases, especially because ineffective assistance claims are among those raised most frequently by convicted offenders in habeas corpus petitions.[11] In *Payton v. New York* (1980), on behalf of a six-justice majority, Stevens's opinion invalidated a New York statute that authorized the warrantless entry into homes to effect routine felony arrests. Stevens's opinion reinforced the sanctity of the home and emphasized the importance of law enforcement officers obtaining warrants before invading that legally protected location. Justice Stevens's majority opinion in *Richards v. Wisconsin* (1997) barred states from creating blanket rules that exempted specific categories of crimes, such as drug offenses, from Fourth Amendment rules that generally require officers to "knock and announce" before entering a home to execute a warrant. In *Ferguson v. City of Charleston* (2001), Stevens's opinion prohibited hospital officials from voluntarily sharing pregnant women's medical test results with law enforcement officials who were interested in initiating prosecutions of expectant mothers who had used illegal drugs.

Among his majority opinions, Stevens announced, and therefore is credited with writing on behalf of the three co-authors, the opinion in *Roberts v. Louisiana* (1976) that narrowed the scope of the death penalty by prohibiting mandatory death sentences. Stevens is similarly credited with writing the three-justice opinion in *Jurek v. Texas* (1976) that was among the trilogy of cases, including *Gregg v. Georgia* (1976), which reactivated the death penalty. However, because Stevens later labeled the decision in *Jurek* as the one vote that he wished he could go back and undo since he ultimately concluded that it was "incorrect,"[12] perhaps he would have preferred not to have that opinion counted as among his most influential. Notwithstanding his regret, the validation of the Texas death penalty statute had significant impact as Texas became far and away the most active state in actually carrying out executions. As of June 2015, Texas had carried out 526 executions since the 1976 reactivation of the death penalty in *Jurek* while the next most vigorous death penalty practitioner-state was Oklahoma with only 112 executions in that time period.[13]

In *Beck v. Alabama* (1979), Stevens's opinion declared that the death penalty may not be imposed when the jury was not permitted to consider conviction for a lesser-included non-capital offense amid evidence that would have supported such a verdict. The case was among several on a theme that continued throughout Stevens's Supreme Court career as he wrote and supported opinions that advocated the narrowing of capital punishment to a limited range of factual circumstances and offenders.[14] A later Stevens majority opinion of exceptional importance in advancing this goal was *Atkins v. Virginia* (2002) which forbade the imposition of the death penalty on developmentally disabled defendants. Justice Stevens's plurality opinion in *Thompson v. Oklahoma* (1988) had a parallel impact by barring the imposition of capital punishment on teenagers below the age of sixteen who were convicted of murder. In both *Thompson* and *Atkins*, Stevens demonstrated the vitality of the *Trop v. Dulles* (1958) test for cruel and unusual punishments by marshaling evidence concerning contemporary societal standards regarding punishment.

Stevens assigned the groundbreaking *Atkins* opinion to himself in his role as senior justice in the majority. The exercise of this authority by Stevens arose most frequently after the retirement of Justice Blackmun in 1994 when Stevens remained as the most senior justice on the Court who frequently supported individuals in criminal justice cases. He used his authority under this role to advance his objective of further reducing the scope of the death penalty so that it would apply only to adults. He assigned to Justice Kennedy the responsibility for writing the majority opinion in *Roper v. Simmons* (2005). The *Roper* decision prohibited use of the death penalty for offenders who committed their capital crimes while under the age of eighteen. The reasoning and evidence that Stevens employed in *Thompson* and *Atkins* unquestionably helped to lay the groundwork for the justifications articulated by Kennedy in the important *Roper* precedent. Stevens contributed to further narrowing of capital punishment by also assigning to Justice Kennedy the majority opinion declaring that defendants convicted of committing non-fatal rapes of children cannot be sentenced to death (*Kennedy v. Louisiana*, 2008).

As senior justice, Stevens deserved credit when his assignment choice served to hold together a potentially fragile majority. For example, Justice Kennedy presumably received these and other important assignments in closely divided liberal decisions because Stevens acknowledged following the practice of regularly assigning majority opinions to the justice who may be least firmly committed to the majority position. In Stevens's experience as a lawyer and jurist, he often found himself more convinced of the correctness of a particular argument as he worked on developing justifications for the argument.[15] Thus his opinion assignments could be based on the idea that a wavering justice will "tend to become more convinced" by working on a draft of the majority opinion.[16] In the *Roper* and *Kennedy* cases assigned to Justice Kennedy, Stevens knew that the loss of a single vote through a justice's change of mind in the opinion-drafting process would lead to a decision preserving a more expansive death penalty. By contrast, *Atkins* was a 6 to 3 decision so Stevens could more readily assign the opinion to himself with less worry about the need to retain the vote of a specific wavering justice.

There are a number of examples of important cases in which Stevens chose the author of the majority opinion. For example, Justice Stevens assigned to Justice Souter the responsibility for writing the plurality opinion in a closely divided *Miranda*-issue case entitled *Missouri v. Seibert* (2004). Souter's opinion on behalf of the narrow majority forbade law enforcement officers from obtaining confessions from suspects and then subsequently providing *Miranda* warnings and asking the suspects to repeat their confessions. Such situations created risks that naïve suspects would assume that their original confession had made conviction inevitable and not realize that those unwarned incriminating statements could not actually be used in court. The decision was important because it served to put an end to many police agencies' expanding practice of actually training officers to give so-called midstream warnings as a way of avoiding and defeating the fundamental purpose of *Miranda* warnings.

In *United States v. Bajakajian* (1998), Stevens had the relatively rare opportunity to assign a five-member majority opinion to Justice Thomas in a criminal justice case. In non-unanimous decisions concerning criminal justice issues, Thomas typically disagreed with Stevens. In this case, however, Thomas's opinion found a violation of the Eighth Amendment's Excessive Fines Clause when a traveler at an airport forfeited $357,000 for failing to file the proper paperwork before transporting that amount of currency out of the country. The decision did not define clear standards for violations of this constitutional clause, but it conveyed a reminder that there were boundaries for permissible fines that courts should stand ready to identify and enforce.

THE GREAT DISSENTER

Because of the historical era in which he served on the Supreme Court, Stevens's attention and energy in many criminal justice cases focused on resisting efforts of the increasingly conservative Supreme Court to diminish the definition and scope of constitutional rights. As a result, Stevens wrote many dissenting opinions concerning *Miranda* rights, capital punishment, prisoners' rights, and the other issues discussed in the preceding chapters. Justice Stevens undoubtedly deserved credit as one of the "great dissenters" in Court history if one evaluates that label in terms of the sheer number of dissenting opinions written. As noted by Craig Rust, "[t]he 720 dissents he authored during his tenure on the Court are more than any other justice in history; indeed, his output is roughly fifty percent greater than that of the second most prolific justice, Justice William O. Douglas (with 486)."[17] While such a large number of dissenting opinions is certainly indicative of assertiveness and energy, it does not necessarily either demonstrate or measure Stevens's influence.

Alternatively, "greatness" as a dissenter may be related to subsequent success in seeing the advocacy of rules and reasoning come to fruition in majority opinions during later terms. Thus the first Justice John Harlan is credited for his important solo dissent against racial segregation in *Plessy v. Ferguson* (1896) that advocated an equality principle which was later to become the law of the land in *Brown v. Board of Education* (1954). Similarly, the dissenting opinion by Justice Oliver Wendell Holmes in *Hammer v. Dagenhart* (1918) that advocated broader congressional authority to regulate products manufactured by child labor was later endorsed in the Supreme Court's subsequent recognition of expansive congressional commerce powers after President Franklin Roosevelt's appointees began to join the Court in the 1930s. However, it is difficult to know whether and how to give credit to such "successful" dissenting opinions. Did their reasoning actually persuade subsequent Supreme Court appointees to move legal doctrine in a new direction? Did they merely anticipate—by either prescience or coincidence—the future social and cultural changes in American society that would help to move legal and policy values in a different direction? Did the existence of the dissenting opinions merely contribute to the legitimacy of new majority opinions reflecting changes in social values? Thus, under the common law process, new doctrines can appear to be the legitimate products of the accumulated wisdom of judges rather than as newly created inventions suddenly imposed by judges upon society. Such questions are not easily answered and they complicate the task of evaluating the importance and influence of a Supreme Court justice whose career in criminal justice cases rested heavily—although certainly not exclusively—on dissenting opinions.

In Rust's empirical analysis of Stevens's legacy as an unmatched writer of judicial opinions, he concluded that "Stevens led by example, prolifically recording his own thoughts on the law and allowing them to influence generations of jurists and scholars, though his position may not have won the day . . . initially."[18] This analysis was not based merely on the large number of opinions, concurring and majority as well as dissenting, written by Justice Stevens. Rust documented that Stevens was cited *by name* in more than 10,858 opinions by federal judges, including 9,818 opinions by federal district and circuit court judges.[19] To Rust, this was an indicator of significant influence because these judges typically could easily have cited just a Supreme Court or Seventh Circuit case without referring to Stevens by name. As a means of direct comparison to illuminate this measure of influence, the study noted that during Chief Justice Roberts's fourth term on the Supreme Court, he was cited by name in sixty federal court cases while, by contrast, Stevens was cited by name 216 times during his own fourth term on the Court.[20] Thus Rust concluded that Stevens should be viewed as an intellectual leader with "profound impact on the thought processes of a generation of federal jurists."[21]

Rust's study highlighted the general presumption about one reason that justices choose to write concurring and dissenting opinions. It should be remembered that in addition to holding the record for most dissenting opinions, Stevens also wrote more concurring opinions than any other justice in Supreme Court history. By devoting so much energy to explaining his viewpoints in these opinions, Stevens placed before the legal community, including future federal jurists, a wealth of thought-provoking reasoning that may potentially shape lawyers' arguments and judges' decisions in the decades ahead. The Rust study was notable because in counting references to Stevens by name it provided empirical documentation of the apparent influence that these opinions have already had even as they remain available to be discovered and utilized in future cases.

The conclusions of the Rust study were based on an empirical examination of Justice Stevens's overall record and career without focusing on individual issue areas. In light of Stevens's extensive record as a dissenter who resisted developments diminishing legal protections in such areas as prisoners' rights and *Miranda* contexts, an assessment of his role and impact in criminal justice requires attention to specific issues. Obviously, dissenting opinions do not automatically, immediately, or necessarily influence the development of law and policy. As indicated in the previous examples of the first Justice Harlan and Justice Holmes, however, there may be dissenting opinions that eventually become regarded as influencing the development of doctrine. In the case of Justice Stevens, his dissenting opinions are credited with laying the groundwork for subsequent important developments in Supreme Court doctrine concerning the role of juries in sentencing.

As Rory Little has noted, Justice Stevens wrote an opinion concurring in part and dissenting in part in *Spaziano v. Florida* (1984) that appears, in retrospect, to have been a foundational element in the Court's eventual alteration of doctrine concerning the jury's role.[22] As described in chapter 6, the jury in *Spaziano* recommended a sentence of life imprisonment after the defendant was convicted of murder, but the judge imposed a death sentence instead. The Supreme Court majority approved this element of Florida's capital sentencing process that placed juries merely in an advisory role. In a dissenting opinion joined by Justices Brennan and Marshall, Stevens insisted that "[h]istory, tradition, and the basic structure and purpose of the jury system persuade me that jury sentencing is essential if the administration of capital punishment is to be governed by the community's evolving standards of decency."[23] Two years later, in *McMillian v. Pennsylvania* (1986), Stevens wrote a solo dissent (Justices Marshall, Brennan, and Blackmun dissented separately). Justice Stevens argued that juries must make a beyond-a-reasonable-doubt finding that a firearm was used in a crime when such a factual finding will trigger a mandatory minimum sentence, even if the firearm's presence was not an element of the crime charged.[24] Four years after that, in *Walton v. Arizona* (1990), Stevens's dissenting opinion argued that the jury, rather than the judge, should determine the existence of aggravating and mitigating factors that determine whether a death sentence will be imposed after a jury finds the defendant guilty of murder.

The groundwork laid by Stevens's dissents came to fruition in 2000 when he was able to assign to himself the majority opinion in *Apprendi v. New Jersey* requiring that juries make determinations according to the beyond-a-reasonable-doubt standard for facts that can trigger sentencing enhancements. Two years after that, the Court overturned *Walton* in a majority opinion assigned by Stevens to Justice Ginsburg in *Ring v. Arizona* (2002). The Court's new emphasis on the jury's essential role for fact-finding in sentencing continued and was solidified in two subsequent cases concerning state and federal sentencing guidelines, *Blakley v. Washington* (2004) and *United States v. Booker* (2005), with the latter having a Stevens-authored majority opinion as one portion of the decision. In the later cases, the arguments that originated with Stevens were reiterated by Justice Scalia and supported even by Justice Thomas. As Jeffrey Fisher noted, however, Stevens did not completely succeed in elevating the jury's role as the Court never overturned *McMillan* and still declined to require jury fact-finding for triggering mandatory minimum sentences in *Harris v. United States* (2002).[25]

Justice Stevens's influence on altering the requirements for the jury's role in sentencing was widely recognized because his dissenting opinions laid the groundwork for later majority opinions by himself and others. According to Professor Fisher, "one might argue that Justice Stevens deserves extra credit for his achievement, because his influence on the Court [for sentencing issues] affected not just new appointees, but also caused some, including Justice Scalia, to change their minds. This reflects Justice Stevens's true power of persuasion."[26] Similarly, Professor Little described Justice Stevens as "the triumphant architect in the *Apprendi-Blakely* line of cases."[27] According to Little:

> The genius of *Blakely* is that Justice Stevens found a way to get the constitutional originalists to come with him in this enterprise. The genius of *Blakely* is that Justice Stevens quietly allowed his idea to percolate, and yet, if you will, allowed the constitutional history to be written in a way so that Justice Scalia and late, but not too late, Justice Thomas [would] come to the table and join him.[28]

Although constituting a less clear-cut instance of influence from dissenting opinions, influential impacts may have developed from Justice Stevens's continuous emphasis on the protection of liberty interests through the Due Process Clause. As discussed in earlier chapters, he was the foremost advocate of liberty interests from his earliest prisoners' rights dissenting opinion in *Meachum v. Fano* (1976) through his extensive valedictory dissenting opinion on incorporation and gun rights in *McDonald v. City of Chicago* (2010). Stevens, by connecting so-called privacy rights directly to "liberty," a word which, unlike "privacy," actually appears in the Constitution, helped to make the right of choice for abortion and other personal autonomy rights more legitimately justified as protected through the concept of substantive due process. The shift in focus from privacy to liberty was first advocated by Justice Stewart, who retired in 1981, and thereafter advocated by Stevens.

Eventually, the liberty concept had significant impact in landmark majority opinions by Justice Kennedy. Kennedy assumed his position on the Supreme Court in 1988. Thus he never served with Stewart but he was Stevens's colleague for the first twenty-two years of his career. According to Randy Barnett, in abortion rights cases Kennedy first employed the liberty concept in place of the right to privacy in his portion of the co-authored majority opinion in *Planned Parenthood of Southeastern Pennsylvania v.*

Casey (1992).[29] With respect to criminal justice, Kennedy emphasized the protection of liberty in writing the monumental majority opinion in *Lawrence v. Texas* (2003) that forbade states from criminalizing the private, consensual sexual conduct of gays and lesbians. Two points are notable about that opinion. First, as senior justice in the majority, Stevens assigned the majority opinion to Kennedy rather than taking for himself the opportunity to write what was destined to be a historic opinion advancing constitutional rights and equality. Second, and more importantly for this discussion, Kennedy's majority opinion quoted at length from Stevens's dissenting opinion in *Bowers v. Hardwick* (1986), the previous precedent in which the Supreme Court had approved the criminalization of gays' and lesbians' sexual behavior. Justice Kennedy quoted Stevens's words, "individual decisions by married persons, concerning the intimacies of their physical relationship, even when not intended to produce offspring, are a form of 'liberty' protected by the Due Process Clause of the Fourteenth Amendment. Moreover, this protection extends to intimate choices by unmarried persons."[30] Kennedy then followed with his own conclusion that "Justice Stevens'[s] analysis, in our view, should have been controlling in *Bowers* and should control here. *Bowers* was not correct when it was decided, and it is not correct today. It ought not to remain binding precedent. *Bowers v. Hardwick* should be and now is overruled."[31]

Justice Stevens's judicial philosophy had a critical influence over a category of criminal laws aimed at adults' choices about intimate, private behavior. Moreover, according to Jamal Greene's analysis, Stevens's liberty-focused approach is likely to have staying power and be applied in future legal debates surrounding various noncriminal justice issues related to personal autonomy, same-sex relationships, and parenting. Indeed, as predicted by Greene, Justice Kennedy's landmark majority opinion recognizing a constitutional right to same-sex marriage in *Obergefell v. Hodges* (2015) focused on liberty as well as human dignity, which Stevens argued was the core element of liberty beginning with his first Supreme Court opinion on prisoners' rights in 1976.[32] According to Greene, the staying power of Stevens's liberty-focused approach will reflect its compatibility with political discourse and interests in society. In Greene's words, "The transformation of sexual intimacy and abortion from privacy to liberty rights accommodates both politically popular liberal demands for a progressive Constitution and legally ascendant conservative demands for a Constitution whose text is authoritative" because the word "liberty" appears in the Constitution in three places.[33] While Justices Harlan and Stewart made arguments for a liberty-focused analysis of due process rights, it was Stevens who further developed the argument, kept it alive in various Supreme Court opinions, and made it persuasive enough to both gain majority support in *Lawrence* and continue its authoritative vitality in the landmark *Obergefell* decision after his retirement.

Justice Kennedy's other notable use of the liberty concept in criminal justice came in the case of *Brown v. Plata* (2011) after Justice Stevens's retirement. The *Brown* case concerned conditions in California's prisons and a lower court's order requiring the state to reduce its prison population because of inadequacies in medical facilities and mental health treatment for California's 156,000 imprisoned offenders. On behalf of the majority in a 5 to 4 decision, Justice Kennedy endorsed the lower court's population reduction order as complying with the requirements for such orders under the Prison Litigation Reform Act. In the opinion, Kennedy wrote:

> As a consequence of their own actions, prisoners may be deprived of rights that are fundamental to liberty. Yet the law and the Constitution demand recognition of certain other rights. Prisoners retain the essence of human dignity inherent in all persons. Respect for that dignity animates the Eighth Amendment prohibition against cruel and unusual punishment. "The basic concept underlying the Eighth Amendment is nothing less than the dignity of man."[34]

The quotation at the end of this paragraph is from Justice Stevens's majority opinion in *Atkins v. Virginia* (2002) which itself quotes *Trop v. Dulles* (1958), the seminal case defining the test for cruel and unusual punishments.[35] Kennedy chose to cite Stevens's opinion as the source of the quotation even though he could have cited directly to *Trop v. Dulles* (1958) if he had not been intent on crediting Stevens's long-standing argument about imprisoned offenders' retention of protected liberty interests. Thus, in both *Lawrence v. Texas* and *Brown v. Plata*, Kennedy appeared to give credit to the influence of Stevens's prior opinions as Kennedy employed with significant effect the liberty concept trumpeted by Stevens throughout his long career.

ROLES ON THE COURT

One other way of attributing importance and influence to a justice is through examination of that justice's informal roles on the Court.[36] This involves consideration of the ways in which a particular justice may have been uniquely influential as an advocate for a particular approach to decision making, the individual who educated other justices about an issue, or otherwise the presenter of unique information and insights. When a justice leaves the Court after having fulfilled a unique role, it raises questions about whether another justice will assume that role and the extent to which the dynamics and direction of the Court may change as a result of losing a particular perspective or voice.

The earlier chapters of this book argued that Stevens was a unique advocate for the protection and expansion of rights with respect to several important issues in criminal justice. From the very beginning of his career, he was the foremost advocate for prisoners' rights. He also strongly advocated preservation of the adversary system when his colleagues sought to diminish the role of defense counsel. He also stood out as a defender of the jury's role in criminal cases. In addition, after the retirement of Justice Marshall in 1991, Stevens clearly established himself as the foremost defender of *Miranda* rights and as the justice most committed to narrowing the applicability of the death penalty.

After the retirement of Marshall, Stevens also stood out as the foremost conscience of the Court with respect to the role of race, especially in criminal justice contexts. His concern about racial equality was very evident and, indeed, caused a minor stir when he arrived in Washington, D.C., after his Senate confirmation. Stevens engineered a major breakthrough for equal opportunity in professional staffing at the Supreme Court. When Stevens arrived at the Supreme Court in December 1975, there were no African Americans employed as professional staff at the Court—other than Justice Thurgood Marshall and an occasional law clerk. Even at that late date, African Americans were hired only as messengers, elevator operators, cooks, and other service occupations that garnered the lowest pay rates and lacked opportunities for meaningful advancement. The prior year, Nina Totenberg, who was soon to become the longtime Supreme Court correspondent for National Public Radio, wrote a scathing article entitled, "The Supreme Court: The Last Plantation," about the Court's blindness to its own lack of equal employment opportunity even as it imposed equal protection decisions on other institutions. Justice Stevens changed the status quo by hiring an African American woman, Ms. Nellie Pitts, whom he knew from the staff at the Seventh Circuit U.S. Court of Appeals in Chicago. He hired her to be his chief administrative assistant and secretary to manage his chambers.[37] In an interview at the end of his career, he said "I was aware [from my clerkship experience] of the fact that there was some Southern culture in the Court. . . . I didn't do it for that reason, it just happened to turn out that way. . . . But it was not—race had nothing to do with [the hiring decision]—even though in retrospect I'm glad it turned out that way."[38] Although he denied that the hiring was motivated by an intent to desegregate staff positions at the Court, his acknowledgment that he was very aware of the "Southern culture" at the Court implied that he knew that his decision would cause a shake-up at the Court. Indeed, he noted that Ms. Pitts "was aware that she was not entirely welcome in some parts of the building."[39] As indicated by this episode, unlike other justices who were apparently insufficiently attentive to issues of equal opportunity and discrimination in their own hiring practices,[40] including members of the Warren Court who had endured controversy and criticism for pro-civil rights decisions, Stevens sought to practice nondiscrimination principles in his own life.

Justice Stevens's unique role as a strong advocate for equal protection of the laws was evident in a number of opinions, including his opinions on discrimination in jury selection that were described in chapter 6. In *Johnson v. California* (2005), as discussed in chapter 4, prison officials had claimed an institutional safety justification for racial and ethnic segregation in individual cells during the first weeks of prison in order to allow officials to identify which prisoners were members of gangs. Justice Stevens, alone among the justices, argued that the Supreme Court should forthrightly rule that the state had violated the Equal Protection Clause by using racial segregation in its prisons. He objected to the Court majority's conclusion that the case should be remanded to the lower courts to determine whether or not California actually had a compelling justification for the racial segregation. His solo opinion was, in effect, a call for direct action by the Supreme Court to extinguish the scourge of racial segregation. Stevens wrote of "the inherent indignity of segregation and its shameful historical connotations" in flatly rejecting a California policy that was imposed without any presentation of evidence to demonstrate that racial separation was necessary to prevent violence.[41]

In *McCleskey v. Kemp* (1987), concerning a five-justice majority's rejection of the use of statistics to prove the existence of racial discrimination in the administration of the death penalty in Georgia, Stevens's dissenting opinion famously asserted: "If society were indeed forced to choose between a racially discriminatory death penalty (one that provides heightened protection against murder "for whites only") and no death penalty at all, the choice mandated by the Constitution would be plain."[42]

In another example, Stevens was the lone dissenter in *United States v. Armstrong* (1996), a case concerning allegations of racial discrimination by one U.S. Attorney's Office in selecting which defendants to prosecute for crack cocaine offenses that were punished by severe mandatory prison sentences. There were indications that only African Americans were prosecuted for crack cocaine offenses despite the fact that crack was also used and sold by whites. While the other justices would not permit anecdotal evidence to provide the basis for initiating an examination of the prosecutor's records, Stevens used his solo dissent to lay out troubling statistics about the differential impacts of crack cocaine prosecutions and sentencing on African Americans and whites:

> Finally, it is undisputed that the brunt of the elevated federal penalties falls heavily on blacks. While 65 percent of the persons who have used crack are

> white, in 1993 they represented only 4 percent of the federal offenders convicted of trafficking in crack. Eighty-eight percent of such defendants were black. . . . [B]lacks on average received sentences 40 percent longer than whites.[43]

Justice Stevens's concerns about the real-world risks of racial discrimination also emerged in cases concerning issues other than the Equal Protection Clause. For example, in *Illinois v. Wardlow* (2000)[44] the Supreme Court ruled that an individual's flight at the sight of police officers in a high-crime area can serve as a consideration to justify a stop-and-frisk search. As described in chapter 7, Justice Stevens's opinion expressed a view that undoubtedly caused consternation among law enforcement officials:

> Among some citizens, particularly minorities and those residing in high crime areas, there is also the possibility that the fleeing person is entirely innocent, but, with or without justification, believes that contact with the police can itself be dangerous, apart from any criminal activity associated with the officer's sudden presence. . . . For such a person, unprovoked flight is neither "aberrant" nor "abnormal."[45]

Stevens had an affluent childhood, education at elite schools, and prestigious career in law that presumably removed him from gaining a close-at-hand view and empathic understanding of the daily lives of less-affluent people in minority communities. Yet, he asserted a unique viewpoint reflecting a sensitivity to and understanding of human experience in poor neighborhoods.

In a further example, albeit from outside the realm of criminal justice, Andrew Siegel credited Stevens with giving voice to righteous indignation in 2007 when the majority of justices endorsed the dismantling of school-initiated desegregation programs in Seattle and Louisville (*Parents Involved in Community Schools v. Seattle School District No. 1*).[46] In his solo dissent, Stevens complained about the "cruel irony" of Chief Justice Roberts's majority opinion purporting to rely on *Brown v. Board of Education* (1954) to insist on racially neutral policies without acknowledging *Brown*'s recognition that the actual discriminatory victimization in that case operated in one direction: against African Americans.[47] Justice Stevens ended his opinion with a strikingly critical comment about how much the Supreme Court had changed since his earliest years on the Court when many school desegregation decisions were being decided through the federal court system: "It is my firm conviction that no Member of the Court that I joined in 1975 would have agreed with today's decision."[48]

These opinions indicate that, especially after the retirement of Justice Marshall in 1991, Stevens possessed a unique awareness of and firm opposition to the existence of racial discrimination. These opinions also highlighted the initial uncertainty about who, if anyone, would emerge with such a strong understanding of discrimination and an outspoken voice for equal protection after Stevens's retirement in 2010. As it turned out, Justice Sonia Sotomayor, the replacement for Justice David Souter in 2009 and someone who had experienced discrimination in her own life, demonstrated her inclination to assume this particular role on the Court.[49]

Justice Stevens also played an important role as a proactive critic of the originalist approach to constitutional interpretation advocated by Justices Scalia and Thomas. In *District of Columbia v. Heller* (2008), for example, Stevens's dissenting opinion went toe-to-toe with Scalia's majority opinion in debating the textual meaning and original intentions of the Second Amendment. Stevens was willing to marshal historical evidence and debate Scalia on his own terms in making the case that the Amendment was intended to protect state militias' access to firearms and not to provide a constitutional right for individuals to own guns. In *Georgia v. Randolph* (2006), a Fourth Amendment case, Stevens wrote a concurring opinion solely to make a pointed criticism of the originalist approach. Stevens noted that if one interpreted the consent-search issue according to the original intent of the framers, the eighteenth-century conception of women's limited property rights would automatically make the husband the sole and final authority on consent searches of a home. Thus Stevens concluded by saying:

> Thus if "original understanding" were to govern the outcome of this case, the search was clearly invalid because the husband did not consent. History, however, is not dispositive because it is now clear, as a matter of constitutional law, that the male and the female are equal. . . . Assuming that both spouses are competent, neither one is a master possessing the power to override the other's constitutional right to deny entry to their castle.[50]

Justice Stevens also played a unique role in reminding the other justices to avoid seeing the Court as obliged to advance the crime control goals of the executive and legislative branches. In *California v. Acevedo* (1991), for example, a vehicle search case discussed in chapter 7, the Court expanded the authority of police to conduct warrantless searches of containers inside vehicles. Stevens's dissenting opinion sharply criticized the majority for its excessively pro-law enforcement leanings. In Stevens's words, "No impartial observer could criticize this Court for hindering the progress of the war on drugs. On the contrary, decisions like this one the Court makes today will support the conclusion that this Court has become a loyal foot soldier in the Executive's fight against crime."[51]

Stevens also highlighted this theme when he regularly complained that the majority too frequently and proactively accepted cases with the goal of limiting constitutional rights in criminal justice, especially when state courts had granted to their own residents more expansive protections than those required by the U.S. Supreme Court. In *Michigan v. Long* (1983), for example, Stevens complained that the Court needlessly accepted a case solely for the purpose of limiting a suspect's rights and reinforcing expanded police authority to conduct a search. As Stevens observed, "[T]he final outcome of the state processes offended no federal interest whatever. Michigan simply provided greater protection to one of its citizens than some other State might provide or, indeed, than this Court might require throughout the country."[52] Justice Stevens also raised this point about the Court's biases in the use of summary decisions. Thus he complained in another case that "[i]n recent years, when we have exercised our discretionary jurisdiction and issued *per curiam* rulings deciding cases summarily, we have most frequently come to the aid of a prosecutor or a warden who has been rebuffed by another court."[53]

A JUDICIAL PHILOSOPHY SHAPED BY EXPERIENCE AND HISTORY

The justices younger than Stevens who were appointed to the Supreme Court in the 1980s and thereafter came into adulthood without witnessing the worst rights-violating abuses routinely practiced by police and prosecutors prior to the 1960s. By contrast, Stevens, who was born in 1920, had direct knowledge of the legal problems and human consequences that arose when constitutional rights were insufficiently defined and protected in the realm of criminal justice. Stevens obviously learned a great deal from representing the wrongly imprisoned victim of police torture, Arthur LaFrana, from representing other prisoners through the Chicago Bar Association committee, and from serving as a Supreme Court law clerk when important legal issues concerning police interrogations, right to counsel, and racial discrimination were under development in the 1940s. As Stevens acknowledged, these experiences, as well as what he learned from his parents and his formal education, contributed to the development of the core values evident in his judicial philosophy. Moreover, Stevens had the opportunity to refine his judicial philosophy and his approach to judicial decision making while serving as a judge on the Seventh Circuit U.S. Court of Appeals just after the conclusion of the Warren Court era. During this period, federal judges in the district and circuit courts bore responsibility for applying the Warren Court's rights-protective precedents to unexplored contexts and situations triggered by the actions of police, prosecutors, and judges in state and federal justice systems. In addition, these lower court judges, including Stevens, played important roles in making initial decisions for still-developing areas of law, such as prisoners' rights.

Justice Stevens's retirement in 2010 represented the final departure from the Supreme Court of a justice whose training in law and initial experience in legal practice predated the advent of the Warren Court era. Certainly, younger justices, such as David Souter, Ruth Bader Ginsburg, Stephen Breyer, Sonia Sotomayor, and Elena Kagan, shared many of the core values evident in Stevens's judicial philosophy, as will, presumably, future justices appointed to the Supreme Court. However, it remains to be seen whether other justices will assume Stevens's mantle as a uniquely strong advocate for prisoners' rights, equal protection, *Miranda* rights, adversarial process, and sensitivity to the human contexts and consequences of court decisions. Future justices will bring to the Court their own unique life experiences and the values and insights derived from those experiences. But no current or future justice will match Stevens's experiences as a World War II veteran, an eyewitness to racial segregation and pre-Warren Court police abuse problems, a law clerk learning at the right hand of a Roosevelt Supreme Court appointee, and a court of appeals judge during an era of initial rights development and refinement.

Justice Stevens was not successful in shaping constitutional rights for criminal justice in accordance with the core values of his judicial philosophy. His impact on certain issues is clear, but the trends in Supreme Court decisions for other issues have been contrary to his interpretation of the Constitution. Yet, he left a legacy that can educate his successors. As the most prolific opinion writer in Supreme Court history, his unprecedented number of concurring and dissenting opinions provide insights and reasoning that undoubtedly will influence contemporary judges throughout the federal courts as well as new generations of jurists in the future.

NOTES

1. Jeffrey A. Segal and Albert D. Cover, "Ideological Values and the Votes of U.S. Supreme Court Justices," *American Political Science Review* 83 (1989): 557–65.
2. Lee Epstein, Andrew D. Martin, Kevin M. Quinn, and Jeffrey A. Segal, "Ideological Drift Among Supreme Court Justices: Who, When, and How Important?" *Northwestern University Law Review* 101 (2007): 1492.
3. Jeffrey A. Segal, Lee Epstein, Charles M. Cameron, and Harold J. Spaeth, "Ideological Values and the Votes of U.S. Supreme Court Justices Revisited," *Journal of Politics* 57 (1995): 816.
4. Ibid.
5. Jeffrey Rosen, "The Dissenter," *New York Times Magazine*, September 23, 2007, 52.
6. Ibid.
7. Epstein, Martin et al, 1502–28.
8. Linda Greenhouse, "John Paul Stevens as Abortion-Rights Strategist," *UC Davis Law Review* 43 (2010): 763.
9. Stefanie A. Lindquist, "Supreme Court Prequel: Justice Stevens on the Seventh Circuit," *Northwestern University Law Review* 106 (2012): 741.
10. Edward L. Rubin, "Question Regarding *D.C. v. Heller*: As a Justice, Antonin Scalia Is (A) Great, (B) Acceptable, (C) Injudicious," *Wayne Law Review* 54 (2008): 1105–6.
11. Roger A. Hanson and Henry W. K. Daley, *Federal Habeas Corpus Review: Challenging State Court Convictions* (Washington, D.C.: U.S. Bureau of Justice Statistics, 1995), 14.

12. Nina Totenberg, "Justice Stevens: An Open Mind on a Changed Court," National Public Radio Online, October 4, 2010, accessed May 21, 2015, http://www.npr.org/templates/story/story.php?storyId=130198344.

13. "Number of Executions by State and Region Since 1976," Death Penalty Information Center website, accessed June 30, 2015, http://www.deathpenaltyinfo.org/number-executions-state-and-region-1976.

14. James S. Liebman and Lawrence C. Marshall, "Less Is Better: Justice Stevens and the Narrowed Death Penalty," *Fordham Law Review* 74 (2006): 1607–82.

15. John Paul Stevens, *Five Chiefs: A Supreme Court Memoir* (Boston: Little, Brown, 2011), 236–37.

16. Rosen, 53.

17. Craig Rust, "The Leadership Legacy of Justice John Paul Stevens," *Journal of Legal Metrics* 1 (2012): 136.

18. Ibid., 137.

19. Ibid., 149–50.

20. Ibid., 152.

21. Ibid., 150.

22. Rory Little, transcript of remarks, "Excerpts from 'The Future of American Sentencing: A National Roundtable on *Blakely*,'" *Ohio State Journal of Criminal Law* 2 (2005): 630.

23. *Spaziano v. Florida*, 468 U.S. 447, 490 (1984) (Stevens, J., concurring in part and dissenting in part).

24. Jeffrey Fisher, "Remarks: Liberty Panel," *UC Davis Law Review* 43 (2010): 879–80.

25. Ibid., 881–82.

26. Ibid., 881.

27. Little, 630.

28. Ibid.

29. Randy Barnett, "Justice Kennedy's Libertarian Revolution: *Lawrence v. Texas*," in *Cato Supreme Court Review, 2002–2003,* James L. Swanson, ed. (Washington, D.C.: Cato Institute, 2003), 33.

30. *Lawrence v. Texas*, 559 U.S. 558, 577–78 (2003) quoting *Bowers v. Hardwick*, 478 U.S. 186, 216 (Stevens, J., dissenting).

31. Ibid., 578.

32. *Meachum v. Fano*, 427 U.S. 215, 233 (1976) (Stevens, J., dissenting).

33. Jamal Greene, "The So-Called Right to Privacy," *UC Davis Law Review* 43 (2010): 742–43.

34. *Brown v. Plata*, 131 S.Ct. 1910, 1928 (2011).

35. *Atkins v. Virginia*, 536 U.S. 304, 311 (2002) quoting *Trop v. Dulles*, 356 U.S. 86, 100 (1958) (plurality opinion).

36. Christopher E. Smith, "The Roles of Justice John Paul Stevens in Criminal Justice Cases," *Suffolk University Law Review* 39 (2006): 719–44.

37. Diane Marie Amann, "John Paul Stevens and Equally Impartial Government," *UC Davis Law Review* 43 (2010): 911–12.

38. Justice John Paul Stevens, interview with author, U.S. Supreme Court, Washington, D.C., July 29, 2010.

39. Ibid.

40. Amann, "John Paul Stevens and Equally Impartial Government," 911–12.

41. *Johnson v. California*, 543 U.S. 499, 521 (2005) (Stevens, J., dissenting).

42. *McCleskey v. Kemp*, 481 U.S. 279, 367 (1987) (Stevens, J., dissenting).

43. *United States v. Armstrong*, 517 U.S. 456, 479–80 (1996) (Stevens, J., dissenting).

44. *Illinois v. Wardlow*, 528 U.S. 119 (2000).

45. *Illinois v. Wardlow*, 528 U.S. 119, 132 (2000) (Stevens, J., concurring in part and dissenting in part).

46. Andrew Siegel, "Justice Stevens and the Seattle Schools Case: A Case Study on the Role of Righteous Anger in Constitutional Discourse," *UC Davis Law Review* 43 (2010): 927–37.

47. *Parents Involved in Community Schools v. Seattle School District No. 1*, 127 U.S. 2738, 2797–98 (2007) (Stevens, J., dissenting).

48. Ibid., 2800 (Stevens, J., dissenting).

49. Joan Biskupic, "Sonia Sotomayor Voices Strong Views on Race in Affirmative Action Dissent," *Christian Science Monitor*, April 23, 2014, accessed July 2, 2015, http://www.csmonitor.com/USA/Latest-News-Wires/2014/0423/Sonia-Sotomayor-voices-strong-views-on-race-in-affirmative-action-dissent.

50. *Georgia v. Randolph*, 547 U.S. 103, 124–25 (2006).

51. *California v. Acevedo*, 500 U.S. 565, 601 (1991) (Stevens, J., dissenting).

52. *Michigan v. Long*, 463 U.S. 1032, 1068 (1983) (Stevens, J., dissenting).

53. *Board of Education of Rogers v. McCluskey*, 458 U.S. 966, 972–73 (1982) (Stevens, J., dissenting).

Bibliography

Abraham, Henry J. *Freedom and the Court*, 5th ed. New York: Oxford University Press, 1988.

Allegrini, Robert V., and Geraldine Hempel Davis. *Chicago's Grand Hotel: A History of the Hilton Chicago*. Lafayette, Colo.: Moonlight Publishing, 2002.

Amann, Diane Marie. "John Paul Stevens, Originalist." *Northwestern University Law Review* 106 (2012): 748–49.

———. "John Paul Stevens and Equally Impartial Government." *UC Davis Law Review* 43 (2010): 885–925.

———. "John Paul Stevens, Human Rights Judge." *Fordham Law Review* 74 (2006): 1569–1605.

American Civil Liberties Union. *Broken Justice: The Death Penalty in Alabama.* New York: American Civil Liberties Union, 2005. Accessed July 2, 2015, http://www.aclualabama.org/WhatWeDo/BrokenJustice_report.pdf.

Ball, Howard, and Phillip J. Cooper. *Of Power and Right: Hugo Black, William O. Douglas, and America's Constitutional Revolution.* New York: Oxford University Press, 1992.

Barnes, Robert. "Over Ginsburg's Dissent, Court Limits Bias Suits." *Washington Post*, May 30, 2007. Accessed July 2, 2015, http://www.washingtonpost.com/wp-dyn/content/article/2007/05/29/AR2007052900740.html.

Barnett, Randy. "Justice Kennedy's Libertarian Revolution: *Lawrence v. Texas*," in *Cato Supreme Court Review, 2002–2003,* ed. James L. Swanson. Washington, D.C.: Cato Institute, 2003.

Barnhart, Bill. "Justice Stevens and the News Media: An Exercise in Exposition." *Northwestern Law Review* 106 (2012): 662–71.

Barnhart, Bill, and Gene Schlickman. *John Paul Stevens: An Independent Life.* DeKalb, Ill.: Northern Illinois University Press, 2010.

Barrett, John Q. "Opinion-Editorial: Commending Opinion Announcements by Supreme Court Justices." National Public Radio *Talking Justice* blog, June 4, 2007. Accessed July 2, 2015, http://www.stjohns.edu/sites/default/files/documents/law/john-q-barrett/070604-commending-opinion-announcements.pdf.

Baugh, Joyce A. *Supreme Court Justices in the Post-Bork Era: Confirmation Politics and Judicial Performance.* New York: Peter Lang, 2002.

Baum, Lawrence. *Judges and Their Audiences.* Princeton, N.J.: Princeton University Press, 2006.

———. *The Puzzle of Judicial Behavior.* Ann Arbor, Mich.: University of Michigan Press, 1997.

Bendiner, Robert. "The Law and Potter Stewart: An Interview with Justice Potter Stewart." *American Heritage* vol. 35 [1] (December 1983). Accessed May 19, 2015, http://www.americanheritage.com/content/law-and-potter-stewart-interview-justice-potter-stewart.

Berman, Douglas A. "Foreward: Beyond *Blakely* and *Booker*: Pondering Modern Sentencing." *Journal of Criminal Law and Criminology* 95 (2005): 655–57.

———. "Should Juries Be the Guide for Adventures Through *Apprendi*-Land?" *Columbia Law Review Sidebar* 109 (2009): 65–72.

Biographies of Current Justices of the Supreme Court, website of the Supreme Court of the United States. Accessed July 2, 2015, http://www.supremecourt.gov/about/biographies.aspx.

Biskupic, Joan. "Justice Stevens to Retire from Supreme Court." *USA Today*, April 12, 2010. Accessed July 2, 2015, http://usatoday30.usatoday.com/news/washington/judicial/2010-04-09-justice-stevens-retire_N.htm.

———. "Sonia Sotomayor Voices Strong Views on Race in Affirmative Action Dissent." *Christian Science Monitor*, April 23, 2014. Accessed July 2, 2015, http://www.csmonitor.com/USA/Latest-News-Wires/2014/0423/Sonia-Sotomayor-voices-strong-views-on-race-in-affirmative-action-dissent.

———. "Supreme Court's Stevens Keeps Cards Close to Robe." *USA Today*, October 18, 2009. Accessed May 19, 2015, http://usatoday30.usatoday.com/news/washington/judicial/2009-10-18-stevens-supreme-court-justice_N.htm.

The Blackmun Papers. Harry A. Blackmun Papers, Manuscript Division, Library of Congress, Washington, D.C.

Blake, William D., and Hans J. Hacker. "'The Brooding Spirit of the Law': Supreme Court Justices Reading Dissents from the Bench." *Justice System Journal* 31 (2010): 1–25.

Bleich, Jeff, Daniel Powell, Aimee Feinberg, and Michelle Friedland. "Justice John Paul Stevens: A Maverick, Liberal Libertarian, Conservative Statesman on the Court." *Oregon State Bar Bulletin* 67 (October 2007): 27.

Bowman, Frank O. "Debacle: How the Supreme Court Has Mangled American Sentencing Law and How It Might Yet Be Mended." *University of Chicago Law Review* 77 (2010): 369.

Boyd, Robert S. "Judge Stevens—His Views on Law." *Chicago Tribune*, November 30, 1975, 6.

Bravin, Jess. "Voter-ID Laws Worry Jurist." *Wall Street Journal Online*, October 17, 2013. Accessed May 21, 2015, http://www.wsj.com/articles/SB10001424052702304384104579141701228734132.

———. "Stevens Evolved From Court Loner to Liberal Wing's Leader." *Wall Street Journal Online*, June 30, 2010. Accessed May 19, 2015, http://www.wsj.com/articles/SB10001424052748703374104575337264290709470.

Bray, Karen. "Reaching the Final Chapter in the Story of Peremptory Challenges." *U.C.L.A. Law Review* 40 (1992): 554–55.

Brennan, Jr., William J. "The Constitution of the United States: Contemporary Ratification," in ed. David M. O'Brien, *Judges on Judging: Views From the Bench*. Chatham, N.J.: Chatham House, 1997, 200–10.

The Brennan Papers. William J. Brennan Papers, Manuscript Division, Library of Congress, Washington, D.C. Accessed July 2, 2015 from website of Professor Paul Wahlbeck, George Washington University, http://home.gwu.edu/~wahlbeck/Personal_Homepage/Home.html.

Breyer, Stephen. *Active Liberty: Interpreting Our Democratic Constitution*. New York: Alfred A. Knopf, 2005.

Bright, Stephen B. "Counsel for the Poor: The Death Sentence Not for the Worst Crime but for Worst Lawyer." *Yale Law Journal* 103 (1994): 1835–83.

Brust, Richard. "Practical Meaning: As the Court Shifted Right, Stevens Kept His Place." *ABA Journal* 96 (May 2010): 53.

Canon, Bradley C. "Justice John Paul Stevens: The Lone Ranger in a Black Robe," in *The Burger Court: Political and Judicial Profiles*. eds. Charles M. Lamb and Stephen C. Halpern. Urbana, Ill.: University of Illinois Press, 1991, 343–74.

Canon, Bradley C., and Charles A. Johnson. *Judicial Policies: Implementation and Impact*, 2nd ed. Washington, D.C.: Congressional Quarterly Press, 1999.

Cassell, Paul G., and Richard Fowles. "Falling Clearance Rates After *Miranda*: Coincidence or Consequences?" *Stanford Law Review* 50 (1998): 1181–91

CBS News, *Sixty Minutes*. "Chicago: The False Confession Capital," December 9, 2012. Accessed May 21, 2015, http://www.cbsnews.com/videos/chicago-the-false-confession-capital/.

Citron, Rodger. "The Last Common Law Justice?" SCOTUS BLOG, May 6, 2010. Accessed May 19, 2015, http://www.scotusblog.com/2010/05/the-last-common-law-justice/.

Clayton, Cornell W. "Supreme Court and Political Jurisprudence: New and Old Institutionalisms," in *Supreme Court Decision-Making: New Institutionalist Approaches,* ed. Cornell W. Clayton and Howard Gillman. Chicago: University of Chicago Press, 1999, 22–30.

"Cook County Board Approves Settlement for Panther Suit," *New York Times*, November 3, 1982. Accessed July 2, 2015, http://www.nytimes.com/1982/11/03/us/cook-county-board-approves-settlement-for-panther-suit.html.

"Court Nominee Is Hard to Label." *New York Times*, November 30, 1975, sec. 4, 1.

Cray, Ed. *Chief Justice*. New York: Simon and Schuster, 1997.

Currey, Josiah Seymour. *Chicago: Its History and Its Builders*. vol. V. Chicago: The S.J. Publishing Co., 1912.

Davis, Ross E., Craig D. Rust, and Adam Aft. "Supreme Court Sluggers: John Paul Stevens Is No Stephen J. Field." *Green Bag* 13 (2010): 475–80.

Dorf, Michael C. "Does Federal Executive Branch Experience Explain Why Some Republican Supreme Court Justices 'Evolve' and Others Don't?" *Harvard Law and Policy Review* 1 (2007): 457–76.

Douglas, William O. *Go East, Young Man*. New York: Random House, 1974.

Douthat, Ross. "The Further Empowerment of Anthony Kennedy." *New York Times,* April 12, 2010. Accessed July 2, 2015, http://douthat.blogs.nytimes.com/2010/04/12/the-further-empowerment-of-anthony-kennedy/.

Duffy, Jill, and Elizabeth Lambert. "Dissents from the Bench: A Compilation of Oral Dissents by U.S. Supreme Court Justices." *Law Library Journal* 102 (2010): 24–37.

Eisler, Kim Isaac. *A Justice for All: William J. Brennan, Jr., and the Decisions that Transformed America*. New York: Simon and Schuster, 1993.

Elsasser, Glen. "Constitution Protects Burning Flag As Protest, Court Rules." *Chicago Tribune*, June 22, 1989, 1.

Epstein, Lee. "Who or What Changed?" *Legal Times,* April 11, 2010. Accessed July 2, 2105, http://legaltimes.typepad.com/justicestevens.

Epstein, Lee, and Jack Knight. *The Choices Justices Make*. Washington, D.C.: Congressional Quarterly Press, 1998.

Epstein, Lee, Andrew D. Martin, Kevin M. Quinn, and Jeffrey A. Segal. "Ideological Drift Among Supreme Court Justices: Who, When, and How Important?" *Northwestern University Law Review* 101 (2007): 1483–1542.

Epstein, Lee, Jeffrey A. Segal, Harold J. Spaeth, and Thomas G. Walker. *The Supreme Court Compendium: Data, Decisions, and Developments*. Washington, D.C.: Congressional Quarterly Press, 2007.

Epstein, Lee, and Thomas G. Walker. *Constitutional Law for a Changing America: Rights, Liberties, and Justice*. Washington, D.C.: Congressional Quarterly Press, 1992.

Farber, Daniel A. "Backward-Looking Laws and Equal Protection: The Case of Black Reparations." *Fordham Law Review* 74 (2006): 2271–99.

Farnsworth, Ward. "Realism, Pragmatism, and John Paul Stevens," in *Rehnquist Justice: Understanding the Court Dynamic*, ed. Earl M. Maltz. Lawrence, Kan.: University Press of Kansas, 2003, 157–84.

Feeley, Malcolm M., and Edward L. Rubin. *Judicial Policy Making and the Modern State: How the Courts Reformed America's Prisons*. New York: Cambridge University Press, 1998.

Feeney, Floyd. "Police Clearances: A Poor Way to Measure the Impact of *Miranda* on the Police." *Rutgers Law Review* 32 (2000): 1–58.

Ferren, John M. *Salt of the Earth; Conscience of the Court: The Story of Justice Wiley Rutledge*. Chapel Hill, N.C.: University of North Carolina Press, 2004.

Fidell, Eugene. "Justice John Paul Stevens and Judicial Deference in Military Matters." *UC Davis Law Review* 43 (2010): 999–1020.

Fisher, Jeffrey. "Remarks: Liberty Panel." *UC Davis Law Review* 43 (2010): 877–84.

Fliter, John A. *Prisoners' Rights: The Supreme Court and Evolving Standards of Decency.* Westport, Conn.: Greenwood Press, 2001.

Fortunato, Stephen. "The Supreme Court's Experience Gap." *Judicature* 82 (1999): 252.

Garner, Bryan A. "Interview with Justice John Paul Stevens." *The Scribes Journal of Legal Writing* (2010): 41–50.

Gibson, James L. "From Simplicity to Complexity: The Development of Theory in the Study of Judicial Behavior." *Political Behavior* 5 (1983): 7–49.

Green, Craig. "Wiley Rutledge, Executive Detention, and Judicial Conscience at War." *Washington University Law Review* 84 (2006): 99–178.

Greene, Jamal. "The Rule of Law as a Law of Standards." *Georgetown Law Journal* 99 (2011): 1289–1300.

———. "The So-Called Right to Privacy." *UC Davis Law Review* 43 (2010): 715–48.

Greenhouse, Linda. "After a 32-Year Journey, Stevens Renounces Capital Punishment," *New York Times*, April 18, 2008. Accessed July 2, 2015, http://www.nytimes.com/2008/04/18/world/americas/18iht-18memo.12124092.html.

———. *Becoming Justice Blackmun: Harry Blackmun's Supreme Court Journey.* New York: Times Books, 2005.

———. "Change and Continuity on the Supreme Court." *Washington University Journal of Law and Policy* 25 (2007): 39–60.

———. "Justice John Paul Stevens as Abortion-Rights Strategist." *UC Davis Law Review* 43 (2010): 749–82.

———. "Justices, 5–4, Back Protesters' Right to Burn the Flag." *New York Times,* June 22, 1989, A1.

———. "Justices, 5–3, Broadly Reject Bush Plan to Try Detainees." *New York Times,* June 30, 2006. Accessed July 4, 2015, http://www.nytimes.com/2006/06/30/washington/30hamdan.html?pagewanted=all.

———. "The Rehnquist Court and Its Imperiled States' Rights Legacy." *New York Times,* June 12, 2005. Accessed May 19, 2015, http://www.nytimes.com/2005/06/12/weekinreview/12green.html?oref=login.

———. "Selective Empathy." *New York Times*, December 3, 2009. Accessed May 21, 2015, http://opinionator.blogs.nytimes.com/2009/12/03/selective-empathy/.

Hanson, Roger A., and Henry W. K. Daley. *Federal Habeas Corpus Review: Challenging State Court Convictions.* Washington, D.C.: U.S. Bureau of Justice Statistics, 1995.

Hensley, Thomas R., Christopher E. Smith, and Joyce A. Baugh. *The Changing Supreme Court: Constitutional Rights and Liberties.* Belmont, Calif.: West/Wadsworth, 1997.

History of McDonough County, Illinois. Springfield, Ill.: Continental Historical Co., 1885.

Hogan, Terry. "The Birth and Death of Abingdon College." *The* (Galesburg, Ill.) *Zephyr*, February 13, 2006. Accessed May 21, 2015, http://www.thezephyr.com/backtrack/abingdoncollege.html.

Hutchinson, Dennis J. *The Man Who Once Was Whizzer White: A Portrait of Justice Byron R. White.* New York: Free Press, 1998.

Irons, Peter. *The Courage of Their Convictions: Sixteen Americans Who Fought Their Way to the Supreme Court.* New York: Free Press, 1988.

Isaacson, Walter. "A Justice Reflects." *The Daily Beast* website, June 29, 2009. Accessed May 21, 2015, http://www.thedailybeast.com/articles/2009/06/29/a-justice-reflects.html.

"James Groppi Dead at 54; Ex-Priest Led Rights Fight." *New York Times,* November 5, 1985. Accessed May 23, 2015, http://www.nytimes.com/1985/11/05/us/james-e-groppi-dead-at-54-ex-priest-led-rights-fight.html.

Jeffries, John C. *Justice Lewis F. Powell, Jr.* New York: Scribner, 1994.

Johnsen, Dawn. "'The Essence of a Free Society': The Executive Powers Legacy of Justice Stevens and the Future of Foreign Affairs Deference." *Northwestern University Law Review* 106 (2012): 467–525.

Kamen, Al. "Court Nullifies Flag-Desecration Laws." *Washington Post,* June 22, 1989, A1.

Kannar, George. "The Constitutional Catechism of Antonin Scalia." *Yale Law Journal* 99 (1990): 1297–1357.

Karlan, Pamela S. "Cousins' Kin: Justice Stevens and Voting Rights." *Rutgers Law Journal* 27 (1996): 521–42.

Kaufman, Irving R. "Does the Judge Have a Right to Qualified Counsel?" *American Bar Association Journal* 61 (1975): 569–72.

Lamb, Brian, Susan Swain, and Mark Farkas, eds., *The Supreme Court: A C-Span Book Featuring the Justices in Their Own Words*. New York: Public Affairs, 2010.

Lamb, Charles M. "Chief Justice Warren E. Burger: A Conservative Chief for Conservative Times," in *The Burger Court: Political and Judicial Profiles*, eds. Charles M. Lamb and Stephen C. Halpern. Champaign, Ill.: University of Illinois Press, 1991, 129–62.

Lane, Charles. "Finding Justice on a Small Scale." *Washington Post*, June 5, 2005. Accessed July 4, 2015, http://www.washingtonpost.com/wp-dyn/content/article/2005/06/04/AR2005060401643.html.

———."Heartbreak Hotel." *Chicago Magazine*, August 2006. Accessed May 21, 2015, http://www.chicagomag.com/Chicago-Magazine/August-2006/Heartbreak-Hotel/.

Lazarus, Edward. *Closed Chamber*. New York: Times Books, 1998.

Lemieux, Scott. "Stevens' Long Battle for Equality." *The American Prospect* (online edition), December 9, 2010. Accessed July 2, 2015, http://prospect.org/article/stevens-long-battle-equality-0.

Lewis, Anthony. *Gideon's Trumpet*. New York: Random House, 1963.

———."The Stevens Nomination." *New York Times*, December 4, 1975, 41.

Liebman, James S., and Lawrence C. Marshall. "Less Is Better: Justice Stevens and the Narrowed Death Penalty." *Fordham Law Review* 74 (2006): 1607–82.

Lindquist, Stefanie A. "Supreme Court Prequel: Justice Stevens on the Seventh Circuit." *Northwestern University Law Review* 106 (2012): 715–42.

Liptak, Adam. "At 89, Stevens Contemplates Law, and How to Leave It." *New York Times*, April 3, 2010. Accessed May 21, 2015, http://www.nytimes.com/2010/04/04/us/04stevens.html?_r=0.

———. "A Justice Slows His Hiring, and Some Wonder About His Future." *New York Times*, September 3, 2009, A14.

———. "Supreme Court Enters the YouTube Era." *New York Times*, March 2, 2009. Accessed July 2, 2015, http://www.nytimes.com/2009/03/03/us/03bar.html.

Little, Rory. Transcript of remarks: "Excerpts from 'The Future of American Sentencing: A National Roundtable on *Blakely*.'" *Ohio State Journal of Criminal Law* 2 (2005): 619–62.

Litwack, Leon F. *Trouble in Mind: Black Southerners in the Age of Jim Crow*. New York: Knopf, 1998.

Maltese, John Anthony. *The Selling of Supreme Court Nominees*. Baltimore: Johns Hopkins University Press, 1998.

Manaster, Kenneth. *Illinois Justice: The Scandal of 1969 and the Rise of John Paul Stevens*. Chicago: University of Chicago Press, 2001.

Mardar, Nancy S. "Justice Stevens, the Peremptory Challenge, and the Jury." *Fordham Law Review* 74 (2006): 1683–1729.

McCall, Michael A., Madhavi M. McCall, and Christopher E. Smith. "Criminal Justice and the U.S. Supreme Court's 2009–2010 Term." *Cumberland Law Review* 41 (2010–2011): 227–82.

———. "Criminal Justice and the 2006–2007 United States Supreme Court Term." *UMKC Law Review* 76 (2008): 993–1043.

McFadden, Robert D. "The President's Choice: John Paul Stevens." *New York Times*, November 29, 1975, 1, 14.

Merida, Kevin, and Michael Fletcher. *Supreme Discomfort: The Divided Soul of Clarence Thomas*. New York: Broadway Books, 2007.

Murphy, Bruce Allen. *Fortas: The Rise and Ruin of a Supreme Court Justice*. New York: William Morrow, 1988.

The Nomination of David H. Souter to be Associate Justice of the Supreme Court of the United States: Hearings Before the Senate Committee on the Judiciary, United States Senate, 101st Congress (1990).

The Nomination of John Paul Stevens to be Associate Justice of the Supreme Court of the United States: Hearings Before the Senate Committee on the Judiciary, United States Senate, 94th Congress (1975).

O'Brien, David M. "The Politics of Professionalism: President Gerald R. Ford's Appointment of Justice John Paul Stevens." *Presidential Studies Quarterly* 21 (1991): 103–26.

Oelsner, Lesley. "Factors in Court Choice: Ford Seems to Have Followed Tradition and Political Aims in Naming Stevens." *New York Times*, November 30, 1975, 31.

Ogletree, Charles J., Jr. "The Rehnquist Revolution in Criminal Procedure," in *The Rehnquist Court: Judicial Activism on the Right*, ed. Herman Schwartz. New York: Hill and Wang, 2002, 55–69.

"Only Four Justices Question Lawyers About Death Penalty." *Deseret News* (Salt Lake City, Utah), April 1, 1976, 2A.

Oyez Project website. Accessed July 4, 2015, http://www.oyez.org.

Penalver, Eduardo Moises. "Treating Religion as Speech: Justice Stevens's Religion Clause Jurisprudence." *Fordham Law Review* 74 (2006): 2241–57.

Popkin, William. "A Common Law Lawyer on the Supreme Court: The Opinions of Justice Stevens." *Duke Law Journal* (1989): 1087–161.

Powe, Lucas A., Jr. *The Supreme Court and the American Elite, 1789–2008*. Cambridge, Mass.: Harvard University Press, 2009.

Ray, Laura Krugman. "Clerk and Justice: The Ties That Bind John Paul Stevens and Wiley B. Rutledge." *Connecticut Law Review* 41 (2008): 211–63.

Redding, Jean. "Evidence of Innocence: The Lloyd Schlup Death Penalty Case." *Variety*, June 18, 1995. Accessed July 2, 2015, http://variety.com/1995/tv/reviews/evidence-of-innocence-the-lloyd-schlup-death-penalty-case-1200441896/.

Rehnquist, William H. "The Notion of a Living Constitution." *Texas Law Review* 54 (1976): 693–706.

Robbins, Ira P. "The Cry of *Wolfish* in the Federal Courts: The Future of Federal Judicial Intervention in Prison Administration." *Journal of Criminal Law and Criminology* 71 (1980): 211–25.

Robinson, Rob. "Does Prosecutorial Experience 'Balance Out' A Judge's Liberal Experience." *Justice System Journal* 32 (2011): 143–68.

Rosen, Jeffrey. "The Dissenter." *New York Times Magazine*, September 23, 2007, 50–57, 72, 76, 78–79, 81.

———. "Interview Transcript: Justice John Paul Stevens." *New York Times*, April 12, 2010 (interview conducted June 22, 2007). Accessed July 2, 2015, http://www.nytimes.com/2010/04/12/magazine/12stevens-interview.html.

Rubin, Edward L. "Question Regarding *D.C. v. Heller*: As a Justice, Antonin Scalia Is (A) Great, (B) Acceptable, (C) Injudicious." *Wayne Law Review* 54 (2008): 1105–30.

Rudoren, Jodi. "Inquiry Finds Police Abuse, but Says Law Bars Trials." *New York Times*, July 20, 2006. Accessed May 21, 2015, http://www.nytimes.com/2006/07/20/us/20chicago.html?pagewanted=all.

Rust, Craig. "The Leadership Legacy of Justice John Paul Stevens." *Journal of Legal Metrics* 1 (2012): 135–54.

Sagona, Brian. "Argument Recap: *Montejo v. Louisiana*." SCOTUS blog website, January 14, 2009. Accessed July 2, 2015, http://www.scotusblog.com/2009/01/argument-recap-montejo-v-louisiana/.

Samuelson, Tracey D. "DC Sniper Execution: Why His Case Moved So Quickly." *Christian Science Monitor*, November 11, 2009. Accessed July 2, 2015, http://www.csmonitor.com/USA/Justice/2009/1111/p02s01-usju.html.

Sandefur, Timothy. "Clarence Thomas's Jurisprudence Unexplained." *NYU Journal of Law and Liberty* 4 (2009): 535–56.

Sarat, Austin, and Neil Vidmar. "Public Opinion, the Death Penalty, and the Eighth Amendment: Testing the Marshall Hypothesis." *Wisconsin Law Review* (1976): 171–206.

Saulny, Susan, and Eric Ferkenhoff. "Ex-Officer Linked to Brutality Is Arrested." *New York Times*, October 22, 2008. Accessed May 21, 2015, http://www.nytimes.com/2008/10/22/us/22chicago.html.

Scalia, Antonin. "Foreword," in *Originalism: A Quarter Century of Debate*, ed. Stephen G. Calabresi. Washington, D.C.: Regnery, 2007, 43–45.

———. "Originalism: The Lesser Evil." *University of Cincinnati Law Review* 57 (1986): 849–65.

———."The Rule of Law as a Law of Rules." *University of Chicago Law Review* 56 (1989): 1175–88.

Schapiro, Robert A. "Justice Stevens's Theory of Interactive Federalism." *Fordham Law Review* 74 (2006): 2133–75.

Schauer, Frederick. "Justice Stevens and the Size of Constitutional Decisions." *Rutgers Law Journal* 27 (1996): 543–61.

Schlanger, Margo. "*Plata v. Brown* and Realignment: Jails, Prisons, Courts, and Politics." *Harvard Civil Rights-Civil Liberties Law Review* 48 (2013): 165–215.

Segal, Jeffrey A., and Albert D. Cover. "Ideological Values and the Votes of U.S. Supreme Court Justices." *American Political Science Review* 83 (1989): 557–65.

Segal, Jeffrey A., Lee Epstein, Charles M. Cameron, and Harold J. Spaeth. "Ideological Values and the Votes of U.S. Supreme Court Justices Revisited." *Journal of Politics* 57 (1995): 812–23.

Segal, Jeffrey A., and Harold J. Spaeth. "Decisional Trends in the Warren and Burger Courts: Results from the Supreme Court Judicial Data Base Project." *Judicature* 73 (1989): 103–7.

Semel, Elisabeth. "Reflections on Justice John Paul Stevens's Concurring Opinion in *Baze v. Rees*: A Fifth *Gregg* Justice Renounces Capital Punishment," *UC Davis Law Review* 43 (2010): 783–876.

Senior, Jennifer. "In Conversation: Antonin Scalia." *New York Magazine*, October 6, 2013. Accessed May 19, 2015, http://nymag.com/news/features/antonin-scalia-2013-10/.

"Settlement Near in Panther Suit." *New York Times*, October 26, 1982. Accessed May 23, 2015, http://www.nytimes.com/1982/10/26/us/settlement-near-in-a-panther-suit.html.

Shaman, Jeffrey M. "The End of Originalism." *San Diego Law Review* 47 (2010): 83–108.

Sherman, Mark. "Obama Legal Team Wants to Limit Defendants' Rights." *Chico* (Calif.) *Enterprise-Record*, April 23, 2009. Accessed July 2, 2015, http://www.chicoer.com/general-news/20090423/obama-legal-team-wants-to-limit-defendants-rights.

Sheppard, Adam. "Justice Stevens' Role in Making Federal Sentencing Matters More Flexible: A Trail-Blazing Opinion." *Chicago Bar Record* 24 (September 2010): 56.

Sickels, Robert Judd. *John Paul Stevens and the Constitution: The Search for Balance*. University Park, Penn.: Pennsylvania State University Press, 1988.

Siegel, Andrew. "Equal Protection Unmodified: Justice John Paul Stevens and the Case for Unmediated Constitutional Interpretation." *Fordham Law Review* 74 (2006): 2339–69.

———. "Justice Stevens and the Seattle Schools Case: A Case Study on the Role of Righteous Anger in Constitutional Discourse." *UC Davis Law Review* 43 (2010): 927–37.

Smith, Christopher E. "An Empathetic Approach to Criminal Justice: Pro Bono Experiences Informed Justice Stevens' Understanding of Prisoners' Rights." SCOTUS BLOG, May 12, 2010. Accessed July 4, 2015, www.scotusblog.com/2010/05/an-empathetic-approach-to-criminal-justice.

———. "Bent on Original Intent." *American Bar Association Journal* 82 (October 1996): 48–52.

———. "Examining the Boundaries of *Bounds*: Prison Law Libraries and Access to the Courts." *Howard Law Journal* 30 (1987): 27–44.

———. "The Governance of Corrections: Implications of the Changing Interface of Courts and Corrections," in *Boundary Changes in Criminal Justice Organizations*, ed. Charles M. Friel. Vol. 2 of *CRIMINAL JUSTICE 2000*. Washington, D.C.: National Institute of Justice, 2000, 113–166.

———. "Justice John Paul Stevens: Staunch Defender of *Miranda* Rights." *DePaul Law Review* 60 (2010): 99–140.

———. "Law and Symbolism." *Detroit College of Law at Michigan State University Law Review* (1997): 935–53.

———. "The Malleability of Constitutional Doctrine and Its Ironic Impact on Prisoners' Rights." *Boston University Public Interest Law Journal* 11 (2001): 73–96.

———."Polarization and Change in the Federal Courts: En Banc Decisions in the U.S. Court of Appeals." *Judicature* 74 (1990): 133–37.

———. "Police Professionalism and the Rights of Criminal Defendants." *Criminal Law Bulletin* 26 (1990): 155–66.

———. *The Rehnquist Court and Criminal Punishment.* New York: Garland Publishing, 1997.

———. "Rights Behind Bars: The Distinctive Viewpoint of Justice Clarence Thomas." *University of Detroit Mercy* 88 (2011): 830–72.

———. "The Roles of Justice John Paul Stevens in Criminal Justice Cases." *Suffolk University Law Review* 39 (2006): 719–44.

Smith, Christopher E., and Joyce A. Baugh. *The Real Clarence Thomas: Confirmation Veracity Meets Performance Reality.* New York: Peter Lang, 2000.

Smith, Christopher E., and Anne Corbin. "The Rehnquist Court and Corrections Law: An Empirical Assessment." *Criminal Justice Studies* 21 (2008): 179–91.

Smith, Christopher E., and Cheryl D. Lema. "Justice Clarence Thomas and Incommunicado Detention: Justifications and Risks." *Valparaiso University Law Review* 39 (2005): 783–813.

Smith, Christopher E., and Madhavi McCall. "Justice Scalia's Influence on Criminal Justice." *University of Toledo Law Review* 34 (2003): 535–57.

Smith, Christopher E., Michael McCall, and Madhavi McCall. "Criminal Justice and the 2004–2005 United States Supreme Court Term." *University of Memphis Law Review* 36 (2006): 951–1011.

Smith, Gregory K. "*Powell v. State*: The Demise of Georgia's Consensual Sodomy Statute." *Mercer Law Review* 51 (2000): 987–98.

Stern, Seth, and Stephen Wermiel. *Justice Brennan: Liberal Champion.* Boston: Houghton Mifflin Harcourt, 2010.

Stevens, John Paul. "Address to the American Bar Association Thurgood Marshall Awards Dinner." Chicago, Ill., August 6, 2005. Accessed May 21, 2015, http://www.supremecourt.gov/publicinfo/speeches/viewspeech/sp_08-06-05.

———. Address at the Chicago Bar Association's 125th Anniversary Dinner and Celebration, September 16, 1998.

———. "The Bill of Rights: A Century of Progress." Keynote Address at the University of Chicago Centennial Celebration and Bicentennial of the Bill of Rights," (October 25, 1991), *University of Chicago Law Review* 59 (1992): 13–38.

———. "Commencement Address." Northwestern University School of Law, Chicago, Illinois, May 13, 2011. Accessed July 2, 2015, http://www.law.northwestern.edu/about/news/newsdisplay.cfm?ID=535.

———. *Five Chiefs: A Supreme Court Memoir.* Boston: Little, Brown, 2011.

———. "Foreword," in Kenneth A. Manaster, *Illinois Justice: The Scandal of 1969 and the Rise of John Paul Stevens.* Chicago: University of Chicago Press, 2001, ix–xii.

———. "A Judge's Use of History—Thomas E. Fairchild Inaugural Lecture." *Wisconsin Law Review* (1989): 223–36.

———. "Judicial Activism: Ensuring the Powers and Freedoms Conceived by the Framers for Today's World." Address at the Third Annual John Paul Stevens Award Dinner (September 25, 2002). *Chicago Bar Association Record* 16 (2002): 25.

———. "Judicial Restraint." *San Diego Law Review* 22 (1985): 437–52.

———. "Learning on the Job." *Fordham Law Review* 74 (2006): 1561–67.

———. "Letter to the Editor." *New York Times*, November 4, 2007. Accessed on May 21, 2015, http://query.nytimes.com/gst/fullpage.html?res=9903E0DF153DF937A35752C1A9619C8B63.

———. "Mr. Justice Rutledge." in *Mr. Justice.* Allison Dunham and Philip B. Kurland, eds. Chicago: University of Chicago Press, 1956, 176–202.

———. "Northwestern University School of Law's 151st Commencement Address." *Northwestern Law Review* 106 (2012): 851–54.

———."A Personal History of the Law Review." *Northwestern University Law Review* 100 (2006): 25–26.

———. "Random Recollections." Speech at the Nathaniel L. Nathanson Memorial Lecture at the University of San Diego (April 7, 2004). *San Diego Law Review* 42 (2005): 269–72.

———. "Remarks at the Dedication of the Arthur Rubloff Building," Northwestern University School of Law, Chicago, Ill., August 4, 1984.

———. *Six Amendments: How and Why We Should Change the Constitution.* New York: Little, Brown, 2014.

———. Speech to Chicago Bar Association, John Paul Stevens Awards Luncheon. Chicago, Ill., October 2, 2012. Accessed May 19, 2015, http://www.supremecourt.gov/publicinfo/speeches/JPS%20Speech(Chicago)_10-02-2012.pdf.

———. Speech at the Federal Bar Council Annual Law Day dinner. New York City, May 3, 2011. Accessed May 19, 2015, http://www.supremecourt.gov/publicinfo/speeches/Federal%20Bar%20Council%20Annual%20Law%20Day%20Dinner(1613_001).pdf.

———. Speech at Georgia State University College of Law. Atlanta, Georgia, April 16, 2014. Accessed May 20, 2015, http://www.supremecourt.gov/publicinfo/speeches/JPS%20Speech_Atlanta_04-16-2014.pdf.

Tate, C. Neal. "Personal Attribute Models of the Voting Behavior of U.S. Supreme Court Justices: Liberalism in Civil Liberties and Economics Decisions." *American Political Science Review* 75 (1981): 355–67.

Thai, Joseph. "Did Justice Stevens Change?" SCOTUSblog, April 29, 2010. Accessed May 21, 2015, http://www.scotusblog.com/2010/04/did-justice-stevens-change/.

———."The Law Clerk Who Wrote *Rasul v. Bush*: John Paul Stevens's Influence from World War II to the War on Terror." *Virginia Law Review* 92 (2006): 501–32.

This Honorable Court: Inside the Marble Temple (documentary film). Public Broadcasting System (PBS), television broadcast September 12, 1989.

Thompson, Rosemary Simota. "Justice John Paul Stevens: Chicago's Native Son." *Chicago Bar Association Record* 24 (September 2010): 34.

Toobin, Jeffrey. "After Stevens: What Will the Supreme Court Be Like Without Its Liberal Leader?" *The New Yorker*, March 22, 2010, 39–43.

———. *The Nine: Inside the Secret World of the Supreme Court.* New York: Doubleday, 2007.

Totenberg, Nina. "Justice Stevens: An Open Mind On a Changed Court." National Public Radio, October 4, 2010. Accessed May 21, 2015, http://www.npr.org/templates/story/story.php?storyId=130198344.

———. "Rehnquist: From Lone Dissenter to Consensus Builder." *All Things Considered* news program, National Public Radio, September 4, 2005. Accessed May 19, 2015, http://www.npr.org/templates/story/story.php?storyId=4832353.

Treanor, William M. "Lesson for Obama in Ford's Selection of Stevens." *USA Today*, April 15, 2015. Accessed July 2, 2015, http://usatoday30.usatoday.com/news/opinion/forum/2010-04-15-treanor15_st_N.htm.

Tushnet, Mark V. *A Court Divided: The Rehnquist Court and the Future of Constitutional Law.* New York: W.W. Norton, 2005.

———. *Making Civil Rights Law: Thurgood Marshall and the Supreme Court, 1936–1961.* New York: Oxford University Press, 1994.

———. *Making Constitutional Law: Thurgood Marshall and the Supreme Court, 1961–1991.* New York: Oxford University Press, 1997.

Unikel, Alan L. "A Supremely Memorable Case." *Chicago Bar Association Record* 24 (September 2010): 48–51.

U.S. Bureau of Census. *Fifteenth Census of the United States: 1930.* Chicago, Cook County, Illinois, Sheet No. 5A, April 1930.

Walker, Samuel. "'Broken Windows' and Fractured History: The Use and Misuse of History in Recent Police Patrol Analysis." *Justice Quarterly* 1 (1984): 75–90.

———. *A Critical History of Police Reform.* Lexington, Mass.: Lexington Books, 1977.

———. *Popular Justice: A History of American Criminal Justice.* New York: Oxford University Press, 1980.

Ward, Stephanie Francis. "A Man of Moderation." *ABA Journal* 96 (May 2010): 49–52, 55–56, 71.

Wedeking, Justin. "Why Do Policy-Motivated Justices Conform to Unfavorable Precedents? The Role of Social-Legal Backgrounds and Precedential Characteristics." *Justice System Journal* 33 (2012): 69–95.

Wermeil, Stephen. "Justices Say First Amendment Protects Burning of Flag—Another Decision Allows Publishing Certain Data Even If Laws Are Broken." *Wall Street Journal*, June 22, 1989, 1.

White, Welsh S. *Miranda's Waning Protections.* Ann Arbor, Mich.: University of Michigan Press, 1999.

Williams, Juan. *Thurgood Marshall: American Revolutionary.* New York: Three Rivers Press, 1998.

Yarbrough, Tinsley E. *David Hackett Souter: Traditional Republican on the Rehnquist Court.* New York: Oxford University Press, 2005.

Case Index

U.S. SUPREME COURT

U.S. COURT OF APPEALS

OTHER COURTS

Index

About the Author

Christopher E. Smith, J.D., Ph.D., is professor of criminal justice at Michigan State University. He is the editor of *The Rehnquist Court and Criminal Justice* (2011). He has also written more than one hundred scholarly articles and twenty-two books, including *The Changing Supreme Court; Constitutional Rights: Myths & Realities; Courts and the Poor*; and *Courts and Public Policy*.